OUT OF ONE, MANY

FRONTISPIECE. Map of the Greek world from Sicily to Anatolia.

OUT OF ONE, MANY

ANCIENT GREEK WAYS OF THOUGHT AND CULTURE

JENNIFER T. ROBERTS

PRINCETON UNIVERSITY PRESS

PRINCETON & OXFORD

Published by Princeton University Press
41 William Street, Princeton, New Jersey 08540
99 Banbury Road, Oxford OX2 6JX

press.princeton.edu

ISBN 978-0-691-18147-9
ISBN (e-book) 978-0-691-24385-6

British Library Cataloging-in-Publication Data is available

Editorial: Rob Tempio and Chloe Coy
Production Editorial: Jill Harris
Text Design: Karl Spurzem
Jacket Design: Karl Spurzem
Production: Erin Suydam
Publicity: Alyssa Sanford and Carmen Jimenez
Copyeditor: Jennifer Harris

Jacket image: *Shards* (2009) by Ruby Sky Stiler. Courtesy of the artist and Nicelle Beauchene Gallery, NY. Screenprint edition published by Forth Estate Editions

This book has been composed in Arno with Trajan Pro 3

Printed on acid-free paper. ∞

Printed in the United States of America

10 9 8 7 6 5 4 3 2 1

To the memory of my husband Robert Lejeune

(b. Paris, 1937; d. New York, 2023)

sit tibi terra levis

Thus at one time they all learned how to grow into one out of many,
And then as they all split apart they again became many from one.

CONTENTS

PREFACE AND ACKNOWLEDGMENTS

My first and greatest debt by far is to my editor, Rob Tempio, whose diabolical plan for me was that I should devote years of my life to this project. Throughout the process Rob has demonstrated both superhuman patience and tremendous insight, and he has been a delight to work with. We should all be so lucky.

To say that this book has been written at a time of adversity would be an understatement. Cancer! Pandemic! Bereavement! I am grateful to my friend and former chair Carlos Riobó and the City College of New York for support when I missed a month of classes for cancer treatment, and to Chris Weimer for taking time out from his dissertation to teach my classes and grade my papers at that time. I am also indebted to the college for a research leave throughout the academic year 2021–22, and to the librarians at the City University of New York Graduate Center for assistance obtaining research materials when the threat of Covid made library visits impossible. My students Keren Freidenreich, Victoria Hsu, and Kiran Mansukhani were kind enough to provide research assistance. Having worked with texts rather than images most of my life, I would have been lost in the quest for illustrations and the attendant permissions without the gracious assistance of Chloe Coy at Princeton and Rachel Kousser and Jennifer Ranck at the City University of New York Graduate Center. Jen was tireless in dealing with all the minutiae entailed in putting together the images in this book, and for this I am boundlessly grateful. I'm surprised she's still speaking to me.

I benefited enormously from the input I received from friends and relations who offered feedback on portions of the manuscript: Maura Gouck, Don Lateiner, Mary Jean McNamara, Nick Pappas, and most of all Rich Weigel, who provided detailed commentary on several chapters, and Walter Blanco, who doggedly plowed through the whole thing. Walter also made a superb suggestion about the rearrangement of material that I think has made the book much more readable. Stan Burstein, Nick Pappas, and Eva Stehle shared unpublished work with me as well as some published work it would have been difficult for me to obtain. I have profited from conversations and correspondence about the Greek world with all these people, as also with Beth Carney, Dee Clayman, Jeff Halpern, Rachel Kousser, Istar Schwager Sarlin, Eva Stehle, and Debi Unger. Artemida Tesho made my stint in administration as stress-free as could be imagined, enabling me to save my energies for seeing this manuscript to its conclusion. Amy Foster enabled me to juggle finishing the book and caring for my ailing husband Bob Lejeune, as did Bob's magnificent caregiver Majorie Gordon. Among the scholarly works I have cited, I take particular delight in the profit I have drawn from the publications of scholars too numerous to mention who did all or part of their graduate work at my home institution, the City University of New York.

As always, members of the hivemind comprised by my Oxford University Press *Ancient Greece* co-authors—Stan Burstein, Sarah Pomeroy, David Tandy, and Georgia Tsouvala—have given generously of their time in reading parts of what I have written and in responding to queries. I am also mindful of how much I learned about early Greece from our co-author on the first, 1998 edition of that book, the late Walter Donlan. Much is also owed to my dictation program, which has not only spared my wrists but offered valuable input into my research, as I learned that the *Parallel Lives* were in fact written by Ozark and the history of the Peloponnesian War by someone known alternately as Facilities, The city flees, Abilities, He silly is, and, incomprehensibly, Frank. I doubt I will ever know what lay behind the sentence it turned out reading "Petting alarm for six and bad odor along founding fathers."

My family has always been a source of tremendous support but never more than in these past years as I juggled the responsibilities of teaching, research, and caring for a sick spouse. (Having used the word *sick* earlier, I just made use of my computer's synonym program to seek alternatives so as to avoid repetition. It suggested I refer to my husband as not sick but rather tasteless, gruesome, revolting, or bilious. I am happy to report that none of these would be accurate.) My sister Page Tolbert and my son Chris Roberts have risen to new heights of greatness, and both my husband and I have benefited enormously from the loving ministrations of our oldest granddaughter Alannah Lejeune, a frequent and most welcome visitor to our home, and her partner Andy Lawson. The other grandkids are pretty nifty too. How fortunate we have been to live long enough to watch them grow into delightful, contemplative young people! Much is also owing to Sneaky, Wiley, and Sandy: you know who you are.

I profited immensely from the comments of the readers for the press, even those emanating from the individual who made clear at every turn that s/he thought I should have written an entirely different book. I am also in the debt of two scholars who have influenced my work profoundly but whom I never had the good fortune to meet: Walter Burkert and Martin West. I spent a good deal of time with their thoughtful scholarship in the course of writing this book, and I think of them admiringly as faithful companions during the months when I was home recuperating from cancer surgery. My late colleague Dorothea Wender has also influenced me in more ways than I can say; I only wish she had been alive to give me feedback on the chapter on myth with which this book begins, which her unerring eye would have improved no end.

All Greek words have been transliterated into the Roman alphabet. Macrons (long marks) over the letter *e* mark it as long, somewhere between the *e* in *led* and the *a* in *lay*, as opposed to the short *e* in *let*; those over the letter *o* mark it as long as in *no*, as opposed to short as in *not*. References to Greek texts follow the protocol laid out in the *Oxford Classical Dictionary*. It is customary to refer to the works of Plato by what are known as Stephanus pages, based on the 1578 edition of Plato's works published by Henri Estienne (Henricus Stephanus, ca. 1530–1598) in Geneva; Estienne also paginated the works of Plutarch. References to Aristotle's works are by Bekker numbers, after the pagination of August Immanuel Bekker (1785–1871). All translations are my own unless otherwise specified.

A list of suggested readings follows each chapter. In addition, Oxford University Press publishes excellent bibliographies on a wide variety of

topics in Greek civilization. These are listed at https://www
.oxfordbibliographies.com/obo/page/classics. Those interested in
learning more about the geography of ancient Greece are directed to the
superb *Barrington Atlas of the Greek and Roman World* edited by Richard J. A. Talbert (Princeton University Press, 2000).

My husband Bob Lejeune was too ill while I was writing this book to
be of much assistance, but I would never have found myself in a position
to undertake it without the unflagging support he gave me over the
preceding thirty years, from long discussions about the methodology
of Herodotus to "Out of the kitchen, woman! You have a book to fin-
ish!" He died just as this book was going into production, and it is to his
memory that it is dedicated.

TIME LINE

All dates in this book are BCE unless otherwise specified.

BRONZE AGE

ca. 2200	Greeks enter what is today Greece
ca. 1200	Destruction of Troy

ARCHAIC AGE

700s	Poetry ascribed to Homer and Hesiod
776	Traditional date for first Olympic Games
ca. 750	Colonization begins
ca. 700	Beginnings of lyric poetry
ca. 670–500	Tyrants rule in several Greek states
594?	Reforms of Solon at Athens
ca. 575	Death of Sappho
ca. 545	Death of Thales
ca. 495	Death of Pythagoras
490–479	Greco-Persian Wars

CLASSICAL AGE

400s	Hippocratics active
477	Foundation of Delian League
461–429	Pericles ascendant at Athens
460–445	"First" Peloponnesian War
	Herodotus at work on his *Histories*
458	Aeschylus, *Oresteia*
ca. 456	Death of Aeschylus
447–432	Construction of Parthenon

ca. 441	Sophocles, *Antigone*
	Sophists active in Athens
ca. 434	Death of Empedocles
431–404	[Second] Peloponnesian War
	Thucydides begins to write
431	Pericles delivers funeral oration over the war dead
431	Euripides, *Medea*
430–426	Plague assails Athens (in two waves)
429	Death of Pericles
428?	Sophocles, *Oedipus the King*
427	Sojourn of Gorgias in Athens
426	Euripides, *Hippolytus*
424	Aristophanes, *Knights*
423	Thucydides forced to leave Athens
	Aristophanes, *Clouds*
415	Euripides, *Trojan Women*
411	Aristophanes, *Lysistrata*
406	Deaths of Euripides, Sophocles
405	Aristophanes, *Frogs*
404–403	Regime of the Thirty Tyrants at Athens
401	Sophocles, *Oedipus at Colonus* (posthumously)
399	Trial and execution of Socrates
399–347	Dialogues of Plato
387	Plato founds Academy
347	Death of Plato
338	Philip defeats Athens and Thebes at the Battle of Chaeronea
336	Philip assassinated and succeeded by Alexander
335	Aristotle founds Lyceum
334	Alexander invades Persia
331	Alexander founds Alexandria in Egypt
327–325	Alexander and his entourage in India
323	Death of Alexander

HELLENISTIC AGE

323	Foundation of Hellenistic kingdoms
322	Death of Aristotle
307–283	Museum and library founded at Alexandria
306	Epicurus founds the Garden at Athens
301	Zeno founds Stoa at Athens
283	Death of Ptolemy I of Egypt
ca. 270	Death of Arsinoë II of Egypt
ca. 260	Death of Herophilus
246	Death of Ptolemy II of Egypt
ca. 240	Death of Callimachus
227	Reforms of Cleomenes III at Sparta
222	Death of Ptolemy III of Egypt
221	Death of Berenice II of Egypt
194	Death of Eratosthenes
31	Octavian (Augustus) defeats Mark Antony and Cleopatra VII at Actium, absorbing last of Hellenistic monarchies into Roman Empire
30	Death of Cleopatra VII

OUT OF ONE, MANY

They Contain Multitudes

The ancient Greeks are still very much with us. The modern city of Athens boasts streets named for the lawgiver Solon, the admiral Themistocles, the god Hermes. The main shopping street in Rhodes is Socrates Street, and a labyrinth of lanes off the southern part of the street leads to Pythagoras Street. Every year on the first Monday of Lent the people of Tyrnavos in northern Greece honor the god Dionysus by parading through the streets bearing phalluses they have made of clay, wood, and bread and inviting passersby to kiss their creations. Although the Greek that is spoken today throughout the Greek mainland and islands differs markedly from ancient Greek—just try to order a meal in the language of Plato!—in the nine small towns that make up Grecia Salentina in south Italy a tongue far closer to the language of the ancients is often heard: the dialect known as Griko. It is the last linguistic survival of the culture of Magna Graecia (Greater Greece), as Sicily and southern Italy were known in antiquity.

We need not be in Europe to feel the Greek presence. Freudian psychoanalysis makes much of the story of Oedipus, and cognitive behavioral therapy is grounded in the teachings of Zeno and the Stoics. Writers in cultures as different as those of France and Nigeria, South Korea and Colombia, Egypt and the United States have found in the story of Oedipus a useful platform for addressing the concerns of their own societies. In New York City, where I live, the Greek heritage is kept alive by the philanthropy of Aristotle Onassis, named for the famous

FIGURE 0.1. Sicily theater. Palazzo Acreide (Province of Syracuse), Sicily: Greek theater of Akrai, 3rd–2nd BCE. The city is mentioned by Thucydides and was part of Magna Graecia. Alfredo Dagli Orti / Art Resource, NY.

philosopher, and of John D. Rockefeller, Jr., who provided inspiration and the funding for the remarkable works of art at Rockefeller Center in midtown Manhattan, including the outsize bronze statues of Atlas and Prometheus. Here in the United States there are more than twenty cities named Athens, and nearly that many Spartas; sixteen states can boast Homers; Achilles Streets can be found in California, in Nebraska, and in New Jersey. Only Nashville, Tennessee, however, can boast its own Parthenon, complete with a statue of Athena by sculptor Alan LeQuire that at nearly forty feet is one of the largest indoor sculptures in the world.

But the ancient Greeks were not a monolithic bunch. Achilles did not look at the world at all in the same way as Socrates, who in turn differed from Aristotle, who differed from the Stoics. Like most people, ancient Greeks were a bundle of contradictions. Given to waxing lyrical about the joys of freedom, they also kept huge numbers of hapless slaves in subjection. Home to an extraordinary proliferation of different schools of thought about both gods and mortals, Greece was also a place where people could be put to death for things they thought or said about religion— even in Athens, where freedom of expression was one of the watchwords of the democracy. Greeks were both contradictory and complex.

We know much more about some than about others. Of the thought patterns of the poor, the female, the enslaved, we have little evidence. We know a good deal about how free Greek men thought about these "muted groups," but little about what people who belonged to these groups believed about anything. Although the Athenian Aristophanes wrote three comedies about women that tell us a great deal about how men imagined women's thought patterns, they reveal little about the thinking of actual women. We would know much more if we knew which sex had invented which myths; surely a number of the Greek myths that have come down to us had been formulated by women, who then as now engaged in storytelling with their children. Even the urban, elite males to whom we owe the bulk of the surviving literature, however, revealed a wide variety of outlooks, and though not many women left a record of their thoughts, some did.

The Spartan Tyrtaeus, a poet of uncertain date, identified martial courage as the only valid measure of a man. I would not take account of anyone, he wrote, just because he is athletic, or rich, or powerful, or handsome, or indeed had every one of these qualities but lacked a fighting spirit; but in warfare, he contended,

Lies excellence, the very finest thing
In all the world, surely the fairest prize
A youth can seek to win, a noble boon
His city and its people share with him,
When someone stands among the foremost spears
Planting his feet with no thought of foul flight,
His soul and steadfast heart superbly trained,
Encouraging the man who stands nearby.
. . .
And he who, fighting in the foremost ranks,
Loses his dear life showers on his city

And all his countrymen, and on his father
The greatest glory, bearing many wounds
In front, through breastplate and through sturdy shield. . . .
    (12, 13–26; Stobaeus, *Anthology* 51. 1, 5)

Those sturdy shields protected not only the wearer but also the man next to him, and it was impressed on Greek soldiers that nothing could be more shameful than throwing away one's shield and running. The outspoken seventh-century mercenary Archilochus from the Aegean island of Paros cannot have been alone in questioning this ideology in eminently unheroic verse:

No doubt some Thracian guy has got my shield.
More power to him. It's in perfect shape,
But I was forced to leave the thing behind
Under a bush. Me, though, I got away!
The hell with that old shield since I can buy
Another one that's every bit as good.
    (Cited in Plutarch, *Spartan Institutions*, 34)

Not surprisingly, the fifth-century poet Pindar from Thebes, north of Athens, who received substantial commissions for composing odes in honor of athletic victories, defines excellence in terms of physical prowess, writing in connection with the Pythian games in honor of Apollo (so named because of Apollo's reported slaying of the serpent/dragon Pytho):

Only a god's heart is untouched by pain,
But fortunate and worthy of acclaim
By all the wisest poets is the man
Who wins a victory by means of excellence
Of hands or speedy feet, the man who gains
The greatest prizes from his daring strength
And in his lifetime sees his stripling son
Duly rewarded with a Pythian crown.
Though he can never reach the brazen sky,
Of all the glories mortals can attain
His voyage takes him to the farthest shore. (*Pythian* 10. 21–29)

The philosopher Xenophanes from Colophon in Anatolia had a different perspective. If a man should win in some event at Olympia, he says, his fellow townsmen would make a colossal fuss over him, but he would not deserve it as Xenophanes does:

> For better than the strength of man or horse
> Is wisdom of the kind I call my own.
> People, though, don't think clearly about this:
> It is not right to value simple strength
> Above the sacred wisdom of the mind.
> For if among the populace there's one
> Who's good at boxing or at wrestling,
> Who wins the arduous Pankration,
> Or the pentathlon, or a runner, say—
> Since racing skill, of all the tests of strength,
> Receives the greatest honor at the Games—
> This would not make his city better run. (Athenaeus, 10. 423–31)

The most famous female poet of antiquity attested to the outsize role war played in the Greeks' frame of reference when she wrote

> Some say of all the sights one could behold
> The loveliest is cavalry; some say,
> No—infantry! Still others say a fleet.
> I see things differently. I say that she
> Whom one loves best is the most beautiful. (16. 1–4)

Sappho goes on to express her sorrow at the departure of her beloved Anactoria, whose radiant face she would rather see than all the armed forces of wealthy Lydia.

Some Greeks hated democracy, while others praised it. Everywhere on earth, claimed an anonymous enemy of popular government,

> The best element is opposed to democracy, for among the best people there is the least licentiousness and wrongdoing but rather the most scrupulous concern for what is admirable, whereas among the people there is the greatest disorder and wickedness, because poverty

drives them to shameful deeds, and the lack of money can result in ignorance and lack of education. (pseudo-Xenophon, *The Athenian Constitution*, 1. 5)

While acknowledging the prevalence of hostility to democracy, the Sicilian politician Athenagoras took a different position. Someone, he concedes, will say

> that democracy is neither intelligent nor fair and that it is rather the rich who are best fitted to govern. I say, however, that "the people" is the name of the whole state, the elite only one segment of it. In addition, the rich are the best at administering the treasury, the wise the best at framing issues, but the people are best at listening to arguments and judging among them, and that all these functions have their place in a democracy. But what actually happens in an oligarchy is that the few give the many their share of risks and then, not content with the lion's share of the profits, take them all. (Thucydides, 6. 39. 1–2)

Plainly there was no such thing as "the Greek value system." Most Greeks believed in the Olympian gods, but a few expressed skepticism. There was no consensus about what people could expect after they died. The Greeks have often been perceived as warlike by temperament, but the war between Athens and Sparta that ravaged Greece from 431 to 404 owed its length in part to powerful ambivalences on both sides, and even after their declaration of war the Spartans sent to the oracle of Apollo at Delphi to inquire whether they should really go ahead with it. Every opportunity for peace throughout the years of fighting was greeted with heated disagreement on both sides. And of course opinions sometimes changed over the course of a lifetime. In the quarter century that separated *Oedipus the King* (*Oedipus Rex*) from *Oedipus at Colonus*, the playwright Sophocles came to think differently about questions of fate, gods, and human agency. The same philosopher who in his *Republic* scandalized public opinion by suggesting that women could govern as well as men dotted his other works with strikingly misogynistic remarks, regularly classing women with children and contending that wicked and cowardly men would be reincarnated as women

FIGURE 0.2. Delphi. The structures at the imposing site of Delphi included this magnificent round temple in the sanctuary of Athena Pronaia. The remains of the twenty Doric columns that surrounded it are still visible. Manuel Cohen / Art Resource, NY.

(*Timaeus* 90e–91a). Some values and beliefs, however, were widely shared. Inscribed on the temple of Apollo at Delphi were the words *mēden agan*: nothing in excess (along with the equally sage caution *gnōthi seauton*: know yourself—that is, recognize that you are a mortal with mortal limitation, and not a god—and with this few would have disagreed.

It is the aim of this book to explore areas of dramatic divergence, areas of subtle difference, and areas of broad agreement. In so doing, we will look at diverse areas of Greek thought and action: politics, religion, performance, competition, literature, and myth. Because myth affected every area of Greek life, we will begin there, bringing onto the stage the rollicking adventures of lovers and warriors, murderers and monsters, and indomitable forces of nature, always asking ourselves: what on earth are we to make of these extraordinary tales that have continued to capture the human imagination over two thousand years into the future?

CHAPTER 1

A World of the Imagination

We are meaning-seeking creatures. Dogs, as far as we know, do not
agonise about the canine condition, worry about the plight of dogs
in other parts of the world, or try to see their lives from a different
perspective. But human beings fall easily into despair, and from the
very beginning we invented stories that enabled us to place our lives in
a larger setting, that revealed an underlying pattern, and gave us a sense
that, against all the depressing and chaotic evidence to the contrary,
life had meaning and value.

—KAREN ARMSTRONG, *A SHORT HISTORY OF MYTH*

But a myth, to speak plainly, to me is like a menu in a fancy French
restaurant: glamorous, complicated camouflage for a fact you wouldn't
otherwise swallow, like maybe lima beans.

—WILLIAM PETER BLATTY, *THE EXORCIST*

Every Greek lived in at least two worlds. On the one hand, there was the
mundane world of the everyday: for women, childbearing and homemaking; for men, farming, sometimes commerce; for citizens, soldier-
ing and politicking; for slaves, backbreaking work of all kinds. On the
other, there was the extraordinarily imaginative world of myth, vibrantly
alive in literature, art, religion, and in simply every Greek mind. Some
fiercely, others with a bemused sense of irony, the Greeks believed in a

glorious past that was in every sense fabulous. Few Greeks had much sense of a historical past. What we would call social studies was not part of the school curriculum, and in any case written records with which the past might be reconstructed were scarce. But to grow up in ancient Greece was to be exposed to a pool of amazing tales about a very different universe, a remote past in which gods and mortals mingled comfortably, indeed interbred—a realm in which Earth, having mated with Sky, produced one-eyed giants and creatures who might sport fifty heads and a hundred arms; where the king of the gods seduced the queen of Sparta in the guise of a swan; where a man accidentally married his mother; where people were transformed into birds and bears and stars and trees; where a goddess killed a giant by picking up Sicily and throwing it at him and a god was so afraid of being overthrown by one of his children that he swallowed each of his offspring at birth. Love affairs both heterosexual and homosexual, jealousy, dismemberment, herbs that restore people to life, prophecies and vain attempts to escape them, fiery battles, thrilling chase sequences—it was all there.

These tales had in turn been invented at some point in the past by other Greeks who had also farmed and reproduced and kept house and fought and traded—mostly by men, to judge from their largely sexist and patriarchal cast, but some surely by women. The story of how the unsuspecting Persephone was kidnapped by her uncle the king of the Underworld as a child but was eventually enabled to spend a good chunk of her time at home with her mother smacks of invention by some female longing for the secure days before she was snatched from the care of her female relatives and compelled to marry an older man she barely knew. Some were invented from whole cloth, some derived from observations of the natural world, some inspired by riveting tales from the Near East. Like all myths, those of the Greeks fall into certain readily identifiable categories, with considerable interconnection and overlap. There are myths of origin designed to explain and justify the existence of the basic building blocks of civilization, which for the Greeks included such phenomena as patriarchy, marriage, law, and animal sacrifice. These stories sometimes overlap with myths about relations between gods and humans. There are myths of conflict between parents and children, particularly fathers and sons. Some of these intersect with myths of origin, as when the reign of Zeus on Olympus is traced first to his overthrow of his father Kronos and ultimately to Kronos's overthrow—and castration—of his own parent, Ouranos. Some myths explain how the universe came to be, while others set up rules for how humans are to define their place in it. (The same can be said of philosophy.) There are myths of progress and myths of decline. A number of myths offer variations on the theme of the hero's quest, while others showcase the rite of passage from one stage of life to another—from virgin to wife, or from adolescent boy to responsible adult member of the community. The latter often intersects with myths of subduing monsters of one kind or another—which in turn intersect with myths of the establishment of order out of disorder.

The Greeks were born storytellers, and what is a myth if not a story? A story, moreover, is a way of organizing information and of explaining the mysteries of life. What science and philosophy would later approach in theory and abstraction, myth approached in concrete stories: told around a campfire, recited beside an altar, related to children by their elders, chiseled in stone or painted on a vase. The stories we call myths made themselves felt in every aspect of culture in the Greek world, where art and literature were unimaginable without them. But what exactly is a myth, and why does myth come into being in all cultures? What need does it fill?

We might say that myths are narratives that have special meaning for a culture, set in a distant past when the universe with which people later became familiar had not yet taken shape: narratives that unveil a sacred world. All Greek myths, for example, posit a world of kings and queens, princes and princesses rather than of oligarchies and democracies; before that a world with no people at all, only gods; and before that a world without either gods or people. The principal characters must include some supra-human beings: gods, demigods, heroes with extraordinary powers no longer accorded to mortals. Greek heroes are not necessarily altruistic or kind like modern heroes, who put others before themselves. They can be very self-centered, like Achilles. Living in a mythical time, heroes do not have paying jobs. Monster-slaying is not so much a job as an avocation (sorry, Heracles). Heroes do not run for office. They do not read or write or trade; they do not come down with colds or develop acne. They may, like Zeus, pile one wife on another, but they never divorce. Myth lies somewhere on the spectrum between history and fiction. It is closer to history in that at least at some time it was believed actually to have happened, closer to fiction in that the events it describes are more exciting and unusual than those of everyday life. Aristotle maintained that poetry—the only kind of fiction he knew—was superior to history because history dealt with a small range of particulars and poetry with a wide range of possibilities (*Poetics*, 1451b). Myth, however, goes poetry one better, for it also deals with impossibilities alternately horrifying and delightful.

A priceless guide to the ideology and organization of a civilization, myth remains of uncertain origin, and we must ask with K. K. Ruthven whether it is "an expression of our freedom to invent alternative realities or . . . merely an agent of those powerful forces (personal and traumatic, or racial and primordial) which determine our lives."[1] In the nineteenth century the Scottish scholar William Robertson Smith maintained that myths were developed to explain rituals, whereas the British classicist and polyglot Jane Ellen Harrison maintained that while myth was closely bound up with ritual, it was not designed to explain it; rather it functioned as the narrative correlative of ritual. For anthropologist Bronislaw Malinowski myth served as a pragmatic charter of wisdom, faith, and values designed to undergird the basic structure and ethos of a society. Structuralist Claude Levi-Strauss saw myth as encapsulating fundamental binary oppositions. Myths, he argued, work to organize perceptions of the world by setting up oppositions like chaos and order, sky and underworld, male and female, old and new. Sigmund Freud viewed myths, much like dreams, as a reflection of a particular society's anxieties and desires, a construction that allotted a substantial role in the formation of myth to the unconscious. Though each civilization's myths are distinctive, however, underlying patterns certainly appear— what psychoanalyst Carl Jung, who saw myth as the product of a collective unconscious, called "archetypes."

Even different practitioners of the same approach can differ widely among themselves in interpreting myths. In his study of myth and psychoanalysis, Robert Eisner has identified several contrasting psychoanalytic approaches to the myth of Oedipus, treated most famously by Sophocles in his tragedy *Oedipus the King*. The story is well known. Having heard a prophecy that their son would grow up to kill his father and marry his mother, King Laius of Thebes and his wife Jocasta give the baby to a shepherd with instructions to abandon him to his fate, with his ankles pierced and tied to prevent his crawling to safety, a development that seems to explain his name *Oedi-pus* (swollen foot), although it's certainly suggestive that the Greek verb for knowing was *oida*, and knowledge plays a large role in his story. The shepherd, however, takes pity on the infant, who is instead adopted by the king and queen of Corinth. Returning as an adult to Thebes, and having no idea of his true identity, he kills Laius in a fight along the road and marries his widow, thus fulfilling the prophecy. For one psychoanalyst, the myth is plainly the story of a deprived child. No, says another; rather it is the case history of a child who has been adopted. A third analyst has a different interpretation: Oedipus has an inferiority complex because of his handicap— the lameness that ensued from having his ankles pierced. Another sees him as a battered child: for heaven's sake, his parents tried to kill him! Still another focuses on his relationship with his mother/wife and sees Oedipus in patients who have been seduced as children by psychotic parents.[2]

No single scaffold can hope to accommodate the rich fabric of Greek myth. Certainly, myth serves to connect people with an imagined past and with another, transcendent dimension of reality. Shared belief enhances community cohesion. It was probably their myths above all that united the far-flung Greeks into a cohesive culture, for myths provided a huge body of shared cultural referents. Some myths are plainly etiological (from Greek *aition*, cause), articulating the rationale behind the organization of society or accounting for natural phenomena. The story of the subordination to Zeus of Hera, previously a powerful goddess in her own right, normalized patriarchy. (Hera's perpetual ill temper is normally ascribed to her husband's compulsive philandering, but

resentment over her demotion might have played a part as well.) Some
explain natural phenomena. The snatching of Persephone, daughter of
the agriculture goddess Demeter, by Hades, god of the Underworld,
accounted for the existence of seasons. When Persephone was with her
husband in the Underworld, Demeter was so disconsolate that nothing
could grow, but when she began to divide her time between her husband and her mother, the land was barren when she was in the Underworld but fruitful when she was on earth. Why are crows black? At one
time all crows were white, but when the crow Apollo had sent to keep
an eye on his beloved Coronis informed the jealous god that Coronis
was having sex with the mortal Ischys, the enraged Apollo, conflating
the message with the messenger, turned it black.

Some myths seem to be etymological. When an irate Zeus decided
to destroy the human race by flooding the earth, the oracle of the goddess Themis instructed the survivors Deucalion and his wife Pyrrha to
repopulate the world by throwing the bones of their mother over their
shoulders, whereupon they picked up stones—*laas*—from "mother
Earth" and tossed them backward. The Greek word for "people" was
laos, though the derivation is fanciful. The island Anaphe (*Revelation*)
owed its name to the rescue of Jason and Medea by Apollo as they were
returning to Greece with the golden fleece. When they found themselves imperiled by a violent storm at sea, Apollo shot an arrow into the
water, causing a flash of lightning that illuminated an island offering safe
anchorage, and this island they named Anaphe because it had been *revealed* to them by Apollo.

Indubitably, some myths do explain a ritual—or at least were believed to do so. Several of these are scattered through the first- or
second-century CE compendium *The Library of Greek Mythology*, sometimes thought to be written by a man known as Apollodorus, although
that was probably not the author's real name. Apollodorus tells how
when Jason and Medea erected an altar to Apollo on Anaphe and sacrificed there, twelve of Medea's slave girls lobbed indecent jokes at the
Argonauts; this, Apollodorus says, is why women make jokes during
sacrifices to Apollo on Anaphe. When Minos received word of his son's
death while he was in the middle of sacrificing to the Graces on the

island of Paros, Apollodorus writes, he completed the sacrifice but cast the ritual garland from his head and demanded that the customary flutes be silent; and that, Apollodorus explains, is why people sacrifice to the Graces on Paros without flutes or garlands.

The women's festival of the Thesmophoria was grounded in several myths, some of which were surely invented to explain the proceedings there. Demeter, so the story went, was so disconsolate after Persephone's disappearance that upon her arrival in Eleusis she at first declined the couch offered to her by the queen Metaneira and only agreed when the queen's slave Iambe offered her a fleece-covered stool:

> The goddess sat a long time on the stool,
> Silent and sorrowing, and by no word
> Or sign would she greet anyone at all;
> She sat, unsmiling, would not eat or drink,
> Pining and longing for her deep-girt child,
> Until astute Iambe intervened
> With jests and quips. Then did the goddess smile,
> The holy lady; then with joyful heart
> Demeter laughed, and ever afterward
> Iambe never failed to cheer her moods.
> (*Homeric Hymn to Demeter*, 198–205)

It was this playfulness that was put forward to explain the cutting jests exchanged by women at the Thesmophoria, and a parallel tale about the elderly Baubo accounted for the evident vulgarity of the women's remarks. Injured by Demeter's rejection of the food and drink she had offered, Baubo evidently lifted her dress and exposed herself to the goddess—which delighted Demeter so greatly that she happily received the proffered sustenance. Iambe's name meanwhile became enshrined in the name iambics given to a genre of Greek poetry that involved invective (usually, though not always, in an iambic meter) aimed sometimes at society as a whole, sometimes at individuals, and very frequently at women. Archilochus, Semonides, and Hipponax were the most famous of the iambic poets. Archilochus was said to have lambasted the family of a young woman whose father had broken their engagement in such savage lines that they hanged themselves; Semonides composed a satire on women, discussed later in chapter 5, in iambics. The searing iambics of Hipponax were said to have had a similar impact on the sculptors Bupalus and Athenis, whose comical likenesses of him had provoked his wrath.[3] From being embedded in a happy story of female bonding, the word came to be associated with punitive verbal assaults.

Still other phenomena were reflective of the particularly dramatic aspects of real life, like kidnappings and rapes and cattle rustling. Tragedies happen that parallel those with which real humans were familiar. Athamas, maddened by an irate Hera, killed his oldest son when he mistook him for a deer; this still happens today, even leaving Hera out of the equation. Snakes abound, and numerous discarded snakeskins dot the Greek countryside. Orpheus's bride Eurydice was said to have died after stepping on a poisonous snake. The poet Anyte from Mytilene on Lesbos commemorated a dog of whom she (or the person who commissioned the verses) was fond who suffered the same fate:

> You too, beside the tangles of a bush
> With all too many roots, dear Locrian hound,
> Swiftest of all the pups who loved to bark—
> Into your nimble paw a gleaming snake
> With speckled throat injected cruel poison. (*Palatine Anthology* 16. 291)

The various myths that congregated around the figure of Prometheus served to explain a good bit. Hesiod tells how Prometheus's theft of fire, which Zeus had hidden from mortals, improved the lot of humankind no end, accounting for both heat and cooking. Another tale explained why it was that sacrifice, the central ritual of Greek religion, was followed by a delightful banquet in which humans got to divide up the meat while the gods luxuriated in the savory aroma of the smoke rising from the barbecue. Prometheus, it seems, tricked Zeus into choosing an offering of the bones of a sacrificed animal rather than the meat by dressing them artfully in glistening fat. Zeus was not best pleased, and the antics whereby Prometheus sought to benefit mankind so angered the king of the gods that he devised a dreadful punishment for man in the form of woman: "An evil thing," wrote Hesiod, "in which they may all delight while they embrace their destruction" (*Works and Days*, 57–58). Ordering Hephaestus to craft the basics—a beautiful, strong female body with the voice of a human but the beauty of a goddess—he commanded the other gods to provide the new creation with a variety of other gifts, hence her name, Pandora, "all gifts." Athena, goddess of crafts, would teach her weaving; Aphrodite, goddess of love and sex, would lavish her with charm and sex appeal; and the versatile messenger god Hermes, also the god of robbers, would be responsible for endowing her with a mind shameful as a dog's and the sly cunning of a thief. She was, in short, trouble. Appearances, the story served to suggest, are not to be trusted. As in the case of Prometheus's deception of Zeus, what looked good on the outside was not good on the inside, and a vast corpus of Greek literature would go on to paint women as deceitful. As if the appearance of woman on earth were not affliction enough, Pandora was also given an ominous jar. For, Hesiod wrote,

> The tribes of men had once lived on the earth
> Free utterly from evils, from harsh toil,
> And innocent of death brought by disease,
> For men who suffer always grow old fast.
> The woman, though, removed the jar's huge lid
> Lifting it in her hands, and then she spread
> Its contents—miseries for men, they were.
> She knew it, too. (*Works and Days*, 90–95)

Prometheus had a great deal to account for. Zeus certainly thought so, since he had him chained to a rock where an eagle fed perpetually on his liver. Not only did his well-meaning appropriation of sacrificial meat and his theft of fire result in saddling man with the plague of women, but man's erstwhile life of ease was also replaced with one of hardship. Before the arrival of Pandora, Hesiod says, men lived free of the hard work and illness that led to early death. The post-Pandora world, by contrast—the world problematically composed of two sexes—was ridden with disease and endless toil. The comfortable relationship that had once existed between gods and mortals (all the mortals evidently being male) had been severed. Once similarly lighthearted, the lives of gods and mortals had now become dramatically differentiated, the one remaining carefree, the other full of apprehension. In Hesiod's construct, then, women were created as a means for separating men—for there had as yet been no women—from the gods.

———

What were these gods like who endowed Pandora with her various attributes? The Greeks conceived their gods as outsize humans in appearance, albeit consistently good-looking where mere mortals varied drastically in pulchritude. They were often surrounded by an aura, although not when they were in disguise (which was a great deal of the time, as they were able to change into animal or human form at will), and sometimes they manifested themselves simply as forces of nature. They had considerable knowledge about the future, but they were not omniscient, as the dynamics of polytheism precluded both omniscience and omnipotence. The gods were temperamental and prone to quarreling with one another: god Alpha often plotted against god Beta, deceived god Gamma, or stymied the plans of god Delta. No god, however, could undo what another god had done. In Euripides' *Hippolytus*, Artemis is helpless to save her devotee Hippolytus and his stepmother Phaedra when Aphrodite has plotted their destruction. She explains:

> This is the custom here among the gods:
> No god can contravene another. We must yield,
> Standing aside, and let things take their course. (137–39)

Greek gods could not simply snap their fingers and will something to be done, as the god of the Hebrew Bible did when he said, "Let there be light." When they want someone dead, for example, they go about it in a very literal way. To gratify his priest Chryses by bringing plague upon the Greeks encamped at Troy, Apollo strides down from Olympus, his bow and quiver clanging on his shoulder, and showers them with poison arrows. In the battle between the gods and the giants, Hephaestus kills Mimas with missiles of red-hot iron while Dionysus kills Eurytos with his wand; Athena for her part does away with Encelados by hurling the island of Sicily at him. At other times, however, gods could be conceived as disembodied principles, possibly even figures of speech, as when people used "Aphrodite" to mean sex.

While not unlimited, however, the gods' powers were extraordinary. Though I have never tried, I should imagine that it takes a great deal of strength to pick up Sicily and throw it. They showed their exceptional nature even in earliest childhood. No sooner had he emerged from his mother Maia's womb than Hermes cast off his swaddling clothes and stole a herd of cattle belonging to his older brother Apollo, concealing them in a cavern except for two that he sacrificed and cooked for his dinner. He then returned to his cave and his swaddling clothes to play the wide-eyed innocent. Not surprisingly, he grew up to be hailed as the god of thieves. Gods developed at an astonishing speed. Zeus reached adulthood within a year of his birth, and his daughter Athena was born fully grown, clad in armor. Their diet was radically different from that of mortals, for in place of bread and wine they dined on ambrosia and drank nectar.

The myths of the Greeks were rife with conflict, struggle, and bloodshed—though the gods did not literally bleed, as their veins were filled not with blood but rather with a thin, watery ethereal substance called ichor. Nectar, ambrosia, ichor: divine DNA was not like yours or mine. The violence that ran like a leitmotif through Greek mythology took many forms. The slaying of monsters was one obvious way in which a hero like Heracles or the Athenian prince Theseus could manifest his heroism and enact his masculinity: monsters were always done in by males, never by females. It is hard to decide which came first, heroes or monsters. Were heroes created to dispatch monsters, or were monsters created to give heroes a way to discharge their energies in a socially constructive way? Greek myth teemed with unnatural creatures of various kinds, some more dangerous than others. By sketching out these inhuman beings the Greeks explored and played with what it meant to be human. Monstrosity defined humanity. Some were rather appealing, such as the satyrs, men with horse features, going on two cloven legs but with equine ears, mane, and tail. Greek satyrs were particularly partial to both drink and nymphs and were associated with Dionysus. They embodied lack of self-control and were regularly portrayed with erections, often masturbating, and they were more amusing than frightening. Also to be found in the woods were centaurs, who sported the bodies of horses but the heads and torsos of men and were more social than satyrs, generally congregating in groups. As nearly all satyrs and centaurs were male (visual evidence shows occasional exceptions), there was some disagreement as to how they reproduced their kind. Centaurs were perceived as every bit as lustful as satyrs but with a tendency toward violence when inebriated, which was a great deal of the time. Relief sculpture on the south side of the Parthenon shows a battle that ensued when the centaurs, guests at the wedding of Theseus's friend Peirithous, king of the Lapiths, tried to carry off the bride and many of their fellow invitees. Although centaurs were generally considered to be wild and uncivilized, one of their number, Chiron, possessed extraordinary wisdom and served as tutor to Achilles, Jason, and Apollo's son the healing god Asklepios (hence Chiron's modern nickname, Centaur for Disease Control). Although they could be dangerous, they were not grotesque.

The same could be said of the Minotaur. Though he fed eagerly on hapless humans who inadvertently wandered his way, he was hardly responsible for the awkward circumstances of his birth. The child who resulted from the Cretan queen Pasiphae's passion for a beautiful bull, he was an embarrassment to his family and thus consigned to the maze of the labyrinth; one wishes the unfortunate creature, blameless in the circumstances of his conception, had been able to enjoy a fuller life. The Cyclops Polyphemus who gobbled up Odysseus's crew might well frighten children, to whom all adult authority figures appear as big as giants, but his creepiness quotient is not high enough to strike cold terror in adults. Still other creatures were positively helpful, like the winged white horse Pegasus who assisted the hero Bellerophon in killing the Chimera. In fact, Pegasus was quite lovely to look at. The Chimera's particular combination of characteristics was fearsome—she was a conglomeration of a lion, a goat, and a snake—and she breathed fire to boot. Bellerophon was finally able to kill her only by approaching on Pegasus and thrusting his spear into her mouth with a lump of lead attached, which, melted by the creature's flaming breath, choked her.

Inevitably, the scariest monsters that sprang from the Greek imagination—the ones who really instilled primal terror—were those who most departed from accepted bodily norms and were most inclined to do harm. Among the most unsettling were creatures who had once been beautiful women, as these occasioned profound anxiety in both women who feared the loss of their looks and men who feared powerful females. Medusa, for example, had been a stunner (with, of all things, unusually beautiful hair) before she had the bad luck to catch Poseidon's eye. When the god raped her in Athena's temple, Athena was so aggrieved that she thought punishment was in order. As so often, this punishment fell not on the rapist but on his victim. The goddess turned Medusa into the forbidding Gorgon she is still known as today, a hideous creature, her lovely locks now hissing snakes, whose gaze turned anyone on whom it fell to stone. The motif of snaky hair crops up again in the dread Furies who leave their homes in the Underworld to avenge murdered kin. Even Athena in Aeschylus's *Eumenides* is taken aback at their appalling appearance. Who might they be? she inquires, for in them she sees

> no race of creatures ever brought to birth,
> neither of goddesses seen by the gods
> nor formed with shapes resembling those of mortals. (410–12)

It is not actually flippant to suggest that both Medusa and the Furies epitomized "bad hair days," symbolizing the inability to tame a serpentine tangle that has taken on a life of its own beyond the control of the head from which it sprang.

Other creatures were horrifying more in behavior than in appearance. The woman-bird hybrids known as the Harpies, though surely disconcerting to behold, repelled not by their looks but by their habits. They seem, like Medusa, once to have been normal women with exquisite hair. In their hybrid incarnation, however, they were given to snatching away the tasty dishes hopeful consultants brought the seer Phineas just as he was about to start eating—and seeing to it that the little they left was disgusting. Apollonius Rhodius tells the tale in the *Argonautica*:

Sometimes they left not a morsel; at other times, only a little.
And thus they ensured that the man would endure a life full of torment.
Over it all they would pour a stench that was utterly loathsome.
Nobody dared even stand near the food, let alone lift it
Up to his mouth, so great was the stink of the creatures' leavings.
  (2. 189–93)

Granted the gift of prophecy by Apollo, Phineus had gotten carried away and revealed the will of Zeus in all its detail, whereupon the king of the gods took away his eyesight and sicced these sadistic creatures on him. Their name derived from the verb *harpazō*, to snatch, but the vile odor they imparted to their leavings made clear their truly fiendish nature. They did not simply want Phineus's food for themselves. Rather, they were determined that he should starve—just as he thought he was about to be fed.

Hurtful deeds are not the province of sadistic monsters alone. It comes as something of a shock when in the *Iliad* the ghost of the exceptionally gentle Patroclus recalls how he came to be so close to the hero Achilles: his father had spirited him away when still a child to safety in the home of Achilles' father Peleus because he was, in effect, wanted for manslaughter. Just like a fool, he says,

> not really meaning to do it, but angry because of a game
> A silly game of dice, I killed Amphidamas's son. (23. 85–88)

The celebrated inventor Daedalus was said to have come to Crete, where he designed the famous labyrinth, because he had been exiled for killing his nephew. The most revered of all Greek heroes, Heracles, in adolescence had struck and killed his music teacher out of frustration during a lesson, and it was as a penance for killing his wife and children in a fit of madness that the priestess at Delphi had ordered him to perform his famous twelve labors.

———

The mythology of the Greeks was both national—if one may use that word of a civilization that spread over hundreds of nation-states—and regional. While some myths were recounted in all parts of the Greek world, others pertaining to deified local heroes were of more limited distribution. Thebes was particularly rich in local myths. Thebans enjoyed telling how Semele had given birth there to Dionysus, how their founder Cadmus had brought the alphabet from Phoenicia, how Teiresias had been born there; they also had the dubious honor of being home to the unfortunate house of Oedipus. Athenians were particularly fond of myths that featured their tutelary deity Athena or their local hero Theseus, whose journey to Athens to assume his rightful place as the king's son afforded one opportunity after another to enact his heroism, dispatching a series of high-profile malefactors. The most famous was the rogue smith Procrustes, known for the iron bed to which he insisted on fitting all passersby, stretching the short and lopping off the legs of the tall; administering a dose of his own medicine, Theseus put an end to Procrustes by fitting him to the very same bed. The Spartans, meanwhile, though they certainly had a temple to Athena, were heavily invested in the cult of Helen—the hometown girl made bad in the *Iliad*, but good, as we shall see, in the *Odyssey*—and Heracles, believed to be the ancestor of the Spartan kings. Like the Spartans, Heracles was renowned more for brawn than for brain. He slept with each of the 50 daughters of Thespios on consecutive nights under the impression that they were all the same person. To be sure, it was probably dark at the time. Nonetheless . . .

The cast of characters tended to be gods, Olympic and otherwise; demigods; and illustrious individuals (along with their families) believed to have lived around the time of the Trojan War. The countryside, moreover, was believed to teem with wild creatures of various kinds, and these regularly made their appearance in myth. Nymphs abounded—tree nymphs (dryads), mountain nymphs (oreads), and water nymphs (naiads). (Champion swimmer Diana Nyad is aptly named.) Nymphs were universally fair of form and face, with appealingly careless locks that never required the ministrations of a professional. They were fond of dancing, and very good at it. The occasional nymph was immortal, like Achilles' mother Thetis, but most nymphs simply lived for a very long time, though they never lost their looks—unless like the unfortunate Callisto, they were turned into animals by wrathful divinities, or like poor Echo, who, falling in love with the self-absorbed Narcissus, so lost her sense of self that she eventually dwindled into nothing but an ... echo. Most nymphs, however, remained beautiful until the end, which came, in the wry calculations of folklorist William Hansen, at the conclusion of 194,400 years. Hesiod, Hansen points out, shows us a nymph declaring that a crow lives for nine human generations, a stag four times as long as a crow, a raven three times as long as a stag, a phoenix nine times as long as a raven, and a nymph ten times as long as a phoenix; and so, calculating a human generation at twenty years ...⁴ The lives of nymphs were largely free of care. The sorrows sparked in Thetis by the sufferings of her beloved son Achilles were exceptional, for few nymphs married or bore children. Nymphs were generally atypical of Greek females in their sexuality. Although some were chaste followers of Artemis (herself something of a super-nymph), many were promiscuous and frolicked uninhibitedly with such males as frequented the forests—satyrs, for example.

Greek myth contained a strong dose of folktale. From folktale comes the motif of the poisoned gift that appears in the story of Heracles' death at the hands of his jealous wife Deianeira. Similarly, the wronged Medea murdered her husband Jason's new bride by bestowing on her the gift of a flammable garment. The stories of both Bellerophon and Jason are built on the folk motif of the man sent on a seemingly impossible quest meant to end in his death. He is then set a series of extraordinarily dangerous and seemingly impossible tasks, which he completes successfully, thereby not only avoiding death but winning the hand of the local princess as well. When Proitos, king of Tiryns in the Peloponnesus, suspects his guest Bellerophon of having tried to seduce his wife, he sends Bellerophon to visit her father King Iobates in Anatolia. With him he sends a letter instructing Iobates to kill him, but, squeamish about killing a guest at his hearth, Iobates instead assigns him three tasks. The first entails killing the fearsome fire-breathing Chimera, which he accomplishes by stuffing a block of lead down her throat. When Bellerophon is equally successful in the other tasks put before him, Iobates marries him to another one of his daughters—and splits his kingdom with him to boot.

The story of Jason and the golden fleece is better known. Alarmed by a prophecy suggesting that Jason might murder him, his wicked uncle Pelias, who has wrested the throne of Iolcos from Jason's father, its rightful occupant, sends the young man off to Colchis on the Black Sea (the modern Sochi, where the winter Olympics were held in 2014) with instructions to retrieve the famous golden ram's fleece in the possession of King Aietes. Setting out on the ship *Argo*, Jason and his crew become known as the Argonauts, sailors of the *Argo*. Their journey requires them to overcome many challenging obstacles, not least of them the terrifying Sympleglades, mobile cliffs that clashed together as ships passed through them, crushing ship and crew alike. When the crew finally arrive safely in Colchis, King Aietes promises to hand over the fleece on condition that Jason perform two daunting tasks, yoking a pair of fire-breathing bulls and sowing dragon's teeth. With the aid of the king's daughter the sorceress Medea, who has conveniently fallen in love with the stranger (as princesses are wont to do), Jason successfully yokes the bulls and defeats the armed men who spring up from the ground sown with the dragon's teeth. Aietes still proving unwilling to surrender the fleece, Jason and Medea make off with it and return to Iolcos, where they take vengeance on Uncle Pelias.

The story of Theseus and the Minotaur offers a variant on the motif. After several years during which the Athenians regretfully accede to King Minos's demand for seven youths and seven maidens to be sent to Crete to be devoured by the Minotaur in compensation for the death of Minos's son Androgeos in Athenian territory, Theseus demands to be one of the youths, hoping to put an end to both the Minotaur and the tribute. After Theseus has slain the Minotaur with the help of the local princess Ariadne, he abandons her (though she has the good fortune to be rescued by, indeed married to, the god Dionysus). Returning to Athens, he forgets to put up the white sail that was to serve as reassurance to his father, Aegeus, that he had survived his ordeal, and it is his father who dies: seeing the black sail Theseus has forgotten to change and believing his son to have perished, he jumps to his death into the sea that now bears his name. Indirectly, then, Theseus too kills the man who had sent him on his mission. Oedipus was only one of many figures who brought about the death of his father in Greek myth, where inter-generational tension plays a prominent role.

Except for Zeus's brother Hades, who ruled the land of the dead, the principal gods were thought to live on Mount Olympus in northern Greece. At nearly 10,000 feet and shrouded in cloud cover, Olympus was sufficiently formidable to discourage any cheeky climbers bent on refuting this belief. In historical times, the Olympian gods formed an extended patriarchal family with Zeus at the head. But it was not always so. It was Homer and Hesiod, said the historian Herodotus, "who taught the Greeks the descent of the gods, giving them names and allotting to them their special skills and honors and describing their appearance" (2. 53. 2). While the *Iliad* and the *Odyssey* depict the Olympian gods manifesting the personality traits and family relationships with which all Greeks came to be familiar, it was Hesiod who took it upon himself to integrate the various tales about the Olympians into a cohesive narrative, and to add to it an account of the very origins of these gods—and indeed of the universe that begat them.

The underlying leitmotif of Hesiod's narrative is the movement from an amoral and unstable universe to a just world subject to Zeus *pater andrōn te theōn te*, father of gods and men. Much of Greek mythology concerns the ill-considered attempts of both gods and mortals to tamper with this order and the punishments that attend them. Hesiod's *Theogony* is organized around the story of Zeus's rise to power and subsequent consolidation of his masculine authority. The poet makes plain, however, that the universe came into existence well before Zeus made his appearance. In Hesiod's construct, the universe is anterior to the gods and was not created by them; indeed various forces of nature are their ancestors. The poet does not say just when or how or why, but at some point *Chaos*, as he calls it in Greek, came into being: not chaos as the English word is understood today, but a yawning gap, an empty space of darkness and disorder. Chaos was soon joined by Gaia (Earth), who literally grounds the previously formless universe; by Tartarus (the deepest part of the Underworld); and by Eros, the dynamic force of desire that will facilitate generation. Most components of what came to be the natural world descended in one way or another from either

Chaos or Gaia, created sometimes by sexual intercourse, sometimes by asexual reproduction, something of which deities were evidently capable. Much later the goddess Hera while estranged from Zeus was said to have engendered Hephaestus in this way, without any sexual partner. Chaos on its own produced Darkness and Night, who in turn mated to produce Brightness and Day. Gaia reproduced parthenogenically as well, giving birth to Ouranos—Sky. After this, however, sex was normally requisite for reproduction.

In no way discouraged by the fact that they were mother and son, Gaia mated with Ouranos. After all, choice of partners was then severely limited. To Ouranos Gaia bore Kronos and eleven other formidable deities of colossal force known as the Titans, as well as a number of unusual creatures: the three one-eyed giants known as Cyclopes (Orb-eyed ones) and the three so-called Hundred-Handers (who also boasted fifty heads). Ouranos, though inordinately fond of sex, was less than enthusiastic about its consequences. In fact, he hated his children so much that no sooner did they appear than he shoved them back into Gaia, causing her no small amount of suffering both emotional and physical. So painfully distended that she was ready to burst, the earth goddess persuaded Kronos to attack his clingy sex maniac father with an adamantine sickle she had wrought from the molten metal deep within her. When next Ouranos visited her, he got quite a surprise:

> Huge Ouranos, full of desire, brought on night,
> And spread himself all over Earth, his mate.
> The son then from his hiding place, his ambush,
> Stretched out his left hand; in his right, he took
> The long and jagged sickle. One fell stroke
> Sufficed to reap his father's genitals
> And cast them off where they would fall to ground.
> Not vainly did they fall from Kronos's hand,
> For earth receiving all the bloody drops
> Bore the strong Furies as the seasons passed.
> She bore the Giants with their gleaming armor.
> . . .

Genitals floating far across the main
Gave rise to shining foam, the product of
Immortal flesh, and in it grew a maiden.

. . .

Her gods and men alike call Aphrodite. (*Theogony* 176–95)

The rage of father against child and child against father gives birth to both sexual passion and a cycle of vengeance, for the Furies, ghastly to look upon with writhing snakes for hair, had as their charge the relentless hounding of those who had murdered the most inappropriate of victims—parents, guests, suppliants. And not only that. Ouranos's vain attempt to stop time and have the earth to himself has been foiled by the maternal love that will move history forward in succeeding generations.

Kronos, however, was no more cut out for parenthood than his father. Having discovered that he was fated to be overthrown by one of his sons, he made a point of gulping down each of his children as it was born. His sister and increasingly unwilling consort Rhea understandably sought a means of both protecting their next child and avenging herself upon Kronos. Hiding her new baby in a cave on the island of Crete, she presented Kronos not with the infant he was expecting but rather with a stone wrapped in swaddling clothes, for which trick, the poet Corinna maintains, "she won great honor from the immortal gods."[5] This stone Kronos obligingly swallowed, leaving baby Zeus to grow to maturity in the care of the nymph Adamanthea. Or the goat Amalthea—who was also sort of a nymph. Or his grandmother Gaia. Greek myths were not known for their consistency. Another female poet, Moero, wrote that Zeus was nursed by birds, who brought him ambrosia from the ends of the earth, with the assistance of an eagle,

Who, ever drawing nectar from a rock.
Brought cunning Zeus the beverage in his beak.[6]

Indeed, another myth made Aphrodite the daughter of Zeus by one of his many consorts, Dione, a Greek word really just meaning "female counterpart of Zeus"; Swiss historian Walter Burkert has wittily dubbed Zeus and Dione "Mr. and Mrs. Heaven."[7]

In the fullness of time Kronos was forced to vomit up the children he had swallowed. Zeus then set about establishing himself as ruler over a well-ordered cosmos, a project in the course of which he underwent many trials. His aunts and uncles the formidable Titans resisted him vigorously, though after a war of ten years Zeus was finally able to prevail. More trouble, however, lay in store, for the monster Typhon challenged Zeus for supremacy, a challenge that threatened everything for which Zeus had worked, as the forces of chaos made one final stand against justice and harmony. Typhon's appearance was so horrifying that upon laying eyes on him even the Olympian gods fled in terror. Out of his shoulders grew a hundred dragons' heads, their snaky tongues flickering ominously. Each fearful head burned with fire, and in each one were voices uttering the most unsettling sounds, the indescribable cries of every imaginable creature. The earth, the sea, and even the Underworld felt the heat generated by the struggle as Typhon's raging fires did combat with the scorching winds from Zeus's lightning bolts, but Zeus at last prevailed and hurled the monster deep into the pit of Tartarus.

It is difficult to know whether the persistent topos in Hesiod's narrative of mothers inciting their sons to harm and displace their fathers derived from the patterns of real life. After all, adolescent Greek girls often as young as fourteen were customarily married off to men of thirty or so, generally in arranged marriages. Frequently having a limited attachment to their husbands, they probably did bond closely with their children, who generally arrived not long after they had put away their dolls. According to Hesiod, however, his remarkable account of how the world came to be as it was had been poured into his ears by the Muses "while he was shepherding lambs by Mount Helicon, reverend and holy" (*Theogony* 23).

If so, we must wonder where the Muses had gotten these stories. Who were the Muses' muses? Similar tales were circulating to the east, and it seems impossible to determine the relationship of these yarns to one another. The narrative traditions of Anatolia and Mesopotamia shared Hesiod's conception of the beginning of time as a period of disorder and anarchy followed by a violent succession of rulers. The discovery of cuneiform tablets recording Hittite myths about the origins of the gods has brought to light striking parallels between Greek and Hittite accounts.[8] The Hittite poem *Kingship in Heaven* tells of a succession of gods similar to the one recounted by Hesiod. After deposing the god Alalu, we read, Anu took over the monarchy and was served by his son Kumarbi, who sat at his feet and gave him his food and drink. In the ninth year of Anu's reign, however, Kumarbi challenged him for the kingship, biting off and swallowing his penis, whereupon his father informed him that he had impregnated him with several gods, including the storm god Teshub. Having heard that Teshub would usurp his power, Kumarbi . . . at this point the tablet is damaged, but it seems that Kumarbi gives birth to another god, whom he announces he will destroy by eating him—and is given what seems to be a stone in the child's place. He subsequently gives birth to Teshub, evidently through his penis.[9]

Both the *Theogony* and *Kingship in Heaven* feature a succession of male gods, the castration of a god by his successor, inappropriate swallowing, male pregnancy, and the conflation of a god and a stone. The parallels are striking, and there are also conspicuous similarities to other Greek accounts. In 1962 a papyrus was discovered near the Derveni Pass in northern Greece. The poem it contained was written around the middle of the fourth century BCE and purports to be the work of the legendary poet Orpheus, who, if he really lived (Aristotle had his doubts, and so do I) would have died centuries earlier. The creation myth the Orphic text contains departs from Hesiod's in several ways, the most arresting of which is that it depicts Zeus swallowing the genitals of a god who appears to be Kronos and thereby becoming pregnant with all the other gods and goddesses, just as Kumarbi gives birth to various gods after swallowing the genitals of Anu.[10]

What are we to make of these parallels? Though the Hittite account is far earlier than the Greek ones, it is not at all clear that Hesiod and his successors were familiar with Hittite literature. Quite possibly they both descended from a common source, but some of these motifs appear in other cultures as well—Egypt and Babylon, for example. It may well be that contact among cultures offered access to a common store of constructs and motifs, or that we need to fall back on Jungian notions of archetypes.

Never dethroned, Zeus ruled eternally. Conflicting family trees accounted for the dozen or so gods who were believed to enjoy carefree lives on Olympus. Zeus, Hesiod reports, first married the clever Titan Metis, profiting from her wise counsel: in many ways Metis was intelligence personified (or, I suppose, deified). Whereas Kronos had swallowed his offspring after hearing that he was fated to be overthrown by one of them, Zeus, having heard that Metis would give birth to a son greater than his father, dealt with the problem by swallowing Metis herself while she was pregnant with Athena, thus ensuring that she would never bear this dreaded boy. Born directly from the head of Zeus (an interesting fantasy of male pregnancy), Athena came to join the small cadre of Olympians already in existence—her father Zeus and his siblings Poseidon, Demeter, and Hades. The rather unexciting Hestia was the goddess of the hearth and its flame. Hades had equal status to the Olympians, though he was not technically one of them, as he presided over the kingdom of the dead in the Underworld—or, as it was called after him, Hades: confusingly, Hades was the name both of the god and of the Underworld over which he presided. The earth not only housed the dead. It was also the source of life in the form of vegetable and mineral products, and thus Hades had another name, Pluto, meaning "wealth," a happier designation by which he came to be known at Rome. Zeus married his sister Demeter, fathering Persephone; his subsequent marriage to a second aunt, the Titan Themis (divine law), produced the Fates and the Horai (hours/seasons). From his final marriage, to Hera, was born Ares, and during that marriage Hera gave birth to Hephaestus—on her own, Hesiod says, the forger god having no father (although other traditions claimed that he was sired by Zeus). Having married both Intellect and Law, Zeus has now brought a just order out of mindlessness and anarchy. Significantly, he does marry, unlike grandfather Ouranos and father Kronos, who simply forced themselves on Gaia and Rhea. Civilization has arrived, and though patriarchy has been tamed a bit, it has also become entrenched as part of the order of things.

Finding marriage confining, however, Zeus expanded the roster of gods through a series of couplings with other females both mortal and immortal, often taking advantage of his Olympian powers to sneak up on them in disguise. Spending nine nights with his aunt Mnemosyne in the guise of a shepherd, he fathered the nine Muses. Perhaps things might have proceeded differently had Hera suggested some role-playing in the boudoir, but then there would have been far fewer gods on tap. His liaison with his cousin Leto produced Artemis and Apollo. On Semele he fathered Dionysus, but poor Semele never lived to see her divine son. Making the mistake of asking her lover to appear to her in his full majesty, she was incinerated by his lightning bolt, whereupon Zeus sewed the embryonic god of wine and fertility into his thigh until the fetus had become viable—a second instance of male pregnancy. The king of gods and men was not above rape. Maia, who became the mother of Hermes, does not seem to have had any choice in the matter, and the busy god also slept with Maia's two sisters. And then there were twelve. Or rather, fourteen, but Hades was really only an honorary Olympian, and to get an even number the Greeks normally left out either Dionysus or the colorless Hestia. There were also many lesser deities who inhabited a variety of places on land and sea, such as the goddesses Calypso and Circe who became lovers of Odysseus.

Following the pattern set down by Zeus, the Olympians were generally prone to restoring order by punishing the hybris that threatened it when humans transgressed their bounds. Determined to drive the chariot of his father the Sun, the inexperienced Phaethon loses control of the horses and falls to his death; disregarding his father Daedalus's caution not to fly too near the sun lest it melt the wax in his artificial wings, Icarus meets a similar fate. When Arachne boasts that she rivaled Athena in weaving, the irate goddess turns her into a spider. It would be a mistake, however, to imagine that the Greeks considered misfortune simply the result of divine punishment in some simplistic sequence of causes and effects. When the gods work their will, an enormous amount of collateral damage frequently ensues. Perhaps the most flagrant example of offspring punished for the sins of their parents is the death of Niobe's children at the hands of Leto's twins Apollo and Artemis. When Niobe boasted that she had seven sons and seven daughters to Leto's mere two, Leto sent her two to kill Niobe's fourteen. Children frequently suffer for the transgressions of ancestors long dead as well, as witness the curse of the house of Atreus, Agamemnon's father.

Both Hestia and Dionysus were outliers among the Olympians. Hestia had too little personality, Dionysus too much. Transgression and disorder were Dionysus's hallmarks, along with a large dose of paradox. Associated with wine and partying and the attendant loss of control, he was male but effeminate and encouraged his followers to cross over into a frenzy of madness; the English word ecstasy, which characterized the condition of his feverish nocturnal followers, means literally standing outside oneself (*ek-stasis*), and appropriately so. Yet though he embodied a life-affirming exuberance, he was also linked to death and the Underworld. The god of play, he would in classical Athens become the god of plays, both tragic and comic: the dramatists that we associate with Athens—Aeschylus, Sophocles, Euripides, Aristophanes—presented their plays at the annual spring festival in his honor, the City Dionysia. Disguised after his birth (sometimes as a girl, sometimes a goat) to avoid the wrath of his divine father's jealous wife, Dionysus was in close touch with an animalistic side. He was often portrayed in art surrounded by wild creatures. Elusive in every sense, he formed a counterweight to the orderly cosmos his divine father had gone to so much trouble to establish. The order of Zeus is all very well, but real life is messy, and in Greek thinking—and feeling—that messiness was embodied in the figure of Dionysus. In the words of French philosopher Luc Ferry, "whenever we need reminding, he makes us newly aware of how the cosmos was constructed out of chaos, and of how fragile is this edifice, stemming from the victory of Zeus over the Titans—all the more fragile if we forget the origins of this precariousness. This is why the carnivalesque frightens us, just as madness frightens us, because we feel undeniably how close it is to us: how it is inside us."[11]

Each of the Olympian gods had a distinct sphere of interest and influence. Zeus was associated with monarchy and justice—"kings," Hesiod proclaimed in a line quoted hundreds of years later by Callimachus in his *Hymn to Zeus*, "are from Zeus" (*Theogony* 96; *Hymn to Zeus* 79)— but also with lightning and thunder, which manifested themselves in the sky; his name was related to the Greek word *dios*, bright or shining.

It comes into English as "day," and the Spanish for "day" is *día*. The first letter of his name had a little bit of a "d" sound in Greek, and from it are descended the English words deity and divine, as well as the words for God in the romance languages, starting with the Latin *deus* and proceeding to the Italian *Dio*, the Spanish *Dios*, the French *Dieu*. (Curiously, the Greek word for a god, *theos*, from which theology derives, is unrelated and comes from a completely different root.) From *Zeus-pater* (Zeus-father) the Romans named their chief god Ju-piter. Zeus's brother Poseidon, generally perceived as the god of the sea, was also the god of horses and earthquakes; the Greeks may have had some understanding of the relationship between earthquakes and tsunamis. Of Zeus's other siblings, Hades ruled the land of the dead, and Demeter governed the fertility of the land and was particularly associated with grain. Hera was the goddess of women, marriage, and motherhood. She had a great deal to contend with, and her lot was not a happy one. Having been dethroned from her original position as a revered goddess in her own right, as consort to Olympus's philanderer-in-chief she came to be characterized as the prototypical nagging wife who never lets her husband have any fun—a disposition easy to understand given that Zeus's idea of fun frequently involved disguising himself as an animal to seduce a mortal woman; Helen, it was said, was conceived after he appeared to the unsuspecting Leda in the form of a swan. Hestia came in a poor sixth, the rather drab goddess of the hearth. Rarely depicted anthropomorphically, she was often represented simply as a flame and symbolized the family and the household, the *oikos*. When she is about to die, Euripides' Alcestis prays to Hestia to take care of her children (*Alcestis*, 163–69). As a symbol of the *oikos*, however, Hestia had great importance, and a deed that would be vile anywhere was considered far more heinous when performed by the hearth. In depicting Clytemnestra's ghost reminiscing at her hearth about the offerings she had made to ward off retribution for the murder of her husband Agamemnon (*Eumenides*, 106–9), Aeschylus is underlining the transgressive nature of her attitude to family, whose integrity women, guardians of the hearth, were charged with preserving.

The gods of the next generation had their own provinces as well. Those of Apollo were numerous: music, arts, medicine, reason, prophecy, the sun. His twin Artemis was in charge of hunting, childbirth, and the moon. The hypermasculine Ares was the pitiless god of war. Unlike that other virgin goddess Artemis, who had unquestioned sex appeal, scrambling across hill and dale in a skimpy outfit suited to quick motion and archery, Athena was rather asexual. She was also something of a gender-bender. She had a good bit to do with war and was often depicted with weapons, but unlike the brutal Ares she was associated more with military valor, strategy, and fighting for just causes, and she was the goddess not only of wisdom but also of handicrafts in general and that prototypically female handicraft, weaving, which embodied wifely virtue. But not the craft of the blacksmith, for that fell to the lame Hephaestus. Smithing was the perfect profession for a god with his handicap, requiring as it did primarily upper body strength. Hermes with his winged sandals served as the messenger of the gods but also was held to be the patron of travelers, including those traveling from the world above to the Underworld after death, and in time he also came to be associated with democracy. When the Athenians awoke one morning to find that the dozens of the images of the god known as herms that served as boundary markers throughout the city had been vandalized during the night, they had no doubt that a conspiracy to overthrow the democratic government was afoot. Aphrodite presided over love and sex. Not surprisingly, none of the male gods was a virgin.

Once the forces of chaos had been overcome, giving birth to a new order over which the "just" Zeus presided, harmony prevailed in the cosmos. In the human community, however, there was trouble. In his *Works and Days*, Hesiod schematizes the history of his own kind in terms of five successive races. First came the men of gold, who enjoyed the carefree life of gods and for whom death was just a tranquil sort of "falling asleep." Next came a race of silver, people who had so little judgment that they not only wronged one another but also failed to sacrifice to the gods; these Zeus destroyed. The race of bronze that followed them required no divine intervention for its extinction, for they were so quarrelsome that they killed one other off. The next race was a major improvement, consisting of the heroes known as demigods. Precisely because of their gallant natures, however, many died fighting in the great wars—at Thebes, at Troy; the others Zeus transported upon their deaths to the isles of the blessed at the ends of the earth. Last came the modern world in the form of the fifth generation, who live in the iron age. Once again fighting is constant, even within families, and the gods are even denied reverence. Finally the time will come, Hesiod says, when the race has degenerated so badly that babies are born already with gray hair, and Zeus will destroy this race too. Curiously, however, Hesiod seems to leave the door open to some improvement at an unspecified time, though he does not indicate how, saying

> If only I were not one of these men,
> Men of the fifth race; would that I had died
> Beforehand, or had been born afterward. (174–75)

———

Most Greek myths originated very early and were passed down by oral tradition before first being recorded in writing. As time went by, variants were rung on the traditional tales. Both Pherecydes of Syros around 500 and Apollodorus much later sought to exonerate Theseus, the legendary founder of Athens, from the charge of abandoning his fiancée Ariadne on the island of Naxos after she had been instrumental in his escape from the labyrinth: Pherecydes claimed that Theseus left the princess on the island at the orders of Athena, and Apollodorus suggested that Dionysus had fallen in love with her and carried her off even before the Athenian prince set sail. Others elaborated greatly on what they had heard, like Apollonius of Rhodes, whose *Argonautica* detailed the adventures of Jason and Medea. The tragedians of the fifth century often presented conflicting versions of the myths that formed their plots. Greeks took their mythical heritage seriously. When they were drawing up their battle lines before Plataea in 479, Herodotus reports, the Tegeans, arguing with the Athenians over which of them should have the honor of holding one of the wings, appealed comfortably to the evidence of myth, maintaining that Sparta had always granted them the honor of holding a wing in all Peloponnesian campaigns since their king

Echemus had defeated Heracles' son Hyllus in single combat when the descendants of Heracles invaded the Peloponnesus. By way of reply the Athenians listed their own good deeds from the heroic age, adducing their hospitality to those same Heraclids, their attack on Thebes to retrieve the dead bodies of those lost in the war between Oedipus's sons, and their defeat in battle of the invading Amazons; "and in the arduous struggle at Troy," they add, "we were second to none" (Herodotus 9. 27). Not even the rationalist Athenian historian Thucydides was able to excise myth entirely from his consciousness. In discussing the Athenians' attempt to ally with the Thracian king Sitalces, he makes a point of stressing that Sitalces' father Teres was in no way related to Tereus, the husband of Procne who with her sister had murdered Tereus's son Itys when she discovered Tereus's rape of her sister and was subsequently turned into a nightingale to escape his wrath. Indeed, he says, the two men lived in different parts of Thrace, Tereus having lived in Daulis, "and it was here the women slaughtered Itys; and many of the poets in seeking an epithet for the nightingale have dubbed it 'Daulian'" (2. 29. 3). Are we to understand that Thucydides believed women can turn into birds?

Late in the fourth century, Euhemerus put forward the theory that myth was nothing but history misremembered: tales that acquired elements of the fantastic as they grew in the retelling. The gods, he claimed, were nothing but illustrious men, generally kings, whose achievements were magnified after death to the point that they were held to be divine. Euhemerus was not the first to explore the origins of the Greeks' myths. In his dialogue *Phaedrus*, written a couple of generations earlier, Plato depicted Socrates and Phaedrus walking along the banks of the Ilissus River on the outskirts of Athens when suddenly Phaedrus realizes that they are in the neighborhood of the spot where Boreas, god of the north wind, was said to have carried off Oreithyia. Do you think, he asks Socrates, that it could have happened in this very spot? After all, the waters here are very clear and pleasant, and this would be a natural place for girls to have been playing. Phaedrus evidently finds the story credible. Actually, Socrates says, the place you're thinking of is a bit farther downstream. But, Phaedrus inquires, do you think the story is true? Socrates replies at length in a speech that alludes to the

famous prescription carved in the forecourt of Apollo's temple at Delphi, "know thyself":

> It would be nothing out of the ordinary if I were to mistrust the story,
> as the wise men do; then I might rationalize the tale by saying that a
> blast of Boreas, the north wind, pushed her off the nearby rocks as
> she was playing . . . and that when she had died in this way she was
> said to have been carried off by Boreas. But I, Phaedrus, think such
> explanations, though as a rule very entertaining, are the inventions
> of a very clever and not altogether enviable man, and a very hard
> worker at that, for he then has to explain the forms of the centaurs,
> and then that of the Chimera, and he is swamped by a whole slew of
> such creatures of peculiar, unimaginable, portentous natures. Anyone
> who disbelieves in these, and with a rustic sort of wisdom, takes it
> upon himself to explain each in accordance with probability, will
> need a great deal of free time. But I, my friend, have no time for them
> at all, for I am not yet able, as the Delphic inscription puts it, to know
> myself; so it seems silly when I have not yet achieved that, to inves-
> tigate irrelevant things. For this reason I just let these things go, and
> allowing myself to accept the customary belief about them, as I was
> just saying, I investigate not these things, but rather myself, to learn
> whether I am a monster more convoluted and more furious than Ty-
> phon or a tamer and simpler creature, to whom a divine and humble
> lot is assigned by nature. (229c–230a)

But what a lovely place this is to which you have led us, he adds. Judging
by the figurines and statues here, it must be sacred to the nymphs!

In response to Phaedrus's question, Socrates punts, giving an eminently reasonable explanation for the myth that he attributes to "wise
men" but then promptly undercutting it by saying that once you start
trying to rationalize myth you find yourself stuck with quite a host of
improbable creatures to explain away. In fact, Socrates—or at any rate,
Plato—reveled in myth when it served his purposes and indeed, as
we will see in chapter 8, enjoyed making original myths of his own. The
centaur problem also captured the imagination of the mythographer
known as Palaephatus, who may have no more been named Palaephatus

than Apollodorus was really named Apollodorus. He probably wrote around 300; he may have come from the area of the Hellespont; and he may have moved to Athens, where Aristotle may have been his lover; but nothing about Palaephatus's biography is certain. What is beyond doubt is that he was exasperated no end by the improbability of so many of the Greek tales and devoted himself energetically to, we might say, "exploding the myths." What kind of idiot, he asks again and again, could fall for this baloney?

A number of myths he dismisses as arising from taking proper names too literally. A sea monster that the Trojans were able to keep from ravaging their land by tossing it young girls to devour? Not bloody likely, he writes: "It is futile for men to make covenants with fish. Can anyone not know that?"[12] No, he insists, the truth is that the area around Troy was once subject to a powerful king who was in the habit of exacting tribute in the form of either livestock or young girls, but because his name, Keaton, was similar to the Greek word for sea monster or whale, *ketos*, the story went around that the girls were being handed over to such a fell creature. And, Palaephatus adds, his depredations continued until Heracles put an end to them. (Evidently the rationalist Palaephatus had no difficulty believing in the historicity of Heracles.) The notion of centaurs, he says, extrapolating from modern times, must have arisen when people saw men on horseback retreating. If there had once upon a time been centaurs, no doubt there would still be centaurs today, but there are not. Besides, horse food and people food are different, so . . . When a real centaur was actually reported in the reign of the Corinthian tyrant Periander, it was considered a very bad omen: while Periander was entertaining guests in honor of a sacrifice to Aphrodite, he was spooked by the birth in his stable of a creature who was reputed to be half human and half horse.[13] Palaephatus appeals to the same line of reason in denying the existence of Amazons, explaining that they must have been simply men who tied their hair back: "as, after all, there are no such armies in the world today, an army of women is not likely ever to have existed" (32).

In this Palaephatus was almost certainly mistaken. Recent research in archaeology and anthropology, as well as the study of the heroic Nart sagas of the Caucasus, suggests that tales of Amazons were grounded in

fact.[14] Abundant finds make clear that there were indeed women warriors in the Caucasus region. Digging has turned up numerous graves of
women buried with weapons whose skeletons show signs of traumatic
wounds, and one of the warrior queens of Caucasus legend was sugges-
tively named Amezan.[15] Greek authors located the Amazons in a variety
of places—basically they were held to live in not-Greece—but the most
common of these was Scythia in Eurasia. Although there was much disagreement among the Greeks as to the details of Amazon life—did Amazons remove one breast to facilitate shooting arrows and throwing the
javelin? did they kill their boy babies? did they live with men or in a
single-sex community?—one thing was clear: unlike Greek women, they
were warriors, and fearsome ones at that. The frequent appearance of
Amazons in art reveals the Greeks' fascination with these outdoorsy
women who followed traditional male pursuits—hunting, riding,
fighting—and had no interest in housework: Amazons were the second
most popular subject for vase painting, eclipsed only by Heracles. They
made wonderful subjects, sporting patterned leggings that emphasized
their shape in a way that draped garments did not and wearing exotic
ankle boots. They were normally portrayed with both breasts, suggesting
that the notion that they removed one breast by searing or cutting was a
false folk etymology derived from their name, a-mazos meaning "absence
of breast" in Greek. (Artemis, it bears mentioning, was in no way hindered from successful hunting by the presence of two breasts.)

Greek men found the notion of such atypical women both titillating
and frightening.[16] The fact that women could bleed every month with
no ill effects and could grow new humans inside their bodies—this was
intimidating enough, but hunting and fighting as well? Terrifying,
indeed almost magical. The only females in their orbit who rejected
domestic duties in favor of hunting or fighting were extremely powerful: Artemis and Athena. Mortal females, Greek men believed, should
stay indoors and be weak—and married. In an imaginary conversation
Socrates' admirer Xenophon portrays the householder Ischomachus
explaining to Socrates that the god fitted woman's nature to indoor tasks
and man's to outdoor ones, and as the woman was in charge of protecting the household stores, the god allotted to woman more timidity than

FIGURE 1.1. Athenian women at work. The weaving of cloth
and production of clothing was a major part of an Athenian
woman's identity, and countless vases reinforced this notion
with depictions of these activities. The Metropolitan Museum
of Art, New York, Fletcher Fund, 1931, https://www.metmuseum
.org/art/collection/search/253348.

to man, since fearfulness is no obstacle to doing a good job of this,
whereas to man he allotted the larger share of bravery. "Knowing then,"
Ischomachus had said to his thirteen-year-old bride, "what responsibilities
have been assigned to each of us by the god, we must each try to carry out
the duties allotted to us as well as possible" (*Oeconomicus* [*On Household*

Management] 7. 22–29). A thoroughgoing media blitz reinforced the requirement that women remain inside, as painters turned out vase after vase depicting citizen women indoors performing household chores.

Amazons, however, conspicuously spent their lives outdoors—they were said even to mate in the open, when and with whom they wished—and were fearless. They were not only the inverse of Greek women; they were the inverse of good Greek wives. Not surprisingly, Herodotus, who devoted a good deal of attention to the Amazons in his *Histories*, found them not only fascinating but admirable and nowhere suggested that they were either frightening or aberrant (4. 110–17).

That the Amazons were real does not in any way alter the fact that a rich mythology grew up around them. The myths that attached to them served important purposes for Greeks. The original "girl gang," they had arrogated to themselves a wide variety of traditionally male privileges, wresting from men even control over marriage and reproduction. This way of life could not be allowed to stand, and their legendary defeat by the Athenians was portrayed as a victory for civilization and patriarchy over barbarism and matriarchy (which, in the Greeks' view, was the only possible alternative to patriarchy). For Athenian men, who boasted frequently of having turned back a purported Amazon invasion of their territory, they represented the antithesis of what they wanted in their women. The sculptural program on the metopes of the Parthenon was devoted to battles with the dark forces of "others" that threatened the Greek world. On the south metope was the battle of Lapiths against the drunken centaurs who had crashed a Lapith wedding, Theseus coming to the aid of the Lapiths; on the north the fall of Troy; to the east the gods were shown putting down the rebellion of the giants; and to the west, the Athenians fending off an Amazon attack on Athens. As rule-breakers, centaurs and giants and Amazons had quite a bit in common. All were monstrous in one way or another. Giants violated norms with respect to size, centaurs violated the norm that separated human from animal, and Amazons violated the norm that separated masculine from feminine pursuits. Unnatural women in the eyes of the Greeks, the Amazons provided fodder for myths cautioning against the breakdown of society and its replacement with barbaric disorder—and celebrating the Greeks' resounding

FIGURE 1.2. Amazons fighting Theseus and the Athenians. The story of the ignominious defeat of the Amazons by Theseus when they dared attack Athens was a central part of Athenian tradition. This mid-fifth-century krater (a bowl for mixing wine and water) shows Theseus in the center fighting the invading Amazons, who are wearing their distinctive leggings and short boots. As is usually the case, the name of the painter is unknown. The Metropolitan Museum of Art, New York, Rogers Fund, 1907, https://www.metmuseum.org/art/collection/search/247964.

victory over these aberrant creatures. As mythologist Adrienne Mayor has pointed out, the Amazon-like women in the Caucasus sagas were frequently victorious in their battles with men, but in Greek myth Amazons are doomed to defeat.[17]

The ability—or inability—to control women was a source of major interest to Greek men. Not surprisingly, therefore, the world of gods and heroes was rife with abductions and rapes, both attempted and successful, and most entailed assaults on females by males. The centaur Nessus was killed when Heracles caught him trying to rape his wife Deianeira. Nessus had the last laugh. With his dying breath he explained to Deianeira that the mixture of his semen and his blood would produce a love potion she could use in an emergency on Heracles. In reality, the concoction was a poison, and Heracles died in agony when Deianeira deployed it. Well, one may say, centaurs; we know all about them. Most mythological rapes, however, were the work of gods, for the Greeks found nothing anomalous about the notion of a god committing rape. Heracles was quite familiar with rape—his son Telephos was born of a priestess of Athena whom he had overpowered. The Athenians proudly claimed descent from a would-be rapist. Their common ancestor was believed to be one Erichthonios, conceived in a botched rape of Athena by Hephaestus: the rejected god ejaculated on Athena's thigh, and when she wiped the semen off and cast it to the ground, the earth goddess Gaia was impregnated.

Numerous myths tied rape to a metamorphosis of one kind or another. When Zeus deflowered Artemis's devotee Callisto after worming his way into her embrace by posing as Artemis, the blameless girl found herself turning into a bear. Some traditions place the responsibility for this on a jealous Hera, some on an appalled Artemis, shocked when the girl proved to be pregnant. Attempts to escape lustful gods figure prominently in myth. When Zeus first tried to have intercourse with his future wife Metis she changed into many different forms in order to avoid him. Similarly Achilles' mother the sea nymph Thetis changed now into fire, now into water, now into a wild animal in her efforts to escape the advances of her future husband Peleus. Psamathe turned herself into a seal in the vain hope of escaping the amorous attentions of Aeacus. The most interesting of these tales features transformation into birds. Conceiving a passion for his wife's sister Philomela, Ares' son Tereus, as we have seen, raped her and in what feminist scholar Helen Morales has aptly termed "the original nondisclosure agreement" cut out her tongue to ensure her silence.[18] Philomela, however, revealed the story to her sister by weaving the story of her assault attack into a robe—another myth that may have been thought up by a woman. On discovering what

FIGURE 1.3. Procne and Philomela. This Attic wine cup depicting Procne and Philomela preparing to kill Itys made early in the fifth century was found in Italy and is attributed to the painter Makron. Louvre Museum, Cp. 929.
© RMN-Grand Palais / Art Resource, NY.

he had done, Tereus's wife Procne punished him by killing their son Itys and serving him up to her unknowing husband. When the enraged Tereus pursued the sisters with an axe, they prayed to the gods to be turned into birds. Procne became a nightingale, Philomela a swallow.

A female fantasy of escape? It is hard not to be reminded of the scene in the 1994 film *Forrest Gump* in which Forrest's beloved Jenny as a child asks Forrest to join her in praying that she be turned into a bird "so I can fly far, far away from here" in order to escape the father who was abusing her. With his heart of gold and limited intellect, Forrest mischaracterizes the father as "a very loving man" because he was "always kissing and touching her and her sisters."

Never punished for his rape of Medusa, Poseidon went on to assault the nymph Caenis. At some point he offered to grant Caenis a wish, and she asked to be turned into a man; the sources are inconsistent about whether this exchange took place before the rape and thus prevented it, or afterward. Caeneus, as s/he was then known, went on to become a formidable warrior among the Lapiths of Thessaly in northern Greece. Indeed, so formidable was Caeneus that in their legendary battle with the Lapiths the centaurs were forced to crush him with the trunks of trees:

> The bards relate that when all on his own,
> Without the other chiefs, he routed them,
> And they in turn rushing at him in force
> Could neither bend nor break him, then unbowed
> He sank, still living, underneath a mound
> Of wood, stout trunks of silver firs with which
> They drove him down into the earth at last.
>   (Apollonius, *Argonautica* 1. 59–64)

It is tempting to associate this near-invincibility with Caenis's having sought a metamorphosis into a sex that is less vulnerable. The Roman poet Ovid tells the story of Caenis/Caeneus at some length, and curiously Ovid is also our principal source for other Greek myths of sexual ambiguity: the story of Hermaphroditus and the story of Iphis and Ianthe (*Metamorphoses* 12. 171–209; 9. 666–797).

———

The silence in Greece regarding tales of ambiguous gender is an index of the discomfort they must have occasioned. Despite Artemis's tomboyish nature and the effeminacy of Dionysus, most Greek myth was not marked by overt gender fluidity. The myths that portray intersex individuals or recount changes in gender can be counted on the fingers of one hand and are late in origin. Ovid writing under the early Roman Empire told how the youth Hermaphroditus, who derived his name from his parents Hermes and Aphrodite, followed Narcissus in his self-absorption and had no interest in bonding with another. As he gazed rapturously at his image in a pool, however, the water nymph Salmacis fell in love with him. No whit discouraged by his rejection, she pounced upon him when he undressed to bathe in her waters and prayed that they might never be separated. Acceding to her request, the gods joined the two bodies into one that bore both male and female sexual characteristics (*Metamorphoses* 4. 285–379). Two other late tales recount sex changes. From Ovid too comes the story of Iphis, raised as a boy because of her mother's fear of disappointing her husband with a female newborn. When she and another girl, Ianthe, fall in love, the goddess Isis grants her mother's prayers and turns Iphis into a man. The story may be modeled on the tale of Leucippus, another female raised as a male, and for the same reason. When her gender began to manifest itself in adolescence, she was changed by the goddess Leto into a real man in answer to her mother's prayers. The story of Iphis and Ianthe stands out for its clear depiction of homoerotic desire between women, for Iphis was still female when she fell in love with Ianthe (and when Ianthe fell in love with her, under the apprehension that she was male). Although tales of lesbian desire are rare in Greek myth, there are other exceptions. Athena, it was said, fell in love with a young woman, Myrmex, but when Myrmex took credit for Athena's new invention, the plow, the enraged goddess turned her into an ant. Typically, the story appears in Servius's late antique commentary on Vergil's *Aeneid*.[19] It may also be that Artemis, traditionally perceived as asexual, enjoyed sexual relationships with some of the nymphs who were devoted to her. In Callimachus's hymn to Artemis, the atmosphere around Artemis and her nymphs certainly seems sexually charged:

> Which nymph do you love the best?
> Which heroine is your companion? (3. 184–85)

he asks, and goes on to list some possibilities:

> Hypsios's daughter Cyrene you have made your companion,
> Giving her two hunting dogs to win the race by the tomb at Iolcos.

The golden-haired wife of Deionios's son Cephalus you chose
To be your hunting partner, Mistress, and they say you loved
Beautiful Anticleia as much as your own eyes. (3. 206–11)

And we might certainly ask why Callisto would have consented to have
sex with Zeus under the impression that he was Artemis if the notion
of sex with Artemis did not appeal, although it may be that she simply
thought Artemis was moving in for a hug.

Homoerotic attraction among males was another story. The Thracian
singer Thamyris was reputed to have been the first man to fall in love with
another male, the young Hyacinthus, with whom Apollo later fell in love
and inadvertently killed in one of those discus accidents that were a common cause of death in myth. Apollo was also believed to have been in
love with a number of other youths, including the seer Carnus; two of
the principal Spartan festivals were the Hyacinthia and the Carneia, both
in Apollo's honor. The cruel fate of Oedipus derived in part from the
family curse incurred when Oedipus's father Laius kidnapped and raped
young Chrysippus, whom he was escorting to an athletic festival in
which the youth was planning to compete. Nobody in this episode ended
well. The grandson of Tantalus, Chrysippus was heir to the same inherited curse that plagued Agamemnon, and he ended up a suicide, while
Laius went on to be killed by his son, Oedipus.

The mythological tales of homoerotic relationships also follow the
pattern of those in real life in generally portraying the infatuation of a
mature individual with a very young person. Such was the case with the
most famous of the same-sex crushes of the gods. Catching sight of the
youth Ganymede, Zeus was reported to have been so captivated by him
that he transported him to Olympus to be his cupbearer, either by sending
an eagle down to snatch him or himself taking the form of an eagle. Most
versions of the story assume an erotic attachment on Zeus's part, but in
the Homeric epics, where there is no mention of homoeroticism, it is
"the gods" who carried Ganymede off (*Iliad*, 20. 230–41). It is not only
Homer who offers a sanitized version of the story. Socrates, according
to his admirer Xenophon, specifically denied the existence of a homoerotic component in Zeus's attraction to Ganymede, maintaining that

whereas Zeus, when seized by a purely physical attraction as in the case of women, never made the objects of his love immortal, he did make those immortal to whom he was drawn because of their beautiful souls, one such being Ganymede. Plainly he was aware that Zeus's abduction of the youth was customarily ascribed to *erōs*, for he says that it was the beloved's spiritual character that motivated Zeus "even in the case of Ganymede." He goes on to deny the erotic element in many of the reputed friendships of myth, including that of Achilles and Patroclus, a denial that makes clear what was commonly believed in his day (though not, it seems, by Homer) (*Symposium* 8. 28–31). In the *Laws*, however, Plato makes clear the usual portrayal of Zeus's response to Ganymede as sexual, writing that

> It is important to note that when male and female unite for the purpose of procreation the attendant pleasure is considered to be in keeping with nature. The pleasure that arises when males mate with males or females with females, however, is against nature, and the first who engaged in this behavior can only have been driven by their slavery to pleasure. And we all accuse the Cretans of concocting the myth of Ganymede since, as they believed that their laws derived from Zeus, they went on to tell this tale so that indulging in this pleasure too they could appear to be just following his example. (636c–d)[20]

Whatever his motivations, in addition to being a serial marrier and serial adulterer, Zeus was also a serial rapist and serial kidnapper, though most of his victims were female. Taken with the princess Europa, the king of the gods was said to have assumed the form of a bull and abducted her to Crete. He also abetted his brother Hades in the abduction of Persephone, whom Hades snatched from a meadow where she was playing with her friends. A mere child, Persephone cries out in terror at the thought of being separated from her mother, but her screams go unheard and unheeded. Chilled to the heart, the devastated Demeter undertakes the search for her daughter that led eventually to the establishment of an international cult of Demeter and Persephone north of Athens at Eleusis—a cult so enduring that the Roman emperor Marcus Aurelius was initiated into it in the second century CE. It was in a parallel act of violence that Boreas, god of the north wind, swept down to the banks of the river Ilissus on the outskirts of Athens with his icy breath and abducted Oreithyia, daughter of the Athenian king Erechtheus. Carried off to wintry Thrace, Oreithyia remained with Boreas as his wife and queen of the Wind—and provided, as we have seen, fodder for a fictional discussion between Socrates and Phaedrus on the topic of myth. One might suppose that gods would be desirable enough as husbands that they would not need to resort to abduction and rape, but then again neither Thrace nor, a fortiori, Hades would have been most brides' first choice of a residence. The twelve-year-old Helen was also abducted by Theseus. In all these cases the kidnap victims were indeed kids. To say that there was a "culture of rape" among the Olympians would be an understatement. So integral was rape to the fabric of Greek myth that Helen Morales was moved to observe that "There are more paintings displayed in art museums in Europe and North America that feature a mythological rape scene than there are paintings displayed by female artists of color."[21]

Helen, one might say—herself born of rape—was created for the very purpose of being abducted. The first surviving works of European literature, the Homeric epics, took as their starting point the seizure of Helen, wife of the Spartan king Menelaus, by the Trojan prince Paris, an international incident portrayed in myth as the cause of the ruinous Trojan War. It is to the rich fabric of these remarkable poems—principal sources for the mythology of the early Greeks—that we now turn.

Suggested Readings

In addition to the readings listed here, Routledge's series *Gods and Heroes of the Ancient World* offers full-length studies of individual deities by outstanding scholars.

Bakker, Egbert. 2001. "The Greek Gilgamesh, or the Immortality of Return." In *Eranos: Proceedings of the 9th International Symposium on the Odyssey*, ed. M. Païsi-Apostolopoulou, 331–53. Ithaka: Kentro Odysseiakōn Spoudōn.

Burkert, Walter. 1992. *The Orientalizing Revolution: Near Eastern Influence on Greek Culture in the Early Archaic Age*. Cambridge, MA, and London: Harvard University Press.

————. 2004. *Babylon, Memphis Persepolis: Eastern Contexts of Greek Culture*. Cambridge, MA, and London: Harvard University Press.

Colarusso, John, ed. and trans. 2016. *Nart Sagas: Ancient Myths and Legends of the Circassians and Abkhazians*, updated with an introduction by Adrienne Mayor. Princeton, NJ: Princeton University Press.

Csapo, Eric. 2005. *Theories of Mythology*. Malden, MA: Blackwell.

Dowden, Ken. 1992. *The Uses of Greek Mythology*. London and New York: Routledge.

Dowden, Ken, and Niall Livingstone, eds. 2011. *A Companion to Greek Mythology*. Chichester, UK, and Malden, MA: Wiley Blackwell.

DuBois, Page. 1982. *Centaurs and Amazons: Women and the Pre-History of the Great Chain of Being*. Ann Arbor: University of Michigan Press.

Eisner, Robert. 1987. *The Road to Daulis: Psychoanalysis, Psychology, and Classical Mythology*. Syracuse, NY: Syracuse University Press.

Hansen, William. 2005. *Classical Mythology: A Guide to the Mythical World of the Greeks and Romans*, illustrated edition. New York: Oxford University Press.

Maurizio, Lisa. 2015. *Classical Mythology in Context*. Oxford and New York: Oxford University Press.

Mayor, Adrienne. 2014. *The Amazons: Lives & Legends of Warrior Women across the Ancient World*. Princeton, NJ: Princeton University Press.

Morales, Helen. 2007. *Classical Mythology: A Very Short Introduction*. Oxford and New York: Oxford University Press.

————. 2020. *Antigone Rising: The Subversive Power of the Ancient Myths*. New York: Bold Type Books.

O'Brien, Joan V. 1993. *The Transformation of Hera: A Study of Ritual, Hero, and the Goddess in the Iliad*. Lanham, MD: Rowman and Littlefield.

Penrose, Walter, Jr. 2016. *Postcolonial Amazons: Female Masculinity and Courage in Ancient Greek and Sanskrit Literature*. Oxford and New York: Oxford University Press.

Rutherford, Ian. 2020. *Hittite Texts and Greek Religion*. Oxford and New York: Oxford University Press.

Sergent, Bernard. 1984. *Homosexuality in Greek Myth*, trans. Arthur Goldhammer, with a preface by Georges Dumezil. Boston: Beacon.

Thury, Eva M., and Margaret K. Devinney. 2013. *Introduction to Mythology: Contemporary Approaches to Classical and World Myths*, 3rd edition. New York: Oxford University Press.

Van Nortwick, Thomas. 1996. *Someplace I Have Never Traveled: The Hero's Journey*. New York: Oxford University Press.

Veyne, Paul. 1988. *Did the Greeks Believe in Their Myths? An Essay in the Constitutive Imagination*, trans. Paula Wissing. Chicago: University of Chicago Press.

Werner, Daniel S. 2012. *Myth and Philosophy in Plato's Phaedrus*. Cambridge, UK, and New York: Cambridge University Press.

West, Martin L. 2007. *Indo-European Poetry and Myth*. Oxford and New York: Oxford University Press.

CHAPTER 2

The Heroic Past

As is the generation of leaves, so is that of us mortals.
Wind scatters some of the leaves on the ground, but the forest in turn
Burgeons with others again that in springtime will come to succeed
    them:
Just so a new generation of men springs up as another must perish.

—*ILIAD* 6. 146–49

We all die. That ineluctable fact permeates the two epics associated with
the name of Homer, from whom so much of Greek myth derives. In the
Iliad, men at war are keenly sensible of their mortality yet struggle valiantly
to live the noblest lives they can within the parameters of the fate that
has been decreed to them; the *Odyssey* depicts a man who rejects the
offer of immortality when it is extended to him, seeking to embrace the
fullness of human life in all its fragility. Along with Hesiod's *Works and
Days* and *Theogony*, the Homeric epics were the foundational texts of
Greek civilization. Although they formed the core of the Greek educational system, their genesis has been the most hotly debated subject in
all classical scholarship. When were the poems composed? With or without the aid of writing? How many people were involved, and over how
long a period of time? What era do the epics depict? This Trojan War—
did it ever take place? Did Achilles and Helen and Odysseus and Penelope
actually live? (The short answer to all the above: we don't know.)

When the Indo-Europeans who became the first Greeks descended on the Greek mainland from the north, they brought with them traditional tales of heroes and heroism, raids and revenge. Meanwhile in the largely Semitic east (the Indo-European Hittites of Anatolia were an exception) modes of storytelling were evolving that would provide vehicles for relating such tales: long verse narratives lacking any division into stanzas but rather proceeding inexorably line by line, making ample use of epithets and repetitions. The trade and travel that brought the Greeks together with these easterners introduced them to these genres, and their bards began to recite longish poems in Greek, many of which came in time to focus on a legendary raid on Anatolia. To be sure, the fact of an event's attaining legendary status doesn't mean it didn't happen. Many things that become legendary did in fact happen—consider the career of American baseball player Babe Ruth or for that matter the 300 (well, 298) Spartans who died at Thermopylae—and there is a wedding planning business in the United States that operates under the name Legendary Events. Regardless of its historicity, the so-called Trojan War had profound resonance as part of the Greek heritage, and the bards of early Greece found ready audiences for their tales about its participants.

In the absence of writing, various "building blocks" facilitated both spontaneous invention and bards' ability to recall their compositions, although no doubt each new narration would differ slightly from the last. Our understanding of just how this worked took a giant leap forward in the 1930s when an American classicist, Milman Parry (1902–1935), traveled to Serbia with a graduate student, Albert Lord, on a hunch that studying the work of illiterate poet-singers who flourished there would shed light on the composition of the Homeric epics.[1] Parry had noticed something curious about the epithets in the poems—phrases like "much-knowing Odysseus" and "swift-footed Achilles." Characters in the epics often had several epithets attached to them, but which one the poet chose at any given time depended, Parry realized, not on context but rather on the place in the line where the epithet fell—and on the meter.

A word on meter: like the poems of Hesiod, the *Iliad* and the *Odyssey* were composed in the meter known as dactylic hexameter. Each "foot" had a long, or "heavy," syllable followed by two shorts, or "lights," and there were six feet in a line, *hex* being the Greek word for six, as in a hexagon. The *dactyl-* root means finger, as in the pterodactyl, a dinosaur with winged fingers; each of the first five feet had a long syllable followed by two shorts, just as the finger has a long joint and two short ones. The last foot of the line was only two syllables, though, a long followed by either a long or a short. To allow for further variation, at most points in the line a foot known as a spondee—two long syllables—could substitute for a dactyl. Otherwise soporific monotony would have set in, and something like this would have resulted:

> Thus did the heroes move forward to battle, the long-haired Achaeans.
> So on and so on forever until you are dying of boredom.

Instead, the poet could slow down the action with one or more spondees, as in the somber third and fourth lines of the *Iliad*, in which he tells how the wrath of Achilles sent many strong souls to Hades (long syllables in capital letters):

POL LAS / D'IPH THI / MOUS PSU / CHAS a i / DI pro i / APS en
HER O / ON, AU / TOUS de he / LO ri a / TEU che ku / NESS in

Literally:

> many stalwart souls to Hades hurled
> of heroes, but their bodies prey made for dogs.

When Parry saw was that it was the demands of meter that dictated which epithet the poet reached for in composing his verses, he realized that the poet was composing not simply in words but in units. Consider the frequency with which Odysseus is, inevitably, mentioned in the *Odyssey*. His name, consisting as it did of a short syllable followed by two longs, would fit nicely into the last position in a dactylic line, and it turns up there with great frequency. Seventy times it is preceded by *dios*—brilliant, divine, godlike. In another seventy we find at the end of a line that "Odysseus full of good plans spoke," accounting for fully ten syllables and over three feet: *prosephē polymētis Odysseus*. Repetitions also filled out a great deal of the Homeric poems. Whole lines were formulaic and recurred frequently: "when early-rising rosy-fingered dawn appeared," "when they had set aside their desire for eating and drinking." One out of every eight lines in the poems is repeated in its entirety somewhere else. Speeches accounted for about half of the *Iliad* and *Odyssey*, and as in the literature of the Near East, when someone ordered someone else to tell someone something, as the message was delivered the speech was repeated word for word. Typical scenes also eased the poet's path—the holding of an assembly, the supplication of the gods, the arming for battle, and of course combat itself. Because of the importance of hospitality in Greek culture, the appearance of a guest initiated an entire sequence of predictable scenes: welcoming the visitor, inviting him in, offering him a meal, inquiring as to his identity, giving him a parting gift.

Sure enough, the Serbian bards whom Parry met built their compositions out of units much like these. Indeed, they used the same Serbo-Croatian word to indicate "word," "sentence," "phrase," "sentence," "episode," and even an entire composition. The most outstanding bard Parry encountered was Avdo Mededović, whose magnum opus, *The Wedding Song of Smailogić Meho*, he recorded. A long catalogue describes each wedding invitation, each hero, each gift; the *Iliad* devotes 384 consecutive lines to the catalogue of all the ships that sailed to Troy. Ornamental expressions are repeated in *The Wedding*: falcon eyes, winged steeds, bone-breaking spears. Longer repetitions also abound: Meho's uncle devotes about 400 lines to recounting for Meho's father the story of young Meho's sadness when things are not going his way, although all this has been related earlier.[2]

Seeing how these devices worked to facilitate the composition of a long epic poem without the aid of writing, many scholars leapt to the conclusion that Homer too worked in the tradition of oral poets. In the tradition, yes, but as an oral poet himself? Perhaps, but perhaps not. Avdo's work, though at 12,323 lines slightly longer than the *Odyssey*, was not the equal of either Homeric epic in depth—or characterization, or motivation, or perspective, or drama. Plainly Homer came at the end of a long oral tradition, incorporating the tales that generations, probably centuries, of oral singers had told before him. He may even have incorporated long passages from existing songs, shaping them to fit his overarching plan, but I am not convinced by the argument that the work that we have is a patchwork of verses by divers hands. The epics are too subtle, too finely wrought. Whether the Homeric poems were composed orally or in writing, however, they were certainly composed for oral delivery without the consultation of a text, and frequent repetition of phrases, lines, and even entire passages were an enormous aid to memorization. We can never know how his predecessors' labors compared in excellence to the *Iliad* and the *Odyssey*. Some no doubt were better than others. But it was the poetry of the genius to whom history has given the name Homer that survived where the rest did not.

The *Iliad* and the *Odyssey* were forged in the crucible of the great creative Archaic Age of Greece, when European and eastern traditions mixed—in religion, in literature, in the plastic arts. Homer had at his disposal not only snatches from the epics of western Asia such as Gilgamesh, whose roots in myth go back to the third millennium, but the powerful Indo-European myths of great heroes and their deeds of derring-do. The most recent of the tales Homer had heard concerned the Greek expedition against Ilion—Troy—sparked by the abduction of the Spartan queen Helen by Paris, son of Priam, the Trojan king. It was a heinous act, for in making off with the wife of his host King Menelaus, Paris had flouted a key building block of the social glue that held Greek society together, that of *xenia*. Although often translated "hospitality," *xenia* yoked both host and guest in a binding relationship, guest-friendship, sanctified by the gods, and because of the involvement of the gods, disrespecting either one's host or one's guest showed an appalling lack of proper *aidōs*: shame/reverence/modesty/respect. One of Zeus's many epithets was Zeus Xenios: Zeus god of guest and host. Since one could never be sure whether a passing stranger might prove to be a god, Greeks considered kindness to strangers a cardinal virtue. As they were short on embassies and consulates, moreover, not to mention telephones and credit cards and online banking, a system of gracious hospitality was essential if people were to move around comfortably, and that principle had categorically to be both appreciated and reciprocated. Herodotus made a point of stressing the piety of the Egyptians, who are scandalized by Paris's behavior. You are damned lucky, their king tells him when he and Helen are carried to his shores by the winds, that

I don't believe in taking the lives of those who wind up in my kingdom after being driven off course, for "otherwise I would punish you on Menelaus's behalf, you lowlife, you who have requited your guest-friend for his hospitality with the gravest of impieties" (2. 115. 4).

A very old Indo-European motif manifests itself in the tale of Paris's misconduct.[3] Originally the goddess Swelénā, Daughter of the Sun, Helen was popular in Baltic myth and was worshipped in Finland, Latvia, and Estonia, and her brothers Castor and Pollux were types of an Indo-European pair of twin horsemen, revered not only in the Baltics but as far east as India—and generally the companions of the Daughter of the Sun.[4] The stories handed down to Homer from earlier poets who sang about the war were probably "nationalistic," showcasing the virtues of the Greeks and giving the Trojans a fairly raw deal. Recognizing that such an approach would make for an impoverished work of art, Homer would have none of it. The poet extends his broad sympathies even to Helen, the adulterous catalyst of the whole miserable business. And so he gave us in the *Iliad* what we would find later on in the history of Thucydides: a work in which a brutal war is depicted from the point of view of both sides. *Mēnin*, the great epic begins, wrath:

> The wrath, Muse:
> Sing to me, Muse, of the wrath of Achilles, son of Peleus,
> That baneful rage. . . . (1. 1–2)

And indeed the poem is all about anger and conflict and their fell consequences. Homer gives us nearly 250 names of people who lose their lives in the course of his narrative, and many others perish anonymously. The skillful poet does not begin with the abduction of Helen from Sparta that provided the trigger for the war. Rather he plunges dramatically *in medias res*, when the war has been going on for nine years. Along with their armies, the Greek leaders are gathered at Troy: Odysseus, the wily king of Ithaca; Nestor, the venerable and long-winded king of Pylos; Menelaus, the cuckolded king of Sparta; his brother Agamemnon, commander-in-chief of the expedition; and Achilles, the best fighter among them and the king of Phthia. The anger we encounter at the outset of the poem is not that of the Greeks at the Trojans but rather that of Achilles at Agamemnon, who finds himself without a war prize and decides to take Achilles' prize instead. Chryses, we learn, a priest of Apollo, had come to the Greek encampment in Troy to ransom his daughter, a prisoner of war who has been allotted to the bed of Agamemnon. Agamemnon's character first reveals itself when he refuses the ransom—over the objections of his soldiers, who cry out, Respect the priest! Take the money! Agamemnon not only sets himself against the army but speaks harshly to Chryses, dropping dark hints about what may happen to him if he is ever again found near the Greek camp.

Predictably, Chryses turns to Apollo. Make the Greeks pay for the tears I am shedding, he implores the god. But he does not say Greeks. Homer does not know this word, indeed no Greek ever used it. Later on the Greeks called themselves Hellenes, but for Homer, the Greeks are, interchangeably, Danaans, Argives, and Achaeans. Here Chryses says Danaans.

> Thus he spoke in prayer, and Phoebus Apollo heard him.
> Down from the peaks of Olympus he strode with a heart full of anger,
> Carrying on his shoulders his bow and his hooded quiver.
> The shafts clanged on his shoulders as he moved, quaking in rage.
> The god came down like the night, and he sat apart from the ships:
> He let go an arrow.
> Frightful the clash that rang from his great bow made of silver.
> First he attacked the mules and the circling dogs, but then
> He let fly a piercing shaft against the men themselves,
> Attacking them. And the corpse fires burned constantly. (1. 44–52)

Characteristically, Agamemnon does nothing. It is Achilles who takes the initiative and, calling an assembly of the army, asks their prophet, Calchas, if he can explain the cause of the plague. In fact, he can: the plague, he reveals, has its origins in Agamemnon's disrespect of Apollo's priest.

Livid, Agamemnon lights into Calchas, complaining that he seems to enjoy prophesying wretched things and has never brought anything good to pass—in effect, of politicizing the issue. Grudgingly, he agrees to accede to Chryses' wishes and return his daughter Chryseis, though not before making unseemly comparisons between her and his lawfully wedded wife Clytemnestra, whom he pronounces inferior to the captive maiden in front of the entire army. But there is a catch. Honor being of great importance among the Greek chiefs, and along with it the prizes that symbolize it, Agamemnon demands another female prisoner of war in exchange for the one he has lost. A quarrel with Achilles immediately breaks out. (This, Homer is telling us, is how wars get started.) There is no store of captive maidens lying ready to hand, Achilles points out. We will certainly give you abundant prizes should Zeus grant us victory over Troy. But you will have to wait until then.

Agamemnon now accuses Achilles of wanting to cheat him, keeping his prize while he himself lacks one, and threatens to go to the quarters of one of the Greek leaders in person and seize a replacement for the girl he has lost. Achilles in turn comes back at him by calling him "clothed in shamelessness" (*an-aideia*, the absence of *aidōs*) and obsessed with profit" (1.148). Then Agamemnon: "To me you are the most hateful of all the kings nurtured by Zeus. . . ." (1.176). Achilles is ambivalent as to how to respond, or so we would say today; what Homer says is that his heart is divided in his shaggy breast: should he draw his sword and kill Agamemnon, or check his rage (1.188–89)? He pulls his sword from its scabbard . . . but then he pauses. He has felt a tug on his hair. Homer reports the appearance of Athena, although nobody but Achilles perceives her. Hearing the goddess promise that he will receive gifts three times over in exchange for the outrage he has endured if he will stay his hand, Achilles decides to content himself with verbal assaults.

Does Homer really think that Achilles' heart was physically split in two, or is this a figure of speech? Does he actually believe that Athena came down from Olympus to reason with Achilles, or is this his way of saying "Achilles pulled himself together"?

In a famous book originally published in 1946, *The Discovery of the Mind: The Greek Origins of European Thought* (translated into English in 1953), German classicist Bruno Snell argued that characters in the Homeric poems did not have the integrated sense of self characteristic of later Greeks and of people in modern times, and that Homer's notion of an inner life was extremely limited.[5] Homeric characters, he maintained, even lacked a concept of the body as a whole; Homer is always speaking of different parts of the body: the *thymos*, the spirit; the *noos*, the mind. Nor do the epics manifest any dualistic distinction between the body and the soul.

This is too extreme. While the body/soul division is indeed under-developed in Homer, it is clear that Homeric characters do have a sense of self and an inner life. Both gods and mortals debate and decide like anyone else. When Hector's brother Deiphobus is on the battlefield and needs to choose the best course of action, he "ponders two ways": should he partner with another Trojan or proceed on his own? And

> it seemed to Deiphobus as he was thinking these matters over
> That it would be the best thing to seek out the aid of Aeneas. (13. 458–59)

This is not to say that the gods play no role; Athena may well have appeared to Achilles. When in the *Odyssey* Penelope learns that her son Telemachus has gone off in a ship seeking news of his father, the wise herald Medon explains:

> I do not know whether it was a god who urged him on
> Or whether it was his own heart that sparked him to go to Pylos
> Hoping to learn of his father's return, or of what fate he had met.
> (4. 712–14)[6]

But decisions are made in the end by mortals, and after hearing Athena assure him that restraint will be rewarded, Achilles does collect himself, and the elderly Nestor tries to make peace. Nestor is given to the wordi-ness that is a liability in his age group, and I suspect that on realizing that he was "at bat" some in Homer's audience might have sneaked off to a nearby tree for a quick bathroom break. Regretfully, Agamemnon agrees to return his war prize to her father, and he sends heralds to Achilles' quarters to grab young Briseis in exchange. The poet then shows Achilles pouring out his heart to his mother, the sea nymph Thetis, thus remind-ing the audience of what it has always known: that Achilles is the off-spring of a mortal man, Peleus, and an immortal nymph. He has, we later learn, the choice of two fates: a long life without glory, or a short life with it. Most of us ordinary folk have to live with the distinct pos-sibility of a short life without glory, but Thetis plainly feels that his situation makes Achilles the most unfortunate of all men, and her the most pitiable of mothers. "Cursed in my childbearing!" she laments, billing her illustrious son as "wretched beyond all others" (1. 414, 417). At Achilles' request, she goes to Zeus and asks him to make things hard for the Greeks in exchange for Agamemnon's dishonoring of Achilles. After showing us some quarreling up on Olympus, Homer has the sun set. Zeus climbs into bed with Hera. Tomorrow will be another day. So ends the first of the twenty-four "books" into which the *Iliad* was divided at some point in antiquity—one book for each letter of the Greek alphabet.

The plot has been set in motion: from the dishonoring of Achilles the rest of the poem will flow. The Greek noun *timē*, honor/reward/recompense, its corresponding verb *timaō*, to honor, and its opposite *atimaō*, to dishonor, appear some dozen times in Book 1. The Greeks have come to Troy to win *timē*, recompense, for the cuckolded Menelaus; Agamemnon *etimes* (dishonored) Chryses; Achilles refuses to remain *atimos* (without honor) in Troy; Achilles claims that Agamemnon *ouden etisas* him, the best of the Achaeans: did not honor him at all. When Thetis implores Zeus to favor Achilles by harming the Achaeans, she uses forms of *timē/timaō* six times in eleven lines.

To slow the breakneck pace of the action—and to provide some leavening from the daily doses of death—Homer introduces dozens of similes, most of them anchored in the universally familiar world of nature. Some are short—Agamemnon is like the most powerful bull in the herd (2. 480–82)—but most extend over a number of lines. Homer likens the swell of the army to a gathering of wild creatures on the move:

> Now when the men on each side had been marshaled by their leaders
> The Trojans advanced like a flock of wild fowl or of cranes shrilly screaming
> In flight from the winter's sharp cold and escaping perpetual rainstorms
> Loudly winging their way to the streaming waters of Ocean,
> Bringing in their train death and destruction to the Pygmies;
> The Achaeans, though, went in silence, breathing valor as they marched,
> Each one fiercely determined to stand fast beside his companions.
> As when the wind from the south spreads a curtain of mist on the
>   mountains,

A terrible thing for the shepherds but better than night for the robbers,
And no-one can make out a thing that lies farther off than a stone's throw,
So from under their feet the dust rose up in a stormcloud
As the men marched over the plain with all deliberate speed. (*Iliad* 3. 1–14)

The carefree Paris compares his more meticulous brother Hector to an axe:

Your heart is forever unyielding and seems to me like an axe
Driven straight through the wood by a man who, skilled beyond measure,
Shapes the wood for a ship, and the swing of the axe aids the carver:
So the heart in your breast is forever steadfast and firm. (3. 60–63)

When Achilles at last returns to the fray after many of his comrades have died fighting the Trojans, the poet offers a powerful analogy in describing the light bouncing off the new shield that the god Hephaestus has wrought for him:

As when across the waters the sailors glimpse a light
From a fire burning high in a desolate farm in the mountains
As the storms carry them, all unwilling, across the sea and its fishes
Far away from their loved ones:
So from the shield of Achilles, beautifully wrought by a master,
A light shot up into the air and reached the highest heaven. (19. 375–80)

The comparison draws its power from the troubled relationship between Achilles and the army he had abandoned in his rage. Like the sailors of the simile, the Greek soldiers are far across the sea, away from home, and Achilles, though he is now returning from his lonely tent, has distanced himself from them as well, and the soldiers are heartened and comforted by seeing his shining appearance, which offers the hope of safety. All these images give our minds a rest from contemplating the conflict and carnage that make up the poem's narrative; there are many fewer similes in the *Odyssey*, where the slaughter is not so relentless.

While Achilles is out of action, the poet introduces us to key players on the Trojan side, particularly the family of the Trojan king Priam: his wife Hecuba; their son Hector, the crown prince and the Trojans' last, best hope; Hector's wife Andromache, consumed by fear that Hector will die in battle; their young son Astyanax; Hector's brother, the dissolute pretty-boy Paris; and Paris's common-law wife Helen, a liminal figure as a Greek living in Troy and struggling to maintain her self-respect in an extraordinary situation. Hector is a man of duty, determined to fight the good fight in defense of his family and his city. His generosity comes out in his interchange with Helen when he visits her home in hopes of rousing her bedmate to battle. The affectionate relationship she shares with Hector despite the war she has brought on his city raises Helen in the eyes of the audience and makes plain that for Homer she is not simply a sexual object but a person to be taken seriously.

Implored by Andromache not to keep risking his life in battle, Hector finds himself in an impossible position. He cannot fulfill his duty of preserving the life of Andromache's husband and Astyanax's father while also fulfilling his duty as the crown prince of Troy. He has been raised to be valiant always and to fight in the front ranks of the army, "seeking to win great renown for my father and for myself" (6. 446). And yet in part of his mind he knows that the struggle is hopeless. For, he says,

> This I know well in my heart, and in my soul I know it:
> There will come a day when sacred Ilion shall perish,
> And Priam of the good ash spear and all of Priam's people. (6. 448–49)

For all this, he could not endure the shame of shirking from battle like his brother. When he holds out his arms to little Astyanax, the boy recoils in terror from his imposing helmet with its waving horsehair crest and shrinks back into the bosom of his attendant, screaming. The child is right to be afraid; armor means death. Homer's audience was well aware that Astyanax would be tossed from the city walls at the war's end by Greeks fearful lest he grow up to avenge his father.

In showing Hector with his family Homer highlights not only his domesticity but also Achilles' essential solitariness. Achilles may be the best of the Greek warriors, but it is lonely at the top. While Hector is fully integrated into his world, Achilles has chosen to alienate himself from his. Achilles' deracination becomes more marked still in Book 9 when things are going so badly for the Greeks that Agamemnon can no longer escape the realization that he needs to bring Achilles back into the fold and sends Odysseus and Ajax to his quarters to engineer a reconciliation, offering the return of Briseis along with lavish gifts.

During his time alone, however, Achilles has been thinking, and in his rumination he has come to some startling conclusions: the game he and all the other Greek heroes have been playing all their lives is meaningless. No amount of glory or material wealth is worth a human life, not his or anyone else's. Three times in three consecutive lines he reiterates the new thought he has had while secluded in his tent, pondering Agamemnon's insult:

> The same lot awaits the shirker and the man who fights his best;
> The self-same honor (*timē*) crowns the coward and the brave man:
> Death comes alike to the lazy man and the tireless worker. (9. 318–20)

He does not need the *timē* that comes from gifts, he says, or from the opinion of others, for he is honored by the dispensation of Zeus. He has taken the first steps toward internalizing what was normally for Greeks a value system dependent on external validation. His words upend the entire social structure in which people like him—and, indeed, Hector— have been raised.

Achilles' rethinking and rejection of the heroic ethos is a key moment in his development, but not in the plot of the poem; the desperate fighting continues all around him as he remains sequestered in his quarters. Homer offers a break in the tension with an uproarious account of high jinx on Olympus as Hera, hoping to keep Zeus occupied while Poseidon helps the Greeks in their war effort, begs from Aphrodite a particularly provocative garment often misleadingly translated "the girdle of Aphrodite." It sounds more like some kind of super-sexy bra, and the sight of his wife thus bedecked propels Zeus into a hilarious speech in which he explains that he has never previously been gripped by comparable lust:

> No, not even when I burned with desire for the wife of Ixion,
> Who bore me Peirithoos, a counselor as wise as the gods;
> Nor when I desired Danaë, her of the shapely ankles,
> Akrosios's daughter who bore Perseus, excelling all men in his valor;

Not when I desired the daughter of the far-famed Phoenix,
Who bore me Minos and godlike Rhadamanthus ... (14. 317–22)

and so on and so forth in a litany that, had Hera's goal not been to distract him from the battlefield, would surely have sunk any prospects for consummation.

Developments on earth are less merry. A constant presence in Achilles' quarters has been Patroclus, Achilles' foster-brother and closest companion, and it is Patroclus who will provide the next turning point in the epic. Though Achilles may find it in him to harden his heart against the deaths of his comrades, Patroclus is not made of such stern stuff. Indeed, his hallmark is a tenderness that engages not only the audience but Briseis, Achilles, and Homer himself, who often addresses him in the second person. Briseis mourns him passionately when he dies—he was, she says, a kind, gentle soul (19. 300). When Achilles finds him weeping over the sufferings of the Achaeans, he compares him to a little girl

who runs after her mother and begs to be carried,
Tugging at her dress, hindering her as she goes,
Tearfully looking up at her until she is picked up. (16. 7–10)

What an utterly remarkable image. In his distress at his comrades' sufferings, Patroclus persuades Achilles to let him enter the fray, wearing Achilles' own armor, to put heart into the Achaeans. It may well be that the fully rounded Patroclus is Homer's creation, like the conflicted family man Hector—that the epic tradition bequeathed to Homer an empty "best buddy" of Achilles and a faceless "enemy chief" out of whom he made vivid and compelling characters that have resonated across the ages.

The fatal encounter between Patroclus and the sympathetic Sarpedon, a Lycian ally of the Trojans and the son of Zeus, is particularly painful, most of all for Zeus, who even toys with snatching Sarpedon from the battle and setting him down in his native Lycia but is won over by the remonstrances of Hera, who reminds him that if he interferes with Sarpedon's allotted fate the other gods will be scrambling to intervene on the behalf of their children as well. As a compromise, she suggests he let Patroclus kill Sarpedon as is fated but send Thanatos, Death, and

FIGURE 2.1. The Sarpedon krater. This krater depicting Hermes directing Hypnos (Sleep) and Thanatos (Death) to carry Sarpedon to his native Lycia for burial and painted around 515 BCE by the renowned Euphronios was illegally excavated from an Etruscan cemetery near Cerveteri, Italy, and stood in the Metropolitan Museum of Art in New York from 1972 to 2008, when it was repatriated to Italy and removed to the Archaeological Museum of Cerveteri. Sarpedon's heroism is accentuated by the resemblance of the fallen youth to a lion. Scala/Ministero per i Beni e le Attività culturali / Art Resource, NY.

Hypnos, Sleep, to carry his corpse away to Lycia for honorable burial at the hands of his kin. This scene of Death and Sleep standing tenderly over the dead Sarpedon formed the subject matter of one of the most beautiful examples of Greek pottery in existence.

Patroclus, however, has ignored Achilles' warning not to get too deeply engaged in the battle, and he does indeed go down to death at the hands of Hector. When he learns that Hector has killed Patroclus, Achilles is so utterly undone that Nestor's son Antilochus grasps his hands preemptively, fearing that he may cut his own throat. This anxiety is remarkable in a culture in which male suicide was almost unheard of.

Throughout the dirge sung for Patroclus, Achilles places his hands on the dead man's chest and lies beside him. Achilles' consuming grief for Patroclus is evocative of the anguish of the Mesopotamian hero Gilgamesh at the loss of his beloved friend Enkidu, over whose body Gilgamesh mourned for seven days, refusing to bury it until a worm falls out of his companion's nose.[7] Patroclus's death is pivotal for the plot, prompting Achilles as it does to return to the battle to avenge his beloved companion. Reconciling with Agamemnon, Achilles reenters the fray and mercilessly cuts down one Trojan after another. Dread suffuses this portion of the poem as the audience realizes Achilles is closing in on Hector—Priam and Hecuba's son, Andromache's husband, little Astyanax's father. The poet reminds us too that Achilles is fated to die soon after Hector. Achilles no longer cares, but our knowledge intensifies the sense of impending doom pervading the poem's last books.

Achilles now betakes himself to Agamemnon to spit out an apology and rouse the troops to battle so that he may avenge the death of his beloved companion. His words on the source of the quarrel that set in motion the fatal chain of events are chilling. Was it really such a good idea, he asks, for us to quarrel "for the sake of a girl"? As for that girl,

> How I wish that Artemis had struck her dead with an arrow
> Beside the ships on the day when I destroyed Lyrnessus and took her.
> (19. 59–60)

So much for his claim in Book 9 that just as any sensible man cherishes his own woman and looks after her,

> So from the bottom of my heart I loved her, even though
> She was a spear-won captive.

What Agamemnon has to say is interesting as well. Although the Greeks have found fault with me, he says, nonetheless *ouk aitios eimi*: I am not responsible. For, he explains, he was in the grips of the dread blindness/folly/delusion the Greeks called *Atē*: It was Zeus, he says,

> it was Fate, and the Fury, walking in darkness,
> Who in the midst of our gathering cast savage *Atē* upon me,

That day I myself undertook to strip his prize from Achilles.
But what could I do? It's the god who brings all things to fulfillment.
Atē, the eldest daughter of Zeus, baneful *Atē*, undoes one. (19. 87–95)

He then segues into a digression about how *Atē* once blinded Zeus himself and follows up this interesting tidbit with over thirty lines of mythological gobbledygook to distract the audience's attention from his own culpability, finally returning to the unpleasant matter at hand with a reiteration of his innocence: in view of the fact that Zeus robbed me of my wits, I'm happy to give you more gifts than you'll know what to do with.

Achilles replies, in effect, "Whatever." He is no longer interested in compensation, only in getting on with the war. But Agamemnon's construction of events is both revealing and intriguing. To some extent he plainly believes that he is not culpable; as someone from another culture might say, the devil made him do it. But we are free to conjecture that this displacement is only partly the Greek mind at work; Agamemnon's own flawed character—this is the same man who in Book 9 could not understand that Achilles wanted an in-person apology, not "stuff"—is very much in play as well. We are not free to say, "Those Greeks, always blaming everything on the gods." This is one specific Greek speaking, and we have come to know him well.

Achilles' quest to avenge Patroclus can now move forward. As for Hector, he is sorely afraid of Achilles. He has much to lose and does not want to leave his life behind. But the decision for his death has been handed down from Olympus: Zeus had briefly toyed with the idea of saving him, but Athena persuaded her father that he must die. Throughout the poem the gods have been weaving in and out of the action on earth or are seen arguing with one another on Olympus about the course of the war and the fates of their favorites, but Athena's behavior here is shameful. Having persuaded Zeus that Hector's time is up, she disguises herself in both appearance and voice as his brother Deiphobus, promising him that they will go up against Achilles together. Hector's joyous response is heartbreaking. Deiphobus! he cries. You were always most precious to me of all my brothers! And the treacherous goddess replies in the voice of his beloved sibling: our father, she says, our mother, all my friends—they begged me not to go, to remain within the safety of the walls,

> But deep within my chest my heart could not stop aching
> with worry for you. (22. 242)

Dastardly, is it not? When Hector, having lost his spear, calls out to his brother for another, he finds that Deiphobus has vanished, and the awful truth dawns on him. "My end has come," he says; but I will fight nobly, earning the renown around which heroes Greek and Trojan organized their lives, *kleos*, from the Greek verb *kluo*, to hear; *kleos* was what future generations would hear about you:[8]

> I see it all now—that the gods have summoned me down to my death.
> I thought that the hero Deiphobus stood right here at my side,
> But he is behind the wall, and the vision I saw was Athena,
> Tricking me. Now dismal death is upon me, not off in the distance,
> And there is no escaping. Long since this was surely the pleasure
> Of Zeus and his son Apollo—Apollo, the deadly archer,
> Who once were accustomed to rush eagerly to my defense.
> But now that my fated doom has finally come upon me,
> Then let me die, but at least not without valiant struggle,
> Not lacking the slightest *kleos*, but doing something worthy
> That men as yet unborn will hear of in the future. (*Iliad* 22. 303–5)

Going down to death at Achilles' hands, he implores the raging avenger to respect his body and return it to the Trojans for proper death rites. Achilles has a different plan: he attaches Hector's corpse to his chariot and drags it around in the dust. Pitying Hector, Apollo protects his body from decay and finally persuades Zeus to let his body be ransomed. Under cover of night and with a safe conduct from the messenger god Hermes, King Priam makes his way through the Greek camp to Achilles' quarters, bearing lavish gifts to exchange for his son's body. The poem that began with an attempted ransom will end with one, but this time the effort will be successful. The tension when the two men meet is almost unbearable. Even for an audience knowing full well that Priam will come away unscathed, the notion of Hector's aged father unarmed in the heart of the Achaean camp is bone-chilling. Show *aidōs* before the gods, Achilles, he says,

> and pity me,
> Thinking about your own father. I am more pitiful by far,
> Having endured what no one on earth has ever suffered:
> I put my lips to the hands of the man who has killed my sons. (24. 503–6)

And Achilles does think about his father. Life is hard, he tells Priam. On the floor of Zeus's halls stand two great jars containing his gifts, one holding miseries, the other blessings. Some people receive from both jars, but others only from the jar of wretchedness. Deep into the night the two men huddle in Achilles' quarters, Priam mourning for his son and Achilles, knowing of his fate to die soon after Hector, grieving for the father who will never see him again, whom he will never see again. Hector is returned to his family, his funeral is held, and Homer brings his poem to an end:

> Thus they conducted the funeral, burying horse-taming Hector. (24. 804)

Just as the poet did not choose to begin with the snatching of Helen or even the mustering of the Greek fleet, neither did he choose to end with the fall of Troy or the death of Achilles. Bringing the poem to a halt where he did was a stroke of genius, for the note on which it concludes is one of gloomy anticipation combined with regretful resignation; the fated ends both of the city and of the Achaeans' foremost champion hover just beyond the horizon.

———

The piercing sorrows the *Iliad* occasions in its audience at the spectacle of people indomitable in their determination to do their best in the worst of circumstances, often forcing themselves into battle in what they know may well be a losing cause; of two armies fighting with might and main when only one can win; of women become the playthings of war; of mortals deserted by gods who once favored them; the inexpressible pain tied up with all this questing after *kleos*: beneath all this runs the counterpoint of the pleasure afforded by the majesty of the language, the poignant family vignettes, the beautiful and thought-provoking similes, the forward thrust of the undulating meter. Did the same intellect that crafted this compelling work of art also compose the other poem associated with the name of Homer, the *Odyssey*? I think so, but I would not stake money on it.[9] Each poem addresses the question of what it is to be a human being, but the answers they present are different. Both poems are suffused with the biting sorrow that comes from a clear look at the nature of life, but one has a (mostly) happy ending and the other does not. Though the gods too are constrained by fate, it is mortals who serve as fate's playthings, and fate operates in disparate ways in the two epics. Whereas fate as justice is impossible in the *Iliad*, where two sympathetic sides war but cannot both prevail, it provides the underlying structure of the *Odyssey*. The later poem (as I believe, though a few would disagree), the *Odyssey* was composed at a time when the determinants of human life had come to be perceived differently. The world of the *Iliad* was one of capricious, quarreling gods; in the *Odyssey*, where fewer Olympians are operative, Zeus and Athena, embodiments of a just and harmonious world order, dominate the stage, ultimately triumphing over the wrathful Poseidon, who is committed to disturbing that order as he pursues his grudge against Odysseus. The principal role of fate is to restore harmony to the sublunary world of mortals by getting Odysseus safely home in one piece—and dealing death to the obnoxious suitors who are violating all laws of civilized behavior.

The *Iliad* shows a poet acutely sensitive to the ways war wears on women. The epic underlines the fragility of family ties during wartime at the same time as it showcases male bonding and the individualism that threatens it. The war has separated the Achaeans and their families from one another and will destroy the family of Hector and Andromache, Priam and Hecuba. Achilles will never see his father again, as Priam will not see his son; Patroclus will never marry and establish a family of his own. The traffic in women drives the *Iliad*'s plot. Helen is the subject/object of the war; the refusal to return Chryseis to her father brings down the plague on the Achaeans; Briseis plays a key role in the quarrel between Agamemnon and Achilles that removes Achilles from the fighting. Yet the female perspective rears its head in the *Iliad* largely to be slapped down by the male protagonists. Helen, Hecuba, and Andromache all attempt to hold Hector back while he is hastening to the battlefield; he needs to assert his manliness by standing up to their entreaties. Hecuba tries to restrain Priam from his effort to ransom Hector's body; Priam's mission, backed by divine will, nonetheless proceeds. At one level Homer shows us women motivating the poem's action; at another he shows us women striving to stop that action in its tracks, something they cannot be allowed to do. Female characters play a greater role in the *Odyssey*, where their importance in the poem is inevitable, given the centrality of Odysseus's quest to return to home and Penelope and the female characters, mortal and immortal, who sometimes hinder him in that quest—but often help as well. Except in the tenuous alliance of the suitors, who unite against Penelope even as they are in competition with one another, male bonding in the *Odyssey* appears only toward the poem's end, after the climactic reunion between Odysseus and Telemachus, when father and son begin plot to kill the loutish interlopers. In contrast, the poet shows us many important interactions in the *Odyssey* between males and females—females whose perspectives and agency, though always subordinate to the interests of men, are nonetheless adumbrated, if not developed in depth.

The higher profile of female characters in the Odyssey points to a major difference in the value system evident in the two poems. As Hellenist Dorothea Wender has written, the central theme of the poem is

that the Wise Man is a greater hero than the simple Soldier, the World is a better proving-ground than the Battle-field, and the Home superior to the Camp. The *Odyssey* criticizes . . . the limited value-system of the typical heroes of the *Iliad*, of Ajax, of Diomedes, and especially of Achilles, and glorifies in their place the more nearly all-embracing values of the flexible Odysseus. In the end, the mighty Agamemnon is only Agamemnon the cuckold and victim, and even the divine Achilles is only Achilles the dead soldier. But Odysseus is Odysseus the traveller, Odysseus the bard, Odysseus the hero, Odysseus the husband, the father, the son, and finally, Odysseus the just king. . . .

The theme is two-fold: the hero's wisdom and his domesticity share equal credit for his ultimate success.[10]

Other contrasts are evident in the poems. The *Iliad* is a saga of days of old—of spears and helmets, kings and princes, battles and more battles and constantly burning funeral pyres. For all its protagonist's tales of fantastic adventures, the bulk of the *Odyssey* is set pretty much in a real world, if not of Homer's day then of not long before; it is a more down-to-earth work in which the poet's interest extends to ordinary people like the swineherd Eumaeus, without whom it would have been difficult for Odysseus to plot his restoration to his patrimony, and Odysseus's childhood nurse Eurycleia, both of them slaves. But it is also a fairy tale. It is the first surviving exemplar of the "returning husband" motif. Before departing, the husband, as is often the case in these tales, specifies a length of time his wife should wait before remarrying (Odysseus says Penelope should wait until their son Telemachus's beard begins to grow). Though wishing to return, he is detained (the nymph Calypso holds him on her island for seven years). From time to time on his journey, he falls asleep. He returns in disguise. He is first recognized by an animal (his faithful dog Argus). Tokens disclose his identity to his family (his childhood nanny Eurycleia recognizes Odysseus by the scar on his leg, and the peculiarities of their marriage bed make clear to Penelope that Odysseus is who he says he is). The hero acquires his wife by winning a contest—the archery contest at the end of the poem. The hero conceals his name—the Rumpelstiltskin motif. Why, Odysseus and Telemachus even have a fairy godmother—Athena![11]

While the *Odyssey* lies in a direct line from the *Iliad*, the Mesopotamian epic *Gilgamesh* is also a clear ancestor. Both men have a chance at immortality but in the end do not obtain it; Gilgamesh loses a magical plant obtained in his travels that would have guaranteed eternal life, and Odysseus turns down the gift of eternal life offered by the nymph Calypso. Each poem concerns a journey that is also a quest: in Gilgamesh's case the quest for eternal life, in the case of Odysseus, who rejected precisely that, the quest for his return to the normalcy of domestic life. Both men overcome an ogre, in Gilgamesh's case the monster Humbaba, guardian of the Cedar Forest, in the *Odyssey* the Cyclops Polyphemus. Both travel extensively by sea; in fact, their journeys both include a voyage of seventeen days.[12]

Andra, the *Odyssey* begins; a man, or the man: Greek lacks words like "a" or "the," but the audience knows the story and they know what man is meant, even though he is not mentioned by name until the twenty-first line of the long poem. Well-informed about their heritage and patient listeners, the ancient Greeks were comfortable waiting to hear the name of their great cultural hero, as were the Mesopotamians; the *Gilgamesh* poet also held back the name of his protagonist for a number of lines. The openings of the two epics are stunningly similar. In the reconstruction of Stephanie Dalley of the Oriental Institute at Oxford, *Gilgamesh* starts out:

> [Of him who] found out all things, I [shall te]ll the land,
> [Of him who] experienced everything, I [shall tea]ch the whole.
> He searched [?] lands [?] everywhere.[13]

The *Odyssey* begins:

> *Andra*, Muse: tell me about that ingenious *andra*
> Who wandered far astray when he'd sacked Troy's sacred citadel;
> Many were the men whose cities he saw, whose minds he learned,
> Many the woes he suffered in his heart as he traveled the seas,
> Seeking to win his safe return and that of his comrades. (1. 1–5)[14]

He did win that safe return for himself, but of his comrades not one survived the journey, and Homer (as I will call the epic's author for the sake of convenience) does not attribute their deaths to fate but rather underlines their own foolhardiness. For, he continues,

> By their own recklessness they perished, every one—
> Fools, for they devoured the cattle of Hyperion the sun god,
> And he took away from them the day of their sweet homecoming.
>   (1. 7–9)

First words mean a lot. It is diagnostic that the first word of the *Odyssey* should be *andra*, man, while the first word of the *Iliad* is *mēnin*, rage.

The *Iliad* is jam-packed with rage of various kinds—that of the Greeks who want to avenge the kidnapping of Helen by murdering unborn Trojan babies in their mothers' wombs, of Hecuba who wants to eat Achilles raw and of Priam who tells his surviving sons he wishes they had died instead of Hector, and of course, the rages of Achilles that drive the plot, first at Agamemnon and then at Hector. For all his musings on the meaning of life, Achilles allows himself to be defined by this rage that alienates him from his peers and from himself. In its grasp, he becomes less than a whole man. It circumscribes his range of emotion until it is spent in the killing of Hector and the defiling of his body; only then can he get in touch with the tenderer, more humane feelings that facilitate his rapprochement with Priam. Odysseus, however, is from the outset the fully developed man that the first word of the poem signals. Achilles is a warrior; the more versatile Odysseus is a warrior, a sailor, a lover, a father, a husband, a son—and, when need be, a liar and a killer. The notion of man has further implications as well. Zeus himself has some choice words for humankind at the outset of the poem. It is amazing, he says, how quick people are to blame us gods, saying that evils come from us when in fact mortals bring trouble upon themselves by their own recklessness (1. 32–34). The burden of Zeus's lament is clear: it is human action, not divine meddling, that causes events to turn out badly or well for people. This way of thinking is a conspicuous departure from the more archaic worldview of the *Iliad*, in which mortals frequently found themselves helpless in the face of divine whim, but not entirely: let us not forget Agamemnon's lily-livered attempt to ascribe his mistreatment of Achilles to *Atē*, a delusory blindness sent by the gods.

———

The *Odyssey* does not unfold in a linear fashion like the *Iliad*. During the first twelve books, the action shifts from place to place, from perspective to perspective, moving from Odysseus's palace in Ithaca, where our hero is not, to the island of the nymph Calypso, where he is, then to the island of Scheria, where he narrates the now-famous adventures that took place where he used to be (in flashbacks that constitutes fully one-sixth of the poem's length), and then, in the audience's mind, to the amazing places about which he tells. Only the last portion of the epic unfolds consistently in Ithaca. The principal mortal characters in the poem, in addition to Odysseus himself, are his wife Penelope and their son Telemachus. Subsidiary roles are played by the royal family of Scheria where the Phaeacians live: King Alcinous, his wife Arete, and their nubile daughter Nausicaä. A variety of immortals are important as well, of whom by far the most prominent is Athena. Her relationship with her protégés Odysseus and, by extension, Telemachus exhibits an intimacy unparalleled by any other mortal-immortal relationship in either Homeric poem, perhaps in all Greek mythology, which depicted gods interacting with mortals primarily by either killing them or raping them.

Disentangled from Homer's nonlinear narrative, the "plot" of the *Odyssey* goes something like this:

After the war at Troy, some of the surviving Greek chiefs get home with ease, others with difficulty. Odysseus, however, is held captive by the nymph Calypso on her island for seven years. Calypso offers him immortality if only he will stay with her, but he declines. To be sure, he is pining for home and Penelope; but it is more than that. If he is to get anything out of the challenges life keeps throwing up, it is that through them he will become a more fully realized human being. His goal is not to step outside of time by becoming immortal but rather to fulfill very mortal goals. Significantly, Calypso's name means "hidden" in Greek. Had he remained with her, he too would have been hidden; and what is concealment but the very opposite of *kleos*?

Pained by Odysseus's suffering, Athena asks Zeus to send the messenger god Hermes to Calypso's island with orders that she let her restless lover go. Before she does so, she gives him her magic veil to keep him safe; it may be worth noting that the innkeeper Siduri, who helped Gilgamesh along in his journey, was called "veiled with veils." Odysseus soon washes up on the idyllic island of Scheria, home of the amiable Phaeacians. There he is taken in by the local princess Nausicaä, into whose mind Athena has put it to come to the shore to do her laundry in anticipation of marriage someday. Marriage indeed; sure enough, an attractive male appears, covering his nakedness with leaves. He is at no loss for words, inquiring whether she is a goddess:

> Looking as much as you do like Artemis, Zeus's great daughter,
> Lovely and tall just like her . . .
>   and unlike any mortal creation,
> No man, no woman I've seen. A reverent awe overcomes me,
> Gazing upon you. Once I saw some such thing,
> In Delos, a fresh young palm that stood by Apollo's altar.
> I marveled at it, for never in all my life had I seen
> A tree such as that one was spring from the soil of the earth.
>   (6. 151–167)

The comparison is from the Near East; just so in the Song of Solomon the singer exclaims

> How beautiful and pleasant you are,
>   O loved one, with all your delights!
> Your stature is like a palm tree,
>   and your breasts are like its clusters. (ESV 6. 6–7)

Three different women in the Old Testament bear the name Tamar, date palm.

Nausicaä arranges for Odysseus to meet her parents the king and queen. At their court he recounts his various adventures, and he is a raconteur beyond compare. We must never forget how much of the poetry of the *Odyssey* comes out of the mouth of Odysseus himself. What readers generally do forget is first of the escapades he narrates, an attack on the tribe of the Cicones in Thrace, northwest of Troy, where our hero loses six men per ship after his crew, drunk on wine, disregard his advice to leave after sacking the town and the Cicones call in reinforcements. In this narrative we are still in the real world. By the second adventure, however, we are in never-never land—specifically, the land of the Lotus Eaters, whose inhabitants share with Odysseus's scouts the delicious fruit that makes them forget all about home; Odysseus has to drag them back to the ships in tears. In this treacherous place both past and future vanish, and there is only a static, unchanging present. Leaving the land of the Cicones had meant passing through an invisible aquatic door into a world of the fantastic.

The excessive drinking that led to the losses in the Cicones' territory flags the opposition of proper to improper consumption that is a persistent theme in this epic—a saga in which the backdrop to Odysseus's escapades is the miserable plight of his wife Penelope back in Ithaca, where her boorish suitors are quite literally eating away at the substance of the household. The third adventure showcases an individual whose truly terrible eating and drinking habits are emblematic of his antisocial nature: the cannibal Cyclops Polyphemus. In the previous adventures, Odysseus appeared as a disciplinarian with his crew. Here he fails signally to discipline himself, with deadly consequences. He is a flawed man. Curiosity leads him to explore the island despite his sailors' desire to leave, and the results prove fatal to those very sailors.

The primitive Cyclopes throw sharply into relief what it means to be civilized—that is, Greek. Each of the males, holed up in his mountain cave, makes laws for his own wife and children, indifferent to what others may do or think. Gigantic in stature, with but a single eye in the middle of their foreheads, they are monstrous in appearance. They are so far out of the mainstream that though they live directly opposite an island whose harbor offers good anchorage, they have never explored it, as they have no shipwrights, no ships. Just imagine: a world without ships! Odysseus is plainly scandalized that no one has seized the opportunity to develop this magnificent real estate. Vines would never fail in its well-watered meadows, and there is rich, level ploughland in abundance. The Cyclopes' indifference to these possibilities makes clear that they lack entrepreneurial instinct: in short, they are not Greeks. The mainland, however, offers sustenance; grain and grapes flourish under the watchful care of Zeus, who sends needful rain to these anti-Greeks (pre-Greeks?) who do not farm, do not sail, do not meet in assembly.

Entering the cave of the Cyclops Polyphemus and coming upon an abundance of cheese, lambs, and goats, Odysseus's men implore him to grab and go, but that is not Odysseus's way. He is eager to see what will happen when they encounter Polyphemus, wondering out loud if the giant will treat him as a guest. And in the event, the Cyclops does not behave as a host is expected to, offering strangers food and drink before inquiring who they are and whence they come; rather he asks them straight off to give an accounting of themselves. From there things go rapidly downhill. In reply to Odysseus's reminder that he and his men are there as suppliants—suppliants of whom Zeus, guardian of strangers, is the protector—the giant explains that he and his fellow Cyclopes pay no heed to Zeus or any of the other gods for "we are mightier that they" (9. 276). And, handily tearing two of the sailors limb from limb, he wolfs them down, bones and all. So far from feeding the strangers at his hearth, he makes of them his own meal.

Odysseus famously engineers the crew's escape from the ill-mannered giant by getting him roaring drunk on unmixed wine he has brought—a concentrate (rather like cola syrup) with which Greeks commonly traveled with the idea of diluting it when they came to a clear stream. When the Cyclops inquires as to his name, Odysseus identifies himself as *Outis*: Nobody. Living outside civilization, the gullible (and not entirely sober) Cyclops fails adequately to scrutinize this improbable response. For this failure he will pay dearly. Sharpening the giant's club into a point and heating it in the fire until it glows, Odysseus drives it with all his might into the Cyclops's single eye and with help from his companions turns it round and round like a drill:

> Eyelids and eyebrows alike were singed by the fiery breath
> From the burning eyeball: its roots now crackled in the heat.
> As when a blacksmith plunges a great axe or an adze
> Into cold water to temper it,
> And it hisses loudly—for this is how iron achieves its greatest
>   strength—
> Just so did his eye now hiss around the olive-wood point. (9. 389–94)

Now the time comes for Odysseus's cunning lie about his name to bear fruit. When his fellow Cyclopes hear Polyphemus's agonized cries and ask who is harming him, he replies, "Nobody," with the result that they see no need to come to his aid.

His interaction with Polyphemus brings out not only the best in Odysseus but also the worst. Not knowing how to quit when he is ahead,

FIGURE 2.2. Odysseus and Polyphemus. This archaic seventh-century amphora (vessel with two handles) of which this is the neck is the earliest surviving visual depiction of Odysseus blinding the Cyclops and stands in the Archaeological Museum of Eleusis. It must have been used as a funeral urn, as it contains the remains of a boy of about eleven. Erich Lessing / Art Resource, NY.

once safely aboard ship he again disregards the pleas of his men, shouting back to the receding shore:

> Cyclops, should any mortal man inquire of you,
> "Why this unseemly blindness in your eye?"
> Tell him it was Odysseus, sacker of cities,

Odysseus of Ithaca, son of Laertes,

Who took your eyesight, took it utterly. (9. 502–5)

What striking hybris. Wanting the *kleos* that he thinks his actions merit, our hero specifically asks Polyphemus to spread the word about what he has done. What glory will he get, after all, unless the news travels? Odysseus pays dearly for his boastful arrogance. Hearing his words, Polyphemus predictably prays to his father Poseidon to avenge his lost eye: see to it, he asks, that this Odysseus does not reach home; but if fate requires him to see his near and dear ones again, grant that his journey be long and harrowing. May he lose all his comrades along the way and find his household in a wretched state.

And so we have the plot of the *Odyssey*.

After further adventures Odysseus and his crew put in at the island home of the witch Circe, who offers shelter but turns the crew into pigs; with Hermes' help, Odysseus avoids this fate himself and persuades Circe to deporcify his men. Again time seems to stop while Odysseus spends two years in Circe's bed and once again finds himself in danger of forgetting who he really is and where his priorities lie. In time, however, the sorceress explains to Odysseus that he must undertake a journey to the Underworld to learn from the blind prophet Teiresias how he might best get home, and she advises him about how best to handle the series of deadly forces he will soon confront—all of them, like her, extraordinary females: the bewitching Sirens, and on either side of a narrow strait the monster Scylla and the whirlpool Charybdis. Unlike Circe and Calypso, females who both (first) hinder and (then) help Odysseus in his quest to return home, these fell creatures are death itself. The Sirens lure sailors to their deaths with their seductive song. Scylla for her part has six gruesome heads with three rows of teeth, each head attached to a very long neck. No vessel ever sails past her unscathed, and she puts an end to six of Odysseus's men. As for Charybdis, three times a day she sends black water up, three times she glugs it down, and great was Odysseus's relief when she spewed back up the ship she had guzzled down.

In the Underworld he encounters the usual suspects: Agamemnon, Ajax, Achilles. Predictably, Agamemnon is still bitter about his murder at his wife's hands. Ajax, who had been enraged when the armor of the dead Achilles was awarded not to him but to Odysseus, is still smarting from the insult and has no interest in Odysseus's peace overtures. When Odysseus contrasts his own recent misfortunes with the glory that has surrounded Achilles both on the earth and below it, honored like an immortal while he lived and now a VIP in the Underworld, Achilles replies in words both poignant and profoundly revealing of Greek values: Do not seek to sugarcoat my situation, Odysseus, he says. I would choose to work for another man, even a pretty poor one with a puny livelihood, if only I could be still alive. Believe me, it would be better than being king down here (487–90). The sentiment is remarkable, but very Greek: he would stoop so low as to actually *have a job* if only he could stay alive! Oh, the indignity!

Teiresias does not in fact tell Odysseus how to get home. He does, however, warn him to refrain from harming the cattle of the sun god, Helios, on the island of Thrinakia. Though at first the crew swear to keep their hands from the god's herds, in time hunger breaks down their resolve, and while Odysseus is sleeping, they slaughter the finest of the animals. Alerted by the familiar smell of meat cooking, Odysseus rushes to the scene of the barbecue, where he encounters unnerving portents:

> The hides were crawling. The meat that sat upon the spits
> Began to moo—the cooked bits, as well as the meat that was raw.
> (12. 395–96)

When Zeus learns of this particularly heinous example of improper consumption, he sends a storm that wipes out the entire crew. Odysseus alone survives to reach Calypso's isle (where time stops for no less than seven years) and make his way from there to the land of the Phaeacians.

Struck with admiration for Odysseus after hearing his account of these incredible adventures, the Phaeacians aid his return to Ithaca. There the action slows considerably as Athena shepherds Odysseus through his defeat of the suitors. The second portion of the poem is rife with irony, as Odysseus is present first in his kingdom, then in his home, but is not recognized because of Athena's masterful disguise of him as an aged beggar. "I wish I were Odysseus's son or even Odysseus himself!" Odysseus says to Telemachus when he hears of the depredations of the suitors. "If only my father would come back home!" Telemachus says— to his father. A series of emotional recognition scenes follow one after another as Odysseus reveals himself to his son Telemachus, the faithful swineherd Eumaeus, his old nanny Eurycleia, and, last but far from least, his wife Penelope, who has been keeping the home fires burning for the full twenty years of his absence. Every bit her shrewd husband's counterpart, she has been holding the voracious suitors at bay by a trick: She cannot marry, she explains, until she has finished a shroud that she is weaving for Odysseus's father Laertes. But the suitors eventually catch on. One told the tale upon his arrival in the Underworld:

> Then every day she would weave at the web, sitting at her great loom—
> But then every night she would undo her work by the light of the torches.
> This was the way that for three years she fooled all the Achaeans.
> But when the fourth year arrived, as the seasons rolled on in their passing,
> As month after month would wane and the days went by in their course,
> One of her girls who knew very well what was really happening
> Told us, and we caught her unraveling the glorious cloth.
> And so we forced her to finish it. That was the end. She just had to.
>   (24. 139–46)

While Odysseus is in the palace in disguise, Penelope, though she does not openly acknowledge his identity, seems to move closer and closer to him. She dreams that someone who looks just like Odysseus did when he left for Troy was sleeping beside her,

> And my heart rejoiced,
> For it seemed like no dream but the truth at last. (20. 89–90)

Hearing Penelope's voice as she tells Artemis, weeping, about her dream, Odysseus stirs from sleep and in his half-awake state:

> Felt that she had recognized him already and was standing by his head.
>   (20. 94–95)

As she is moving closer to him, he is moving closer to her. No less crafty than her sly husband, Penelope asks that the marriage bed that Odysseus built be carried out from the master bedroom and made up for Odysseus. Her husband cries out in outrage: WHO MOVED MY BED? For he had built it around a live olive tree that served as a bedpost. His cry resolves any lingering doubts Penelope might have had as to his identity. When the two fall into one another's arms at last, Homer introduces a simile that unites them in an extraordinary way, seeming as it does to be about him but turning out to be about her:

> Welcome as is the sight of land to swimmers whose well-built ship
> Poseidon has smashed on the sea, driven on by the wind and the
>   swollen wave,
> And but a few have made their escape from the gray sea to the shore,
> Swimming, and thickly are their bodies crusted with brine,
> And with delight have they set foot on the welcome land,
> Escaping their evil circumstances; even so welcome to her
>   was her husband,
> As she gazed upon him. (23. 233–39)

The cunning husband and the devious wife are at last one. Penelope, however, endures a stunning loss that offsets her recovery of her missing husband: learning that they have had sex with the suitors, Odysseus orders Telemachus to butcher the enslaved women in the house, who had offered some of the only companionship Penelope experienced during Odysseus's two decades away. Instead, Telemachus hangs them. I quote the passage in the translation of Emily Wilson to be discussed later in the epilogue:

> The girls, their heads all in a row,
> Were strung up with the noose around their necks
> To make their death an agony. They gasped,
> Feet twitching for a while, but not for long. (2. 471–74)

While wandering the seas, Odysseus has not been without a partner. Far more significant than his liaisons with Calypso and Circe, the extraordinary connection he enjoys with Athena marks him out as a very special mortal. Athena's bond with Odysseus is almost one of equals. When Odysseus fails to see through the disguise she wears to greet him on his return to Ithaca, she remarks on the similarities in intellect and temperament that draw them together and reminds him of her unflagging care for him:

> We are both well versed in cunning. You are by far the best
> Of mortals when it comes to planning, storytelling,
> And I am known among the gods for cleverness and craft.
> You failed to recognize me—me, Pallas Athena, daughter of Zeus.
> I can always be found near you, guarding you,
> In all your hardships. Indeed it was I who saw to it
> That you were welcomed by all the Phaeacians.
> And now I have come here to weave a plan with you. . . . (13. 296–303)

Who better to weave a plan than the goddess of weaving herself?

Athena makes her first appearance early in the poem, plotting with Zeus to thwart his vengeful brother Poseidon and arrange Odysseus's homecoming. Down she flies on her golden sandals to Odysseus's palace in Ithaca, where she appears to Telemachus in the guise of an old friend of Odysseus and urges him to journey to Nestor in Pylos and Menelaus in Sparta in search of information about his father. On his journey, Telemachus is mentored in growing up and receives all the education of which he has been deprived in his irregular childhood and adolescence on Ithaca, a land of misrule where he has seen no models of appropriate behavior and many of its opposite. He arrives in Pylos to find a magnificent and pious sacrifice of eighty-one bulls in progress, and before Nestor proffers the standard inquiries about who they are and whence they come, the aged king makes a point of offering his guests food and drink: no Cyclops he.

Once Odysseus and Telemachus are reunited in Ithaca, Athena is their constant companion and advisor; from this point on, the three are thick as thieves as they plot the downfall of the suitors. (She also gives both Odysseus and Penelope periodic beauty makeovers, as needed.) The killing of the suitors and the reunion of Odysseus and Penelope proclaim the triumph of human and divine justice. Zeus had declared at the outset of the poem that evildoing was repaid with punishment, and the theme continues to be developed by the poet. Penelope articulates the importance of good behavior in telling Odysseus, in his beggar's disguise, why she must treat him well:

> People are born to short lives.
> Those who themselves are hard and have hard hearts to boot—
> On them all mortals call down wretchedness for all their lives,
> And mock when they have died, not some but all of them;
> But those who have no faults, those who live lives that are
>   blameless—
> Their *kleos* strangers bear among all folk, and many
> Praise their great nobility. (19. 328–35)

When Odysseus and Telemachus have dispatched the suitors and Medon the houseboy has been spared at Telemachus's instigation, Odysseus says to him

> Take heart, for he has rescued you. He saved your life,
> That you yourself may know, and also spread the word,
> That doing good is better far than wickedness. (22. 372–74)

Though fate often appears as a synonym for death, the word is also used frequently to refer to the just resolution of Odysseus's affairs—the return to Ithaca, however difficult, and the death of the suitors. It is Odysseus's fate, Zeus tells Hermes, to return home, news that the messenger god then carries to Calypso. Penelope predicts that not a single suitor will escape death and the fates, and her prediction is fulfilled. Unlike in the *Iliad*, where fate is divorced from a unified grand scheme, in the *Odyssey* it guides the plot. In both Homeric poems, the world is badly out of joint. In the *Iliad*, there can be no real resolution. The damage done to the social order by the snatching of Helen can be resolved only by inflicting terrible suffering on men, women, and children who have harmed nobody. Achilles' maturation and the return and burial of Hector's body are small consolation for so much death and loss. The *Odyssey* does restore order: though we are free to wonder (as many have) how Odysseus will adjust to a settled life, and free as well to recoil (as many have) from the slaughter of the unfortunate slave girls, as the curtain falls Odysseus is safely back in Ithaca, he and Penelope are reunited, and the hybristic suitors are no more.

Suggested Readings

Austin, Emily P. 2021. *Grief and the Hero: The Futility of Longing in the Iliad*. Ann Arbor: University of Michigan Press.

Beye, Charles Rowan. 1968. *The Iliad, the Odyssey, and the Epic Tradition*, 2nd edition. New York: Gordian Press.

Clay, Jenny Strauss. 1983. *The Wrath of Athena: Gods and Men in the Odyssey*. Princeton, NJ: Princeton University Press.

Edmunds, Lowell. 2016. *Stealing Helen: The Myth of the Abducted Wife*. Princeton, NJ: Princeton University Press.

Griffin, Jasper. 1980. *Homer on Life and Death*. Oxford: Clarendon and New York: Oxford University Press.

Lord, Albert B. 1951. "Composition by Theme in Homer and Southslavic Epos." *Transactions of the American Philological Association* 82, 71–80.

———. 2000. *The Singer of Tales*, ed. Stephen Mitchell and Gregory Nagy. Cambridge, MA: Harvard University Press.

Nagy, Gregory. 1999. *The Best of the Achaeans: Concepts of the Hero in Archaic Greek Poetry*, revised edition. Baltimore, MD: Johns Hopkins University Press.

Morris, Ian, and Barry B. Powell. 2011. *A New Companion to Homer*, illustrated edition. Leiden and New York: Brill.

Powell, Barry B. 2007. *Homer*. Malden, MA: Blackwell.

Redfield, James. 1983. *Nature and Culture in the Iliad: The Tragedy of Hector*. Chicago: University of Chicago Press.

Schein, Seth L. 1972. *The Mortal Hero: An Introduction to Homer's Iliad*. Berkeley and Los Angeles: University of California Press.

Scodel, Ruth. 2002. *Listening to Homer: Tradition, Narrative, and Audience*. Ann Arbor: University of Michigan Press.

Wender, Dorothea. 1977. "Homer, Avdo Mededovic, and *The Elephant's Child*." *American Journal of Philology* 98 (1977), 327–47.

———. 1978. *The Last Scenes of the Odyssey*. Mnemosyne Supplement 52. Leiden: Brill.

West, Martin L. 1997. *The East Face of Helicon: West Asiatic Elements in Greek Poetry and Myth*. Oxford and New York: Clarendon.

———. 2014. *The Making of the Odyssey*. Oxford: Oxford University Press.

CHAPTER 3

Meeting the Greeks

You know very well what it is to be a slave, but having never tasted freedom, you do not know whether it is sweet or not. Believe me, if you should get a taste of it, you would advise us to fight for it not with spears but with axes.

—SPARTANS TO A PERSIAN ARISTOCRAT,
HERODOTUS 7. 135. 3

(this from people whose way of life was entirely dependent on
the labor of thousands upon thousands of slaves)

The Homeric epics were accorded unparalleled reverence throughout Greek history. Along with other poems about the war at Troy that are now lost, the *Iliad* and the *Odyssey* provided countless plots for Greek poetry, drama, and visual arts. They also enshrined in the Greek consciousness the notion that war should be the organizing principle for a long narrative as well as a central focus of endeavor. When in the Classical Age men sat down to write history, for all their reservation about war's value it was nonetheless war that formed their subject matter and gave us the magisterial narratives of Herodotus and Thucydides. Fortunately Herodotus's interests extended far beyond the war that was the ostensible subject of his work, and having examined myth and epic, we might choose as a third point of entry into Greek thinking his remarkable opus, the first sustained Greek prose text that survives.

In the year that we know as 492 BCE, the little city-states of Greece that dotted the Aegean and Mediterranean basins were faced with a terrifying prospect. Darius I, king of the wealthy and powerful Persian Empire, sent his son-in-law Mardonius west with the idea in mind of adding Greece to his already substantial domains. His forces were defeated at the famous Battle of Marathon, and when his son and successor Xerxes sought a rematch a decade later, the result was the same. The Greeks were exhilarated by their surprising victory over vastly larger numbers, a victory that soon passed into the realm of nationalistic myth as the defeat of disorder, *chaos*, by *cosmos*—order. The western coast of what is today Turkey was then dotted with flourishing Greek cities, and one young man from the city of Halicarnassus toward the south thought there might be a book in it. Over many years, he wrote that book, and it is easily purchased today both in the original Greek and in translations into many modern languages. It is the *Historiē*, the research, of Herodotus, the first surviving piece of prose in any length written in Greek. Although Herodotus was an outlier in several respects, his rich narrative offers a wealth of information about the common scaffolding and parameters of the Greek worldview.

The opening sentence of the *Histories* offers an explanation of his undertaking:

> The researches of Herodotus of Halicarnassus have been set forth here so that the memory of things people have done may not be forgotten with the passing of time, and so that great and wondrous achievements, whether of Greeks or foreigners, may not become *aklea*.

Aklea: lacking in *kleos*—without fame, without glory. The noun *kleos* shares the same Indo-European root as *slava*, glory, which came to prominence in the Russian invasion of Ukraine in 2022 in the slogan *Slava Ukraini*, revived from its use in earlier conflicts: Glory to Ukraine. *Kleos* as a motivating factor in human life persists throughout Greek literature. As we have seen, Homer's heroes both Greek and Trojan show enormous concern for their *kleos*. Achilles' mother, a sea nymph, has told him that he has a choice of two fates. Should he stay in Troy and fight, he will die, but he will have *kleos aphthiton*, glory imperishable; if he returns home, he will live a long time but without *kleos* (*Iliad*, 9. 410–16). In the fourth century Plato would include in his dialogue *The Symposium* ideas that Socrates ascribes to Diotima, a wise woman from the Greek city of Mantinea. Consider, she says in a verse of her own composition, people's eagerness for

laying up immortal *kleos* for all time to come.

For this, she says—more in fact than for their children—people are prepared to run all manner of risks, even to the extent of giving up their lives (208b–d).

From this programmatic opening sentence Herodotus moves on to explore the origins of the conflict between East and West. He begins by repeating the salacious tales Persians and Phoenicians tell about a series of tit-for-tat woman-snatchings: the seizure of the Greek princess Io from Argos by some Phoenicians, the retaliatory abduction of the Phoenician princess Europa from Tyre and the Colchian princess Medea by Greeks, and finally the capture of the Spartan queen Helen by the Trojan Paris, who calculated that he could safely help himself to Helen seeing that the previous kidnappers had never been compelled to give restitution. *Dikas*, Herodotus calls the restitution. Various forms of the Greek word *dikē*— justice, fairness, compensation—dot Herodotus's version of the tale: eight of them, in fact. Deriving from a verb meaning to straighten, *dikē* had been terribly important for Greeks since the time of Homer. Its original opposite was crookedness, and indeed those who did not practice *dikē* were often crooks. In time it became a common word in court procedure, but it also carried a strong connotation of requital—of giving, and getting, one's "just" deserts. That enemies should be punished in kind was a key Greek belief. The seventh-century poet Archilochus was famed for the tongue-lashings his verses delivered to those by whom he had been wounded. "I know one really important thing," he wrote:

How to requite with evil reproaches the person who has wronged
    me evilly.[1]

In seeking to persuade his contemporaries that injuring their enemies was not, in fact, the ultimate in justice, Plato would have an uphill fight on his hands. The notion of distinguishing justice from vengeance was novel, and a hard sell.

Personally, Herodotus says, he cannot vouch for the truth of any of these racy anecdotes. Rather, "I will identify the one whom I myself know to have first behaved unjustly toward the Greeks and thus move ahead in my narrative" (1. 5. 3). This was the Lydian ruler Croesus, whose life story epitomized for the historian the nature of the human condition.

Croesus's family, Herodotus explains, came to power in the following way: Because he was "fated to come to a bad end," Croesus's ancestor King Candaules became thoroughly infatuated with his own wife, and being thus smitten, made a habit of expatiating on her beauty to his favorite bodyguard, Gyges. Sensing that Gyges was not fully persuaded of the queen's incomparable loveliness, he promises to contrive for him to behold her naked. Gyges is scandalized, but despite his horrified protests, the king insists. Compelled to observe his master's wife as she strips for bed, Gyges is seen, and the enterprising queen summons him in the morning and informs him that he can escape with his life only if he will agree to assassinate Candaules, after which he may rule Lydia together with her. "He chose," says Herodotus, "to live" (1. 11. 4). The priestess of Apollo at Delphi, however, cautioned him that vengeance would come for the regicide in the fifth generation, and the man who paid for Gyges' transgression was none other than his great-great-grandson Croesus.

This Croesus received many visitors at his lavish court, and when the Athenian lawgiver Solon came by, the Lydian king, having seen to it that he was taken on a tour of the treasury, inquired pointedly whether perhaps in his travels Solon might have encountered someone he considered to be more fortunate than anyone else. Disappointed in his hope of being awarded this slot, Croesus was forced to listen instead to Solon's admiring accounts of several Greeks of humble station who had lived virtuously and ended their lives well. And so, Solon concluded, "human life is entirely a question of chance." One may, after all, be immensely wealthy but still unfortunate, and even if someone appears to be fortunate, you cannot assess his good fortune until he is dead, as "You need to wait and see how everything turns out, for the god often gives a glimpse of happiness to someone—and then rips him to shreds" (1. 32. 4, 9). The poet Archilochus had voiced much the same sentiment some years before when he wrote

> Entrust all to the gods, who frequently
> Raise up the men misfortune has cast down
> Upon the black, black earth; and often too
> Men standing firm those same gods will lay flat.
> Great evils then ensue, and such men roam
> With hungry bellies and distracted minds.[2]

Indeed for all his wealth there was much suffering ahead for Croesus, including but not limited to the death of a beloved child. Consulting the Delphic oracle about the advisability of going to war with Cyrus, the Lydian king had been told that if he were to cross the Halys River, he would destroy a mighty empire. Elated, he failed to consider the possibility that the empire he destroyed might be his own. When upon meeting defeat he lodged a complaint, the priestess informed him sternly that "Not even a god can escape the fate that has been ordained for him. Croesus has paid for the crime of his ancestor four generations ago" (1. 91. 1).

Belief in inherited family guilt was powerful in antiquity, when people were not as individualistic as many moderns.[3] The accursed house of Tantalus, who had presumed to serve his son to the gods at dinner, provided numerous plots for Greek tragedies, as did the family of the notoriously unfortunate Oedipus. The notion that punishment for a transgression might come in future generations was a valuable deterrent to wrongdoing in a society with limited forensic capabilities and next to no police force. Zeus, Solon wrote, catches up with everyone sooner or later:

> One pays today, another pays tomorrow.
> Though some, it's true, appear to circumvent
> The fate decreed on high, yet destiny
> Always pursues and will not be denied.
> Their blameless child, however innocent,
> Will pay a heavy price, or that child's child. (13. 27–32)

The story of Croesus is a mini-tragedy, as the whole of Xerxes' arrogant attempt to conquer Greece is the tragedy that undergirds Herodotus's entire *Histories*. (It is likely that Herodotus's concern about the excess he identified in Persian ambitions contained warnings as well for the far-flung Athenian Empire, about to go down to defeat in its ruinous war with Sparta.)

In life as on the stage, fate and character interact and are prone to bring about catastrophic reversals of fortune when it is in a person's nature to overreach. This overreaching, Greeks believed, was grounded in the arrogance, *hybris*, that rejects the gods' ordained limits on human aspiration.[4] Like most Greeks, Herodotus found this behavior deeply troubling. That Asia and Europe should be ruled by a single individual violated a deeply held Greek conviction about limits and boundaries. Xerxes had no respect for such natural limits, and Herodotus pointedly depicted the Persian king crowing that at such time as he subdues the Greeks he "will show that Persian territory is coterminous with the sky where Zeus reigns." Passing through the whole of Europe, he boasts, "I will make all lands a single country" (7. 8c. 1–2). When the stormy waters of the Hellespont destroy the bridge he has built to link the two continents, in his infantile rage he actually orders them whipped and tattooed. Fate, chance, hybris, excess, transgression, reversals of fortune—all these play prominent roles in the tragic drama that was contemporaneous with Herodotus's project, and all would play important roles in the tragedies that were being performed in Athens in Herodotus's lifetime: Clytemnestra's murder of her war hero husband Agamemnon, Oedipus's patricide and incest.

Just as bad as transgression was excess. That excess incurs the gods' displeasure is axiomatic in Herodotus's worldview. When Arcesilaus, the ruler of Cyrene in North Africa, had exiled a number of his political opponents and slaughtered others, the exiles in nearby Barca murdered him in revenge. His mother Pheretime, Herodotus reports, responded by impaling Barca's most prominent citizens on stakes—and embossed the city walls with the breasts she had chopped off their wives. Herodotus plainly takes satisfaction in reporting her grisly end:

For as soon as she had taken vengeance on the people of Barca and left Libya for Egypt, she died horribly, teeming with maggots while still alive, as if to show people that excessive retribution will exact a proportionate response from the gods. (4. 205)

The sixth-century poet and moralist Theognis also advocated the avoidance of excess:

> The middle way is best in everything,
> And thus you will attain to excellence,
> A thing it is not easy to achieve. (335–36)

When the inventor Daedalus devised mechanical wings on which he and his son Icarus might escape from Crete, he cautioned Icarus to take the middle way, avoiding both the sun's heat and the ocean's spray. As children will, Icarus disregarded his father's counsel, flying higher and higher, with the result that the wax in his wings melted and he fell to his death. In the *Republic*, Plato depicts Socrates as stressing the importance of knowing "how to choose the life that is situated on the mean and shun the excess on either side" (619a).

Greek thought, however, was far from monolithic, and as interesting as the overlap between Herodotus's thinking and that of other Greeks is the wide assortment of differences. The divine watchfulness Herodotus saw at work in quashing transgression and excess is nowhere evident in the more or less contemporary history of the Athenian Thucydides, and another contemporary, Protagoras from Abdera in northern Greece, questioned whether the gods even existed, or what they might look like if they did, arguing that numerous obstacles stood in the way of gaining certain knowledge about these things, "such as the shortness of life and the difficulty of the subject matter."[5] Herodotus's narrative takes a long running jump in the lead-in to the clash between Greece and Persia as he details the customs of the many peoples who made up the Persian Empire and its environs. As we will see in chapter 5, most Greeks had limited interest in foreigners, whom they called *barbaroi*: people whose language sounded like *bar bar bar*; babblers. It is ironic that the man who is our principal source for many generations of Greek history should have been an exceedingly atypical Greek, and yet it is also necessary that this should have been so. For although the world-view that shines through in the *Histories* was in many respects quintessentially Greek, what made Herodotus's enterprise possible was an eminently un-Greek openness that manifested itself not only in an affinity for intelligent, resourceful women but a lively curiosity about non-Greek peoples. The author of the wide-ranging *Histories* took enormous delight in recording the many examples of ingenuity in meeting logistical challenges that he encountered throughout the non-Greek world in his researches. Consider the people of Scythia, he says, a vast area extending from Ukraine across southern Russia and embracing much of southwestern Kazakhstan. It was quite a challenge to cook an ox in Scythia after it had been sacrificed, as there was no wood about with which to build a fire, and cauldrons were hard come by. Consequently the Scythians fill the ox's paunch with the flesh, mix in some water, and boil it over a fire they have made from the animal's bones. A self-cooking ox! He was impressed by the Babylonian system for ensuring that no women were left without husbands. Every year the Babylonians would put up their young women for auction in descending order of beauty. The wealthiest men, consequently, would keep raising the bids on the most beautiful women, and the money collected in this way would provide dowries for the least good-looking. Everyone went home happy (or so Herodotus was persuaded).

Neither Herodotus's curiosity about the customs, the *nomoi*, of non-Greek peoples nor the respect he accorded them, was characteristic of his fellow Hellenes. And much of his work concerned these *nomoi* (sing. *nomos*). In his lifetime the concept of *nomos* and its opposite *physis*, nature, had become a hot topic. A major concern of his contemporaries was whether it was *nomos*, custom/law that held primacy in human affairs, or *physis*, nature; the debate was central to the thought of the itinerant intellectuals known as sophists. *Nomos*, which encompassed both informal mores and statutes "on the books," was determined by people and could therefore be changed, whereas *physis*, it was believed, was dictated by the gods and thus immutable. The notion of nomos raised troubling questions of moral relativism. Herodotus himself tells a diagnostic tale designed to show that it is decidedly *nomos* that dominates. When Darius was king in Persia, he writes, he gathered together the Greeks who happened to be at his court and inquired of them how much money it would take to get them to eat the dead bodies of their fathers. Horrified, the Greeks replied that they would never do such a thing, no matter how much they were paid. Next the king summoned some Indians who were in the habit of doing just this—eating the bodies of their deceased parents—and asked them, in the presence of the Greeks, how much money it would take to persuade them to allow their parents to be cremated, and the Indians were similarly scandalized. "We see from this," Herodotus observed, "how deeply rooted a thing custom is" (3. 38. 3).

Most Greek men, moreover, found women at the very least problematic, and they devised a variety of mechanisms to circumscribe the spheres in which they might be permitted to operate—religion and the household, but certainly nothing else. The ideal Greek woman was to be neither seen nor heard. Herodotus saw things differently. Ancient historian Carolyn Dewald has identified 375 mentions of women or femaleness in the *Histories*.[6] By contrast, the fingers of one hand would suffice to count such mentions in the history Herodotus's contemporary Thucydides wrote of the war between Athens and Sparta, a work of nearly the same length. Greek men varied radically in their responses to the opposite sex. Greeks were fascinated by the existence of sex differences, and a central purpose of Greek social organization was to steer these differences into productive channels. A potent strain of misogyny was evident in Greece in both literature and life, and one regard in which Herodotus plainly found non-Greek cultures more advanced was in the opportunities they afforded to women of talent. Resourceful women crop up constantly in his *Histories*, from Candaules' wife, who orchestrated her husband's assassination, to the Babylonian queen Nitocris, who quashed a potential attack by diverting the course of the Euphrates River to make it near-impossible to navigate (1. 185). The Greek city-states were far less hospitable to enterprising females. For most of antiquity, Greek women were excluded from all offices except priesthoods, and in most states they were subject to their male relatives throughout their lives: first their fathers, then their husbands, and then, if widowed, their sons. Though the Homeric epics gave some space to women's voices and feature many estimable female characters both human and divine, the perspective of Homer's approximate contemporary Hesiod was radically different. Before the creation of woman, he maintained, men lived carefree lives free of toil and illness, but now that women have become part of their lives

> Plagues beyond number wander among us:
> Now earth and sea alike are crammed with ills.
> (*Works and Days*, 100–101)

A few generations later the poet Semonides from the Aegean island of Amorgos composed a diatribe against the female sex, explaining that

> women are the biggest single plague
> Zeus has created. (7. 115)

With the development of democracy at Athens came a host of practices limiting the rights of women. Plato's radical inclusion of women in the government of the ideal state he sketched out in his *Republic* appalled his pupil Aristotle, who characterized women as "deformed men" (*Generation of Animals*, 737a25) who could only function under the guiding hand of a male intellect. When toward the end of Aristotle's life the Macedonians from the north conquered first the states of mainland Greece and then the empires of the east, destroying the autonomy of the Greek city-states and creating vast multi-ethnic empires, tensions between the sexes eased. Deprived of the satisfaction once afforded by politics, Greek men turned their energies to their friends and families, and accordingly the situation of women improved somewhat. Herodotus would have been most pleased.

Athenian democracy flourished in Herodotus's day, but though there were numerous other democracies in Greece (most of them in the empire the Athenians had built for themselves in Herodotus's youth), oligarchy was common as well, as was one-man rule, particularly outside the Greek world. Herodotus included in his history a debate that he

swore actually took place in Persia in 525 between three of the conspira-
tors who had just overthrown the previous government. What manner
of regime shall they institute, they wonder, now that they seem to have
a clean slate? One praises democracy, another oligarchy, another monarchy, and they end by choosing monarchy—democratically: by voting!
Herodotus's entire history was eminently democratic, incorporating as
it did a wide variety of viewpoints and voices: it was his business, he
wrote, to report what he had heard, not necessarily to believe it (2. 123;
7. 152). His contemporary Thucydides, on the other hand, sifted through
his sources in his mind before crafting every sentence, producing a uni-
vocal narrative that except in reported (or invented) speeches gave no
space to claims he did not endorse. Not surprisingly, Thucydides was
highly critical of democracy. As we have seen in the prologue, Greeks
also disagreed passionately on this topic. The persistent conflict between the aristocratic ethos manifest in the early centuries of Greek
civilization and the egalitarian principles of later eras led not only to a
diversity of political views but to frequent and bloody civil wars.

To illustrate the Persian failure to understand the mentality of the
Greeks, Herodotus deploys a conversation between two Persians,
Mardonius and another of Xerxes' commanders, Tritantaechmes. On
discovering that the prize at the Olympics was a crown of olive,
Tritantaechmes revealed what Herodotus viewed as stereotypical Persian limitations, exclaiming "Good grief, Mardonius, what kind of men
have you brought us to fight against, people who compete to be recognized for excellence rather than to be rewarded with money!" (8. 26. 3).
The word I have translated "excellence" here is *aretē*, and it was one of
the cornerstones of the Greek value system. Often translated into
English as "virtue," *aretē* did not necessarily carry an equal ethical burden. In Homer it is closely identified with distinction in battle. The word
in fact derived from Ares, god of war, and its corollaries included the
adjective *aristos*, best, hence the word aristocracy, semantically speaking
the rule of the best although in reality nearly always the rule of the
wealthiest. In one of the most unbearably painful scenes of the *Iliad* the
Greek champion Achilles and the Trojan prince Hector realize they are
finally about to fight to the death. When Hector implores Achilles not

to mutilate his body, Achilles informs him coldly that agreements between the two of them are no more possible than between men and lions, wolves and lambs. This is the time, he suggests, to get in touch with your *aretē* and prove yourself a worthy spearman (22. 260–69). In the fifth century the sophist Gorgias would argue that the nature of *aretē* varied according to a person's station in life, status, age, and gender all being factors, and defined a woman's *aretē* as managing the household well, preserving the property within it, and obeying her husband (Plato, *Meno* 71–72a). The iconoclast Plato had radically different ideas. He too identified particular kinds of *aretē*, each specific to a particular function. A field possessed of *aretē* would be highly fertile; a horse possessed of *aretē* would be marked by swiftness; a knife possessed of *aretē* would be singularly sharp. But in Plato's construct the *aretē* of all people was the same, for the *aretē* of the human being was quite simply justice.

———

Herodotus reached fairly far back in his narrative, relying on oral traditions handed down for generations, but his knowledge of the first centuries of Greek history was nonexistent. When we seek to learn about the early acts and thoughts of the people we call Greeks, we must turn to material remains; to the clay tablets of the late Bronze Age found in Crete and on the Greek mainland; to documents that survive in the Near East; and to early poets like Homer and Hesiod. And a good bit of what we infer will be guesswork.

Although they wouldn't have recognized the word "Greek" or the expression "BCE," the people who would turn into the Greeks seem to have entered what is now the country of Greece around 2200 BCE, originating perhaps in Hungary or Romania. Like about half of us who are alive today, they spoke a tongue belonging to the Indo-European language family; there are more than 400 such languages. This book is written in an Indo-European language, English, and printed in the alphabet of an Indo-European people, the Romans. The proto-Greeks brought with them their characteristically Indo-European sky-god Dyeus, who became Zeus—a deity whose name in fact means "sky" or "shining." As they settled among a new, southern people more prone to worshipping female deities, Zeus acquired some high-profile relatives—a wife, Hera, and a daughter, Athena.

At some point in the 3000s, someone in the Near East had discovered that combining copper with a little tin or arsenic would produce bronze, an alloy far harder and handier than any of its components. When they arrived in Greece, the proto-Greeks added themselves to the Bronze Age societies like the successful river valley civilizations already thriving in Mesopotamia and Egypt. Like other Indo-European societies, that of the proto-Greeks was patrilineal and patriarchal. Descent was reckoned through the paternal line, and men ruled both in families and in the state. As in the largely non-Indo-European states of the Near East, the prosperity of the Greek states was considered to depend on divine favor. If the gods did not receive their due, the crops would fail, women would give birth to deformed children (or no children at all), and the armed forces would not win wars. This belief persisted throughout Greek history. In 399 the philosopher Socrates was put to death for, among other things, failure to acknowledge the gods of the state.

The proto-Greeks did not establish a single nation in their new territory. Rather, archaeology has turned up hundreds of independent settlements on mainland Greece and in the islands of the Aegean Sea. One of the most substantial of these was at Mycenae on the Peloponnesus. Home of Agamemnon, Mycenae has given its name to the notion of "the Mycenaean Age" beginning around 1600, and from this point on when referring to Greeks of the Late Bronze Age historians speak not of Greeks but of "Mycenaeans."

Around 1500 the Mycenaeans took over a thriving civilization on Crete. We have no idea what the Bronze Age Cretans actually called themselves, but today we call them Minoans after their legendary king Minos. At the Cretan capital of Cnossus and in Pylos on the west coast of the Peloponnesus, archaeologists have found samples of an early form of writing known as Linear B. (Some script labeled "Linear A" was also found at Cnossus, presumably the language of the Minoans, but it has yet to be deciphered.) Hopes that deciphering Linear B would uncover a great literature were disappointed when the code was finally cracked in the 1950s and it was found to be an embryonic form of Greek. The Linear B tablets proved to consist of palace records that revealed the existence of an intricate bureaucracy and an elaborate system of economic redistribution focused on the royal palaces. But in all the Linear B tablets, literature there was none. The Homeric epics remain the first surviving literature of Greece, indeed of Europe.

The Mycenaeans were raiders. The weapons that predominate among their grave goods testify to the role that warfare played in both their lives and their self-concept. One town with which they seem to have interacted was the town referred to in the archives of the Indo-European Hittites as Wilusa, or Taruwisa, a city on the coast of northwest Anatolia, the modern Turkey. Though Homer's tale of a protracted war at Troy may be nothing more than fiction, Wilusa must surely have been the Greek Ilios, hence the title the *Iliad*—the story of a war at Taruwisa/Troy. Archaeology shows that someone destroyed Wilusa by fire at the end of the Bronze Age, but it need not have been the Mycenaeans. Wilusa had plenty of other enemies.

Around 1200 BCE, the world the Mycenaeans knew collapsed around them. The powerful Hittite Empire in Anatolia disintegrated. Syrian Ugarit, the most successful emporium in the Mediterranean, was burned to the ground. Though in the end it was the one major Mediterranean state left standing, even Egypt experienced many attacks from outsiders. A variety of peoples experienced pressures that forced them to move around, looking sometimes for new markets, sometimes for new homes. Archaeologists have found remains of many cities that had been sacked and burned, with bodies lying unburied in the streets.

Many explanations have been put forward for the dramatic systems collapse that befell the Mediterranean. Egyptian records refer to attacks by raiders they called "Sea Peoples" or "The Foreigners in Their Islands," but it is unclear just who these were or what role their marauding played in the disintegration of Bronze Age civilization.[7] The obstruction of trade in the Aegean may have cut off the supply of tin and copper needed for the production of bronze. A natural disaster such as drought, earthquake, exhaustion of the soil or some combination of these could have undermined the food distribution systems of the Mycenaean and Near

Eastern palaces. There may have been an epidemic of some kind. The fallout from the Covid-19 pandemic is a stark reminder of the ripple effect such an event can trigger. As is often the case in times of food scarcity, civil wars may have broken out. The extreme political, economic, and social inequalities that characterized the Bronze Age could easily have sparked revolution from below.

Whatever the cause, not long after 1200, Greeks found themselves living in a different world. The Iron Age that set in was much poorer than the preceding era. Numbers plummeted. By 1000 the population of the Greek world was probably one-third of what it had been 300 years before. Entire towns disappeared. Many craft skills were lost, and the art of writing was forgotten. It would be a long time before Greek society and culture reawakened. When it did, however, the Greek mind would take great leaps forward. Sadly for those who had lost their lives in the collapse of the Bronze Age, the disintegration of the hierarchical palace bureaucracies was necessary to pave the way for the more open society that was to come. In the words of global historian Walter Scheidel, "the miserable equality of near-universal impoverishment of the postpalatial period may arguably have prepared the ground for the resilient egalitarianism of later centuries of Greek history."[8]

It was probably during the eighth century that some clever person, perhaps a bilingual one, adapted the script of the Phoenicians into an alphabet for writing Greek.[9] The ability to record not only thoughts but doings in writing would ultimately make possible a broadly based government responsible to the people for its actions—a government on which citizens could keep tabs. Power generally passed first to small circles of aristocratic families who held the bulk of the land and replaced the weak monarchies that had succeeded the centralized bureaucracies of the Bronze Age, then to successively larger groups. Not always: many states remained oligarchic, like Corinth; monarchy persisted in Herodotus's birthplace of Halicarnassus on the southwest tip of Anatolia; the Spartan constitution defied categorization. The city-states (*poleis*, sing. *polis*) that developed as the Greek world revived experimented with a variety of governments. A mountainous terrain, mainland Greece had always been broken up into small poleis. Now these poleis became host to the exchange of exciting new ideas—many of them about the polis itself. And soon democracy would become a force to be reckoned with.

Cross-fertilization with both Semitic and Indo-European civilizations sparked the flowering of Greek culture in this period, as many skills besides the alphabet resulted from Greek contacts with the east. Already by the end of the ninth century Greek traders could be found at Al Mina in Syria. By the middle of the eighth, trade routes passing directly through the Greek mainland connected Italy and the Near East, placing the Greeks in an ideal position to absorb influences of all kinds, from handicrafts to literature. Eastern imports—and local imitations of them—appear increasingly in mainland Greece by 700. Although many potters still followed the custom of adorning their creations with the geometric designs that gave the early Archaic Age the name of the "Geometric Era," vases adapting new motifs like floral patterns and animals from the Near East begin to pop up around 725. It is a great disappointment that we know the names of very few of the talented individuals who century after century painted Greek pottery with amazing scenes; surely some of them were women, but we have no idea how many. Even painters whose distinctive style is recognized from one vase to the next are often known only by the names or current locations of their most memorable creations: the Pan painter, the Madrid painter, the Princeton painter. The statuary of the Egyptian Saite dynasty (664–525) took Greek form in the monumental statues known as *kouroi*, stylized depictions of young men in somewhat unnatural, formal poses with their lips artificially shaped in what art historians call the "archaic smile," and their female counterparts, *korai*. In a conspicuous departure from Egyptian practice, Greek *kouroi* were unabashedly naked, though their female counterparts most decidedly were not.

It was also during these formative years of Greek civilization that the first great works of European literature (though far younger than the epics of the Ancient Near East) came into being in the form of the *Iliad* and the *Odyssey*, possibly with the aid of the alphabet. These works too show marked Near Eastern influence, particularly from *Gilgamesh*, which manifests the same profound concern with mortality and whose protagonist offers a striking parallel to the concern of Homer's heroes with *kleos*: Gilgamesh expresses his determination to "establish forever a

FIGURE 3.1. Egyptian and Greek statuary. (a) This statue of the twenty-fifth century BCE pharaoh Menkaure and his wife is typical of the Egyptian statuary that provided a prototype for the Greek *kouros* and *korē*. Erich Lessing / Art Resource, NY. This sixth-century *kouros* (b) and *korē* (c) show the distinctive Greek adaptations of the Egyptian prototype. The *kouros* is naked and has a certain artificial, stylized pose and facial expression; the *korē* is clothed and appears more lifelike. 3.1b: The Metropolitan Museum of Art, New York, Fletcher Fund, 1932, https://www.metmuseum.org/art/collection/search/253370. 3.1c: Marie Mauzy / Art Resource, NY.

name eternal!" As we have seen, the roughly contemporaneous *Theogony* (*The Genealogy of the Gods*) of Hesiod shows dramatic parallels to the Hittite poem *The Kingship in Heaven,* and the two may derive from a common source. Eastern influence also helped shape the structure of elite social life: from Assyria by way of Lydia the Greeks learned the

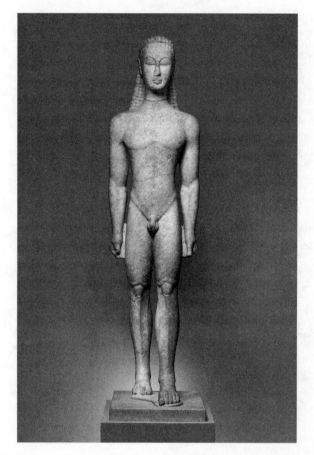

FIGURE 3.1B. (*continued*)

habit of reclining on couches at the elite drinking parties known as *symposia* (literally, "together-drinkings"). The position was more than a little conducive to the flirting that often went on there.

The opening up of trade and development of sailing skills combined with population growth and land hunger to spark excursions abroad in order to found new settlements. Though these *apoikiai*—homes away from home—are generally called colonies, they should not be confused with the New World colonies founded in more recent times, for despite sentimental ties with their founding states, Greek colonies were politically independent from the start. Greek states founded hundreds of

FIGURE 3.1C. (*continued*)

colonies; Miletus in Anatolia alone established dozens. Beginning in the eighth century, colonization spread Greek people, goods, and ideas from Spain to Turkey, from North Africa to the Black Sea. With their combination of seafaring and farming interests and skills, and spurred on by curiosity, a sense of adventure, and a willingness to take risks, the

Greeks were in many ways ideal colonists (although no doubt the populations on which they descended saw things differently). Unlike the
Phoenicians, who settled only in ports, the Greeks also spread out into
the hinterland, delighted to find arable turf. By 500 the population of
colonies accounted for some two-fifths of all Greeks. Wherever the
olive would grow, there they were.

During this period new military developments evolved that would
shore up the power of the developing middle class in politics, as armies
were increasingly composed of heavily armored infantrymen called
hoplites, so named for the round shield or *hoplon* that they carried. The
full hoplite panoply of helmet, breastplate, and greaves was not prohibi-
tively expensive, but neither was it cheap. Those who served in the phalanx were men of middling status, while the rich served in the cavalry
and the poor served as light-armed troops and, as navies developed, as
rowers. With the hoplite phalanx forming the core of a city's defense, it
was now more difficult for the aristocrats to claim a monopoly on
political power. The social and political ferment of the late Archaic Age
in his native Megara forced the poet Theognis to confront the aristocrat's greatest nightmare: social mobility. In verses probably designed
for recitation at symposia, he makes clear his horror at the rise to power
of a new class. Addressing Cyrnus, the real or fictional young man to
whom his poetry was directed, he laments:

> This city, though allegedly the same,
> Is peopled by completely different folk.
> Those who before knew no judgments, no laws,
> But wore goatskins to shreds around their sides
> And used to pasture out of town like deer—
> These people, son of Polypaüs, now
> Are held in high esteem, and, even worse,
> Those who were once accounted excellent
> Are thought today to be of no account.
> Who can endure to look upon such things? (53–58)

One serious challenge to aristocratic rule, however, would come from
within the aristocrats' own ranks, as strongmen, usually of distinguished

heritage, made power grabs in a variety of poleis. Taken over from Anatolian autocrats, the word "tyrant" can be misleading. The rule of the tyrants could be arbitrary, but it was not always harsh. Though the tyrants generally had the support of the populace, tyrannical rule was felt to be un-Greek, and in time (except to the far west, in Sicily) it died out.

Fearing just such a tyranny, the Athenians addressed the unrest in their city by setting up a respected citizen admired by rich and poor alike to overhaul their government. A man of vision and conviction, Solon devised a system that allotted officeholding to citizen males in accordance with income rather than lineage. (No women could participate in government, although some held prestigious priesthoods.) This was a radical change from what had gone before, when power lay in the hands of a small group of men in rich, prominent families known as "Eupatrids"—literally, "men with good fathers." Nine magistrates known as "archons" would govern along with a body that met on a hill sacred to the war god Ares and thus was called the Council of the Areopagus. There was also an assembly of adult male citizens, and a pool of 6,000 of these was available for service on juries. Solon's fundamentally egalitarian mindset shines through in his poetry:

> Equal in wealth, I think, is he who has
> Enough to eat, and clothes and shoes as well,
> To one who has much silver and much gold
> And wheat and mules and many horses, too.
> For mortals, having just enough is fine.
> This is abundance, for no one at all
> Can take his goods along when Hades calls,
> Nor can his money keep him safe from death
> Or dread diseases or a cruel old age.[10]

Solon wrote a good deal, always in verse. Prose had not yet come into its own as a literary form. Today prose is the default format for expression; like Molière's Monsieur Jourdain, all our lives we have been speaking prose without even being aware of it. In Greece literature well into the Classical Age, the opposite was true: poetry was the default, prose the exception. Until shortly after Solon's day, no Greek intellectual whose work is known to us wrote in prose. Few people could read, and prose relies on readers more than on listeners. Greek verse was commonly sung to the accompaniment of a stringed instrument, usually the lyre, hence the English word "lyrics." Verse continued to be the primary medium of Greek literature for centuries. It was the prescribed format for both comedy and tragedy, and at the festivals in honor of the god Dionysus at which these dramas were presented, other poetry was performed as well. The authors taught in school were all poets, as instruction was largely oral and poetry is far easier to memorize than prose, especially when sung. Even the first works of philosophy were composed in verse.

A variety of poets were active in the Archaic Age, as epic gave way to more individualistic genres. Instead of the omniscient author hiding behind his persona as a teller of tales, the new poets had names and personalities and opinions—strong ones. Where epic poetry had been about the past, lyric poetry was very much about the present, which took on a powerful immediacy. The Homeric epics had depicted individuals whose fulfillment lay in their relationship to their communities. Achilles must have the admiration of other Greeks living and yet to be born; Odysseus must become the king of Ithaca once again and restore order in his beleaguered palace. Lyric, on the other hand, reached inward to the deepest recesses of the soul, and what it found varied enormously depending on the interests and temperament of the individual poet. In verses composed for both choral and individual performance, the lyric poets experimented with fairly short poems in a variety of meters that touched on a wide range of subjects. Choral compositions were cast as the voice of the community rather than reflecting the mind of the individual poet and tended to be religious or ritual in nature: songs in honor of a god, most frequently Apollo or Dionysus; dirges; songs for groups of young women called *partheneia* (maiden songs); and in time also songs in praise of prominent people and epinician odes, odes commissioned *epi-nikē* (upon a victory) celebrating a winning athlete. Gone from the lyric are the comfortable certainties of epic, a value system in which all could readily concur.

The more daring of the lyric poets composed verses meant for solo performance, writing personally and passionately about concerns ranging from politics and warfare to love and drinking. The Greek cities of the east, in Anatolia and on the islands offshore, provided much of this verse. Anacreon hailed from Teos; the most famous of the lyric poets, Sappho, was from the offshore island of Lesbos a little farther north, as was Alcaeus, whose brother got even farther to the east when he served in the army of the Babylonian king Nebuchadnezzar II. The varied subject matter of the lyric poets pointed to the individualism of this new kind of poetry, a genre born in a world where people were developing more of a sense of themselves as unique and private persons who believed that their thoughts and emotions mattered. Anacreon wrote of the sorrows of old age—and the fear of death and what lay beyond:

> Gray are my temples, white my head,
> The carefree days of youth are gone;
> My teeth have gotten old.
> I'm in a state of constant dread,
> Facing the pit of Tartarus,
> And Hades, deep and grim.
> Grievous enough the journey down,
> And as for coming back:
> That's not an option. (395; Stobaeus, *Anthology* 4. 51. 12)

Only eight fragments of her poetry seem to have survived, but Praxilla lives on in her more soulful comments about death, placed in the mouth of Aphrodite's dying lover the mortal Adonis:

> Most precious of the things I leave behind
> Is sunlight; after that, the brilliant stars,
> The bright face of the moon shining above,
> And ripe cucumbers; apples too, and pears. (747)

Mimnermus from one of the Greek cities of Anatolia combined pain at the loss of love and sex with the sorrows and ignominy of old age:

> What, then, is life, what is joy, in the absence of bright Aphrodite?
> When the day comes that I care
> No more for secret intrigues,

Or for the gifts that seduce or delights that take place in the bedroom,
  All those sweet blossoms of youth
  Loved by both sexes alike—
Frankly, I'd sooner be dead, for when grievous old age comes upon one,
  Turning the best-looking man
  Into a hideous wreck
Cares wear away at the heart; there's no joy in beholding the sunlight.
  Hateful to boys he's become,
  Loathsome to women as well.
Such is the curse that the gods made for us of that monster, old age.

Far more fragments of Sappho's poetry survive than of any other female poet, for she was widely admired for the passion to which her work gave voice:

I want to die. That's all.
Weeping, she left me
And said these things:
"Things have turned out so dreadfully for us!
Believe me, Sappho, it is against my will that I leave you."
  And I replied,
"Be happy and remember me,
Knowing how we cared for you.
It not, I want to remind you . . .
. . . and lovely times we enjoyed.
  Many crowns of violets,
Roses and crocuses
You put on at my side
And many garlands of soft flowers
Around your soft throat . . .
Anointing us . . .
with pure, sweet oil . . .
And on a soft and gentle bed . . .
You gave way to your longing . . .
. . . We were absent from
. . . no holy site

Nor grove . . .
nor dance
nor sound . . ."(94)

   Evening, you bring back everything that dawn
In shining splendor has driven apart.
You draw a lamb, you draw a kid,
You draw a child back to its waiting mother. (104a)

You came and I was simply mad for you
You cooled the longing in my burning mind. (48)

I don't know what to do; there are
Two states of mind warring within me. (51)

Her images of desire sometimes convey tenderness, sometimes the feeling of being overpowered:

Sweet mother, I cannot manage the loom,
Undone by slender Aphrodite as I am
With longing for a boy. (102)

Eros shook my senses
As if it were a mountain wind falling on oak trees. (47)

Plato dubbed Sappho "the tenth muse," and her adroit articulation of her helplessness in the face of desire captivated even men who disapproved of educated, literary women. Predictably, she was nonetheless suspected of inappropriate sexual behavior, although not necessarily the kind associated today with the word lesbian (which does derive from Sappho and her poetry); she was often accused of heterosexual promiscuity, and the Greek verb *lesbiazein* appears to have referred to fellatio, not homoerotic behavior.

   The uncertainty in the scholarly world about Sappho's sexuality is a little puzzling in light of the burning love she declares repeatedly for others of her gender, but the disposition of nervous commentators through the ages to deny her bisexuality was facilitated by the delicacy of the language with which she described lovemaking between women.

Greeks might be extremely circumspect about sex, or they might be strikingly open. Homer is the soul of discretion. He assumes that we can easily use our imaginations to summon up images of what Odysseus did with Calypso, and Circe, and Penelope. At the other extreme, Aristophanes' comedies overflowed with raw physicality and were rife with crude sexual and scatological humor. The plays are dotted gleefully with words like *binein* (fuck), *kusthos* (cunt), *peos* (prick), *skōr* (shit), *prōktos* (asshole), *perdesthai* (fart), and the homosexual love affairs that were standard operating procedure among the elite were quite literally the butt of many jokes.[11] Statuary tended to portray people in dignified pursuits. Scenes of sexual intercourse were not unusual on vases, but they fell more into the category of pornography than of erotica. Though many such works were surely designed for use at symposia, there is no reason to doubt that such pottery was regularly viewed by children. These were not objects that could be obtained only at the "adult vase store." Orators, however, preferred to manipulate their audiences by using euphemisms for genitalia and sexual acts, underlining their own propriety while at the same time making it clear that their opponents engaged in conduct so shameful (principally passive homosexual acts) that it could not even be mentioned in polite company. Even Herodotus, who makes frequent reference to sex, is not graphic in its portrayal. The Athenians' hope of avoiding tyranny was dashed when Peisistratus seized power in 561, but Herodotus tells how he was expelled not long afterward when one of his supporters, whose daughter he had married, discovered that he was having intercourse with the young woman *ou kata nomon*: not according to custom (1. 61). We are left to conjecture just what Peisistratus did with his new wife, although it is not difficult to imagine.

Engineering his restoration to power in Athens, Peisistratus endeared himself to many by public works that beautified the city while creating an abundance of jobs, but his popularity did not prove hereditary, and in 510 his son and successor Hippias was driven out with Spartan help. Not long afterward ingenious reforms were pushed through by the democrat Cleisthenes. Previously Athenians had been divided into four kinship groups in which aristocratic families wielded significant power. To erode the power of the aristocracy, Cleisthenes created ten new artificial tribes out of the 139 neighborhoods called demes that made up the peninsula of Attica, the territory of Athens.

Each tribe was to choose one man to serve on a board of ten *strategoi* (sing. *stragegos*, generals who also served as admirals) and fifty men to a new Council of Five Hundred, which would prepare business for the assembly and manage financial and some foreign affairs.

The extraordinary institution of ostracism is usually ascribed to Cleisthenes as well. In accordance with the rules of this quirky procedure, the Athenians would vote each spring as to whether they wished to hold an ostracism. If they did, each voter would scratch on a broken piece of pottery (*ostrakon*), the name of the man—no women were ever ostracized—whom he would most like to see exiled for a period of ten years. No charge needed to be laid against anyone, let alone proven. Winning this inverse popularity contest carried no shame with it; after their ten years were up people who had been ostracized generally returned to Athens, resumed possession of their property, and took up participation in public life once again.

———

This was the Greek world as it stood when the city-states faced a powerful challenge from the East. To general astonishment, the hardy Greek hoplites from Athens and nearby Plataea defeated the vastly larger Persian armament at Marathon in northern Attica, but Darius's son and successor Xerxes returned ten years later with a far larger force. Hearing of the ships Xerxes was having built, the Athenians threw together a formidable navy in a very short time. But what of the other Greek states?

Shortly before 500 the Spartans had organized an alliance under their leadership known today as the Peloponnesian League. The purpose of the league was twofold. Each state would offer the others protection from states outside the league, but this was not all. The Spartan citizen body was small, but the population of the territory it controlled was large, for early in its history Sparta had conquered both the surrounding territory of Laconia and Messenia to the west. This freed the Spartans from all labor, for the more fortunate inhabitants became *perioikoi*, "people who lived round about," enjoying no civic rights in Sparta but providing pots, pans, weaponry, and the like, living in their own communities largely without Spartan interference, while the far less fortunate became slave/serfs known as helots. State property, helots were assigned to citizen families whose food they provided through farming. While the Spartans benefited tremendously from the exploited helot labor that freed up their time for military training, the existence of this dispossessed underclass, which at the time of the Persian Wars outnumbered the citizen class some seven to one, posed a grave security threat, and a principal function of the league was to provide support for Sparta in the event of an uprising.

Early in their history, moreover, the Spartans had overhauled their way of life and instituted a rigorous system that became famous throughout Greece, turning Sparta in effect into an armed camp. Boys were removed from their families and taken to live in military academy, where they were broken down into groups according to age. Designed as they were to prepare young people for the rigors of military life, days were disagreeable. So were nights, when the youths slept on rough mats they had made themselves by pulling up reeds from the banks of the frigid Eurotas River with their bare hands. To harden the soles of their feet and prepare them for mastering all sorts of terrain, the children went without shoes, and often naked as well, receiving only one cloak a year to wear in all kinds of weather, and no tunic to wear underneath. Fed on an unappetizing mixture of pigs' legs, blood, salt, and vinegar known as "black soup," they were always kept a little hungry. To develop skills in subterfuge, they were encouraged to supplement their skimpy rations by theft, with the threat of a beating hanging over them in the event of discovery. All Spartan youths upon reaching adulthood were required to contribute a fixed amount of food to the common mess. When the boys reached the age of eighteen, a select group would be chosen for the secret service known as the *krypteia*, whose charge it was to lie in wait in the countryside at night keeping an eye out for potentially seditious helots and kill them; to lend a semblance of legality to this chilling system, the government annually declared war on the helots.

The problem with putting the organization led by this murderous elite in charge of defense against the Persians was its location: the Peloponnesian League's center of gravity lay too far to the southwest for it to function as an effective bulwark against the Persian onslaught, and in 481 a new league, the Hellenic League, was formed to fight the invaders. The Spartans sent 300 men under their king Leonidas to guard the Thermopylae pass in northern Greece. The oracle at Delphi had warned that if Leonidas died, Greece might be saved. Leonidas perished along with 298 of his fellow Spartans, and Greece was in fact saved, for the heroic Spartans had bought some time for their fellow Greeks to the south. The Greeks construed the holding operation at Thermopylae as a moral victory, and Leonidas was revered ever afterward. Among the many sayings attributed to him was his terse reply to Xerxes' demand that he hand over his weapons: *molōn labe* (come and get them). The holding operation was celebrated by the poet Simonides from the island of Ceos in the Cyclades in a famous epitaph for the Thermopylae dead:

> Go, tell the Spartans, stranger passing by,
> That here, obeying their commands, we lie.

Although Xerxes then moved down on Athens and sacked the city, his forces were defeated by the navy of the Hellenic League in the bay of Salamis off Attica. The king then returned home, leaving the war in the hands of his cousin Mardonius, who also went down to defeat in a land battle at Plataea in Boeotia, north of Athens. Around the same time— tradition placed it on the very same day—the Greek fleet defeated the Persian navy at Mycale near Miletus, liberating the rebellious Greek cities on the coast of Anatolia at last.

In 479, when the Persians had won one battle on land but lost another by sea, Mardonius sent an envoy to Athens in hopes of persuading the Athenians to abandon their fellow Greeks and go over to the Persians.

Herodotus reproduced in his narrative the response of the Athenians, or at least the response he imagines they might have made. Tell Mardonius, he portrays them as saying,

> that as long as the sun maintains its present course, we will never come to an agreement with Xerxes. Instead, we will fight against him unceasingly, trusting in the aid of the gods and heroes for whom he had no regard—whose homes and statues he burned. (8. 143. 2)

Too many factors militated against capitulation:

> First and most important of all, the burnt and ruined temples and statues of our gods. We are constrained to avenge these with might and main, not to come to terms with the author of this destruction. Next, the things we have in common: our fundamental Greekness, if you will—our shared blood and language, not to mention the temples of the gods and our sacrifices and our shared way of life, all of which it would hardly befit the Athenians to betray. (8. 144. 2)

At least from the time of Herodotus, all Greeks had a strong belief in the unity of Greek civilization. Although there was no one political entity, no sovereign nation, called Greece as there is today, the residents of the many far-flung city-states believed firmly they were all ultimately descended from a small pool of ancestors, and they were correct that all Greeks shared a single language. Every Greek, they thought, was related to every other Greek through their common ancestor Hellen (no relation to Helen of Troy), from whom they took the name Hellenes. Hellen was believed to have fathered three sons: Xuthus, Aeolus, and Dorus. From these were descended the three ethnic groups to which all Hellenes belonged and their corresponding three dialects; Greece today is called Hellas. Through Xuthus's son Ion, the Ionian Athenians were tied to the cities of Ionia on the west coast of Anatolia, around Smyrna (modern Izmir); the Aeolians originated in Thessaly in northern Greece and included the Boeotians and Corinthians of central Greece as well as the inhabitants of Lesbos and Aeolia just north of Ionia; Dorians were found mostly in the Peloponnesus, where Sparta and its territory of Laconia were located. (From Laconia we get the English word "laconic," as the Spartans were notoriously economical of speech.) Despite these dialectical variations, a Briton might well have more trouble understanding a Scot or a New Yorker a Texan than would a Greek fail to understand another Greek—excluding the exception that proved the rule: Thucydides observed that the tribe of the Eurytanians, who lived in the hills north of the Corinthian Gulf in central Greece and spoke an incomprehensible dialect of Greek, also ate their meat raw (3. 94. 5). Plainly he considered them outliers in every respect.

These heroes whom Herodotus's Athenians had coupled with the gods were not contemporaries who had distinguished themselves in war but rather quasi-divine figures who had once been alive, performed amazing deeds or had special connections with the gods, and after death had been venerated in the area where they had lived and been buried. Thebes was particularly rich in heroic lore. The Thebans sought protection from the tombs they ascribed to Semele, the mother of Dionysus, to the twins Amphion and Zethus, who were credited with building the city's fortifications—the stones, it was said, were so enchanted by Amphion's music that they easily followed Zethus and fell into place—and to numerous others including even the Trojan Hector, whose body they claimed had found its way to Thebes after his death. Attica alone contained shrines to 170 heroes, and the Spartans regarded their kings as heroes after their deaths. The goodwill of heroes was held necessary to the well-being of both the individual and the group, and most Greeks believed that heroes would, if properly revered, rise from the dead and come to their aid in times of trial. After the Greek triumph over the Persians, Herodotus wrote, the Athenian admiral Themistocles proclaimed that

> It is not we who brought this victory about but rather the gods and the heroes, who recoiled from the notion that one man—and an impious and wicked man at that—should rule over both Asia and Europe. (8. 109. 3)

In ascribing their improbable success against the Persians to the gods and heroes, Greeks had very specific thoughts about which gods and which heroes. A generation later, a mural in Athens portrayed Athena fighting by the Greeks' side at Marathon along with the demigod Heracles and the legendary Athenian king Theseus. The depiction of Theseus was particularly dramatic, as he was shown rising out of the ground to offer aid (Pausanias 1. 15. 3).

Fear of a third invasion compounded by the desire for vengeance drove the Greeks to form a brand-new naval alliance. With the defeat of the Persians, however, the balance of power among the Greek states shifted significantly—and, as it proved, ominously. Although the Spartans had led the Hellenic League during the wars with Persia, their commander Pausanias, stationed in Byzantium, alienated the Greeks by adopting the manners of an eastern potentate, dressing in Persian garb and going about with a distinctly un-Greek bodyguard. His violent behavior toward Greek citizens in Anatolia, particularly women, infuriated the forces under his command. The isolation of Spartan males in military academy from boyhood, their education largely limited to the skills that would be useful in war—fortitude, self-denial, stealth—resulted in stunted social skills. Even when they married, Spartan men would remain in camp, seeing their wives only during surreptitious visits, as the Spartans believed that the passion engendered by the combination of infrequency and secrecy would generate robust offspring. This way of life produced outstanding soldiers, but not necessarily well-rounded human beings. Though it resulted in remarkable freedom for Spartan women, their cloistered existence left Spartan men—Spartiates, as the citizens were called—ill prepared for the complexities and temptations of life in the outside world, and it was not unusual for them to misconduct themselves when away from home.

The leadership of the new alliance thus fell instead to the Athenians, and tensions between Athens's new league and Sparta's Peloponnesian League would shape the political and military history of the entire fifth century. The new league needed money to maintain its navy, and soon the annual contributions from the subject allies—tribute, modern historians call it—amounted to the equivalent of some quarter of a million dollars or 175,000 pounds sterling in contemporary terms. This was quite a tidy sum for a population of about a third of a million, many of them enslaved workers who were largely cut off from the fruits of empire.

Because the league treasury was established on the Aegean island of Delos, modern historians refer to the organization as the Delian League, though contemporaries called it simply "the Athenians and their allies." The alliance had an assembly of representatives that would, in theory, shape policy, but in reality decision-making lay with the hegemon, Athens, which soon began to flex its muscles in preventing restive league members from withdrawing—and compelling reluctant states to join. In 454 the Athenians moved the league treasury to Athens, and historians refer to the league from this time onward as the Athenian Empire.

Shortly before 460 an up-and-coming politician named Ephialtes persuaded the Athenians to pass legislation that transferred many of the powers of the venerable Council of the Areopagus, composed of former archons, to the assembly, the council, and the popular juries. Ephialtes' name, however, is not well known, for people who disliked the democratic direction in which his policies were taking the city arranged his assassination. The man who became famous in connection with Athenian democracy was rather Ephialtes' charismatic associate Pericles, who would be the most prominent politician in Athens until his death in 429. Although he held no official job in the state beyond his position on the board of ten *strategoi*, to which he was reelected nearly every year, his prestige and eloquence were so great that the Athenians did little during this period of their history that did not meet with his approval, and in time he came to be the author of most Athenian policy. It was Pericles who, drawing on the funds pouring in from the imperial tribute, began to coordinate the adornment of the Athenian Acropolis with the buildings that still crown it today. The most conspicuous of these was the temple of Athena known as the Parthenon, now one of the most recognizable buildings on earth. In it stood a magnificent gold and ivory statue of Athena crafted by Pericles' friend Pheidias, also credited with the statue of Zeus in his temple at Olympia that was considered one of the seven wonders of the ancient world. Nearly 40 feet tall, the statue of Athena in the Parthenon commanded an audience of worshippers and tourists who came from hundreds of miles around to gaze on it; fifth-century sculpture was characterized by extraordinary grandeur and was remarkably awe-inspiring.

FIGURE 3.2. The discobolos statue. This superb fifth-century bronze statue of an athlete, the work of Myron, survives only in a marble Roman copy. The lifelike nature of the athlete's pose is striking as he is captured in the moment just before he hurls the discus. © Vanni Archive / Art Resource, NY.

The fifth century was a glorious age for the arts throughout Greece. Sculpture reached great heights in works like the discobolus (discus-thrower) of Myron, a stunning portrayal of pent-up energy in solid marble, and the outsize bronze warriors recovered from the sea near Riace in southern Italy.

Magnificent theaters began to mark the spread of Greek culture throughout the Mediterranean and beyond. In literature, Herodotus and Thucydides produced the first major prose works. Even as literacy increased, however, verse remained the medium of comic and tragic drama, both of them genres associated with Athens. Although numerous Athenians wrote comedies, only those of Aristophanes survive intact from this period. Written largely during the long war between Athens and Sparta known as the Peloponnesian War, Aristophanes' raucous and ribald plays, overflowing with topical humor, skewered the politicians of his day mercilessly and were filled with a longing for the Athens of old, free of war and sophists. Among the tragedians, the famous Aeschylus, Sophocles, and Euripides were just three of the admired playwrights of their day. Sophocles' trilogy that included *Oedipus the King* was awarded only second prize at the annual festival of Dionysus where plays were presented, while the first prize went to Aeschylus's nephew Philocles. The stark contrast between the unrelenting obscenity of Aristophanes and the lofty diction of the tragedians reveals the richness and diversity of Athenian culture.

This flowering was the product of the democratic polis. All citizens were engaged in the life of the state, whose religious festivals brought them together on a regular basis; Athenians celebrated some 170 festivals a year, nearly one every other day. Clubs of various kinds and kinship organizations also fostered fellow feeling. There was somewhat less sense of commonality in poleis that remained oligarchies, but throughout the Greek world the polis inspired loyalty and affection. How free people bonded varied to some extent on class and gender; we know far less about those who were enslaved, many of whom had been dislocated from the cultures into which they had been born. Athenian citizen males of all classes were drawn together in politics and government. Those who harbored aristocratic inclinations often belonged to the oligarchic drinking clubs that were rightly suspected of hatching antidemocratic plots. Women were involved in extended family networks and gathered for female-only festivals as well as the festivals that were open to everyone. Men moved around the classical polis in a way that only some women could. Upper- and middle-class ideology dictated seclusion at home for citizen women: a speaker in an Athenian courtroom boasted his nieces had been "so well brought-up that they were ashamed to be seen even by their male relatives" (Lysias 3. 6–7).

Not all women were constrained by this dogma. Poor women frequently ventured from home to do various jobs, mostly in the clothing and sex industries, and many women were not citizens but rather slaves or resident aliens. Athens, the polis about which we know most, was home to a large community of resident aliens: metics, they were called, *met-oikoi*, "with-livers," that is, people who live with us, but are most emphatically not us. Metics might become wealthy and might travel in exalted social circles: Plato's dialogue the *Republic* opens in the home of Cephalus of Syracuse, a rich metic whose son Lysias became one of Athens's most prominent orators. But during the Classical Age neither they nor their descendants could become citizens. Not laboring under the same restrictions that confined citizen women, a number of female metics became *hetairai*—paid companions (the word actually means companion) to men who could afford them. For this reason it was not unusual for metic women to have their chastity called into question, although in reality most of them were probably dutiful housewives.[12] More cultivated than citizen women, who had been minimally educated and married off by the age of fourteen or so to much older men, *hetairai* could often not only sing and dance and play musical instruments but also discuss philosophy and public affairs. After the dual descent citizenship law of 451, however, they could not give birth to citizens. As a result, Athenian men of means frequently had both a wife from among the citizens and a succession of liaisons with *hetairai*. Pericles lived after his divorce with the cultivated metic Aspasia, who bore his youngest son.

Relations between Greek husbands and wives seem to have entailed a certain amount of anxiety. Misogyny had a long history in Greece, where women were frequently regarded as rapacious, wanton, given to drink, and lacking in both brainpower and self-control. Ironically, the same women who left no records of their thoughts and desires and thus now have no voice were perceived by their husbands as never shutting up. The loyalties of married women, it was suspected, were divided between their families of origin and the families into which they had married. In the intensely homosocial society of Greece, elite men often met in the evenings at symposia that offered wine and conversation. Though *hetairai* might attend such events, citizen women other than prostitutes were probably excluded—certainly in classical times, and perhaps earlier as well.

———

Like modern ones, Greek alliances were held together not by love but by self-interest. The members of the Peloponnesian League had no more affection for Sparta than did the members of the Delian League for Athens. Around the same time as Ephialtes' death, the little state of Megara on the narrow isthmus that linked Attica with the Peloponnesus defected from the Peloponnesian League and joined the Delian League instead. The defection of Megara sparked tensions between the two leagues that resulted in a decade and a half of on and off fighting that historians call the "First" Peloponnesian War to distinguish it from the later, more consuming war that raged between the two alliances from 431 to 404. In 445 the two sides finally agreed upon the optimistically named Thirty Years' Peace, but in the 430s a series of crises brought the two leagues into conflict with one another once again. Under pressure from its allies and concerned about the growing power of Athens, the Spartans declared war in 432. Most of our knowledge of Greek history during this period comes from the narrative of Thucydides, an Athenian aristocrat who wrote up the history of the Peloponnesian War down to 410, when his narrative breaks off. A member of the board of generals during a pivotal year in the war as well as a towering figure in ancient historiography, Thucydides spent the bulk of the war in exile after being impeached for losing a key outpost to the Spartans. Deprived of the opportunity to hear deliberations in the Athenian assembly, he used his exile to meet with participants on both sides of the war, thus gaining a variety of perspectives that he might otherwise have lacked. His account is utterly devoid of Athenian chauvinism. For the most part, the calculating and imperialistic Athenians come off badly.

A conflict between a land power and a sea power, the war dragged on for years. A horrific plague broke out in Athens shortly after the war broke out, carrying off perhaps a third of the populace, including Pericles. We know from the intensely emotional and irrational responses to Covid-19 how a pandemic can unbalance both societies and individuals. Thucydides' narrative includes an astute description of the social and psychological consequences of the pestilence:

> When they saw instantaneous change from prosperity to death and paupers becoming comfortable from sudden inheritances, people became nonchalant about undertaking things openly that they had once done in secret. So, regarding both their lives and their possessions as equally ephemeral, they resolved to spend quickly and enjoy themselves. Nobody had the stomach to persevere in conventional ideas about goodness and honor when they had no idea whether they would live long enough to profit from a spotless reputation. Whatever felt good, and whatever conduced to feeling good, was now judged to be the good, useful thing. Neither divine punishment nor human law held anyone back. As for the first, people figured it made no difference whether you worshipped the gods or not, since they saw everyone dying, good and bad alike; and as for the last, no one expected to live long enough to be brought to trial and take his punishment. Rather, people all felt that a far more terrible verdict had been delivered against them and was hanging over their heads, and the only sensible thing seemed to be to enjoy life while they could. (2. 53. 1–4)

After a decade of fighting, the two sides made a treaty known as the Peace of Nicias after the chief negotiator on the Athenian side. Fighting, however, soon resumed, and in 415 Athens undertook an expedition to Sicily that was costly in every sense of the word. The campaign ended with a cataclysmic defeat in the harbor at Syracuse and proved a disaster for the Athenians and the hapless allies they had dragged along with them. The collapse of the expedition, Thucydides wrote,

> was the most decisive military development in the war, and from what can be gathered from oral tradition, it seems, to me at least, to have been the most significant in Greek history, at the same time the most glorious to the victors and the most disastrous for the vanquished. For the Athenians were beaten in every which way imaginable, and they suffered on a massive scale. Men, ships—absolutely everything was lost, and of those who set out, few ever saw their homes again. (7. 87. 5–6)

Cheered by the Athenians' stunning defeat in the west, the land-lubbing Spartans set about building a quite respectable fleet and negotiating for Persian support, and for the remainder of the war, the Persians played one side off against the other, supporting now the Athenians, now the Spartans. The catastrophic outcome of the Sicilian expedition, moreover, opened the door for dissidents to undermine faith in Athens's democracy. In 411 these men pressured the Athenian government into voting itself out of existence and placing power in the hands of an oligarchy, putting forward the fraudulent claim to be restoring the true democracy of Solon and Cleisthenes, an imaginary "ancestral constitution" that limited the franchise to 5,000 men who could afford to serve the state without pay. After a few months, however, the democracy was restored when the oligarchs proved unable to improve the Athenians' situation through either a negotiated peace or a more successful war.

A new star now arose in Sparta in the form of the dynamic naval commander Lysander, who improved Sparta's position dramatically by gaining the friendship and financial support of the teenage Persian prince Cyrus the Younger. Because their principal source of grain lay in the Black Sea area, in 404 the Athenians (quite imprudently) stationed the imperial fleet, 180 ships strong, at Aegospotami in the Hellespont. Lysander saw his opportunity and pounced, seizing all but a handful of the ships and cutting the Athenians off from their source of bread to boot. The war was over. Lysander then installed an oligarchy of thirty pro-Spartan Athenians at Athens, but this crew—known to history as the Thirty

Tyrants—was so bloody that they alienated even the Spartan king Pausanias, and within a few months Pausanias sided with the Athenian democrats who overthrew the oligarchy.

Years of fighting had taken a heavy toll throughout the Greek world, where an incalculable number of people had died—or been enslaved. The Greek economy had suffered enormously. Families had fallen apart in the protracted absence of men on campaign. An additional casualty was the philosopher Socrates, who was brought to trial and executed in 399 on charges of impiety and corrupting the young. Suspicion of oligarchic sympathies was one factor in the verdict against him, but another was his close friendship with the Athenian traitor Alcibiades, who had defected to Sparta while serving as a general in Sicily. The comic dramatist Aristophanes used the hardships the war inflicted on women as the springboard for his still famous play *Lysistrata*, in which the title character leads the distraught women of Greece in a sex strike in hopes of ending the war that is making them so miserable. A confirmed peacenik and deeply suspicious of career politicians, Aristophanes clearly sympathized with the women's suffering and their frustration at the mess men had made in managing public affairs. Presenting a female protagonist was a striking innovation. The playwright had plainly given serious thought to Athens's problems, for Lysistrata proposes bulking up the citizenry not only by the enfranchisement of immigrants but even by the restoration of citizen rights to those who have lost them as a result of owing money to the state treasury. That she does not suggest citizen rights for women as well is a clear indication that the playwright intends her proposals to be taken seriously; *Lysistrata* is not a fantasy like his later *Congresswomen*, in which women disguise themselves as men, take over the assembly, and introduce a communistic government—under which no man can make love to a young woman until he has had sex with an old one. The premise of the *Congresswomen* is hardly feminist. Just as a play in which pets take over the government would aim at showing that the people in power are so incompetent that even cats and dogs could do better, the *Congresswomen* does not so much praise the administrative abilities of women as show up the ineptitude of Athens's politicians. It also contains the longest word not

only in Greek but, at 183 letters, in any known language, the playful *lopa-
dotemachoselachogaleokranioleipsanodrimhypotrimmatosilphioparaomeli-
tokatakechymenokichlepikossyphophattoperisteralektryonoptekephalliokig-
klopeleiolagoiosiraiobaphetraganopterygon* (1169–74), designating the
spicy casserole made of assorted seafood, birds, and hare served at the
banquet that concludes the play.

In many ways the war years marked a watershed in Greek civilization.
The great age of tragedy ended with the deaths of Sophocles and Euripides
around 405. Aeschylus had died in the 450s. Aristophanes continued to
produce thought-provoking comedies, but he was a war playwright at
heart, and his postwar plays lacked the punch of his earlier work.
Socrates was executed in 399. Drama had served the fifth-century Athenians as a vehicle for the exploration of human nature and the human
community. Thinkers of the fourth century would examine many of the
same questions in treatises and dialogues. The comedians who followed
Aristophanes wrote in a more light-hearted genre, as biting political
satire gave way to more domestic dramas and romance became a common theme. Although examples of the genre known as "Middle Comedy" have not survived, it seems to have moved in the direction we see
exemplified in the New Comedy of Menander, whose surviving fragments were augmented in 1952 by the discovery of one whole play, *The
Grouch*, and good chunks of some others.

———

The Spartans squandered the supremacy they had won in the long war
by pursuing a graceless foreign policy that bought them many enemies,
and in 371 they experienced a devastating defeat at the hands of their
former ally Thebes. Democrats throughout the Peloponnesus began
staging revolutions in their cities, and the Thebans' swelling army ravaged Laconia and freed Messenia from Spartan rule, liberating the helots there. With the loss of such a large chunk of the underclass that had
sustained its economy, the Spartans were finished. The Thebans' hege-
mony in Greece was brief, and the leaderless condition of Greece that
followed on its collapse in 362 provided an opening through which the

brilliant new king of Macedon in the north was all too happy to charge, bringing Greek freedom to an end on the field of Chaeronea in Boeotia in 338 and organizing the conquered Greek states into an association known as the League of Corinth. It was the army of this league that Philip II intended to carry with him in his projected invasion of Persia. In the event, it was led by his son Alexander, for Philip was assassinated in 336.

Philip's son by his wife Olympias, a formidable princess from Epirus in the Balkans, Alexander was 20 at the time of his father's death. His extraordinary promise was evident already in his youth, and his natural gifts were enhanced by the years he spent studying under a remarkable tutor, the philosopher Aristotle. His vision extended far beyond Macedon and Greece, but his interests and his talents lay more in conquest than in government. As it happens, he was never forced to confront the problem of administering the vast empire he acquired through conquest, for shortly after his troops finally mutinied and insisted on returning home, he died, whether from poison or from natural causes.

Alexander was a remarkable general. Defeating the Persians handily in two battles, he then moved down to Egypt, where he dragged his men some 300 miles through the desert to the oracle of Zeus-Ammon at the oasis of Siwah. There he was convinced that the chief priest greeted him as the son of Ammon, the Egyptian god Greeks associated with Zeus. While in Egypt he also established the city of Alexandria, the first of many such foundations he named for himself. When King Darius III was assassinated in 330, Alexander adopted a new style of combined Macedonian and Persian dress and declared himself his legitimate heir. He went on to cross the Hindu Kush mountains in the summer of 327, where it seemed to him that he was approaching the end of the inhabited world. In the construction of his tutor Aristotle, all that lay beyond was a great desert, and then ocean. He spent some time in Taxila with a group of ascetic Indian holy men, who fascinated him. Among them was a man who came to be known as Calanus, although it is possible that this appellation arose from a misunderstanding: Plutarch, a Greek historian and biographer writing under the Roman Empire, maintained that his real name was Sphines but that Alexander and his companions dubbed him "Calanus" because of his habit of greeting him with the

Indian greeting "kale" (*Alexander* 65. 3). Alexander was much taken with Calanus, who despite some original hesitation agreed to accompany the Macedonian king's retinue, where he probably served as an interpreter as well as engaging in philosophical discussions with Alexander. Their association came to an end in 324 when Calanus, having suffered for some time from an intestinal disorder from which he doubted he would ever recover, fell ill in Persepolis and insisted on having a funeral pyre erected for him, on which he duly perished. Some were impressed with his fortitude in enduring pain, while others found the display rather showy.[13]

With his last words Calanus bade the onlookers tell Alexander that he would see him in Babylon, an odd remark since at that time Alexander had no particular plans to go to Babylon (Plutarch, *Alexander* 69. 3). Not long afterward, however, homesick, exhausted, and apprehensive about the campaigns that might lie ahead, the king's troops refused to go farther, and he was forced to make plans for a return march. The many who perished on the trip home included Alexander himself, who died in Babylon in June of 323, just a few weeks shy of his thirty-third birthday.

Alexander's sweeping conquests ushered in a new era and new hybrid cultures, both known to historians as Hellenistic: Greek-like, but not entirely Greek. The absence of an obvious successor led almost immediately to the breakup of the sprawling domain the Macedonian king had acquired, with three individual kingdoms springing up each headed by one of his generals: the Ptolemaic kingdom in Egypt, founded by Ptolemy I; the Seleucid kingdom in Anatolia founded by Seleucus I; and the kingdom of Macedon, ruled from 276 by Antigonus Gonatas, a descendant of Alexander's general Antigonus the One-Eyed. In the 230s a fourth empire emerged on the west coast of Anatolia when Attalus I claimed power at Pergamum. Greece, while it did not belong to any of these kingdoms, was nonetheless very much under the thumb of Macedon. Sparta, though it managed to remain independent for some time, was finally defeated by Macedonian forces in 222. Until the Romans installed an oligarchy in Athens in 86, the Athenians, although no longer independent, nearly always enjoyed democratic government, and some form of democracy became the norm throughout the Hellenistic cities, at least in theory. In reality, however, much of the real power lay with aristocratic oligarchies that operated behind the scenes.

In the countryside, life went on much as before, although even in small villages Greek was taught in schools and used for many business transactions. Since it was the language of government, those who wanted to petition the bureaucracy for one reason or another were required to hire translators if they did not themselves know the language. At court, society was sometimes more Greek/Macedonian, sometimes less so. Though the royal families did not tend to intermarry with the locals and thus remained Macedonian—the famous Cleopatra, Cleopatra VII, was Macedonian—others certainly did, particularly in the countryside, and even in royal families there were exceptions: Seleucus married the Persian Apame, thus making the dynasty of the Seleucids a mixed Macedonian–Iranian one. The big cities, meanwhile, were instrumental in spreading Greek culture throughout the Hellenistic world. Tens of thousands of Greeks fanned out throughout the eastern kingdoms into these urban centers, taking with them their traditions and their educational systems. In time the population of major urban centers like Alexandria in Egypt and Antioch in Anatolia grew to several hundred thousand, far exceeding even the largest cities of old Greece. Greek schools, gymnasia, theaters, and temples proclaimed the Hellenic underpinnings of city life. Excavations at Ai Khanoum in northern Afghanistan have revealed a large city with wide streets, imposing homes, and the customary trappings of a Greek polis: a gymnasium, a theater, and the combination market/gathering place ideal for business and conversation of various kinds known as an agora. A palace built in traditional Persian style nonetheless sported Greek columns. In 1966 a Greek inscription was discovered in Ai Khanoum, dating from the first half of the third century BCE, at the sanctuary of Cineas, the city's founder. Erected by a certain Clearchus (probably Clearchus of Soli in Cyprus, an associate of Aristotle), it includes the last five of the 147 maxims associated with Apollo's oracle at Delphi:

These sage instructions of the men of old,
The words of men whose wisdom was well known,

Brought from Apollo's holiest of shrines
Clearchus, who had copied them with care,
Wishing that they should shine from far away
Set up here in the shrine of Cineas:
As a child, be well-mannered,
As a youth, self-disciplined,
In middle age, be just,
As an old man, give sound advice,
At the end, be without regret.[14]

The elites of the eastern cities learned the Greek language and studied Greek literature. Precisely because politics no longer offered the same satisfaction it once had, affluent citizens increasingly sought recognition and affirmation in other ways. The cities of the Hellenistic world benefited enormously from the ensuing philanthropy, as not only men but women undertook to fund schools, gymnasia, libraries, temples, and other amenities. The city of Pergamum not far from the Aegean in Anatolia was one of the most beautiful of all the Hellenistic cities, adorned by an extraordinary library and a variety of artwork collected from all over the Greek world (though superb works of art were also produced in Pergamum itself). Tourists and worshippers alike were open-mouthed at the sight of the imposing altar of Zeus erected there in the second century BCE, a structure that was so large as to dwarf most buildings.

The very meaning of "Greek" came to refer not only to those who hailed from old Greece and their descendants but also to a wide variety of people who had adopted Greek customs, had received a Greek education, and in many cases had even taken Greek names. This notion was not unprecedented before Alexander: history rarely affords clean breaks. The orator Isocrates had boasted that the attainments of the Athenians had created a situation in which "the name Hellenes indicates no longer a race but an intellect, and people are called Hellenes who share our culture rather than those related to us by blood" (*Panegyricus* 50).

The most illustrious and enduring of the many cities Alexander had founded, Alexandria in the Nile delta became both a multiethnic city and a cultural center. Known as the Museum because of its dedication

FIGURE 3.3. The Pergamum altar. This monumental altar some 117 feet wide and 110 feet deep was constructed in Pergamum in the first half of the second century BCE in the reign of Eumenes II. The reliefs on the base show the battle between the Giants and the Olympian gods. The altar was reconstructed in Berlin and now stands as the centerpiece of the Pergamonmuseum there. bpk Bildagentur / Art Resource, NY.

to the nine muses, the Ptolemaic think tank housed distinguished intellectuals who obtained government stipends to pursue their research. Scholars received further support in the form of a magnificent library originally intended to contain a copy of every book ever written in Greek. The library grew to an unprecedented size, boasting several hundred thousand rolls of papyrus. Scholars flocked to Alexandria from all over the Mediterranean. Euclid, the founder of geometry, worked there, as did the physician Herophilus, the first scientist to conduct systematic dissections of human cadavers and the discoverer of the fallopian tubes. Chief librarians at Alexandria included Apollonius Rhodius, the author of a bravura epic the *Argonautica* on the quest for the golden fleece, and the scientist Eratosthenes, whose calculation of the circumference of the earth was more accurate than those with which Columbus was working in the fifteenth century CE. The formidable scholar and poet Callimachus from Cyrene in Libya, a librarian at Alexandria although perhaps never chief librarian, made a catalogue of the library's holdings and was credited with some eight hundred other works in both poetry and prose: sacred hymns, epigrams, and essays on a broad range of topics. Titles of his treatises included *On Winds, On the World's Rivers,* and *Customs of Foreign Peoples,* all of which are lost today, though a good chunk of his poetry survives. His hymns to the gods combined learned references to the whole corpus of Greek literature and mythology with delightful wit. The lovely hymn to Artemis includes a charming portrait of the goddess as a toddler, interacting with the grown-up gods; sitting on Zeus's knee, she asks to have as many epithets as her brother Apollo and begs for an archery set. Like the so-called Homeric Hymn to Demeter (not actually by Homer), that of Callimachus leads off with the goddess's desperate search for her missing daughter, but instead of proceeding like the original to a discussion of the Eleusinian mysteries, it turns instead to an account of the goddess's punishment of the Thessalian Erysichthon, son of Triopas, when he tried to cut down the trees in her sacred grove. In hilarious mock epic style the poet tells how Demeter infected him with an insatiable desire for food and drink. Even with twenty slaves preparing his dinner and a dozen pouring his wine, he had no success in assuaging his hunger. His embarrassed mother and father covered for him frantically, piling excuse on excuse:

> His parents were mortified. Him at a feast,
> Or disgracing a banquet? The thought was unbearable.
> Every excuse they could think of, they used.
> Here were the Ormenidae, come to invite him
> To games being held for Athena. She put them off.
> "Truly, he isn't at home. Only yesterday
> Off he went over to Crannon to pick up
> Some oxen—a hundred!—he figured were owed to him."
> Then came Polyxo, Actorion's mother,

Eager to have both the son and the father
Attending a wedding her daughter was having.
"Triopas will come, but . . . well . . . our Erysichthon, he's
Taken to bed, the poor lad—for nine days, no less.
Up on Mount Pindus a boar got the best of him.
Now he lies wounded. He just can't go anywhere!" (72–82)

She continues piling pretext on pretext to prevent her son from appearing in public. He was struck by a discus! He . . . uh . . . fell out of his chariot!

Each of the kingdoms enjoyed a distinct culture. Greek influence on architecture was less conspicuous in Egypt, for example, which enjoyed particularly strong architectural traditions of its own and whose architecture and sculpture had exercised strong influence on that of Greece. The Ptolemies made a point of adopting a strong overlay of Egyptian traditions, marrying their sisters, having themselves portrayed on public monuments in Egyptian dress, and taking part in Egyptian religious life. They never intermarried with locals, however, and thus the royal line remained purely Macedonian. It was said that only the last of the Ptolemaic line, the gifted Cleopatra VII, took the trouble to learn the Egyptian language, although surely some of her predecessors knew the rudiments. Macedonia proper never reached the cultural level of the other kingdoms, but it did embrace old Greece, which flourished in the area of philosophy. The philosophies of the Hellenistic Age like Stoicism, Epicureanism, Cynicism, and Skepticism (discussed later in chapter 8) addressed the needs of people in large multi-ethnic states who no longer looked to the polis to fulfill their spiritual needs, and they prospered throughout the Hellenistic world. Both the prolific philosophers of the Classical Age, Plato and Aristotle, had assumed an audience composed largely of males who wished to become the virtuous citizens of a virtuous polis, and Aristotle believed that no state should be so large that a herald could not address the citizens or that the people meeting in deliberation could not get to know one another's characters. The Hellenistic philosophers by contrast sought to help people of both sexes and from all social classes find meaning in a world in which an active civic life in a sovereign polis was no longer an option.

The decrease in real power experienced by men under the Hellenistic monarchies conduced to a degree of relaxation in tensions between the sexes; concomitantly, at least some women began to enjoy more freedom. Whereas the classical polis had been marked by the exclusion of women from the public sphere and by severe restrictions on women's economic rights and personal freedoms, in the Hellenistic Age, as men's preoccupation with their roles as political actors was forced to take a back seat to their personal lives, women came to appear as less different from them. In many places women were accorded more legal rights, and family life became an increased source of interest and satisfaction. With the reappearance of monarchic government, moreover, came the rise of an aristocracy of both sexes, and beginning with Alexander's determined mother Olympias (who deployed her power and prestige to order brutal killings of women and children who seemed to threaten her son's position), royal women played increasingly important roles in government and sometimes warfare, a phenomenon that culminated in the reign of the formidable Cleopatra VII in Egypt. When Olympias invaded Macedonia to support the accession of Alexander's young son, the wife of Alexander's brother Arrhidaeus, Adea Eurydice, marched out with her own troops. Never before had two female-led armies opposed one another. Women were abundant in Macedonian royal families, for certainly as far back as Philip Macedonian kings were polygamous. The fact that women in the east, and particularly in Egypt, had always enjoyed higher status than women in mainland Greece also played a role in the dignity now accorded to them. More and more parents sent daughters to school (although never as often as sons), and some women became writers, artists, and physicians. Wealthy women in time came to be chosen as honorary magistrates, and during their terms of office they often deployed their wealth in donating buildings or sponsoring civic events. Just as men had frequently gained prestige in this way, these women were now rewarded with the admiration and gratitude of the community.

It is likely that Hellenistic queens were wealthier than any females of classical times, when many states outlawed the owning of land by women, and unlike in the Classical Age, when women generally needed the consent of a male *kyrios* (guardian) to conduct any financial transaction of significance, they were frequently able to administer their own resources. They were often lavish philanthropists, using their money in support of religion and in shoring up their own relations with the gods by way of dedications to individual deities and donations to sanctuaries. The highly educated intellectual Arsinoë II was the daughter of Alexander's friend Ptolemy I and the wife first of the Seleucid king Lysimachus, then of her half-brother Ptolemy Keraunos, and finally of Ptolemy II. Wielding enormous power, Arsinoë came to be a role model for subsequent Hellenistic queens, sharing the titles of Ptolemy II and enjoying considerable input into his policies. She was much interested in religion and seems to have been an initiate in the temple on the island of Samothrace during her tenure as a Seleucid queen; she paid for a rotunda to be erected there. A priestess at Mendes in the Nile delta, she would have been most gratified to learn that she was deified there upon her death. All temples in Egypt were required to include a cult statue of her. At her husband's insistence, temples were constructed for her worship throughout Egypt, and a regular portion of annual taxes was dedicating to funding her cult. Berenice II, wife of Ptolemy III, also ruled jointly with her husband, and the two were worshipped as *Theoi Euergetai*, Benefactor Gods. Particularly associated with protection against shipwrecks, Berenice herself was assimilated to both Isis and Aphrodite. She also had a celebrated afterlife in poetry. When Ptolemy left on campaign shortly after their wedding in 246, Berenice vowed a lock of her hair to the gods in exchange for his safe return, and after the lock mysteriously disappeared and the astronomer Conon announced the discovery of a new constellation that strongly resembled it, Callimachus composed a famous poem in which the lock lamented its separation from Berenice's head; it became instantly famous and was widely imitated both in antiquity and afterward.

The world had changed, and it would soon change still further. Beginning around 200, Rome fought a series of wars in Macedonia and Greece that would culminate in the destruction of the flourishing port of Corinth in 146 and the absorption of the region into the growing Roman Empire. More of Alexander's former territory farther to the east fell into Roman laps when Attalus of Pergamum, dying childless, bequeathed his kingdom to Rome. When the fleet of Julius Caesar's adopted son Gaius Octavianus defeated the forces of Mark Antony and Cleopatra VII at Actium in 31 BCE, driving the pair to suicide the following year, Roman power, by absorbing the kingdom of the Ptolemies, finally brought the Hellenistic Age to an end. The Mediterranean Sea now belonged to a people who would refer to it by a new Latin name: *mare nostrum*—our sea.

Suggested Readings

Adkins, Arthur W. H. 1960. *Merit and Responsibility: A Study in Greek Values*. Oxford: Clarendon.

Ager, Sheila L., and Reimer A. Faber, eds. 2013. *Belonging and Isolation in the Hellenistic World. Phoenix Supplementary Volumes* 51. Toronto: University of Toronto Press.

Boardman, John. 1980. *The Greeks Overseas: Their Early Colonies and Trade*. 1964; new and enlarged edition. London: Thames and Hudson.

Boardman, John, Jasper Griffin, and Oswyn Murray, eds. 1986. *The Oxford Illustrated History of Greece and the Hellenistic World*. Oxford: Oxford University Press.

Budelmann, Felix, ed. 2009. *The Cambridge Companion to Greek Lyric (Cambridge Companions to Literature)*, illustrated edition. Cambridge, UK: Cambridge University Press.

Budin, Stephanie. 2009. *The Ancient Greeks: An Introduction*. New York: Oxford University Press.

Bugh, Glen R., ed. 2006. *Cambridge Companion to the Hellenistic World*. Cambridge, UK: Cambridge University Press.

Carney, Elizabeth Donnelly. 2013. *Arsinoë of Egypt and Macedon: A Royal Life*. New York and Oxford: Oxford University Press.

Cartledge, Paul. 1993. *The Greeks: A Portrait of Self and Others*. Oxford and New York: Oxford University Press.

———, ed. 1998. *The Cambridge Illustrated History of Greece*. Cambridge, UK, and New York: Cambridge University Press.

———. 2002. *Sparta and Lakonia: A Regional History 1300–362 BC*, 2nd edition. Oxford and New York: Routledge.

Clayman, Dee. 2014. *Berenice II and the Golden Age of Ptolemaic Egypt*. New York and Oxford: Oxford University Press.

Cline, Eric H. 2021. *1177: The Year Civilization Collapsed: Revised and Updated. Turning Points in Ancient History* 6. Princeton, NJ: Princeton University Press.

Demand, Nancy. 1996. *A History of Ancient Greece*. New York: McGraw-Hill.

Dover, Kenneth J. 1974. *Greek Popular Morality in the Time of Plato and Aristotle*. Oxford: Blackwell.

Eidinow, Esther. 2011. *Luck, Fate and Fortune: Antiquity and Its Legacy*. Oxford and New York: Oxford University Press.

Errington, R. Malcolm. 2008. *A History of the Hellenistic World: 323–30 BC. Blackwell History of the Ancient World Series*. Malden, MA: Blackwell.

Fine, John V. A. 1983. *The Ancient Greeks: A Critical History*. Cambridge, MA, and London: Belknap Press.

Fisher, N.R.E. 1992. *Hybris: A Study in the Values of Honour and Shame in Ancient Greece*. Warminster, UK: Aris & Phillips.

Green, Peter. 1996. *The Greco-Persian Wars*. Berkeley and Los Angeles: University of California Press.

———. 2013. *Alexander of Macedon, 356–323 B.C.: A Historical Biography*, with a foreword by Eugene N. Borza. Berkeley and Los Angeles: University of California Press.

Hall, Edith. 2014. *Introducing the Ancient Greeks: From Bronze Age Seafarers to Navigators of the Western Mind*. New York: W. W. Norton.

Hammond, N.G.L. 1986. *A History of Greece to 322 B.C.* 3rd edition. Oxford: Oxford University Press.

Holland, Tom. 2005. *Persian Fire: The First World Empire and the Battle for the West*. New York: Doubleday.

Jaeger, Werner. 1939–44. *Paideia: The Ideals of Greek Culture*, 3 volumes, trans. Gilbert Highet. New York: Oxford University Press.

Lateiner, Donald. 1989. *The Historical Method of Herodotus*. Toronto: University of Toronto Press.

Manning, Joseph G. 2009. *The Last Pharaohs: Egypt under the Ptolemies, 305–30 BC*. Princeton, NJ: Princeton University Press.

Martin, Thomas R. 2013. *Ancient Greece: From Prehistoric to Hellenistic Times*. 2nd edition. New Haven, CT: Yale University Press.

McInerney, Jeremy. 2018. *Ancient Greece: A New History*. London: Thames and Hudson.

Munson, Rosaria. 2001. *Telling Wonders: Ethnographic and Political Discourse in the Works of Herodotus*. Ann Arbor: University of Michigan Press.

Ober, Josiah. 2015. *The Rise and Fall of Classical Greece. The Princeton History of the Ancient World*. Princeton, NJ: Princeton University Press.

Pomeroy, Sarah. 1984. *Women in Hellenistic Egypt*. New York: Schocken.

Pomeroy, Sarah, Stanley Burstein, Jennifer Roberts, David Tandy, and Georgia Tsouvala. 2017. *Ancient Greece: A Political, Social, and Cultural History*. 4th edition. New York: Oxford University Press.

Raaflaub, Kurt A., and Hans van Wees, eds. 2009. *A Companion to Archaic Greece. Blackwell Companions to the Ancient World*. Malden, MA: Wiley-Blackwell.

Roberts, Jennifer T. 2011. *Herodotus: A Very Short Introduction*. Oxford: Oxford University Press, 2011.

———. 2017. *The Plague of War: Athens, Sparta, and the Struggle for Ancient Greece*. New York: Oxford University Press.

Scheidel, Walter. 2017. *The Great Leveler: Violence and the History of Inequality from the Stone Age to the Twenty-First Century. The Princeton Economic History of the Western World*. Princeton, NJ: Princeton University Press.

Strauss, Barry. 2005. *The Battle of Salamis: The Naval Encounter That Saved Greece—and Western Civilization*. New York: Simon & Schuster.

Tritle, Lawrence, ed. 1997. *The Greek World in the Fourth Century: From the Fall of the Athenian Empire to the Successors of Alexander*. London and New York: Routledge.

Walcot, Peter. 1978. *Envy and the Greeks*. Warminster, UK: Aris & Phillips, Ltd.

Waterfield, Robin. 2020. *Creators, Conquerors, and Citizens: A History of Ancient Greece*. New York and Oxford: Oxford University Press.

CHAPTER 4

The Polis—City and State

A little state, well-governed, on a sheer cliff
Is stronger than Nineveh gone mad.

—PHOCYLIDES OF MILETUS, CA. 500 BCE

The most distinctive political form to develop in Greece was the polis, and without an exploration of its dynamics we will not understand what it meant to be a Greek. There were well over a thousand poleis in the Greek world. Although they did not wish to share in a single polity, the multifarious city-states of Greece shared much: their language, their gods, their patriarchal social and political structure, and many of their customs. One of the more famous passages in Greek literature comes from Aristotle's *Politics*, composed around the middle of the fourth century. There the philosopher wrote that

> The polis is a natural growth, and a human being is by nature an animal designed to live in a polis. Someone who is by nature and not merely by fortune without a polis is either a paltry creature or something greater than human. . . . Why this should be the case for humans more than for, say, bees, or other gregarious creatures, is clear; for . . . it is the special property of humans as opposed to the other animals that they alone are capable of perceiving good and bad and right and wrong and the other moral qualities, and it is sharing in these things that makes a household and a polis. (1253a)

The polis, Greek writers believed, made a man what he was. *Polis andra didaskei*, Simonides wrote: It is the city that educates a man. Women were another story. Essential to the polis, they both were and were not part of it. Even Aristotle was not certain. At times he describes the polis as a collection of voters, at times as a collection of households; the latter necessarily included women but the former did not. Some Greeks lived not in poleis but more rustically in *ethnē* (tribes), but if any of the rustic *ethnē* produced literature that would illuminate their worldview, it has not come to light. Neither by and large did women, though there were a few exceptions, or enslaved people; nearly all the literature that has come down to us is the work of a free, urban male elite.

———

The economies of even the most commercially successful poleis relied to a considerable extent on agriculture. A polis would embrace an urban area and its surrounding countryside, the *chora*, and most city-dwellers who were not dirt-poor owned property in the *chora*. Many walked out to their farms and back daily. Every man aspired to own his own land; those who didn't and were forced to work for another felt not only deprived but embarrassed. Women were precluded from owning land in most places, though not in some Dorian states like Sparta and the city of Gortyn in Crete. A householder who owned no slaves was poor and doubtless was saving up for one. Though the quality of life experienced by enslaved people varied enormously depending on the duties assigned and the temperaments of owners, slavery was a wretched and degrading condition. For Greeks, the freedom/slavery dichotomy was a powerful one. As would happen in the antebellum South of the United States, the presence of slaves in, but not entirely of, the polis played a role in shoring up a degree of unity in the citizen body, fostering as it did an alliance between free people both rich and poor who were united in distinction to the unfree, and giving the poor someone to look down on.

Some states traded widely, others little. Most were near the shore, but some were inland. Some belonged to leagues, while others were unaffiliated. Some were large, some small, and some downright tiny. Though warfare and famine might at times render the citizen body minute to the point of danger, Greek states were jealous of their citizenship and loath to extend it. Naturalization was rare. At least one citizen parent was required to claim citizenship, and sometimes two. Poleis were linked to other poleis by a variety of networks, some more benign than others. Already in the seventh century twelve cities in Ionia formed a league that held regular festivals and met to explore strategies in times of crisis. During the Classical Age some states joined organizations like the Delian or Peloponnesian League voluntarily, but others had been forced to join or prevented from leaving, and in all cases they were subject to interference by the hegemon. Athens preferred democracies in member states, while Sparta pushed for oligarchies. Though a key member of the Peloponnesian League, Thebes also belonged to a federation of eleven cities in Boeotia of which it continually sought domination. During the early decades of the fourth century, an area of some 4,000 square miles in the eastern part of the island was subject to Syracuse, and the poleis on the west coast of Anatolia and the islands nearby frequently found themselves under Persian rule. In the Hellenistic Age a number of cities in the Peloponnesus formed the Achaean League, with a league assembly, council, and a *strategos*; the league often came into conflict with the Aetolian League in central Greece that comprised both poleis and *ethnē*.

Of the hundreds of little city-states that made up the Greek world, many were colonies founded by older states. Those intending to establish colonies were expected to run their intentions by Delphi. This made good practical sense since the body of information the oracle had amassed from its various far-flung consultants put it in an excellent position to give advice. In addition, the priestess (known as the Pythia) and her associates enjoyed the benefit of a hot line to Apollo. Gods knew a lot. They had been around for a long time and, from their perch on Olympus, had seen much. Herodotus cites the beginning of a Delphic oracle:

> I know the number of grains of sand and the measure of the sea,
> I understand the deaf-mute and hear those who lack speech. (1. 47. 2)

For colonists in Italy, perhaps from the city of Graia north of Athens or from the tribe of Graikoi in Epirus in northwestern Greece, the Romans

used the word *Graeci*, and the name stuck: the people who called themselves Hellenes are now more commonly known as Greeks.

Though politically autonomous, colonies generally enjoyed sentimental and religious ties to their founding cities, and sometimes more; Potidaea
in Chalcidice actually took its magistrates from its mother city of Corinth.
The small size of the polis worked against self-sufficiency, as no one state
was satisfactorily diverse in natural resources or local talent. Trade accordingly tied the various poleis together. Religious festivals brought together
participants from all over. Citizens—and indeed slaves—of all poleis were
free to participate in the annual rites of the mystery religion that celebrated
the goddess Demeter and her daughter Persephone at Eleusis northwest
of Athens, and many did. Private individuals and public delegations
fanned out to consult oracles throughout Greece and Anatolia, and athletes were sent off to participate in the Panhellenic games, where little
villages of pop-up stores would materialize for the occasion. Every year
tens of thousands of people traveled to see the Olympics and thousands
to view the lesser games. Individuals, moreover, were linked with people
in other states by ties of family or friendship. Hereditary relationships
of *xenia* tied families of two poleis together, and the frequency of inter-
marriage in the upper classes, where a strategic union might yield substantial political capital, prompted restrictions like the Athenian law of
451 that limited citizenship to those with two Athenian parents.

There were many resident aliens (metics) at Athens, but resident
aliens were just that: residents, but aliens nonetheless. Metics labored
under substantial legal disabilities. They could not own land; unlike
citizens, they could be enslaved for debt; and a citizen who murdered a
metic did not run the risk of capital punishment as s/he would do if
convicted of murdering a citizen. The size of the metic community in
Athens was unusual, but other states housed immigrant populations as
well. Doctors, teachers, philosophers, exiles, craftspeople, mercenaries
all joined a substantial group of merchants as they circulated around the
Greek world and, often, settled down away from home. One reason Greek
culture remained cohesive despite its lack of political unity was that
Greeks tended to be adventurous, and many of them moved around,
taking their skills with them.

Greeks had many ideas not only about the polis in general but about their own state in particular. The near-total absence of surviving texts going back significantly before the Classical Age facilitated the invention of patriotic myths about the earliest times and fostered a habit of mind that disposed people to invent affirming tales going back only a few generations. Though Greece produced any number of fine historians (many of whose works survive only in fragments), a historical mindset was the exception rather than the rule. Every polis had its own founding lore, its own Plymouth Rock and Simón Bolívar. The purported founders of colonies were not necessarily the people who had really set out in ships from their mother states, nor is it clear that they were guided by talking animals or heavenly portents. Early lawgivers like Solon in Athens, Lycurgus in Sparta, and Zaleucus in Locri played large roles in the oral traditions of their states. No doubt some legendary founders had really lived, but probably not all. They certainly did not all do everything ascribed to them; it is not likely that the Spartan system sprang fully formed one day from the brain of Lycurgus. The Greeks were consummate inventors of tradition. For a strikingly innovative race, they were profoundly anxious about change, and it was a point of pride in a polis that its laws should have existed without change since time immemorial.

Belief that they had always lived in their territory, indeed that the land itself had given birth to them, was not unusual. This notion was grounded in a preference for racial uniformity in the polis. Beginning in 451, as we have seen, Athenian citizenship required two citizen parents, although some states in times of crisis granted citizen status to children with only one such parent. In Thasos in northern Greece, children with noncitizen fathers could be citizens, and in Siphnos in the Aegean, children with noncitizen mothers. It was not until the Hellenistic Age that Greek states began granting citizenship to immigrants, generally in exchange for money, though in radically different amounts. Dyme in the Peloponnesus, apparently hard up for funds, charged a talent, a huge sum that put it off limits to nearly everyone. At the other end of the spectrum, Phaselis in Anatolia, hard up for people, charged only a sixtieth of that—a mina. The Spartans were extreme in their xenophobia; their unwillingness to expand their citizen body to the *perioikoi* during the fourth century was beyond remarkable in light of the parlous oliganthropy that affected their city.

Attachment to the land in these predominantly agrarian societies took many forms, from the conviction that farming (or having others farm your land) was the only really respectable way of making a living to the belief that birth in alien territory precluded membership in the citizen body. Many Greeks took the notion of Mother Earth literally. Even after the establishment of Olympian religion, the idea of the earth as a primal life force persisted. Prometheus, the story went, had molded the first humans out of mud. The archaic poet Asius of Samos maintained that the earth had given birth to Pelasgos, the legendary ancestor of the entire Greek people "so that the race of mortals might exist."[1] The orator Dio Chrysostom from Prusa in Anatolia ascribed the belief in gods to the fact that Zeus was plainly provident in supplying people with food. "The first humans," he claimed, "those who were born from the earth—autochthonous—had the earliest sort of food, which came from the soft, moist loam that then prevailed on the earth, licking it up from the earth as if she were their mother just as plants now draw up moisture" (12. 29–30). Individual poleis had their own more local versions. The Thebans claimed descent from men who sprang from the ground when their founder Cadmus of Tyre, having slain the local dragon, sowed the ground with the creature's teeth. This was a particularly useful myth in view of Cadmus's distinctly non-Greek origin. Birth from a river provided an alternative form of autochthony. The Dryopes of southern Thessaly traced their ancestry to one Dryops, son of the river Spercheios, while the Argives claimed to be descended from Phoroneus, whose father was the river Inachos. Snake ancestry also provided "grounding," so to speak, in the land, since the tendency of snakes to emerge from the earth unexpectedly led many Greeks to believe that they in fact were born from the soil.

Autochthony was overdetermined in the charter myths of the Athenians. Not surprisingly, the autochthony myth crops up in Athenian literature just as the Athenians were establishing their controversial empire.[2] In Athenian minds autochthony was good, its opposite bad, and who better to hold sway over the Greeks than these very good people?

Serpentine themes tied together the nexus of myths regarding the ancestral kings Cecrops and Erichthonios. Said to have been born from the earth, Cecrops nonetheless had a name that was not Greek. He was also called *diphuēs*, of two natures and perceived as being human above the waist but a snake or fish below; the Sicilian historian Diodorus conjectured that this epithet alluded to the fact that he was both Greek and not Greek (1. 28. 7). Cecrops had three daughters, and these link up with another myth of autochthony, that of Erichthonios, whose name of course contains the *chthon* root—earth.

The god Hephaestus, so the story went, lusted after Athena, but the determined virgin goddess succeeded in keeping him at bay, with the result that he ejaculated on her thigh. When she wiped the semen off with a tuft of wool (*erion*) that she then cast to the ground, it impregnated Ge, with the result that the baby who sprang from this unusual conception, Erichthonios, was born literally from the earth thus ensouled by the forger god. Placing him in a small box, Athena entrusted the newborn to Cecrops's three daughters, cautioning them never to look inside. Of course, such prohibitions ("no matter what happens, make sure you don't . . .") are invariably disobeyed in myth and folklore, and when some of the girls predictably opened the box, something snaky happened, followed by something fatal, though there is some inconsistency in the various myths as to what. In some versions the girls were horrified to find a snake coiled around the infant; in others the infant they saw was himself part snake. Some said they then went mad and threw themselves from the Acropolis, others that they were killed by the snake. It was alleged that Erichthonios, when he grew up to rule Athens, invented the four-horse chariot because he was lame and had trouble getting around. Certainly being half snake could impede an individual's mobility.

Like other Greek poleis, Athens advertised itself not as a melting pot but rather as a fictive kinship group. When the Athenian assembly was contemplating the fateful expedition to Sicily, the aristocrat Alcibiades, eager for the glory that would attend on a military command, argued that the mixed and unstable nature of their population would hinder the Sicilians' resistance. Since people there don't feel like the cities in which they live are their own homeland, he says, "they don't provide themselves with weapons or even develop their land if they live in the country. They figure that even if they should fail at getting what they want from the public treasury by clever rhetoric or political intrigue, they can always settle down someplace else. It isn't likely," he claims, "that a mob like this will ever be able to agree on a plan or carry it out" (Thucydides 6. 17. 2–4). Such was the view of a mixed populace that a speaker thought would play well in the assembly. In reality, many poleis housed populations far more mixed than they liked to admit. In states located on the fringes of the Greek world, many citizens could not even claim Greek descent. On the coast of Anatolia, both Miletus, the birthplace of Greek philosophy and science, and Herodotus's hometown of Halicarnassus, were populated by a mix of Greeks and native Carians, a people identified in Homer as Trojan allies and "men of barbarian speech" (*Iliad* 2. 867–68).

———

The Spartans, who certainly believed in an impermeable boundary that separated Spartiates from all others, demonstrated their racialism not only in the institution of helotry but also in their suicidal refusal to expand their citizenship during the fourth century, even as far as the *perioikoi*. Although the Athenians sustained substantial manpower losses during the Peloponnesian War, losing perhaps some 20,000 in battle and several times that in the plague, their numbers at the war's outset were robust enough to take a substantial hit. The situation was different in Sparta. There the code of honor that pressured Spartiate soldiers to fight to the death rather than surrender reduced numbers substantially throughout the Peloponnesian War; when Spartan soldiers marooned on an island off the Peloponnesus in 425 stunned the Greek world by surrendering, a large number died in Athenian custody. King Agesilaus's bellicose policies throughout the fourth century shrank the population still further. The terms of Spartan inheritance laws knocked many men off the citizen rolls, so that even at times when the absolute number of adult males was not declining, the fighting body was: whereas in most other parts of Greece daughters received a portion of the family wealth by way of their dowries, in Sparta they actually inherited land, albeit only half as much as sons. Aristotle was deeply distressed at how much Spartan land had fallen into female hands by his day—fully two-fifths, he claims (*Politics* 1270a). Men affected by these inheritance laws often lost their civic rights and fell into the ranks of the *hypomeiones*—the "inferiors." In democracies, a man who fell on hard times simply became poor, but in Sparta he ceased to be a citizen. Fully 8,000 at the time of the Battle of Plataea in 479, by the Battle of Leuctra in 371 the Spartan male citizenry numbered no more than a tenth of that.

Solving this problem was the easiest thing in the world. The monthly contribution to the common mess that was required of all Spartiates could have been reduced. The *perioikoi* could easily have been enfranchised; they already fought and indeed were billeted alongside the Spartans on campaign. Tunnel vision, however, prevented the Spartan elite from contemplating any such radical steps. What classical Sparta desperately needed but did not get was the kind of radical redistricting enacted during the Hellenistic Age by its imaginative king Cleomenes III, who pooled the land, redistributed it in equal lots to citizens, and, at last, incorporated a good number of *perioikoi* into the citizen body. But so powerful was the Greek commitment to restricting citizenship to the descent group that there would be no thinking outside the box as Sparta tottered to its destruction.

The organizing principle of Spartan society, the production of stalwart hoplites affected Spartan life in a variety of ways. Elsewhere in Greece the father would determine the future of a newborn, male or female, by either picking it up and deciding to raise it or declaring that it should be abandoned out of doors to be ravaged by the elements or picked up by a passing slave-dealer. In Sparta, government officials decided which baby boys would live and which would be left to die in a chasm at the foot of Mount Taygetus. Baby girls, who were more likely than boys to be exposed in other states, were spared this rigorous examination. Altogether, it is likely that Spartan females were more fortunate than those elsewhere in Greece, who received less food than their brothers and were kept indoors. What we know of their marriages when they were grown is both limited and mixed. On the one hand, Spartan wives were closer in age to their husbands than Athenian brides, resulting in a bit more common ground between husband and wife; unlike Athenian girls who were married off at puberty to grown men, most Spartan women were not married before the age of eighteen or twenty—a healthy practice, since it reduced the chances of death in childbirth. One might imagine that the Athenians would have learned from this, but their concern about the legitimacy of the heirs who would inherit the oikos trumped their concern for adolescents' well-being, and they persisted in marrying daughters off in late childhood; Greek men were convinced that women were inclined to be immensely eager for sex and did not want them to have any experience of it except with their lawful husbands. Spartan men, however, around thirty at the time of their marriage, remained intensely invested in military life even after they were permitted to leave barracks and resume domestic life. They continued, for example, to eat at the common mess with their dining companions rather than at home. This left their wives considerable freedom. Were they also lonely, especially in the absence of their sons as well, or did they delight in the liberty they enjoyed—or both?

In Sparta state and society were completely fused. From an early age Spartan males spent their lives in barracks, and the labor that in other states was performed by household slaves was relegated to helot families who lived mostly on their own. Sparta thus had the only professionally trained army in Greece; all the other poleis relied on citizen militias. It also had the only system of public education, although the skills taught focused on the shaping of future soldiers and seem to have involved comparatively little in the way of the music and poetry that formed the core of the education for which affluent parents in other states paid. Growing Spartan girls were educated by the state in music, dance, and gymnastics. Far from Sparta's preoccupation with warfare leading to a devaluation of women on the grounds that they did not fight, the Spartiates' concern with their military prompted eugenic considerations that inevitably involved both sexes. It is possible that roles for women in Sparta were designed and applauded by women as well as men; Spartan women have certainly been portrayed as both assertive and respected. Groups of young women in Sparta performed at festivals, singing and dancing, and they were encouraged to include in their songs (which they often composed themselves) teasing reproaches of the young men in the audience whose conduct was less than ideal, while praising the most outstanding.

Plainly captivated by Sparta, Plutarch preserved a number of "sayings of Spartan women" he had come across, most of them insufferably smug and sanctimonious. One hopes that not all Spartan women fit the off-putting profile of these heartless creatures, who would appear to have taken a ghoulish delight in the deaths of their sons in battle—and proposed suicide to those who had the misfortune to survive. When a passerby made the mistake of lamenting the misfortune of a woman she had found burying her son, Plutarch reported, the mother was quick to correct her, insisting that her fortune could not have been better, for "I bore him so that he might die for Sparta, and this is precisely what happened" (*Sayings of Spartan Women* 6. 8). Another woman, he wrote, when she asked her son about the outcome of Sparta's most recent battle and learned that all the Spartan soldiers had died, killed him by throwing a tile at him, saying "So you're the one they sent to bring us the bad news?" (6. 5). To be sure, these snappy ripostes fall into a genre that invites both caricature and invention, and we have no way of determining the veracity of these "laconic" zingers.

As future bearers of warriors, citizen women and girls in the militaristic society of Sparta were well-nourished from birth and strengthened by frequent exercise outdoors, running, wrestling, and throwing the discus. Strong mothers, it was believed, would produce strong sons. As far as we know, only in Sparta did women strip for athletics. Other Greeks found this shocking. Throughout the Archaic and Classical Ages, female nudity was avoided throughout most of Greece. Naked women depicted on vases were probably *hetairai* and prostitutes. Statues depicted males unclad and females draped unless they were goddesses, although not even goddesses were permitted to appear naked before the fourth century; only in the Hellenistic Age did the nude female come into its own in art. Physical fitness conduced to somewhat less onerous childbirth, and by exercising outdoors Spartan women also escaped the deadening confinement to the house prescribed for women by Athenian men. Sparta produced at least two women poets, Megalostrata and Cleitagora, and several Spartan women became disciples of the philosopher Pythagoras. All this was very different from what we hear about Athens, where bourgeois ideology dictated narrow roles for females: religion and the household. Not a single word written by an Athenian woman has survived to give us a sense of her thoughts.

Because the Spartans did not themselves write literature (even their laws were unwritten) and were so inhospitable to visitors that they practiced a periodic expulsion of foreigners known as *xenelasia*, knowledge of what went on in their government was limited. This ignorance lent credence to an impression of tremendous stability, something greatly cherished in the Greek world, where civil strife was alarmingly common. In a culture that persisted in defining a man's worth by his performance on the battlefield, moreover, the Spartans' highly disciplined military was an object of great admiration. Herodotus included in his *Histories* a pointed conversation between Xerxes and the exiled Spartan king Demaratus. Tell me, Herodotus portrays Xerxes as saying, are those Greeks really going to stand up to me? (Herodotus, to be sure, was not present at this conversation, but Greek historians followed Homer in lending immediacy to their narratives by reporting verbatim speeches they had never heard.) The question Herodotus puts in Xerxes' mouth is calculated to reveal to the reader the king's inadequate grasp of the situation—his failure to understand what makes Greeks Greeks. Confining himself to responding for his countrymen alone, Demaratus assures Xerxes that the Spartans will never permit Greece to be enslaved. They will fight no matter how few men they can raise. Come now, Xerxes replies; let's be reasonable. Say there are, hypothetically, five thousand Greeks. Why, we will outnumber them by over a thousand to one! If they were under the rule of a single man the way it is in Persia, then they might, I suppose, in fear of him become better than they naturally are and go up against greater numbers under the compulsion of the lash. As it is, though, being free and rulerless, how could they possibly withstand an army like mine? Demaratus replies in words that would become famous for their embodiment of the Spartan ethos:

> To be sure, they are free, but not entirely so. For they do have a master over them, and that is *nomos*. And believe me, they stand in far more

awe of it than your men do of you. Whatever it commands—they will do it. And its command is always the same: never to flee the field, no matter how vast the enemy, but remain at their posts either to prevail there, or to die there. (7. 104. 4–5)

Throughout his narrative Herodotus undertook to set forth the mindsets of the various peoples he had studied, and here he places in the mouth of Demaratus a classic expression of the Spartans' code of behavior, one the admiring Greeks understood very well, but Xerxes, with his autocrat's perspective, not at all. On the whole Socrates' admirers thought well of Sparta. Xenophon composed a history of the Spartan constitution, and his friendship with the Spartan king Agesilaus bore fruit when he was exiled from Athens for his Spartan sympathies and Agesilaus granted him an estate at Scillus, near Olympia. Alienated by what he perceived as the disorderly democracy of his native polis, Plato was impressed by the systematic nature of Spartan government and society, with its thoroughgoing regimentation of every aspect of life, but even he was disturbed by the gearing of Spartan education to war alone. Aristotle shared his concern, complaining that

> the whole legal system is directed toward a single part of virtue only, namely, military valor, as this is helpful when it comes to conquest. For this reason the Spartans remained secure as long as they were at war, but everything fell apart as soon as they had acquired an empire, for they had no idea how to use the leisure they had acquired, trained as they were in none of the things that are more important than the art of war. (*Politics* 1271b)

———

Most theorizing about the polis that has survived derives from Athens, a circumstance that yields a limited perspective even though the most prolific political theorist to work there, Aristotle, was a metic from Stagira in northern Greece. Atypical in many ways, Athens throughout the Classical Age was by far the largest polis in mainland Greece, with a population that usually hovered around 250,000, including free and enslaved, adult and child, citizen and alien, and it left behind unusually abundant remains, both literary and material. Every polis had an agora, but some were so small that archaeologists had difficulty locating them; at around 24,000 square yards, the Athenian agora extended over several acres. Government buildings, statues, monuments, and temples sat side by side with vendors' stalls; many are still there today. Trees specially planted for the purpose supplemented the shade afforded by spacious colonnades known as stoas. The followers of the philosopher Zeno from Citium in Cyprus, who met in one of the stoas starting around 300, were named Stoics for that reason. Citizens and noncitizens alike swarmed around, doing what we today would call networking. One might go to the agora to meet a friend or blackmail an enemy, to serve on a jury or discharge a public office, to sue or be sued, to listen to a sophist, to buy shoes or sell honey. Men of all classes could be found there, seeing and being seen. A woman found in the agora was likely to be fairly far down on the social scale, either a slave who had been sent shopping or a poor woman selling ribbons used in religious rites or foodstuffs like olives, figs, garlic, grapes, or bread.

Though much power-broking was conducted in the agora, the highest authority in the Athenian state was the assembly of all adult male citizens. Meeting on the hill called the Pnyx dozens of times a year, it debated vigorously and voted by show of hands. Some spoke rarely, others frequently; some surely must have seemed to speak constantly. Shouting and heckling was common, and issues ranged from smallish matters of finance to life and death questions of war and peace. Even some trials—impeachments, for example—might be held in the assembly, but most were heard by juries of several hundred men. The jury that sentenced Socrates to death numbered 501. Widespread participation in government was fostered in other ways as well. Many officeholders were chosen by lottery, although the frequency of war meant that the board of ten generals—the *strategoi*—who served for one-year terms, renewable, was elected, and the system of *prokrisis* (literally, before-judgment) winnowed the pool, knocking suspected kooks and malcontents off the list prior to the selection. By this practice the Athenians may well have done themselves out of input from some of their more interesting and iconoclastic citizens. Terms of office in Athens were short, generally a year, the high turnover designed to discourage the development of a bureaucracy.

As the philosophers never tired of complaining, Athenian democracy was truly amateur government. It is a tribute to Athenian democracy that it produced its own sternest critics. Xenophon was such a fierce opponent of the democracy that he was eventually exiled from the city, and such a strong anti-democratic strain ran through the teachings of Plato and Aristotle that hostility to democracy, Greek and otherwise, dominated the western tradition and was still firmly entrenched in political thought in the eighteenth century, when revolutionaries in France and America turned not to democratic Athens but to republican Rome for models. As political scientist J. S. McClelland pointed out at the end of the twentieth century, "It could almost be said that political theorizing was invented to show that democracy, the rule of men by themselves, necessarily turns into rule by the mob."[3]

Aristotle was quick to label democracy government by the poor (*Politics* 1279b). Indeed the Athenian poor exercised considerable power both in the assembly and in the courts, for their role as rowers in the huge imperial fleet prevented the upper classes from disenfranchising them. Although the Athenians placed sovereignty in an assembly dominated by men who were distinctly not rich, in Athens as elsewhere a disproportionate number of the literate, urban males who left writings behind were quick to condescend to anyone who made a living doing anything but working his own land—or directing slaves to work it. A sentimental attachment to the land led Aristophanes to idealize farmers in his comedies and disparage the new breed of politicians who made their living in business. Xenophon grounded an entire system in such beliefs. Aristotle, unhappy about political power being placed in the hands of anyone who did hard work, grudgingly conceded that farmers might make adequate citizens, since a benign apathy would discourage them from exercising their civic rights too often.

For these thinkers the category of undesirables included the poorest Athenians, who worked as hired hands on other men's farms; craftspeople who worked in "factories," large or small, making shoes, armaments, kitchenware, and the like; and even the wealthy owners of such shops, like the *strategos* Cleon, who owned a tannery. Cleon seems to have succeeded Pericles for a while as the most popular politician in Athens and was plainly despised by both Thucydides and Aristophanes. Aristophanes' heroes are rather the stalwart farmers of Attica—the men who form the chorus of his play *Peace*, performed in 421 when the Peace of Nicias that seemed to promise an end to the Peloponnesian War was in sight. We have peace now, exclaims his protagonist Trygaeus,

> we can trade in all that arming
> for a happy, happy song as we march home to do some farming.

The chorus of farmers replies:

> What a day, not just for farmers but for anyone worthwhile!
> What a yearned-for, hoped-for vision! See how joyously I smile
> As I think about how soon I'll see the vines upon my land
> And the fig trees that I planted as a youth with my own hand! (553–58)

A champion of the agricultural life, Aristophanes had no use for pompous politicians of any stripe, but particularly not the upstart Cleon, who had upset the natural balance of Athenian politics. At one time, voters both rich and poor had regularly elected affluent men from the landed aristocracy to the generalship, but in the new world of post-Periclean politics, men of business too might hope to hold the office. Aristophanes devoted his entire *Knights*, produced in 424, to savaging Cleon, even making so bold as to mention him by name there, as the chorus burst out:

> What a sweet day, what a bright day,
> What a filled-with-all-delight day
> What a treat for those who live here,
> Also people passing through,
> The day that Cleon meets his doom! (973–76)

The scaffold on which Aristophanes hangs the play's plot is the manipulation of an elderly Athenian householder by his slaves, two of them of long standing and a new one who has upstaged them: Paphlagon, whose background, of course, is in tanning. From oracles the two original slaves learn about others who will become influential, including a hemp seller (plainly Eucrates) and a sheep dealer (Lysicles) (129, 132). To make clear that his play is an allegory for the ease with which the Athenian people can be manipulated by self-seeking politicians, Aristophanes has given his householder the name Demos, the word by which the populace of the city was known and which lies at the root of the word democracy: people-power.

Socrates' admirer Xenophon believed strongly that men were disqualified from good decision-making by the work that Greeks called "banausic": literally, work done over a hot furnace, but by extension any hard labor that was not agricultural. In his essay on household management the *Oeconomicus*, a free composition not thought to represent the views of the real Socrates, Xenophon gives vent to his ideas on the various professions. "We have agreed with our states," he portrays his mentor as saying, "in rejecting those arts that are called 'banausic' because they seem to ruin both the body and the mind." An enemy invasion, "Socrates" maintains, would show the wisdom of disfranchising those who practiced banausic trades, for in such a crisis the farmers would step up and vote to defend the land, while the craftsmen would vote against fighting or taking any risks. Husbandry, he concludes, is the best occupation for a person of character, for it is liable to endow the body with "the greatest measure of strength and beauty, and to leave to the mind the most leisure for attending to the interests of one's friends and one's city" (*Oeconomicus* 6. 5–11).

Aristotle put forward an entirely different reason for the superiority of farmers as citizens, maintaining that though they are every bit as devoid of judgment as artisans, shopkeepers, and day laborers, the fact that they live farther from town and are constantly struggling to keep their heads above water renders them less prone to attend the assembly. Only a life of leisured contemplation, he maintains, can bring wisdom. Thus his ideal state will grant citizenship only to citizens who enjoy such leisure: "the class of workmen merits no share in the state" (*Politics* 1329a). Along the same lines, slaves, who engaged in hard labor, could never be suitable citizens, and about this his fellow Greeks were in agreement. Unlike in imperial Rome, where at least every other citizen could, if one went back far enough, trace his or her descent to a slave, neither Greek slaves nor their descendants became citizens with any frequency.

Praise of farmers over other kinds of citizens also appears in Plato's *Laws*. The premise of the dialogue is that a new city is to be founded on Crete, and in a three-way discussion an Athenian, a Cretan, and a Spartan explore the optimal government and laws for this city. Proximity to the sea, the Athenian warns, brings with it a host of problems, including retail trade and naval power. In a clear allusion to the seven boys and seven girls who legend claimed had been sent at regular intervals to Crete as offerings to the Minotaur, he maintains that his countrymen

> would have done better to lose seventy times seven children rather than to become, as they did, sailors in place of staunch infantrymen; for sailors are accustomed to jumping ashore frequently and running at full speed for their ships; they do not realize that honor calls for them to die bravely at their posts when the enemy attacks. (706c)

States dependent for their power on navies, he complains, give honors to a segment of society that is "not too respectable" (707b).

Although Thucydides was quick to dismiss the Athenian assembly as a fickle mob, he also included in his history of the Peloponnesian War a paean to democracy in the form of a speech delivered by Pericles at the funeral for those who had died during the first year of the war. There Pericles makes a point of explaining why the word is attached to the government of the Athenians: "Because it operates for the many rather than for the few, our government is known as a democracy" (Thucydides 2. 37. 1). Pericles used the occasion to remind his audience of the way of life they were fighting to defend, and he spared no opportunity to contrast it with that practiced by the Spartans. Whoever composed the speech—Pericles, Thucydides, or, it has even been speculated, Pericles' common-law wife the metic Aspasia—it is worth citing at some length:

> We do not emulate the customs of our neighbors in our way of life but rather serve as a pattern for others.
>
> . . .
>
> With respect to our approach to military matters, we also differ from our antagonists in the following ways. We throw open our city to

everyone, and we do not by periodic expulsions of foreigners, preclude them from seeing or learning things lest someone hostile to us profit from what is readily available to be seen. We place less trust in our preparation and our cunning than in the spirited nature of our citizens. As far as education is concerned, where our rivals from the time they are children train painstakingly to develop manly courage, we who live in a less pressured way will advance just as readily to meet the same dangers as they.

. . .

We cultivate refinement without ostentation and knowledge without effeminacy; we consider wealth something to use, not to boast about. As for poverty, we do not view it as shameful; what appears to us shameful is failing to take steps to escape from it. . . . We alone consider a man who takes no part in politics not as someone who minds his own business, but as someone useless, and we are also the only people who, even when we cannot originate proposals, are nonetheless able to make good decisions about them, and instead of regarding discussion as a stumbling-block to action, we consider it a crucial preliminary to taking prudent action. . . .

In summation, I tell you that for all these reasons we are the school of Greece, and I doubt if anyone in any other city is as well-rounded and fully developed as each and every Athenian citizen. (2. 37. 1. 2. 39. 1; 2. 39.4–41.1)

Pericles' grudging injunction to the war widows of Athens sat oddly on the lips of a man living with a woman who attracted more gossip than any other female in the city:

And since I suppose I need to say something about female excellence to those of you who will now be widows, let me sum the situation up like this: your glory will be greatest in simply being no worse than your natures, and in being least talked about by men for either good or ill. (2. 45)

Pericles also takes care to praise Athens in areas in which Sparta was perceived as strong. Since Spartans were famous for revering their laws,

Pericles stresses how law-abiding the Athenians are. With its large and fertile territory, Sparta was self-sufficient, so Pericles praises the Athenians for their self-sufficiency—a most peculiar claim in light of their dependence on imported grain: in 405 the Spartans would end the war that Pericles had begun by cutting off the grain supply from the Black Sea. Sparta was the only state in Greece that offered free public education, so Pericles bills Athens as the school of Greece.[4]

Athens and Sparta were both strikingly similar and dramatically different. Sparta shared many features with Athens and other Greek poleis. Its citizens had a strong sense of civic consciousness and identified strongly as Hellenes. They spoke Greek. They worshipped the Olympian gods; indeed, they were famous for their piety. They were not open to expanding the franchise to newcomers. They welcomed slavery as an agreeable fact of life. While some Greeks found Spartan rigidity and asceticism comical, many admired Sparta for its tight organization, mixed constitution, and record of military success. Any man over sixty might be elected to its twenty-eight-man council of elders, the gerousia, although these were usually men of high status. Members of the gerousia served for life, and the approval of the gerousia was needed for bills passed by the assembly of male citizens, which voted but did not, like the vociferous Athenian assembly, debate; Spartans seem to have had a deep-seated suspicion of public deliberation.[5] Candidates over the age of thirty might present themselves for the board of five ephors (overseers), who served for one-year terms and oversaw the kings, with the right of impeaching and deposing them. Most curious of all was the Spartan dual kingship, held concurrently by representatives of two ancient royal houses.

Although it is easy to fall into the trap of conceiving monarchy as unaccountable government, such was not at all the case in Sparta. Each Spartan king served as a check on the other as the two men functioned as military and religious leaders, and their political power was hemmed in by the watchful supervision of the ephors. Greeks were mistrustful of too much power concentrated in a single pair of hands, and elaborate machinery existed to hold officials to account. Plato engages the question in the Laws when he depicts his Athenian spokesman explaining that since "there exists no mortal soul who, when he is young and irresponsible, will ever be able to tolerate holding the highest office on earth without becoming victim to the greatest of mental disorders, folly"; consequently some god must have been watching over the Spartans when he devised the dual kingship (691c–e). Trials of Spartan kings were not unusual, and the consequences were often catastrophic for the defendant. King Pleistoanax was banished when he withdrew Spartan troops from Attica after a conference with Pericles during the First Peloponnesian War, the same conference that led to Pericles' impeachment at Athens. Pericles was returned to office at the regular elections after a few months, but Pleistoanax remained in exile until 427, when he was recalled at the instigation of Apollo's oracle at Delphi (which he was suspected of having bribed to bring about his restoration). When Agis II made a humiliating battlefield truce with Argos in 418, he was threatened with the destruction of his house and a huge fine, though in the end the Spartans contented themselves with saddling him with ten advisors for future campaigning. Thinking they had lost a valuable opportunity to deal Sparta a decisive blow, the Argives were equally incensed at their commanders and began to stone their general Thrasyllus. Though Thrasyllus saved his life by taking asylum at an altar, he lost his property, which the citizens confiscated. The Spartan king Pausanias was condemned to death in 395, ostensibly for lateness in arriving to reinforce Lysander at Haliartus in Boeotia, though the real cause was plainly that he had aided in the restoration of the democracy at Athens in 403.

The Athenians had their own methods of preventing the concentration of power, designing their government to function with no president, no premier, and dividing the highest office in the state, that of *strategos* (general/admiral) among ten men elected for one-year terms. The machinery of control was particularly rigorous in Athens, where despite the brevity of their terms all officials had to undergo a rigorous scrutiny both before entering on their terms of office and upon leaving them, and many were subjected to monthly votes of confidence. Because of the risks attendant on military failure, the ten generals were the most vulnerable. The orator Demosthenes was probably exaggerating when he maintained that every general was impeached two or three times in his life, but he was certainly onto something (4. 47).[6] For this reason, military discipline in the Athenian armed forces was lenient, for the last thing a general wanted to do was to alienate those under his command who might be called upon to testify at some future hearing. The threat of ostracism, moreover, hung over all citizens active in politics.

Athens and Sparta were far from the only states concerned about accountability. Throughout Greece, the desire to diffuse authority had prompted a movement from monarchy to narrow oligarchy to broader oligarchy and in many cases to democracy. Democratic Argos also held audits of outgoing officials and seems to have practiced some form of ostracism, and for a while the Syracusans had a similar practice as well.[7] The notion that officials should be accountable to the populace arose from the profound Greek conviction that the state was an association of free men who voluntarily invested greater power in a smaller group who served at their pleasure, pending periodic review of their competence. Authority lay in the office, not the official. Male citizens enjoyed the privilege of *parrhesia*, freedom/frankness of speech, a right that enabled them to say to their officials what one could not say to a tyrant—or an eastern potentate such as Xerxes—without taking one's life in one's hands.

Many Greek states—by no means all—proclaimed commitments to equality among citizens, but not even democratic poleis sought to eliminate inequality. The goal was rather to manage relations among citizens by entrusting the people with the power, and the responsibility, of arbitrating conflicts among those in authority, giving officials strong motivation to behave honorably. Like the Athenians, the Spartans evinced an equality among citizens that was more theoretical than real. To the Spartiates, known as the *homoioi*—equals/similar/peers—was attached the legend that an early lawgiver, Lycurgus, had divided the land into 9,000 equal allotments, *klaroi*, and assigned each one to a Spartiate. Indeed, most of the institutions of Spartan political, social, and economic life were ascribed to Lycurgus, although it was generally agreed that the ephorate came later. Lycurgus was credited with creating the common messes and the institution that came to be known as the *agogē*, the "upbringing," the rigorous system in which boys were instructed in martial skills and virtues. Though it is not clear that Lycurgus ever existed, what

is certain is that the principle of equality among Spartiates was passionately cherished. While one man's land might be more productive than
another's and not everyone was an equally successful hunter, resulting
in differential contributions to the common mess, the wealthier Spartiates were careful not to parade their prosperity in front of others.
Though partible inheritance and the attendant division of land among
offspring led to inevitable real-world inequality, the ideology of equality
among the *homoioi* was fiercely maintained in theory. All Spartiates were
careful to dress just like their peers and avoid ostentation at all costs.

The Athenians, by contrast, could be impressed by wealth, especially
when it was channeled into public service. Although private displays of
ostentation such as elaborate funerals could induce envy in the masses
and were for that reason discouraged by sumptuary laws, an ingenious
system of indirect taxation in the public interest worked to mediate the
inevitable tensions between rich and poor. Harnessing the wealth of
the elite into enforced public service, the institution of "liturgies" required substantial outlays. The liturgy of the trierarchy entailed maintaining a warship for a year and training its crew; the *chorēgia* involved
training the choruses that would sing and dance at competitions in tragedy, comedy, and poetry in the various Attic religious festivals. Another
liturgy required leading and financing a delegation to a public festival in
another state. The government assigned over a hundred of these liturgies, and they were excellent investments in public relations. Despite
Pericles' claim that Athenians did not boast about wealth, defendants
in court regularly adduced the liturgies they had performed as evidence
of their fine character and good citizenship.

Notions of equality did not extend to the sexes. Greeks were heavily
invested in gender differences and had no desire to attenuate them. We
know most about the *nomoi* that constricted the lives of female citizens
in Athens, where women were perpetual minors at law. Although the
dignity and value of women was affirmed in their depiction on funeral
stelai—particularly after the law of 451 that limited citizenship to the
offspring of a citizen wife—their freedom was substantially restricted.
Throughout her life, every female was in the power of a *kyrios*—in childhood, her father, if alive, otherwise another close male relative; upon

marriage, her husband; in widowhood, her son; in the event of divorce (which a woman could initiate only by appearing before the archon with the backing of a male relative from her family of origin), again her father or another male relative from her birth family. Men could divorce their wives at will, and if adultery were involved the woman was forbidden not only to wear jewelry but to participate in public religious activities, a grave interdiction in a world in which such activities were some of the only ones available to citizen women outside the home.[8] Like children, Athenian women could not own property and were not considered competent to engage in any but the most minor financial transactions. Athenian laws sometimes paired women and children. "The law," we read in a speech of the orator Isaeus, "expressly forbids any child or woman to enter into a contract for more than a medimnus of barley," a medimnus being about one and a half bushels (Isaeus 10. 10).

Restricted in any case to children whose parents could afford to spare the loss of their labor on the farm, formal education was almost exclusively limited to boys, although the occasional girl with unusual parents might be sent to school as well. In any case, a girl's education would cease around the age of fourteen, at which point she was generally married by her father to a man of about thirty. It is not clear how much of an emotional bond formed between spouses. The dramatic age gap—a disparity aggravated in more affluent families by the gap in education—meant that husband and wife began their marriage with little in common. In the absence of records, we have no idea how frequently Athenians divorced. By law children always remained with the father, a powerful disincentive for women to leave their marriages; most divorce proceedings consequently were initiated by men. Women were never fully integrated into any family except the one into which they were born. In their husbands' homes they were merely sojourners who could be returned to their fathers at any time, with no grievance alleged. When in Euripides' *Alcestis* Heracles, finding the house of Admetus in mourning, asks solicitously if the deceased was a relative or not, Admetus replies that no, she was not (533). He is correct; a wife remained technically an outsider throughout her marriage. It may be that some of the mistrust of wives on the part of poets like Hesiod and Semonides (discussed later in chapter 5) derived in part from the fact that a woman's loyalty was always divided between the natal family that had raised her and the husband to whom she had been given. The figures of Medea and Ariadne seemed to offer cautionary tales in this regard. Medea had betrayed her father Aeëtes to help her lover Jason relieve him of the golden fleece (and indeed dismembered her young brother as a distraction to aid in the couple's escape), and Minos's daughter Ariadne had enabled Theseus to escape her father's labyrinth after killing the Minotaur. These daring females betrayed not only their families of origin but their countries. Women might well construe their biographies differently, remembering that Medea and Ariadne had both been subsequently discarded by the men whose lives they had saved at great peril to themselves.

———

For men, however, equality of a sort obtained under tyranny, which leveled distinctions among all those outside of the immediate circle of the tyrant's family and friends. A significant number of Greek states fell at one time or another into the hands of despots, some more benevolent than others. The word tyrant (*tyrannos*) is not Greek and was probably borrowed from neighboring Lydia, where, as Herodotus recounted, Gyges—probably a Carian—had seized power by killing the legitimate king Candaules. The first appearance of the word *tyrannos* in Greek literature is in a poem by Archilochus:

> The wealth of golden Gyges leaves me cold.
> I envy men like him not one whit more
> Than I'd be jealous of the works of gods.
> No, not for me a haughty tyranny;
> That kind of life is too rich for my blood.[9]

Archilochus's indifference was atypical. Both admired and resented, tyrants typically attracted considerable envy and substantial anxiety. Acutely aware of the human drive to power and concomitantly anxious about surrendering power to others, Greeks were both appalled by tyranny and impressed by the audacity of the men who dared to undertake it.

The power wielded by political authorities made Greeks nervous even when it was diluted between two men, as in Sparta, or even among ten, as in Athens. It is remarkable how frequently the Athenians impeached and deposed members of their Board of Generals in light of the fact that their terms were only one year and their authority shared with nine others.

Greeks could not but find the unbridled power of a tyrant unsettling, yet this very power often brought with it advances of many kinds. Peisistratus, for example, undertook numerous public works projects that supplied many jobs, sponsored an authoritative edition of the Homeric epics, and initiated the festival of the Dionysia, where crowds (certainly of free men, less certainly women and enslaved people) gathered to see tragedies and later comedies performed. Many Athenians looked back on the era of Peisistratus as a golden age of cultural blossoming and economic prosperity, and the period of Gelon's tyranny in Syracuse was held to be a magnificent era even in its own day.

One of the largest Greek states to experience tyranny was the commercial dynamo of Corinth. For the Corinthians, geography was destiny. Their location on the narrow isthmus that linked Attica and northern Greece with the Peloponnesus won them ports facing both west and east, making them natural sailors and traders. With its substantial navy, Corinth was a cherished member of the Peloponnesian League. Archaic Corinth was ruled by a particularly narrow aristocracy, the intermarrying clan of the Bacchiads. Around 650, however, Cypselus, himself part Bacchiad, seized sole power and established a tyranny.

In light of the allure that attends on absolute power, it is not surprising that colorful anecdotes tended to congregate around tyrants, some quaint, some lurid, some pithy. Thanks to a long speech preserved (or invented) in the *Histories* of Herodotus, tales about the Corinthian tyranny check all these boxes. When the Spartans were seeking to persuade their allies to help restore the exiled tyrant Hippias to Athens, Herodotus says, a Corinthian by the name of Socles quashed the proposal by a speech recounting of the Corinthians' bad experiences with the family of Cypselus. He leads off with an account of Cypselus's birth and accession to power, which, he explains, had been foretold by the Delphic oracle. Because of the prophecy, he says, when Cypselus's mother Labda, a Bacchiad, gave birth, the Bacchiads sent ten men to her house asking to see the baby. Imagining them to be friends of her husband, Labda placed the child in the arms of one of the visitors. The men had agreed that the first one to hold the infant should dash it to the ground, but when Labda handed over the baby, "by divine chance" it smiled up at the would-be murderer, and that was the end of that. The men passed the baby from hand to hand, but nobody was able to steel himself to do the deed. Standing at the door upbraiding one another, they finally decided to give it another try. Labda, meanwhile, who had overheard their conversation, prudently hid the baby in some sort of container—in Greek, a *kypselē*—from which the future tyrant got his name. And the rest is history. Unable to find the child, and not really having the stomach for the infanticide anyhow, the visitors returned to their superiors and reported that they had carried out their orders. This improbable tale provided the quaint anecdote associated with founding of the Cypselid tyranny.

Like that of many tyrants, Cypselus's birth was problematic. As his mother was lame, no Bacchiad would have her, and so she was married to someone outside the clan, and a prophecy had warned of dire results from his birth. It is possible that Cypselus himself was lame. Although Herodotus's charming tale suggests one etymology for his name, others are possible. The Greek word *kypselos* meant sandpiper, and Aristotle reports that some Greeks called sandpipers *apodes*, footless.[10] It may also be significant that the Greek word *psellos* was used to describe someone with a speech impediment: people seem to have perceived something "off" about Cypselus.[11] That Cypselus had some sort of a disability that set him off from others would fit a pattern. The lyric poet Alcaeus accused the tyrant of Mytilene, Pittacus, both of being lame and of being *kakopatridan*, "of bad father" or "fathers"—rather like Cypselus, whose father Eëtion was outside the Bacchiad clan.[12] It was not illegitimate power alone that attracted such tales. The imputation of anatomical peculiarities to both legitimate and illegitimate rulers suggests that there was something charged about power that prompted Greeks to label these rulers as in every way exceptional. In addition to stories imputing some physical handicap to tyrants, there were a number that ascribed these to founders and legitimate kings. Battus, the founder and first king of Cyrene, was said to have received his name because he stammered, and he was the son not of his father's wife but rather of a concubine—one, moreover, who had been accused of promiscuity, thus also calling Battus's paternity into question.[13] It was suggested, as we have seen, that the legendary Athenian king Cecrops was a man above the waist but a snake or fish below, and much the same was said of King Erichthonios. Myskellos, the founder of Croton in Italy, seems to have had some deformity, whether a limp or a hunched back.[14] The story of Agesilaus's accession in Sparta offers a historical corollary. Following the death of Agis II in 401, the heir apparent Leotychidas claimed to be in possession of an oracle from Delphi warning the Spartans against a "lame kingship" and pointed to the handicap of his uncle Agesilaus, who was challenging him for the kingship on the grounds that he was in fact not Agis's son. (He was rumored to have been fathered by the Athenian defector Alcibiades.) The Spartans, however, were persuaded by the argument of Lysander, who had been Agesilaus's lover, to the effect that the lameness was metaphorical and referred to Leotychidas's illegitimacy, and they chose Agesilaus for their king.

Tyrants also drew to themselves imputations of sexual and marital peculiarities. By having sex with his wife *ou kata nomon* (Herodotus 1. 61. 1)—not in keeping with custom—the Athenian tyrant Peisistratus gave offense to his father-in-law and political ally, resulting in his expulsion from the city. Herodotus reported that Peisistratus's son Hippias dreamed that he was having sex with his mother (6. 107. 6). Dionysius I of Syracuse defied convention by marrying two women in a single ceremony. When his Locrian wife Aristomache bore a child, his Syracusan wife Doris remaining long childless, Dionysius accused Aristomache of using drugs to prevent Doris from conceiving and murdered her. He would not be the only Greek tyrant to kill his wife. Cypselus's son and successor Periander was reported to have murdered his wife Melissa and had sex with her corpse, an act for which he was later chastised by her ghost. If we are to believe the third-century CE biographer Diogenes Laertius, he also burned alive the concubines who had prompted his wrath against her by filling his ears with slanderous stories.[15] A tyrant's lack of accountability, says a supporter of democracy in the text of Herodotus, breeds hybris. A tyrant will flout a country's ancestral *nomoi*, rape women, and put men to death without trial (3. 80. 5). If the prototypical tyrant was a rapist, however, so was the prototypical god; raping with impunity was the common province of both. Tyrants, then, took on a power beyond what was appropriate for a mortal, and the response was ambivalent. While on the surface the sexual irregularities were disapproved, there was still envy of the tyrant's options, and envy was a two-edged sword, combining as it did resentment with admiration. It is a truism in Plato's dialogues that the average unthinking person finds the life of a tyrant enviable. Seeking to refute Socrates' claim that unbridled power does not bring happiness, the rhetorician Polus puts forward the example of Archelaus, who had usurped the throne of Macedon in 413, as an example of absolute power bringing happiness. Polus concedes at once that Archelaus is a profoundly unjust man, having murdered the rightful ruler and his son as well as his own seven-year-old brother, but, he insists, Archelaus is nonetheless happy (*Gorgias* 470d–471d). Predictably, Socrates does not agree. Both here and in Book 9 of the *Republic* he portrays the tyrant as a miserable prisoner of his own uncontrollable impulses.

That tyrants were international celebrities added to their mystique. Renowned for their wealth and power, they made marriage connections with other states, often other tyrannies. Anaxilas, tyrant of Rhegium in south Italy, married Cydippe, the daughter of Terillus, tyrant of Himera on the north coast of Sicily. Cylon, who attempted unsuccessfully to become tyrant of Athens, was married to the daughter of the Megarian tyrant Theagenes. Of the two women whom Dionysius I of Syracuse married on the same day, one was from Epizephyrian Locris in Italy, a union that led ultimately to his son's seizing power there and ruling as tyrant. They also had friends and allies among other rulers. Periander, Herodotus reports, sent an envoy to his fellow tyrant Thrasybulus of Miletus to garner some tips on maintaining security, whereupon Thrasybulus led the fellow

> out of town into a field of grain, and as he walked through the wheat, constantly asking questions about the envoy's trip from Corinth, he

kept lopping off all the tallest ears of wheat he could see and tossing them away, until he had destroyed the loveliest and richest part of the crop. Then, after passing through the place and speaking no word of advice, he sent the herald away. When the man returned to Corinth, Periander naturally wanted to know what he had learned, but the envoy reported that Thrasybulus had given him no advice at all. (Herodotus 5. 92F2–3)

Periander, however, recognized at once that Thrasybulus was advising him to make away with all those who were in any way outstanding, and he at once began a campaign of murder and banishment.[16] He was a savage and bloodthirsty ruler, and after his death Corinth reverted to oligarchy; in the Hellenistic Age it was under the suzerainty of Macedon. Because its thriving trade seemed to threaten their own, the Romans destroyed the city in 146, killing all the men and enslaving the women and children.

A late archaic phenomenon, tyranny died out in most of the Greek world during the Classical Age with the striking exception of Sicily. Not surprisingly, the exceedingly fertile island was a big draw for colonists, and along with the Greek settlements on the Italian peninsula the glittering Greek civilization that developed there came to be known in Roman times as Magna Graecia: Greater Greece. Sicily was literally a land of milk and honey—and beef and pork and timber and fish and fine horses and boundless grain. But Sicily was not only the golden west; it was also the wild west. Like the Americans of European descent who headed for the wide-open spaces to the west only to discover that there were people living there already who regarded the land as theirs, the Greek settlers encountered a variety of well-established peoples in Sicily, some of whom were already at odds with one another. Carthage made no secret of its desire to control the whole island, and although the Greek cities there experimented with a variety of governments, the tensions among the various groups combined with fear of the Carthaginians to make them particularly vulnerable to tyranny. Other factors conduced to tyranny as well. Skyrocketing wealth in the upper class fostered unrest among others, and ambitious men, of whom there were many, seized the opportunity to take power outside the law, swelling their power bases by the enfranchisement of mercenaries and immigrants. Mass murder was often on the agenda. Though sensational tales tended to attach themselves to tyrants, the stories associated with Phalaris, tyrant of Acragas, were extreme. Not only was he rumored to eat suckling babies; he was reputed to have had a hollow brass bull created in which he roasted alive those who had given him displeasure, delighting in the shrieks of agony that simulated the bellowing of an actual bull. What grounding these tales had in reality is impossible to know.

The wealth of these men dwarfed that of the mainland tyrants. Gelon, tyrant of Syracuse, was the most powerful man in Greece, perhaps in all of Europe, and garnered undying gratitude in Sicily when he turned back the invading Carthaginians at Himera on the north coast in 480. To commemorate his victory, his brother-in-law Theron erected the Temple of Zeus at Acragas. Measuring roughly 360 by 165 feet, it was one of the largest Greek temples ever built; sadly, it now lies in ruins. Gelon's rule was considered by many a golden age, and on his death in 478 he was mourned widely, though by no means universally. A dedicated patron of the arts, Gelon's brother and successor Hiero lured the Athenian tragedian Aeschylus more than once to Sicily, where he composed his lost play *Women of Aetna* in honor of Hiero's newly founded city of that name.

If the Sicilians believed that only tyranny could protect them from overseas invaders, they were mistaken. Around 465 the violent tyrants of Acragas and Syracuse were expelled and democracies installed there that endured for generations. When the Athenians invaded Sicily in force in 415 and invested Syracuse, it was the democratic government that mobilized the resistance. The invaders found themselves slaughtered, imprisoned, or enslaved, and the triumphant Syracusans, stripping the bodies of the Athenian dead, decorated the tallest trees by the banks of the Assinarus River with their armor.[17] In 405, however, Dionysius I was catapulted to power in Syracuse and soon became the most powerful Greek ruler of his day.

Although monarchy did not persist much past the collapse of the Bronze Age, there were exceptions. Atypically, Halicarnassus was governed by a monarchy throughout its history, first a series of independent rulers and then Alexander and his successors. A Dorian colony, it was populated, like Miletus to the north, by a mixture of Greeks and Carians. Halicarnassus's most famous son, the historian Herodotus, was surely part Carian, perhaps accounting for the breadth of his interests and perspective. His narrative includes a vivid portrait of one of the most remarkable Halicarnassians, Artemisia. Queen during the Persian Wars, Artemisia was a formidable individual who called into question traditional sex roles. This gutsy woman had come to govern Halicarnassus after her husband's death and followed Xerxes' army to Greece on her own initiative, prompted, Herodotus says, by her *andreia*—a striking word to use in connection with a woman, signifying as it did both courage and, literally, manliness (7. 99. 1). It was all the more striking as Aeschylus had already produced his *Persians*, in which Xerxes' mother complained that her son had been pushed to invade Greece by evil men who taunted him with accusations of the opposite, *anandria*— cowardice/effeminacy (755). Alone among the Persian commanders Artemisia counseled Xerxes against fighting the Greeks at Salamis, pointing out the foolhardiness of risking his forces when there was every reason to think the Greeks, left to their devices, would scatter to their homes and the victory would go to him by default. Though she could not have been more right, Xerxes was eager for the glory that would attend on a victory at sea, and he engaged the Greeks anyway. Finding herself chased by an Athenian ship, Artemisia executed a maneuver that earned Herodotus's fervent admiration. In an impressive display of quick thinking, she rammed and sank another ship fighting for Persia— whereupon the Athenian captain, assuming she was on his side, immediately abandoned his pursuit. Xerxes, Herodotus tells us, believing that Artemisia had sunk a Greek vessel, exclaimed, "My men have turned into women and my women into men!" (8. 88. 3).

In the following century another Artemisia appeared in Halicarnassus, the able sister and wife of the ambitious Mausolus. A man of tremendous drive, Mausolus extended his power both north and south and took it on himself to fan the flames of opposition to Athens. His plans came to fruition in 357 when the city of Byzantium rebelled from the Second Athenian Confederacy, accompanied by Rhodes, Cos, and

Chios. Other defections followed, and the Athenian military was unable to quell the rebellion. Though the Athenian Confederacy continued for some time, it was never the same without its eastern members.

Artemisia and Mausolus spent lavishly to adorn and fortify Halicarnassus, and upon Mausolus's death in 353 Artemisia began construction of a magnificent tomb that they would share—an extraordinary creation that became one of the wonders of antiquity and bequeathed to the world the word mausoleum. Resembling a Greek temple atop a wedding cake, it was a striking blend of Greek restraint and eastern opulence, towering some 138 feet above the ground and displaying impressive larger-than-life statues of the royal pair that thousands of visitors to the British Museum in London now admire every year. When Alexander invaded Caria in 334, another sibling of the royal couple, Ada, thought it prudent to ally with him, and she joined him in taking Halicarnassus by siege. Like both Artemisias, she was a gifted commander, and Alexander rewarded her with the title Queen of Caria. She ruled until her death in 326, and as she had adopted him as her son, Caria then passed into Alexander's hands.

Though gender roles were more narrowly circumscribed in classical Greece, this was not equally the case in all poleis. Sparta, where women had considerably more freedom and higher status than elsewhere in the mainland, was connected in Greek thought both with Locri in Italy and with the island of Crete. In 680 or so, "Epizephyrian" (western, from Zephyr, the west wind) Locri near the toe of the "boot" of Italy was founded by settlers from Sparta and perhaps also from the original Locris on the Greek mainland. The Locrians were known for their excellent laws; the geographer Strabo may be mistaken in his claim that they were the first to use written laws, but the existence of this claim makes plain the high regard in which Locrian law was held in Greece. Locri and Sparta were linked in the Greek mind as "well-lawed cities."[18] Each was associated with a legendary lawgiver. The Locrians' version of Lycurgus was Zaleucus, and tradition connected the two men in various ways. Each was rumored to have had only one eye and to have studied under the Cretan poet and musician Thaletas of Gortyn. Even in that most forward-looking of poleis, Athens, oligarchs who wanted to replace the democracy with an aristocracy claimed that they merely sought a reversion to the *patrios politeia* (ancestral constitution) of earlier days. Plato, who did not even want new measures in music to be introduced, was an extreme case; in his mind, change and decline were synonymous. The nostalgia for the good old days that pervades the plays of Aristophanes is another example. More reactionary societies like Sparta and Locris were still more wedded to the notion of an unchanging universe. The Spartans were heavily invested in the notion that Lycurgus, a perfect individual in every way, had fixed the Spartan *politeia* for all time, and the Locrians were a paragon of immutability. The Athenian orator Demosthenes cited a Locrian custom in an Athenian courtroom on the grounds that it would be helpful to hear an example from a "well-lawed city." The Locrians, he said,

> are so confident that long-established laws should be obeyed and ancestral usage preserved, that laws should never be made for the gratification of whims or to accommodate the transgressions of criminals, that anyone who wants to propose a new law must do so with a noose around his neck. If the law is found to be good and beneficial, the proposer leaves alive, but if not, the noose is tightened and he dies. (24. 139)

Not surprisingly Plato describes the Locrians as enjoying the best laws of any state in their part of the world (*Laws* 638b).

Despite their rigid conception of law, the Locrians seem to have been rather open-minded when it came to gender relations. It is likely, though not certain, that women exercised in Locri. A fourth-century pot found in a Locrian cemetery portrays a young woman wearing a very short garment similar to those found in Spartan art, and strigils (the instruments with which Greek athletes scraped down their bodies after exercise) were found in the graves of some Locrian women.[19] The historian Polybius, who visited Locri several times, reported that it was a matrilineal society. The Locrians, he wrote, told him that all hereditary honors among them were traced through the female side. The noblest traced their descent to the early female colonists, not to the men. When they expelled the Sicels from their territory, moreover, and learned that it was a Sicel custom to have processions at their sacrifices led by the highest-born boy available, in adopting the custom they also adapted it, substituting a girl for a boy, since they reckoned noble ancestry through the female line (12. 5). The Locrian poet Nossis follows this practice in her epigram to Hera:

> Most reverend Hera, you who frequently
> Descend from heaven to behold your shrine
> Placed on Lacinia's bold promontory
> Fragrant with incense:
> I beg you take this woven linen wrap
> Made by Theophilus, Cleucha's child,
> In tandem with her noble daughter Nossis. (*Greek Anthology* 6. 265)

Describing a picture of Melinna in another epigram, she observes with pleasure how closely Melinna resembles her mother and exclaims "Children resembling parents is so good!" (*Greek Anthology* 6. 353) appropriating the more common Greek claim that it is good that sons should resemble their fathers. The poet to whom she alludes most often in her surviving work, moreover, is Sappho, another writer who lived in a world hospitable to women. Plainly in Sappho's day young women on Lesbos enjoyed a measure of freedom and education; whether this persisted in the Classical Age is unclear. Whereas the opening poem in her collection offered a nod to Sappho by its claim of the primacy of *erōs*—than which nothing, Nossis says, is sweeter—the concluding epigram names Sappho openly. Functioning as her own epitaph, the verses link the two poets in a powerful bond:

> Stranger, if you sail
> To Mytilene of the lovely dance
> To be inspired there by Sappho's grace
> Say was born here in the Locrian land,
> One precious to the muses—and to her.
> Know that the name I bore is Nossis. Go. (*Greek Anthology* 7. 718)

Two impressive sanctuaries were built in Locri, one of Persephone and another of Aphrodite. Demeter was also worshipped, but, exceptionally, in a sanctuary of her own, separately from her daughter Persephone. The material remains point to the centrality of females in Locrian culture. Locri appears to have been the point of origin of the so-called Ludovisi Throne, a block of marble adorned with stunning relief sculpture discovered in 1887 on the grounds of the Villa Ludovisi in Rome.[20] Evidently sculpted during the first part of the fifth century, it is about four feet wide, three feet high and four and a half feet deep and is generally taken to depict Aphrodite rising from the sea at the time of her creation, clothed in a clinging garment that defines her form as well as indicating her wetness; alternative interpretations identify the figure as Persephone or Pandora, rising from a cleft in the earth. The goddess, whoever she is, is flanked by two attendants, probably the Hours, daughters of Zeus and Themis. Other panels also depict only females. When we combine this remarkable work of art with the report of matriliny, a picture emerges of a society far more oriented toward females than most Greek cultures. To be sure, the Athenians' tutelary deity was female, but as the goddess herself observed pointedly in Aeschylus's *Eumenides*, she was conspicuously male-identified: no mother gave birth to her, and in all respects except marriage

> I'm for the male, and that wholeheartedly;
> I am entirely on the father's side. (737–38)

She was also a goddess of war. Persephone and Aphrodite were associated with fertility, death, and love/sex, distinctly different provinces.

As the Locrians' much-admired laws do not survive, we have no access to what women in Locri were able to do when they were not writing poetry or tracing their descent through their mothers. We know much more about women's rights in another polis in a very different part of the Greek world: the city of Gortyn in Crete, where a remarkable document literally carved in stone survives to this day. The text known as the Gortyn Code—actually a series of codes—is the longest extant inscription from classical Greece. Running to some 600 lines, it was carved into a wall about twelve feet high and thirty feet long. It makes plain that women in Gortyn had substantially more freedom than those in, say, Athens. Gortynian women could not only own property; they could manage it themselves without the supervision of a *kyrios*. They could also appear in court as either plaintiffs or defendants without an intermediary. As in Sparta, daughters could inherit, though they received only half what their brothers got. Girls appear to have had significant input into the choice of husbands. In the event of divorce, a wife might well move into her own house, although she might also move in with relatives or a new husband. She was entitled to take with her half of what she had woven. Presumably this means the monetary value of her work: a good deal of her weaving would have been clothing for other family members, and it is hard to see what use she would have had for these items (although it is not hard to imagine a vengeful divorcée taking half of every garment she had made for her former spouse).[21]

The polis was a way of life as well as a constitution. The Greek word for constitution, *politeia*, embraced every aspect of polis living—and thinking. The Platonic dialogue on the ideal state normally translated into English as *The Republic* actually bore the title *Politeia*. The advantages of the polis system were many. It enabled a significant percentage of residents to take part in government; its smallness encouraged a strong sense of belonging, not least by the easy access it afforded to the frequent festivals, which, though religious in origin, also served as the social glue that bound communities together. Yet before we succumb to a romantic polis envy, we need to remember the problems that beset the city-state system. The very smallness of the polis gave politics an intensity that often led to bloody civil strife—*stasis*, as the Greeks called it. Every city, Aristotle maintained, was in fact two cities, a city of the rich and a city of the poor. Thucydides in his history of the Peloponnesian War described with biting sorrow the *stasis* that erupted in Corcyra in 427:

> For seven days the Corcyraeans busied themselves butchering those of their fellow citizens whom they regarded as their enemies. Although they were ostensibly accused of seeking to dissolve the democracy, some died on account of private feuds, and others because they owed money. Every imaginable kind of death could be seen, and as usually happens at such times, there was no extreme to which the violence did not go. Sons were killed by their own fathers; suppliants

were dragged from altars or killed on top of them; some were even walled up in the temple of Dionysus and left to die there. (Thucydides 3. 81. 2–5)

This behavior, the historian tells us, became the paradigm for numerous such episodes throughout the war, as the populace hoped to bring in the Athenians on their side, the oligarchs the Spartans. Words changed their meaning; audacity was now courage, hesitation cowardice, moderation unmanliness. *Stasis* struck one city after another as it always would, Thucydides wrote, for as long as human nature remained the same; in times of peace and prosperity, both cities and individuals can afford lofty ideals, but war, which robs people of their daily needs, is a *biaios didaskalos*: a violent teacher (3. 82. 2).

If Thucydides imagined that civil strife would abate when the war ended, he was mistaken. *Stasis* was the bugaboo of the fourth century. Xenophon mentioned over thirty instances. In addition, the aversion of the Greek states to uniting combined with a naturally competitive disposition to leave them open to the dangers of constant warfare. Throughout their history, Greek families lived with the knowledge that at any time the men could be called upon to fight and the women to adjust in their absence—and that the loss of a war could mean death for some and enslavement for others. This was the price to be paid for the rewards of living in a small, cohesive community.

The conquests of Alexander put an end both to the corrosive wars of the city-states and to their existence as independent agents on the diplomatic scene. The polis, however, remained the center of communal life throughout the Hellenistic Age, thriving as a vital social, civic, and cultural entity. Eastern cities like Alexandria and Antioch were far bigger than any of the cities of old Greece. To be sure, in an age when many cities had given up their armies and navies the polis could no longer be conceived as a community of warriors, but this construct had begun to lose meaning already in the fourth century, when more men served as mercenaries in foreign armies than in the militias of their home states, and it had never taken women into consideration. The polis to end all Hellenistic poleis was Alexandria in Egypt, the largest city in antiquity until it was eclipsed by Rome. Sporting both the great research center of the Museum and the most remarkable library of antiquity, Alexandria drew scholars from all over the world, and the exchange of ideas was not limited to venues specifically designated as centers of intellectual life; the many ethnicities that jostled one another in the busy streets generated a climate of constant discovery. Overall, the Ptolemies did not establish new cities, but Seleucus, who had vast tracts of cultivable land available to him, founded many, including Antioch and several Seleucias, one of which, Mesopotamian Seleucia, served as a second capital along with Antioch; it was said to be just as large, with a population of over half a million. To keep the discombobulation of the Greek settlers in this alien land to a minimum, Seleucus and his successors decked out their foundations with the standard amenities that would make transplants feel at home—theaters, schools, temples to the Olympian gods. Every new city came complete with an agora. Alexandria and the glittering cities of the Seleucids proclaimed the advent of a new cosmopolitan world order.

Suggested Readings

Allen, Danielle. 2003. *The World of Prometheus: The Politics of Punishing in Democratic Athens.* Princeton, NJ: Princeton University Press.

Börm, Henning, and Nino Luraghi, eds. 2018. *The Polis in the Hellenistic World.* Stuttgart: Franz Steiner Verlag, 2018.

Brock, Roger, and Stephen Hodkinson, eds. 2000. *Alternatives to Athens: Varieties of Political Organization and Community in Ancient Greece.* Oxford and New York: Oxford University Press.

Cartledge, Paul. 2002. *Sparta and Lakonia: A Regional History, 1300–362 B.C.* New York: Routledge.

———. 2009. *Ancient Greece: A History in Eleven Cities.* Oxford: Oxford University Press.

Chamoux, François. 2002. *Hellenistic Civilization.* Malden, MA: Wiley-Blackwell.

De Angelis, Franco. 2018. *Archaic and Classical Greek Sicily: A Social and Economic History. Greeks Overseas.* Oxford and New York: Oxford University Press.

Gagarin, Michael, and David Cohen, eds. 2005. *The Cambridge Companion to Ancient Greek Law.* New York: Cambridge University Press.

Gorman, Vanessa B. 2001. *Miletus, the Ornament of Ionia: A History of the City to 400 B.C. E.* Ann Arbor: University of Michigan Press.

Hansen, Mogens H. 1991. *The Athenian Democracy in the Age of Demosthenes: Structure, Principles, and Ideology,* trans. J. A. Crook. Oxford and Cambridge, MA: Blackwell.

Joint Association of Classical Teachers. 2008. *The World of Athens: An Introduction to Classical Athenian Culture.* Cambridge, UK: Cambridge University Press.

Kennell, Nigel. 2010. *Spartans: A New History*. Chichester, UK, and Malden, MA: Wiley-Blackwell.

Landauer, Matthew. 2019. *Dangerous Counsel: Accountability and Advice in Ancient Greece*. Chicago and London: University of Chicago Press.

Lape, Susan. 2004. *Reproducing Athens: Menander's Comedy, Democratic Culture, and the Hellenistic City*. Princeton, NJ, and Oxford: Princeton University Press.

Ma, John. 2024. *Polis: A New History of the Ancient Greek City-State from the Early Iron Age to the End of Antiquity*. Princeton, NJ: Princeton University Press.

Mackil, Emily. 2015. *Creating a Common Polity: Religion, Economy, and Politics in the Making of the Greek Koinon*. Berkeley and Los Angeles: University of California Press.

Munn, Mark. 2000. *The School of History: Athens in the Age of Socrates*. Berkeley and Los Angeles: University of California Press.

Ober, Josiah. 1991. *Mass and Elite in Democratic Athens: Rhetoric, Ideology, and the Power of the People*. Princeton, NJ: Princeton University Press.

Powell, Anton, and Stephen Hodkinson, eds. 2002. *Sparta: Beyond the Mirage*. London: Classical Press of Wales and Duckworth.

Raaflaub, Kurt. 2004. The *Discovery of Freedom in Ancient Greece*, trans. Renate Franciscono, revised by the author. Chicago and London: University of Chicago Press.

Robinson, Eric W. 2011. *Democracy beyond Athens: Popular Government in the Greek Classical Age*. Cambridge, UK, and New York: Cambridge University Press.

Rose, Peter W. 2012. *Class in Archaic Greece*. Cambridge, UK, and New York: Cambridge University Press.

Salmon, J. B. *Wealthy Corinth*. 1984. Oxford and New York: Oxford University Press.

Simonton, Matthew. 2019. *Classical Greek Oligarchy: A Political History*. Princeton, NJ: Princeton University Press.

Vlassopoulos, Kostas. 2007. *Unthinking the Greek Polis: Ancient Greek History beyond Eurocentrism*. Cambridge, UK: Cambridge University Press.

CHAPTER 5

Foreigners, Slaves, and Sex[ism]

I am grateful to fortune for three things: first, that I was born a human
being rather than a beast; next, a man rather than a woman; and third,
a Greek rather than a barbarian.

—DIOGENES LAERTIUS

Attributed alternately to the sixth-century Milesian protoscientist Thales
and the fifth-century Athenian philosopher Socrates, this proclamation
could probably have come from the mouth of almost any free Greek man.
It appears in different forms in various places in the Talmud, substituting
the dichotomy Jew/Gentile for Greek/barbarian and sometimes adding
the free/slave antithesis; plainly Greeks were not unique in their propensity to assimilate foreigners to women and animals. Aeschylus in his *Persians* associated the Persians with slavery and femaleness. For him the
troika of barbarian/slavish/feminine made up the essence of what a
Greek man defined himself against. While Plato had scandalized his contemporaries by according exceptional women equal power to men in the
ideal state he sketched out in the *Republic*, his writings nonetheless reveal
a generally low opinion of the typical woman, flighty and emotional, and
he often groups women with slaves, children, and animals.[1] Aristotle put
forward a different triad, presenting as he did three forms of rule: the rule
of free people over slaves, males over females, and grown men over
children (*Politics* 1260a). Although the formulation was always slightly

different, the sentiment was the same. It was the free Greek man alone who could live a truly blessed, fully realized life.

———

Although some nineteen out of every twenty Greek states declined to fight for Greece, the Persian wars forged a strong sense of Hellenic identity among the Greek belligerents. The Homeric epics had not portrayed Greek culture as distinct from that of the enemy Trojans, and the beleaguered Trojans were drawn with considerable empathy; Homer's account of the death of Hector was so poignant that it still causes almost unbearable pain in readers today. The Persians' attempt to deprive the Greek states of their freedom changed this. A Greek/Asiatic opposition undergirded Aeschylus's *Persians*, produced in 472, only seven years after the invasion had been turned back. Aeschylus's choice of venue set the tone for the tableau. The play takes place at the Persian court as Xerxes' mother Atossa, flanked by a chorus of Persian elders, awaits word of her son's expedition to Greece. The audience, of course, knows the dire news: the Persian forces have been defeated decisively at Salamis. The very fact of setting the play in Persia with exclusively Persian characters works against the audience's instinctive loathing for their recent invader, as Aeschylus shows the Persians first fearing and then hearing the horrendous news from the west. The chorus members evoke compassion by virtue of their advanced years, the queen mother by her vulnerability as a worried parent. The ghost of Darius, a man once the paramount enemy of Greece, sparks sympathy because of his helplessness, qua ghost, to do anything to curtail the rashness of his son, the messenger who brings word of the near annihilation of the Persian host by virtue of the misery he has observed and of which he has partaken. Even Xerxes, by far the least appealing character in the mix, gains a measure of empathy as he staggers into the tableau an utterly beaten man.

The patent compassion for the invaders is striking in a man whose brother Cynegirus, after all, had bled out when the Persians chopped off his hand as he was trying to hold back one of their ships bent on escaping from the disaster at Marathon; given the organization of Athenian forces, Aeschylus himself may have witnessed his brother's death. The differences between Greek and Persian culture, however, are drawn in the starkest of terms. Aeschylus takes pains to contrast the small states of Greece with the sprawling Persian Empire, its army enormous, virtually incalculable (40, 431–32, 926). Unlike Greece, Persia is immensely wealthy (250–52). Sardis and Babylon are rich in gold (45, 52–53). Accused by his compatriots of *anandria*, Xerxes is anything but the picture of masculinity. His weeping and wailing would have been considered extraordinarily demeaning to any Greek male. In Greece, as we will see in chapter 9, mourning was the job of women, who were often hired to do it. In her important essay "Asia Unmanned: Images of Victory in Classical Athens," British classicist Edith Hall writes that we see in Aeschylus's play

> an elision of non-Greek, defeated, and female. Since woman was the ancient Athenian's primary "other" and, with barbarian slaves, one of the primary objects of his power, he used her as an image for the ethnically other, thus transferring the asymmetrical power-relation embedded in her difference from the patriarchal male to the sphere of international power struggle.[2]

The Persians are plainly the anti-Greeks. Even should Xerxes fail, his mother reminds the chorus (and reassures herself), he will continue in power as before. He is not, she says, accountable to the state for his actions—not *hypeuthynos polei* (213). Her words mark a jarring intrusion of the language of Athenian democracy into the Persian court. The reference is to the annual hearings, the *euthynai*, to which outgoing Athenian officials were subjected. It sits incongruously on the lips of the wife of King Darius, a man later compared by the chorus to a god (857), and functions as a pointed reminder that Persia is very much not Greece, where officials are accountable and distinctly mortal. Aeschylus deploys a conversation between Atossa and the chorus to underline the difference between the ethos of the polis and that of the Persians, in which one man is "master." Who, Atossa inquires, is in charge of the Greek army? The chorus replies:

> They are the slaves or subjects of no man (242).

Persia's size and wealth, however, avail nought against the determination and discipline of the Greeks fighting for their freedom and their homeland, crying as they row into battle

> On, sons of Greece! Free now your fatherland!
> Free now your children, wives, free now the shrines
> Of your ancestral gods, and your ancestors' tombs!
> We fight today for everything we prize. (399–405)

Like Aeschylus, Herodotus refrains from demonizing the Persians. Despite the latent triumphalism discernible in his account of the Greco-Persian Wars, it is from Herodotus that we learn that the Persians taught their sons only three things: to ride, to shoot with the bow and arrow, and to tell the truth. While the "only" highlights the literary element that is lacking in their education and thus distinguishes it from the upbringing on offer among the more affluent Greeks, the nobility of the truth-telling lends a virtuous cast to the Persian trivium. As a historian, Herodotus had enormous respect for truth.

The Persians are only one of the many peoples whose customs Herodotus, eager to lay a kaleidoscope of cultures before the provincial Greeks, recounted in his sprawling narrative. So far from sharing the more common Greek view of "barbarians," Herodotus was one of the first globalists. The Atlantes, he reported, never dream. When one of the Padaeans falls ill, he is at once killed by his friends—and eaten. The Massagetae wait until their relatives are elderly, and then they kill and eat them. The Issedones do not act until their relatives have already died; only then do they chop up the deceased and mix the meat with that of cattle before feasting on it. They also clean out the dead man's head and gild the skull. The Gyzantes eat monkeys![3] All this Herodotus delighted in discovering—and sharing. In Arabia, he reports, live certain sheep with extra-wide tails a foot and a half across—and nearly five feet long. Were the sheep permitted to trail their tails behind them as they walked, the tails would become terribly sore. The shepherds, however, make little carts that they affix under the tail of each sheep. Problem solved![4]

Look! Herodotus often seems to be saying, how very different from us. That is by no means always a bad thing, but it is the Greeks who set the standard for normalcy. All of Herodotus's accounts of the *nomoi* of the various peoples he encounters are ethnocentric, and the center is always and forever Greece. When he says that a culture does things "differently," he means "differently from us Greeks." The notion of opposition is particularly conspicuous in his treatment of the Egyptians, of whom he writes:

> Just as they have a climate that is peculiar to themselves and a river different in its nature from all other rivers, similarly they have instituted customs and laws that are practically the complete opposite of those followed by the rest of mankind. For instance, the women go to the market to buy and sell while the men stay at home and weave, and whereas in weaving everyone else pushes the woof upwards, the Egyptians pull it down. Men carry burdens on their heads, but women on their shoulders. Women urinate standing up, men squatting. They move their bowels indoors but eat outside in the street, explaining that unseemly necessities should be performed in private whereas those things that are not unseemly should be done openly. (2. 35. 2–3)[5]

He goes on to list a number of other practices that strike him as the opposite of what is customary elsewhere, that is, in Greece; plainly he was well aware of the entertainment value of such contrasts. Herodotus was quick to perceive differences as opposites.

The very notion of polarity was profoundly Greek. It was in fact built into the language. One of the first linguistic habits a student of Greek encounters is the propensity of Greek authors to divide sentences into "on the one hand . . . on the other hand," or as the Greek has it *men . . . de*. The construction can be found by opening any Greek text at random. Herodotus's *Histories* begin with a *men . . . de* construction, as the historian proclaims in his own first sentence his intention to memorialize the glorious deeds of the Greeks, *men*, and barbarians, *de*. The defense Plato ascribes to Socrates at his trial begins, "How you, fellow Athenians, *men*, have been affected by those who have brought these accusations against me, I do not know, but they spoke so persuasively that I, *de*, very nearly lost track of my own identity. . . ." (*Apology*, 17a).[6]

Greeks were as captivated by Egypt's uniqueness as many today still are. Scarcely any Greek writer whose words have come down to us failed to make some reference to Egypt. Herodotus was quick to point out the Greeks' multifarious debts to the Egyptians. Geometry, the notion of seasons and months, contempt for artisans, astrology: all these Herodotus claimed had originated in Egypt and then been taken up by the Greeks (2. 109. 3, 4. 1, 167. 1–2, 82. 1). It was the Egyptians, he maintained, who first developed the idea of the transmigration of souls, a doctrine that some of the Greeks adopted "as if were their very own" (2. 123. 3). "The names of nearly all the gods," he wrote, "came to Greece from Egypt" (2. 50. 1), and "what the origin was of each of the gods, or whether all of them had always existed, and what they looked like, the Greeks did not know until yesterday, so to speak, or the day before," since Homer and Hesiod, who had laid out the pantheon of gods for posterity, had lived only some four hundred years before his time (2. 50. 1; 2. 53. 1–2). Although he saw the Greeks as having taken a great deal from other civilizations as well, no one land had contributed as much to their development as Egypt. From the Phoenicians they had gotten the alphabet; from the Babylonians the sundial and the division of the day into hours; the goatskin shield of Athena was modeled on the dress of Libyan women, and from Libya too were derived the four-horse chariot and the *ololugē*, the celebratory cry of ululation heard at sacrifices and other celebrations (though sometimes also in mourning) (5. 58. 1–2; 4. 189. 1–3; 2. 109. 3). When most Greeks thought of Egypt, they thought not of a culture contemporary with themselves but rather of the vast expanse of Egyptian history, of an Egypt removed from their own world not only in space but in time. It seemed to exist at the intersection of fact and fiction. Herodotus was preoccupied with the antiquity of Egyptian civilization, which he greatly exaggerated; no wonder he believed so many inventions could be traced to this land whose beginnings were virtually coterminous with the creation.

Egypt loomed large in the imagination of Plato, whose writings refer to it far more often to than any other country outside the Greek world. Egypt functioned for Plato as both not-Athens and not-democracy, and he esteemed it accordingly. The seemingly timeless and static culture held a powerful allure for a man with a revulsion from the idea of change, which he associated with decline and decay. In the words of classicist Phiroze Vasunia, Plato seems to fetishize Egypt, which "serves as a substitute location for the realization of his philosophy and politics; at the same time, his texts mystify the country by stripping it bare of historical practice and change."[7] Plato pegged the idealized Egypt of his imagination as the source of the Atlantis myth, which for him was also the myth of an ancient, idealized Athens. In his *Timaeus*, his relative Critias told how when Solon, while traveling in Egypt, tried to calculate the chronology of Greek history, one of the priests cried out, "O Solon, Solon, you Greeks are forever children; there is no such thing as an old Greek!" For, he argued, the Greeks do not possess "a single belief that is venerable and derived from ancient tradition, or a single field of learning that is hoary with age" (22b). There have been many, many cataclysms in past times, he said, that wiped out all memories of previous achievements (including the knowledge of writing), and you Greeks invariably have to start all over again, but here in Egypt our meticulous record-keeping combines with the polite regularity of the Nile to preserve knowledge of the past, so we Egyptians do not lose all the accumulated skills of earlier eras. And it is for this reason, he maintained, that we here in Egypt know what you in Greece do not: that at one time, before the greatest of the floods,

> what is now the Athenian state was the most valiant in war and su-premely well ordered in all other respects as well. It possessed, it was said, the most beautiful works of art and constitution of any nation on earth of which word has come down to us. (23c)

It was this idealized Athens that turned back the hybristic attack of the legendary island of Atlantis on all of Europe and Asia as well. Only the *aretē* of the ancient Athenians prevented the powerful and imperialistic Atlantis from enslaving all of the known world (24c–25c). Afterward, however, both Atlantis and Athens perished in a cataclysm, vanishing into the sea. Plato, who had no use for Athenian democracy, deployed the venerable records of that most record-keeping of civilizations, Egypt, to forge his own version of the fictional "ancestral constitution" touted by the fifth-century oligarchs who sought to ground their notion of good government in a polity that had actually existed in an Athens of the past.

Though some, like Plato, made an exception for Egypt, neither Herodotus's enthusiasm for cultural variety nor his admiration for "barbarian" ingenuity was widely shared by his fellow Greeks. Beginning shortly after Herodotus's death, a variety of scientific writings explored explanations for the differences among the races and concluded unanimously that the Greeks were far superior. Around 400 the physician Hippocrates or one of his followers composed a treatise on the effects of climate and environment on health and character. Known as *Airs, Waters, Places*, the tract argued that the dispositions of each ethnic group corresponded to the nature of the country in which it lived. The dramatic change of the seasons, for example, combined with frequent rains, droughts, and wind to make the inhabitants of northern Europe wild and unsociable, albeit courageous. In Asia, on the other hand, the consistent climate was conducive to cowardice, indolence, and baseness (23, 24). Evidently the Greeks, with their homes in southern Europe, were not vulnerable to these disabilities. Aristotle too viewed the Greeks, who had the good fortune to live neither in chilly northern Europe nor in unduly mild Asia, as possessing an ideal character, writing that

> the peoples inhabiting the cold places and those of northern Europe are full of spirit but somewhat deficient in intelligence and skill, so that although they remain generally independent, they are lacking in political organization, and unable to govern others. The peoples of Asia, on the other hand, are naturally both intelligent and skillful, but they lack spirit, with the result that they are always in subjection— indeed, slavery. But the Greek race, just as it dwells in the middle position geographically, partakes of both characters. For it is both spirited and intelligent, and so it continues to be free and to enjoy excellent political institutions, and to be capable, were it to be united, of ruling the whole world. (*Politics* 1327b)

So little an Athenian booster that he was exiled for Spartan partisanship, Xenophon nonetheless suggested that Athens lay at the center of the world, praising its climate—plants that will not even grow in many places actually bear fruit in Attica—and natural resources. It would not be unreasonable, he concluded,

> to conjecture that the city lies at the center of Greece, indeed of the whole inhabited world. For the farther we go from it, the more oppressive is the heat or cold we encounter, and anyone who would cross from one end of Greece to the other whether by land or sea passes by Athens as the center of a circle. (*Ways and Means* 1. 6)

Some generations later an essay devoted solely to physiognomy outlined an elaborate system of classification by which different physical types were identified with distinct characters, most of them rather unappealing. The *Physiognomics* was evidently a composite text embracing the work of two men who followed the Hippocratics and Aristotle in deriving the dispositions of each ethnic group to the nature of the country in which it lived. The authors were in no doubt about the close connections between physiology and character. A nose broad around the nostrils, they maintained,

> indicates laziness, as witness cattle: but if thick at the tip, it means dullness of sense, as in swine; those whose noses are sharp at the tip are irascible, like dogs, while a round, blunt tip points to magnanimity, as in lions. Those with a nose thin at the tip have the characteristics of birds. When such a nose is hooked and rises straight from the forehead, it indicates shamelessness, as in ravens. (811a 28–36)

Like the author of *Airs, Waters, Places*, and like Aristotle, the physiognomists advocate a mean in all things. Those with small ears, they argue, have the disposition of monkeys whereas those with large ears are more like donkeys, while one will observe that the finest breeds of dogs have ears of moderate size (811a 10–12). Very short men being hasty and very tall men sluggish, "the man likely to prove most effective in accomplishing what he sets out to do and is most able will be the man of intermediate stature" (813b 30–35)—a stature characteristic of Greeks. The drawbacks of extremes form a segue to the insufficiencies of the various races. "Too swarthy a complexion," they write, "marks the coward, as witness

FIGURE 5.1. Janiform cup. This "Janus-form"—that is, double-faced—drinking cup dating to around 475 BCE demonstrates that already in the early fifth century the Greeks perceived themselves as radically different from Africans: indeed, as virtual mirror images. Princeton University Art Museum / Art Resource, NY.

Egyptians and Ethiopians," but so does too pale a complexion—as one may see from the complexions of women. So, they conclude, "the complexion that makes for courage must be intermediate between these extremes" (812a 13–15). Once again, the Greeks win out. They also drew connections between the cowardice of the Ethiopians and their extremely woolly hair: "southern peoples are cowardly and have soft hair" (812b 30). Mixing the races would have been an excellent method of attaining the mean, but this was not proposed, since Greeks conceived of ethnic mixing as a source of degeneration, not hybrid vigor. Greeks were not alone, of course, in identifying their own race as embodying the salutary mean between extremes. The tenth-century Persian geographer Ibn al-Faqih al Hamadham maintained that the Iraqis had "sound minds, commendable passions, balanced natures" as well as well-proportioned limbs and "a pale brown colour which is the most apt and proper colour," as they have been "well baked in wombs that do not expel them [prematurely] with a blondish or reddish colour, with grey-blue eyes and whitish eyebrows such as occurs to the wombs of the Slav women or those like them." The wombs of the Ethiopians, on the other hand, overcook children "until they are burnt, so that the child comes out something black or pitch-black, malodorous and pungent-smelling, with peppercorn hair, unbalanced limbs, a deficient mind, and depraved passions."[8]

———

In putting cultural distinctions on a firm racial basis, the pseudo-scientists of the *Physiognomics* conveniently justified much of Greek slavery. But not all. Although Greeks liked to believe that they did not enslave other Greeks, this was patently false. The helots were Greek. Toward the beginning of the Peloponnesian War the Spartans enslaved the women and children of Plataea (Thucydides mentions only women, but it is uncertain whether all the children had escaped to Athens); the Athenians then enslaved the women and children of several cities including Scione and Melos—and in the last years of the war the blood-thirsty Spartan admiral Lysander enslaved the inhabitants of Iasus and Cedreae in Caria, selling off the Greek and non-Greek inhabitants alike. Upon their victory over the Athenians and their allies in 413, the Syracusans happily enslaved thousands of fellow Greeks, and in 405 when news of Lysander's victory at Aegospotami in the Hellespont arrived at Athens, the Athenians were petrified, foreseeing that slavery might well lie in store for them as well. If Aristotle wanted to make an air-tight defense of slavery, he would have to develop arguments that went beyond race.[9] And he did. That some should rule and others be ruled, he argued, "is both necessary and expedient, for from the very moment of their birth, some are plainly marked out for the one, some for the other"

(*Politics* 1254a). The relationship of the householder to other members of the *oikos*, therefore, will be hierarchical in nature, but he will relate to them differently, for

> the free man rules over the slave in a different way from the manner in which the male rules over the female or the man over the child; although the various parts of the soul are present in all of them, they are different in each case. For the slave lacks deliberative capacity entirely; the female has it, but of an inoperative, unauthoritative kind; and the child possesses it, but in an immature, undeveloped form. (*Politics* 1260a)

The very fact of being defeated in war confirmed for Aristotle the inferiority that marked a person out as slave material. As for slaves who had not been captured in war, they demonstrated their naturally slavish nature by being . . . slaves.

Along with ancient commentaries on them, the body of Aristotle's work is one of our principal sources for the existence of anti-slavery sentiment in Greece. Some, Aristotle wrote in the *Politics*, "argue that slavery is against nature, since it is only by convention that one person is a slave while another is free even while they do not in fact differ in their natures, and that therefore slavery, being based on force, is unjust" (1253b). In keeping with their sensitivity to issues of *nomos* versus *physis*, several sophists pointed out that slavery was grounded in illogic and injustice. God, said Aristotle's contemporary the sophist Alcidamas of Elaea, "left all people free; nature has made nobody a slave." We know this from an ancient commentator's note in Aristotle's *Rhetoric* (Scholiast on 1373b 18–19). Though the occasional Greek questioned the rationale behind slavery, however, never in all Greek history did any abolitionist movement develop.

Aristotle was forced to concede that there were a few bugs in the system. Free people of noble natures might be captured in war, for example. The legends of the Trojan War had driven home to the Greeks the problems attendant on the enslavement of prisoners of war. The misery inflicted on the women of Troy after the city's capture formed the painful subject matter of Euripides' play *The Trojan Women*, and it

FIGURE 5.2. Banquet scene. This fourth-century BCE marble relief depicting a banquet was dedicated in a *hērōon*. The status of the individuals is indexed by their comparative size: the hero himself, reclining on the right, is by far the largest, his wife a little smaller, and the slave to the left far smaller, a common convention in Greek art. Michael C. Carlos Museum of Emory University, Carlos Collection of Ancient Art. © Bruce M. White, 2004.

was evidently in response to the destruction of Plataea during the Peloponnesian War in 427 by Sparta and its ally Thebes that Euripides composed his *Andromache*. The chilling execution of all the Plataean men who had not escaped the Theban night raid in 431 and the enslavement of the Plataean women and children seem to have made a deep impression on Euripides. The horror was surely heightened by the Athenians' close association with those Plataeans who upon their escape had been welcomed into the Athenian citizen body. *Andromache* provides a valuable window into the poet's thinking about the human community. In it the sympathetic characters voice an inclusive and egalitarian view of society while the patently unsympathetic ones speak harshly to and about non-Greeks and slaves. Andromache herself opens the play by pointing out the contrast between her position in Troy as the wife of Hector and mother to his son and her present condition, lamenting the harsh fate that became hers when she fell into slavery *anaxiōs*, undeservedly (99). The woman who had served her in Troy makes a point of continuing to address her as *despoina*, mistress, upholding the status differential between them, but Andromache, unfailingly presented in this play as a paragon of virtue, corrects her gently, addressing her as "fellow slave" and pointing out that the two of them are now in much the same boat (59–66).

The premise of the play places Andromache in a replay of the situation she endured at Troy. Once again she is helpless in the face of force majeure, once again a sentence of death is passed on her son. This time, however, it is not Astyanax, her son by Hector, who has been doomed but rather the boy she has borne to her Greek master Neoptolemus, Achilles' son, whose war prize she has become. For Neoptolemus now intends to take a Greek bride, Hermione, daughter of Helen and Menelaus, and Hermione has no intention of sharing her home with the foreigner and her brat.

The savage Hermione has back-up in the person of her powerful and thoroughly brutal father. One would be hard put to decide which of the pair is more disagreeable. Hermione sneers at Andromache, reminding her that she is nothing but a slave won by the spear. Fall at my feet! she says; sweep my house; take the water from my golden pails in your hands and sprinkle it (165–69)! Menelaus has Andromache dragged from the shrine where she has taken refuge, shouting that Hermione will choose whether her son will live or die. She must learn, he says, now that she has become a slave, to stop committing hybris against free people (433–34). Asia appears if anything morally superior as the Greek characters condemn themselves by their hostility to the "barbarians." The odious Hermione indeed has the nerve to echo the words of Homer's Achilles as she snickers at Andromache for sleeping with the son of her husband's killer:

You, wretch that you are, now have brought yourself
To sleep beside the son of that same man
Who killed your husband. (170–72)

Her words would inevitably have brought to the minds of Euripides' audience those of Priam to Achilles in Book 24 of the Iliad:

> I am more pitiful by far,
> Having endured what no one on earth has ever suffered:
> I put my lips to the hands of the man who has killed my sons. (24. 503–6)

But Hermione is no Priam. Typical, she goes on. That's the way all barbarians are: parents have sex with children and siblings with each other, people murder close relations (173–76). Plainly, however, the Bronze Age myths of incest and family murder that were the stuff of tragedy involved Greeks, not foreigners; inevitably the thoughts of Euripides' audience would have turned to Oedipus and the House of Atreus. It is for Andromache, the "barbarian," to assume the role of arbiter of morals. When Hermione is dismissive of her criticisms on the grounds that she is applying "barbarian" values to Greece, Andromache replies that matters of right and wrong are judged by a universal standard:

> Shameful is shameful, here as well as there. (244)[10]

Throughout the play Euripides undermines any notion that Greeks were superior to "barbarians," the free superior to the enslaved, and the elite superior to ordinary citizens.

The absence of any abolitionist movement in ancient Greece points to a stunning blind spot in the Greeks' purported proclivity for original thinking. So integral were slaves to Greek life that even utopias like the ideal city of Plato's *Laws* made abundant use of them—Plato devoted considerable space there to laws regarding slaves—and the ideal constitution framed by Phaleas of Chalcedon provided that "all the artisans should be slaves owned by the state."[11] All free people who were not poor owned slaves, and to the best of our knowledge it was poverty, not scruples, that constrained those who did not. We know little about the thought patterns of slaves. We do know how their owners thought of them. Comparison of slaves to animals both wild and tame were common; indeed slaves in Greece were often referred to as *andrapoda*, "man-footed things," on the model of *tetrapoda*, "four-footed things," used to describe livestock. Although in general, Xenophon wrote, people can be made obedient simply by pointing out the desirability of following orders, in dealing with slaves it is also "quite useful to employ the same strategies used with wild animals," giving them, for example, their favorite foods in abundance (*Oeconomicus* 14. 9). Although Plato's *Laws* specifies that in dealing with slaves both violence and excessive familiarity are to be avoided (777d), in fact, he advocated substantial violence against slaves. Many of the punishments for slaves listed in the *Laws* involve flogging, and as far as I know, the Greeks had not invented nonviolent "virtual" flogging over Zoom. The methods of controlling slaves that were standard fare are enumerated by Xenophon in a conversation he re-creates between Socrates and another philosopher, Aristippus. Consider, he depicts Socrates as saying, how people customarily treat shiftless slaves: "Don't they starve them to keep them from lechery, lock things up to keep them from stealing, clap chains on them to keep them from running away, and banish their laziness with blows? Tell me, what do you do when you discover that you have someone like that among your slaves?" "I punish him," Aristippus replies, "in every way possible, until I can get him to serve me as he should" (*Memorabilia* 1. 16).

Abuse of slaves did not necessarily hurt a man's reputation. Up to 30,000 slaves worked in the silver mines at Laurium in southern Attica. When the wealthy Nicias increased his already substantial income by renting out a thousand of his slaves for use in the mines, a particularly dreadful job that greatly shortened life expectancy, he promised that "all casualties would be promptly replaced" (Xenophon, *Ways and Means*, 4. 14), and Nicias was revered as one of the most upright men in Athens. The young Spartiates for whom a rite of passage entailed the nocturnal murder of particularly troublesome helots were rewarded, not punished. It was not only fear for their lives, moreover, that kept the helots in line. The Spartans practiced a thoroughgoing system of ideological warfare designed to overwhelm and demoralize their exploited servile labor force. To terror was added degradation. For easy identification, helots were required to dress in a humiliating costume featuring animal skins and a distinctive cap, and to impress on Spartan youth the evils of inebriation, the Spartans would compel helots to drink large quantities of very strong wine and parade them before the public messes in their drunken state; they might also command them to perform ridiculous songs and dances.[12]

The vital services provided both to individuals and to the state by enslaved people were routinely ignored. A particularly insidious conspiracy of silence concealed the participation of slaves in warfare. The geographer Pausanias in treating the Battle of Marathon states bluntly that "slaves fought then for the first time." Indeed, he says, they have their own grave there, and he adds later on that Miltiades freed them prior to the battle (*Description of Greece* 1. 32. 3–4, 7. 15. 7). One would never guess such a thing from Herodotus's account of the battle and the surrounding events. In recounting the heroic last stand of the 300 full-blooded Spartans at Thermopylae, Herodotus does not directly discuss the participation of anyone else from Sparta, but in his eagerness to underline the Persians' naiveté, he lets it slip. When the Persians went to inspect the Greek dead, he says, they assumed that all the bodies they saw were those of free men, "although they were also looking at helot corpses" (Herodotus 8. 25. 1).[13] Thucydides' narrative reveals that the immensely successful campaigns of the Spartan general Brasidas in northern Greece during the Peloponnesian War were fought with an army that contained 700 helots, and the Athenians' disastrous loss in Sicily in 413 was due in considerable part to the arrival of a force that included a significant helot contingent (4. 80. 5, 4. 78. 1, 7. 19. 3, 7. 58. 3).

Thucydides' narrative makes plain that slaves served in the Peloponnesian War as sailors. At 1. 55. 1 he identifies most of the Corcyraean sailors captured by the Corinthians at the Battle of Sybota in 433 as slaves. Probably a number of the Corinthian sailors were too, since at 2. 103. 1 he reports that not long afterward the Athenian admiral Phormio, following two victories over a Peloponnesian navy consisting primarily of Corinthian vessels, brought back to Athens such of the captives as were free men. Some, then, must not have been. The pattern seems to have persisted. In 411, when the Peloponnesian sailors were grousing about not having received their pay, it was the crews from Thurii and Syracuse who were most aggressive in confronting the Spartan admiral Astyochus, since they contained the largest proportion of free men (Thucydides 8. 84. 2). Where there is a proportion of free men, there is a proportion of unfree ones; plainly slaves were abundant throughout the Peloponnesian fleet. Yet of slaves in the fleet of Thucydides' own polis we read nothing. The chances that there were none are slim. It seems far more likely that Thucydides was as squeamish about acknowledging it as Herodotus had been about fully accepting the role of slaves in the heroic victory over the mighty Persian Empire. The conviction that fighting was the province of free men alone disposed Greek historians to gloss over the important role of slaves in fighting for the very people who had taken away their freedom.

———

If Greeks preferred that slaves be of a different race, many of them were convinced that women were. From Pandora, Hesiod wrote, came

> the deadly race and tribe of femalekind
> who live with mortal men, a thing of bane,
> no help in hateful poverty, but glad
> to share in wealth. (*Theogony* 590–93)

The notion that women were a race apart was echoed a few generations later by Semonides in verses probably meant for performance in front of a sympathetic male audience. "From the start," he explains, "the god made woman's mind to be different from man's" (7.1).[14] The various sorts of women, he contends, were created each from a different substance, each retaining the fundamental characteristics of the material from which she was made. He traced their descent from the earth, the sea, and most of all from various animals. From the earth was constructed a useless woman whose only skill is eating; from the sea, a changeable, volatile one, serene on one day, stirred up to ungovernable rage the next. Another sort of woman derives from the donkey:

> No easy thing to get this one to work,
> Although with blows and threats she'll buckle down.
> . . .
> Eating's her thing. She'll eat beside the fire,

Off in her room, she'll eat—all day, all night.
It's just the same with sex. She's glad to take
The first friend of her husband's who turns up. (44–49)

The weasel woman is equally eager for sex but is unable to find partners because she is so unappealing. The sole good female type derives from the bee; she will be a superb household manager and a source of illustrious and good-looking offspring. Most of all, perhaps, she has distaste for the one activity by which men felt most threatened:

She doesn't care to chat with other wives
When it appears the topic will be sex. (90–91)

Altogether women's mouths are trouble, used for overeating and overtalking. A married man, Semonides cautions, will always have hunger knocking at his door,

For women are the biggest single plague
Zeus has created. (115)

Greek men tended to believe that women were altogether too highly sexed. The blind seer Teiresias, it was said, had been born with normal vision. He had been changed into a woman by Hera after he impiously struck a pair of copulating snakes, and seven years later he was changed back. When Zeus and Hera were arguing about which sex experienced greater pleasure in sex, Zeus appealed to Teiresias to settle the dispute. Hera was so infuriated by Teiresias's revelation that women had not only more pleasure but indeed nine times more that she blinded him, and in exchange, Zeus granted him the power of prophecy. It is not surprising, then, that the ideal woman should have been identified with the bee, who was believed to reproduce asexually. In the mind of many Greek men, the less sexuality in a woman the better.

Not all Greek men who have left records of their thoughts shared the dim view of women put forward by these poets. Intelligent and sympathetic women play important roles in the Homeric epics, from Andromache and Helen to Nausicaä and Penelope. Someone plainly thought the clever sayings of Spartan women to merit preservation someplace where

Plutarch found them centuries later. Several tragedies of Sophocles and Euripides were grounded in considerable admiration for women's character and empathy for their lot: the devoted sister Antigone who risks—and eventually loses—her life to bury her brother's body, the dutiful wife Alcestis who agrees to die in her husband's place. Yet that lot was determined largely by laws and customs (*nomoi* in both senses) that purposefully circumscribed women's opportunities in a wide variety of ways—laws made entirely by men, and customs primarily by men as well. As feminist historian Marilyn Arthur Katz has put it, in the social and political structure of the polis, "women were recognized as an aspect of men's existence rather than as existants in their own right."[15]

Greek medical texts regularly discussed the female body by reference to the normative, male body, compared to which it was found wanting. The common belief that women's bodies were both moister—spongier— and cooler than men's was accompanied by a conviction that this difference resulted in females being weaker and more prone to disease, although modern science suggests that the opposite is true. The Hippocratics also identified another key difference between the sexes in the existence in the female body of a second sentient being—the uterus—and ascribed ill health in women to the roamings of this "animal within an animal." When the womb strays to the upper abdomen, they cautioned, women may have difficulty breathing and experience sharp pains in the heart; their mouths may fill with fluid; they may become unable to speak; their teeth may chatter, and their legs may become cold (*Diseases of Women*, 2. 126). Women who did not have intercourse, they argued, were particularly subject to "wandering womb" syndrome (*Diseases of Women*, 1. 7). Endowed with the power of movement, the uterus was considered by many to have a will of its own, and what it willed was to conceive. Plato attributed a variety of ills in older women to the wanderings of the post-menopausal uterus, cantankerous and frustrated because of its inability to bear a child. The origin of intercourse, he explained, was as follows: because cowardly men became women when they were reincarnated, the gods devised the desire for sexual intercourse as a means to unite the two sexes. Men developed sperm, which produces "a love for procreating by implanting a powerful desire for emission." For this reason the male genitals are ungovernable like an animal that is deaf to reason. In women, meanwhile, and for the same reason,

> whenever the womb, being an animal desirous of childbearing, is infertile for an overly long time, it becomes irritated and disagreeable, and wandering every which way through the body it blocks up the breathing passages and in so doing throws the body into the utmost distress and causes every kind of illness until the passion and desire of the two sexes unite them. (*Timaeus* 91b–c)

Greek men commonly believed that abstention from their natural purpose of childbearing was likely to make women ill and were prone to recommend marriage and motherhood as the cure for a variety of ailments—not coincidentally, the very conditions that suited men's need for the perpetuation of the *oikos*. Girls who remain unmarried, the Hippocratics explained, suffer during menstruation from impulses both homicidal and suicidal.[16]

Aristotle did not share his predecessors' belief in the "wandering womb," but he did share the conviction of Apollo—and presumably Aeschylus as well—put forward in Aeschylus's *Oresteia* (discussed later in chapter 7) that women contributed no genetic material to their offspring but rather simply babysat the embryo until the child was ready to be born. It was the insufficiency of heat in the female, he believed, that accounted for this and indeed formed the basis of the distinction between the two sexes. It also underlay his characterization of women as deformed men. Just as it can happen, he argued, that deformed parents sometimes produce deformed offspring but not always, similarly "the offspring produced by a female are sometimes female but sometimes male instead. This is because the female is, as it were, a deformed male" (*Generation of Animals* 737a25). No wonder he believed that men needed to exercise authority over such deficient creatures. Women, he maintained, albeit more compassionate than men, were less truthful, more impulsive, and prone to mischief. The authors of the *Physiognomics* viewed sex differences similarly, contending that women and the female animals "have a more malicious nature than the male, as well as being more impulsive and less courageous," whereas "males are in every respect the opposite, being braver and more just" (809b 1–4, 12–14). A large, shapely and well-articulated foot, the text argues, betokens a strong character, as witness the male sex, whereas "a small, narrow, ill-articulated foot, attractive to the eye but feeble, indicates a weak one, as in the female sex" (810a 18–20). Pointy, bony hindquarters are the mark of a strong character, as witness males, fat and fleshy ones of a weak one, as witness females (810a 85–87). Similar contrasts are made with respect to calves, backs, sides, necks, and hair. Overall, the authors conclude, the clearest distinction offered by nature is the principle of female inferiority, both physical and characterological (814a 6–10).

Viewed as lascivious, unstable, deceptive, and of limited capacity, throughout much of Greece, and certainly in Athens, women were, at least in theory, confined to their homes unless constrained by poverty to leave them. Citizen woman and industrious housewife were synonymous; it is in this context that vase paintings normally portray her.

Householders who could afford to do so often constructed their homes so as to provide separate quarters for the sexes, with the result that dinner guests—men sometimes accompanied by *hetairai*—ate unseen by the women and girls of the house, who remained sequestered in their own quarters. Not surprisingly, reality threw obstacles in the way of these bourgeois ideals. As Aristotle observed, it is hopeless to prevent poor women from leaving their houses (*Politics* 1300a). Since many families throughout Greece were extremely poor, there must have been a good number of women in the streets and the marketplaces. Both literature and vase painting, moreover, make plain that women visited one another, attended funerals, visited male relatives in prison, gathered at wells to not only draw water but also converse, and were eager participants in the religious festivals that dotted the calendar.[17] The frequency with which Greek men were prone to cite the line from Sophocles' *Ajax* "Adornment for a woman lies in silence" (284) makes clear that Greek women were not naturally inclined to be timid and self-effacing. For people who were supposed to be neither heard nor seen, women in the Greek world were plainly both heard and seen a good deal. Socrates' mother Phaenarete, a midwife, certainly made house calls, as did others of her profession.

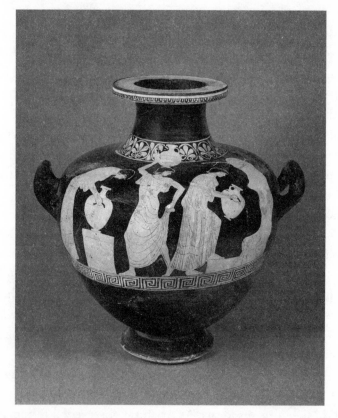

FIGURE 5.3. Women at a fountain house. Leaving their homes to gather water from a fountain house offered women a welcome opportunity to gather and chat with friends from other households. © RMN-Grand Palais / Art Resource, NY.

It is no coincidence that the man best known to us for taking females seriously as fully developed beings was born a good distance from Athens in Ionia, where the little evidence we have suggests that women's lives were less constricted. Women are mentioned hundreds of times in Herodotus's *Histories*. Greeks who read Herodotus's work or heard him recite from it learned of societies as different from the universe they knew as those of science fiction are from daily life today. In the strange new worlds of which Herodotus spoke, women might aspire to an agency from which they were cut off in classical Greece except on the stage. They play pivotal roles in history. When Astyages, king of Media, tries to make away with his grandson Cyrus, it is Spaco, a shepherd's wife, who rescues the infant and raises him as her own child (1. 110–113). Given a new lease on life by one woman, Cyrus, who goes on to found the Persian Empire, eventually meets his death at the hands of an army commanded by another—the formidable Tomyris, queen of the Massagetae (1. 214).

Women in mainland Greece did not enjoy similar opportunities, at least not before the Hellenistic Age. The intensely competitive civic environment of the polis affected out-groups in a variety of ways. Not only were the perquisites of citizenship carefully guarded against outsiders, with participation in government withheld from immigrants and manumission of slaves unusual; in most poleis, the fact that women were second-class citizens worked to diminish the regard in which they were held by men. Greek public life was strikingly homosocial, and the bonds that seem to have mattered most in a man's life were those they developed with other active citizens and citizens-to-be, that is, boys. This left women in the cold. Though the women of the polis might be citizens in the sense that they were neither slaves nor resident aliens, were able to bear citizen children, and could hold priestesshoods, they were decidedly not citizens in the sense that they performed citizenship daily in the assembly, in the council, in the courts, and in the animated discussions about policy that took place in the agora (although the occasional spunky women might intrude herself into the agora chit-chat). They could not offer a man the ego boost of being singled out as a partner by a member of the men's club that was the beating heart of the polis. While this may go a long way toward explaining the high incidence of homoerotic relationships among the elite, to whom politics was the stuff of life—these relationships were less common in other social classes—it fails to account for the customary age difference. The paederastic relationships in Greece by definition (the word comes from *pais*, child/adolescent and *erōs*, sexual passion) involved a grown man (the *erastēs*, in Greek: the lover) and a teenage boy, (the *erōmenos*: the beloved).

The origins of the custom are much debated, as is its connection with education. It seems to postdate Homer and Hesiod—or at least its respectability does. Such relationships are lacking in the Homeric epics—some

Greeks like Aeschylus were confident that the relationship between Achilles and Patroclus was sexual, but there is no evidence for that—and Hesiod's vast corpus of myths includes no homoerotic ones. As we have seen, the myth of Zeus and Ganymede, normally perceived as involving erotic attraction on Zeus's part, was sanitized in the *Iliad*. It may have originated in initiation rituals and rites of passage. Certainly this was the case in Crete, where traditionally an adult male, having obtained the approval of his beloved's father, would enlist his friends in the abduction of an adolescent boy. Once carried off, the youth would retire for two months to the countryside with his suitor, where they would spend their time hunting and feasting on their prey. At the conclusion of this interval, his suitor would present the youth with gifts that included military attire, marking his entry into the adult world of warriors.

Paederastic relationships between a grown man and a teenage boy were common and approved among the elite throughout Greece. It may be that heterosexual relationships were more fulfilling in the stratum of society that did not hold out much hope of guiding government policy. I suspect that marriages were happier in nonelite households, where spouses were less likely to have been chosen for political advantage. Certainly Aristophanes' *Lysistrata* suggests that in many family units the marital bond was anything but inconsequential. Indeed, given that poor women were compelled to go out of the house while richer ones were under orders to guard their chastity by remaining always indoors, some girls from the lower classes may have struck up relationships with males whom they later chose as husbands. Among the elite, however, the segregation of the sexes meant not only that married couples were often strangers to one another at their wedding but that outside of his immediate family, the people a man was likely to encounter in his daily life were nearly all male. An elite youth would learn the values of his society by socializing with older men at symposia, where homoerotic connections were celebrated and homoerotic verses recited—and where a great deal of flirtation went on. The body that most interested Greek men of the Classical Age was the beautiful young male body, and it was that form that dominated sculpture. Only in the Hellenistic Age did women's bodies become objects of interest and imagination. The symbol of fertility was the phallus rather than the breast, and it was often on display, whether attached to a body or not; its image might well be carried in religious processions.

These relationships by no means precluded future heterosexual marriage. Every Greek man was expected to marry, and nearly all did (Solon and Plato being glaring exceptions to the rule), for the perpetuation of the *oikos* was a major preoccupation. The Theban poet Pindar wrote of the way a man's heart swells with delight when his wife surprises him in his later years with a son at last:

> For to a man who finds himself on the verge of death
> Nothing can be more hateful than the thought of a stranger,
> Master of some other home, coming in and taking possession
> Of everything that he owns. (*Olympian* 10, 88–90)

Some men continued to have sexual relations with adolescent boys after marriage. Same-age homoerotic relationships, however, were frowned on, and it is here that the most conspicuous element of the paederastic relationship comes to the fore: its clear definition of roles, marking out the *erastēs* as the pursuer and the *erōmenos* as the pursued, the *erastēs* as the active partner and the *erōmenos* as the passive one, the *erastēs* as the giver of gifts (something not so easy for poor men) and the *erōmenos* as the recipient, the *erastēs* as the one who contributed his wisdom and status and the *erōmenos* as the one who offered his youth and beauty.

The *erastēs* was riding a wave of passion for the youth, while the youth was graciously allowing him access, basking in his lover's admiration. Among the countless vase paintings depicting paederastic courtship, none portrays the *erōmenos* with an erection. Although there were surely many exceptions, protocol dictated that whatever the adolescent derived from the relationship, it was only the adult who would experience arousal and ejaculation.

The passive role in sex, however, was completely unacceptable for a male citizen. It made the adolescent into a surrogate female, blurring gender boundaries, and no such individual could perform the role of citizen. Convention suggested that the relationship had to end when the

FIGURE 5.4. Suitors bringing gifts. The inequality in the relationship of the *erastēs* and the *erōmenos* was reflected in the custom of the older male courting the younger with gifts, never the other way around. Erich Lessing / Art Resource, NY.

teenager began to grow a beard. Although this was by no means always the case, it was not acceptable for a Greek adult active in politics, speaking and voting in the assembly, to be the passive partner in a sexual relationship. It was one thing to be temporarily "feminized" in adolescence and another to continue this behavior into adult life. The extreme of passivity, the allowing of anal penetration, was a subject of some anxiety, and it seems likely that what the *erastēs* aspired to was to ejaculate between the thighs of the *erōmenos*. In both comedy and oratory a standard insult was to accuse a man of playing the passive role in homoerotic sex. Aristophanes' standard term of disparagement was *euruprōktos*, "wide-anused," and the playwright manifested a concomitant fascination with anal activities in general. Farting, defecation, and constipation receive frequent mention, although invariably in the context of men: to peruse the corpus of Aristophanic comedy, one would imagine that Greek women were born without anuses. Because of the exclusion of women from political life, homoerotic relationships afforded men the only opportunity to be accepted by a partner of their own status— another male citizen—in a way that heterosexual relationships did not. Although to some extent the same power differential obtained in paederastic relationships, there was still something of an even trade between the status of the *erastēs* and the youthful beauty of the *erōmenos* (much as there still is in many heterosexual relationships today).

We cannot know what it was like for women to know that rivals for a man's affection included not only other women but teenage boys as well. Although there was in theory no conflict between impulses heterosexual and homosexual, the attraction felt by men for other members of the "men's club" that was the Greek polis must surely have had some effect on those who found themselves out in the cold. A fragment of Pindar opposes the appropriateness of desire for a lovely boy to the ignobility of materialism and the baseness of attachment to a woman:

> Ah, any man who catches with his glance
> The rays that flash from Theoxenus's eyes
> And is not tossed upon desire's waves
> Must have a heart that's black indeed—of steel
> Or iron, forged within a chilly fire!
> By Aphrodite with her crescent brow
> Such a man has been scorned. Perhaps he toils
> Compulsively for money; then again, perhaps
> The insolence of woman drags him down
> Along the cold, cold path of slavery.
> But I, by Aphrodite, when I gaze
> Upon the fresh limbed youth that graces boys,
> I melt just like the wax of holy bees
> That softens underneath the sun's hot rays. (Fragment 123)

Pindar may well not be speaking in his own voice here—the poem may have been commissioned by Theoxenus's suitor—but the construct in which attachment to a woman is compared to crass acquisitiveness and contrasted with the purer passion for a boy is striking. The decreased preoccupation with politics and the turn toward family life in the Hellenistic Age seems to have accentuated a shift in the balance between paederastic and marital relations that began in the fourth century, when heterosexual romances undergird the plots of New Comedy. One of the most celebrated passions of the third century was that of Seleucus's son Antiochus for his young stepmother Stratonice; Plutarch and Appian both tell how Seleucus generously allowed them to marry.[18] Paederasty, however, continued as a prominent feature of social life throughout Greek history; much Hellenistic love poetry, such as that of Theocritus and Callimachus, concerns the love of men for boys.

Did the male paederastic relationship have a female counterpart? This may be what we see in Artemis's passionate attachments to her nymphs. Sappho in Lesbos certainly expressed *erōs* for other females, but it's not clear that these were younger women to whom she was in a mentoring relationship. The conjecture that much of Sappho's poetry was addressed to the young pupils at a school of some kind that she ran may well arise from a modern discomfort with female eroticism. There is no evidence of this purported school.[19] Plutarch maintained that institutionalized paederasty was so highly thought of in Sparta that worthy Spartan women became lovers of adolescent girls, but no other evidence supports this contention.[20] Art historian Lauren Hackworth Petersen's search for homoerotic scenes of two women turned up only three images, and in these it is not possible to determine the age of the participants.[21] But of course this paucity may attest only to male unease with, even revulsion from, love between women.

It is a profound irony that it should have been a pupil of Aristotle who forged a new world that called into question many of the distinctions and hierarchies so integral to Greeks' construction of their world. By uniting west and east, Greek and non-Greek, into a huge empire, Alexander laid the groundwork for a much more fluid perception of Greek identity. Even in old Greece, a fragment from the comic dramatist Menander dating from around 300 depicted a character defending non-Greeks to his mother by citing the example of the Scythian philosopher Anacharsis, that rare metic who actually became an Athenian citizen:

> Mother, the man whose natural bent is good
> Counts as well-bred. No matter if he comes
> From Ethiopia! A Scyth, you say
> Is someone we should fear. Not so!
> Was Anacharsis not a Scythian? (9. 72 Fragment 533 Koch)

When Greeks fanned out to the cities of the former Persian Empire, multi-ethnic states developed that redefined the concept of Greekness. In managing their kingdoms Alexander's successors built a bureaucracy made up of both transplanted Greeks on whose loyalty they could count and on native elites whose knowledge of local customs, languages, and personnel was irreplaceable in ensuring cooperation from their subjects. As a knowledge of English was in colonial India (and still is in many countries today), a knowledge of Greek was a prerequisite for advancement. The term "Greek" came to embrace not only those who hailed from old Greece and their descendants but a wide variety of people who had adopted Greek customs, received a Greek education, and in many cases even taken Greek names, like the Babylonian governor of Gilgamesh's city, Uruk. Born Anu-Ubllit, he adopted the name Cephalus, married a Greek woman, and gave his children Greek names.[22] The Carthaginian philosopher Hasdrubal adopted the Greek name Clitomachus and settled in Athens, becoming the head of Plato's school the Academy in 129 (Diogenes Laertius 4. 10). We might call these people "honorary Greeks."

Women, moreover, found many more avenues open to them in the Hellenistic world. Marriage was often (not always) less confining; many marriage contracts granted wives the right to end their marriages entirely on their own initiative, whereas in classical times they generally needed the support of a male relative and the approval of a magistrate. Although the only people who could take advantage of land grants from the Ptolemies in exchange for army service were men, women could and did inherit such land, first as wives and finally in the first century BCE as daughters. In terms of rental, the papyri show some women as both lessors and lessees, and as both lenders and borrowers of money. Women worked outside the home to a far greater extent than they had during the Classical Age, mostly in the same professions as before: wet nursing, the clothing industry, and the preparation of food and drink. Beer had been popular in Egypt for centuries, and women there both brewed and sold it; one mother-daughter business was a beer shop.[23] More women became educated, some even studying medicine and practicing obstetrics, and we hear of women painters and poets.

It is to this era that nearly all female-authored ancient Greek texts date. Not until the fourth century did women in the Greek world learn to read and write in significant numbers, and though some archaic and classical women were no doubt active in the plastic arts, we are not able to identify their work. Recovering female consciousness from the male-authored texts and works of art of these eras is a challenging, often hopeless, task. The sentiments put into the mouths of female characters by the fifth-century playwrights, for example, may or may not be an accurate reflection of women's thought patterns. Female-authored texts from the Hellenistic kingdoms, however, offer a window into what women might be thinking and feeling, although all that survives is some letters and some mostly short poems. Letters make clear that not all Hellenistic women were shy about asserting themselves and their claims to respectful treatment. Zenon, a bureaucrat and estate manager in Egypt, was on the receiving end of numerous complaints. Simale complains about the beatings administered to her son Herophantus. Haynchis asks for help recovering her daughter from the married man who has run off with her; she is getting on in years and needs her daughter's help in her beer emporium. Senchon needs her donkey back, which one Nicias had taken.[24] In 168 BCE Isias wrote an exasperated letter to her husband Hephaestion, whom she suspected of inventing excuses for not returning home on schedule from some sort of religious retreat. Although she was delighted (or so she says) to learn from his letter that he is well (for which she thanks the gods), nonetheless, she writes,

> about your not coming home, when all the others who had been secluded there have come, I am ill-pleased, because after having

piloted myself and your child through such bad times and been driven to every extremity owing to the price of corn I thought that now at least, with you at home, I should enjoy some respite, whereas you have not even thought of coming home nor given any regard to our circumstances, remembering how I was in want of everything while you were still here, not to mention this long lapse of time and these critical days, during which you have sent us nothing. As, moreover, Horus who delivered the letter has brought news of your having been released from detention, I am thoroughly ill-pleased. Notwithstanding, as your mother also is annoyed, for her sake as well as for mine please return to the city, if nothing more pressing holds you back. You will do me a favor by taking care of your bodily health. Goodbye.[25]

Antipater of Thessalonica in northern Greece assembled a list of female poets, nine in number. They were, he said,

> women with voices divine whom Helicon nurtured in song,
> Helicon and the rock of Pieria in Macedon. (*Greek Anthology* 9, 26)

Praxilla, Moero, Anyte ("the female Homer"), Sappho, Erinna, Telesilla, Corinna, "female-tongued" Nossis, and Myrtis all found places on the list. The nine corresponded both to the nine muses and to a list made up in Alexandria of nine canonical lyric poets: Alcman, Sappho, Alcaeus, Anacreon, Stesichorus, Ibycus, Simonides, Bacchylides, and Pindar. Of the women catalogued by Antipater, most date from the Hellenistic Age, although Sappho wrote during the late Archaic Age and Corinna's date is uncertain. Women do not seem to have composed in as many genres as men. As classicist Kathryn Gutzwiller has pointed out,

> The reason that women seem not to have composed in the genres of epic, elegy, and drama has to do not only with the often public, sometimes even Panhellenic, setting for the performance of these genres, but also with their traditional function in defining Greek patriarchal culture. The grand epics that memorialized the military achievements of mythical heroes, the elegies that conveyed the ethical standards of Greek culture to male citizens at symposia, the dramas that

reinforced or interrogated civic values in democratic Athens were, through origin and custom, the province of male poets. Women, however, had their own traditions of oral song—including lament, love lyric, and lullaby—which must have been passed down from mother to daughter without the scrutiny of a male audience.[26]

The verses by women that were written down and survived represent a tiny fraction of these compositions. Most poems are, or appear, short, either because only a fragment survives or because they were intended to be so. An exception is the *Distaff of Erinna*, a plangent lament for the poet's childhood friend Baucis quoted later in this chapter, in which Erinna utilizes the tradition of a woman's lament for a war hero reported in epic (such as those for Hector included in the *Iliad*) to speak directly to a dead person who was not a famous man but rather a beloved female friend. Laments for women who died young account for a good deal of women's surviving poetry. Anyte mourned the death of young Thersis:

> Your mother gave you not the solemn rites
> Of marriage, Thersis, but instead, a maid
> Looking much like you, beautiful and tall,
> To stand in marble on your tomb; still now
> That you have passed from us, we speak to her
> And feel that we are reaching out to you. (*Greek Anthology* 7. 649)

The delights of children's play come alive in Anyte's lines about a billy-goat:

> The children, billy-goat, have decked you out
> In purple reins, muzzled your bearded face,
> And train you now to race just like a horse
> Around the god's temple; they all rejoice
> To think he looks upon their childish joy. (*Greek Anthology* 6. 312)

Women might put words in a male speaker's mouth just as male poets did in those of women. In one of her hymns Praxilla from Sicyon in the Peloponnesus depicts Aphrodite's mortal lover Adonis enumerating the most beautiful things he had left behind in dying:

Most precious of the things I leave behind
Is sunlight; after that, the brilliant stars,
The bright face of the moon shining above,
And ripe cucumbers; apples too, and pears. (747)

Others admired and preserved female-authored compositions. Meleager, for example, a famous collector of epigrams, made a point of including in his collection the work of the Locrian Nossis quoted in chapter 4. Inevitably, some men snickered at women poets. The very collocation that takes this poem beyond the realm of cliché won Praxilla nothing but contempt from the second-century CE Greek rhetorician Zenobius, who in his *Proverbs* explained why stupid people were known as "sillier than the Adonis of Praxilla." Citing these lines, he maintained that "nobody with half a brain would classify cucumbers and the rest with the sun and the moon."[27] Nossis, whose lost love poetry appears to have been addressed to women, was savaged by Herodas, the originator of the new genre of mime-iamboi, *mimiamboi*. Though he seems to have been based in the east and spent a good bit of time in Alexandria, Herodas was plainly familiar with Nossis's work, and one of the characters in his sixth mimiambos is referred to as "Nossis, daughter of Erinna" (6. 21), plainly an allusion both to Nossis as the literary heir of Erinna and to her identification of herself in terms of her mother and grandmother. Mimiambos 6 deals with the origin of a scarlet dildo seen in the possession of this "Nossis." She is plainly in bad odor with her neighbor Coritto, who insists that it was not she who had lent it to her. Even if she had a thousand dildos, she exclaims, "I wouldn't give one to Nossis, not even an old ratty one!" (6. 34–36). The mimiambos that follows is set in the shop of the cobbler Cerdon, which seems to be a front for an adult toy store, where "shoes" are in fact dildos, and he offers his admiring customers a choice of any number of styles, including not only the Nossis "shoe" but also the Baucis "shoe," evoking the lost beloved of Erinna's *Distaff*.[28]

Although the age was not devoid of longer works like Apollonius's epic the *Argonautica*, shorter ones were very popular. The Alexandrian court poet Callimachus is still remembered for his proclamation *mega biblion, mega kakon*: big book, big bad. From the time Greek civilization recovered after the Bronze Age collapse and began groping its way to the incarnations it would enjoy throughout the Archaic, Classical, and Hellenistic Ages, a vibrant and diverse literature that has offered us insights into the way their inhabitants viewed themselves and the world around them marked the various Greek states. From Hesiod's *Theogony* to the hymns of Callimachus, an enormous amount of that literature focused on religion, the topic of the chapter that follows.

Suggested Readings

Akrig, Ben, and Rob Tordoff, eds. 2013. *Slaves and Slavery in Ancient Greek Comic Drama*. New York: Cambridge University Press.

Arthur [Katz], Marylin. 1973. "Early Greece: The Origins of the Western Attitude Towards Women." *Arethusa* 6 (1973), 7–58.

Bettini, Maurizio. 2013. *Women & Weasels: Mythologies of Birth in Ancient Greece and Rome*. London and Chicago: University of Chicago Press.

Blundell, Sue. 1995. *Women in Ancient Greece*. London: British Museum Press.

Bowman, Laurel. 2004. "The 'Women's Tradition' in Greek Poetry." *Phoenix* 58, 1–27.

Bradley, Keith, and Paul Cartledge. 2011. *The Cambridge World History of Slavery*. Vol. 1, *The Ancient Mediterranean World*. Cambridge, UK: Cambridge University Press.

Demetriou, Denise. 2012. *Negotiating Identity in the Ancient Mediterranean: The Archaic and Classical Greek Multiethnic Emporia*. Cambridge, UK: Cambridge University Press, 2012.

Derbew, Sarah F. 2022. *Untangling Blackness in Greek Antiquity*. Cambridge, UK: Cambridge University Press.

Dover, Kenneth J. 1989. *Greek Homosexuality*, updated and with a new postscript. Cambridge, MA: Harvard University Press.

DuBois, Page. 2010. *Slavery: Antiquity and Its Legacy*. London and New York: I. B. Tauris.

Ferguson, John. 1975. *Utopias of the Classical World*. London: Thames and Hudson.

Figueira, Thomas, and Carmen Soares, eds. 2020. *Ethnicity and Identity in Herodotus*. Abingdon, UK, and New York: Routledge/Taylor & Francis.

Finley, Moses I. 1998. *Ancient Slavery and Modern Ideology*, expanded edition. Princeton, NJ: Markus Wiener Publishers.

Greene, Ellen, ed. 2005. *Women Poets in Ancient Greece and Rome*. Norman: University of Oklahoma Press.

Gruen, Erich. 2020. *Ethnicity in the Ancient World—Did It Matter?* Berlin: De Gruyter.

Hall, Jonathan M. 2002. *Hellenicity: Between Ethnicity and Culture*. Chicago: University of Chicago Press.

Halperin, David M. 1990. *One Hundred Years of Homosexuality and Other Essays on Greek Love*. London and New York: Routledge.

Hartog, François. 1988. *The Mirror of Herodotus: The Representation of the Other in the Writing of History*, trans. Janet Lloyd. Berkeley and Los Angeles: University of California Press.

Haubold, Johannes. 2013. *Greece and Mesopotamia: Dialogues in Literature*. Cambridge, UK: Cambridge University Press.

Isaac, Benjamin. 2004. *The Invention of Racism in Classical Antiquity*. Princeton, NJ: Princeton University Press.

Jensen, Erik. 2018. *Barbarians in the Greek and Roman World*. Indianapolis, IN: Hackett.

Keuls, Eva. 1985. *The Reign of the Phallus: Sexual Politics in Ancient Athens*. New York: Harper & Row.

McClure, Laura, ed. 2002. *Sexuality and Gender in the Classical World: Readings and Sources*. Malden, MA: Blackwell.

———. 2019. *Women in Classical Antiquity: From Birth to Death*. Hoboken, NJ: Wiley-Blackwell.

McCoskey, Denise. 2012. *Race: Antiquity and Its Legacy. Ancients and Moderns*. London and New York: I. B. Tauris.

Morrow, Glenn R. 1939. *Plato's Law of Slavery in Relation to Greek Law*. Urbana: University of Illinois Press.

Pomeroy, Sarah. 2002. *Spartan Women*. Oxford and New York: Oxford University Press.

Roisman, Joseph. 2005. *The Rhetoric of Manhood: Masculinity in the Attic Orators*. Berkeley and Los Angeles: University of California Press.

Romm, James S. 2021. *The Sacred Band: Three Hundred Theban Lovers Fighting to Save Greek Freedom*. New York: Scribner.

Sassi, Maria M. 2001. *The Science of Man in Ancient Greece*, trans. Paul Tucker. Chicago: University of Chicago Press.

Skinner, Joseph E. 2012. *The Invention of Greek Ethnography: From Homer to Herodotus*. Oxford and New York: Oxford University Press.

Skinner, Marilyn B. 2014. *Sexuality in Greek and Roman Culture*, 2nd edition. Malden, MA: Wiley-Blackwell.

Stoneman, Richard. 2019. *The Greek Experience of India*. Princeton, NJ: Princeton University Press.

Snowden, Frank, Jr. 1970. *Blacks in Antiquity: Ethiopians in the Greco-Roman Experience*. Cambridge, MA: Belknap Press of Harvard University Press.

Vasunia, Phiroze. 2001. *The Gift of the Nile: Hellenizing Egypt from Aeschylus to Alexander*. Berkeley and Los Angeles: University of California Press.

Winkler, John J. 1989. *The Constraints of Desire: The Anthropology of Sex and Gender in Ancient Greece*. New York: Routledge.

Wrenhaven, Kelly. 2012. *Reconstructing the Slave: The Image of the Slave in Ancient Greece*. London: Bristol Classical Press.

CHAPTER 6

Giving the Gods Their Due

Zeus, first cause, prime mover; for what thing without Zeus is done among mortals?

—AESCHYLUS, *AGAMEMNON*

Something has got to hold it together. I'm saying my prayers to Elmer, the Greek god of glue.

—TOM ROBBINS, *STILL LIFE WITH WOODPECKER*

Religion permeated Greek life at nearly every turn. Placating the gods who determined the success or failure of the crops was crucial to survival. Most Greeks were farmers, and even those who were not had to eat. Human fertility also depended on divine favor, as did success in war. The goodwill of the gods was also believed to reduce the dangers of seafaring, which posed a constant risk to both life and livelihood in an age lacking in navigational instruments—so much so that Greek literature contains numerous references to the fear of boarding a ship with someone who has offended them.[1] These gods were not always reasonable—they were capricious and changeable in the *Iliad*, and Euripides' *Hippolytus* showed a murderously vengeful Aphrodite—but they were always to be feared and revered. Although one could not except in the whimsies of Aristophanes and other fantasists visit them on Mount Olympus—it was nearly 10,000 feet high and was never scaled until the twentieth century—one could certainly pay homage to them in their temples and sanctuaries. The Greek calendar revolved around festivals of these gods, and myths about them also served to account for natural phenomena. Religious belief made sense of the world, and the prescribed rituals, if they did not guarantee success in it, at least made failure less likely. In contrast to many modern religions, it was ritual rather than belief that formed the core of Greek religion. When Achilles at the beginning of the *Iliad* proposes asking a seer or a priest why Apollo has sent a plague upon the Greek camp, he conjectures that the god has found fault with a vow or a sacrifice (1. 65), and when Phaedra is wasting away for love of her stepson in Euripides' *Hippolytus*, the chorus speculates that perhaps she is being punished for having failed to make the proper offering to the Cretan hunting goddess Dictynna (146–47). The conscientious performance of ritual was an obligation not only of an individual to a deity but of an individual to the community, for in the words of classicist Robert Parker,

> there was, in Greek belief, no such thing as non-contagious religious danger. Some dangers were more commonly seen as communicable by contact, while others threatened the guilty party's descendants; but the difference was one of degree rather than kind. Every member of any community lived in principle under threat of suffering for his neighbours' offences.[2]

In a speech written for a defendant in a murder case, the orator Antiphon adduced as evidence of his client's innocence the fact that his presence on shipboard had not caused the vessel to sink, nor had his involvement in a sacrifice prevented its successful conclusion, as would surely have been expected if he had been such a polluted individual as a murderer (5. 82).

———

Religion was both private and public, individual and communal, and in both its central ritual was sacrifice; it was when the polis came together to enact and celebrate the killing of a large mammal while asking for divine favor that it was most a community. The gods, it was believed, were delighted by the smoke that rose up to Olympus as the flesh from the sacrificial victim was roasted, a convenient fact that left the succulent meat to be devoured by the populace. Although small animals and, more frequently, vegetable matter—cakes were particularly popular—might be sacrificed at private shrines in the home, large mammals were the sacrificial object of choice at public events, chiefly pigs, sheep, goats, and cattle, cows and bulls being the largest, most expensive, and most prestigious animals. Elaborate rituals governed what took place before, during, and after.

Why of all things should the fundamental religious act of a community be gathering for the ritual slaughter of an animal? The story of how Prometheus tricked Zeus into accepting the fat and the bones while leaving the succulent meat for mortals explained why the animal was divided up in this way, but it did not explain why sacrifice should take place at all. Does it trace its origins back to a time when there was human sacrifice—or cannibalism? Was the animal a surrogate for something/someone else, and if so, what/whom? Does the sacrifice reenact some primal event early in the civilization's history, perhaps the killing of a father? Was it some sort of scapegoat rite in which all the transgressions of the community were concentrated in a single creature marked out as guilty while all others are innocent? Was the elaborate ritual surrounding the sacrifice a means of compensating the victim for putting it to death, and/or was it designed to build solidarity among the worshippers? Walter Burkert has suggested that banding together on the occasion of the animal's death militated against life-threatening divisions within the human community, as the animal absorbs all the internal tensions and rivalries within the group.[3] As Aeschylus observed, nothing binds a community together like a shared enemy:

> The cure for many an evil in the world
> Is hating the same object with a single mind. (*Eumenides*, 684–87)

And how important was the feast that followed the sacrifice? Was the taking of nourishment from the sacrificed animal fundamental to the ritual, a procedure whereby the killing is legitimized as necessary for the biological continuity of the group, or must the group partake of the sacrificed animal in order to dilute the guilt attendant on its slaughter? Is it all about the need to kill in order to stay alive, that is to say, to obtain nourishment/protein, or is it partly about that and partly about something else, or is it not really about that at all? To be sure, elaborate civic sacrifices resulted in substantial distributions of meat, but was this the purpose of the ritual or simply its result? Focusing on sacrifices in classical democracies, scholars like Jean-Pierre Vernant and Marcel Detienne have stressed the equal distribution of meat throughout the community and privileged the feasting aspect of the sacrifice over the killing aspect (though there was not likely to be enough meat for the entire citizenry).[4]

And where are the gods in all this? The previous questions explore sacrifice as a social phenomenon, which it most certainly was, but it was also an act of religious devotion. Why did the gods appreciate sacrifices—or not? After all, some offerings were not accepted, their concomitant prayers denied: chapter 4 of Fred Naiden's study of sacrifice, *Smoke Signals for the Gods*, is titled "When a God Says No." In Naiden's view, the social aspect and the emphasis on killing has obscured the central aspect of the ritual: an offering to, and interaction with, the gods.[5]

Greeks needed their gods—to ensure the prosperity of the community; to uphold justice in public and private life (oaths were sworn by the gods); and to provide a measure of comfort and security to individuals. And yet it was questionable whether the gods needed them back—indeed, whether the gods cared for them at all. Although gods might favor individual mortals as Athena favored Odysseus, they also might abandon their favorites at any time. In the *Iliad* Aphrodite threatens Helen:

> Do not provoke me, wretch. In my anger I might well forsake you
> Hating you just as ferociously as even now I do love you
> And might contrive grievous loathing of you in both warring parties,
> Danaans and Trojans alike; in an evil fate you would perish. (3. 414–17)

Zeus allows himself to be persuaded by Athena to abandon Hector to his death at the hands of Achilles. To be sure, the Zeus of the *Odyssey* is committed to seeing that fairness prevails among mortals, and both Hesiod and Aeschylus identified the king of the gods with justice. Even in the *Odyssey*, however, Olympian peevishness was a major problem, as witness the endless miseries heaped on Odysseus by Poseidon, and even when they acted in the service of restoring or reinforcing some sort of divine order, the gods were not always very nice. The pervasiveness of divine caprice posed a serious problem. What could mortals possibly do to gain the favor of such deities, favor that was indispensable for success on both an individual and communal level? Though the gods needed nothing from humans, surely there were things they might like?

Homer provided a number of suggestions. Only a few dozen lines into the *Iliad* he showed Chryses at prayer as he beseeches the god he has served so well to requite him by punishing the Greeks for the rough handling he has received at the hands of the hybristic Agamemnon, despiser of gods and men:

> Hear me, lord of the silver bow, you who guard Chryse
> and sacred Cilla, and rule in might over Tenedos.
> O Smintheus, lord of mice!
> If ever I roofed over a pleasing shrine for you,
> If ever I burned for you fat thigh pieces of bulls, or of goats,
> Fulfill for me this wish:
> With your arrows may the Danaans pay for my tears. (1. 33–42)

One answer, then, is prayer, and in prayer it is appropriate to speak of the services one has performed for a god. That, evidently, in addition to prayer, is what pleases gods: temple-building and sacrifice. And we know that Apollo hearkened unto Chryses' prayer and did indeed requite his tears, by sending a devastating plague into the Greek camp that wrought havoc with their war effort.

Part of Telemachus's education in the Odyssey involves spending time at the home of Nestor, who knows how to do things right, and his devotion to lavish sacrifice is the emblem of what is right in his palace—a pointed contrast to what is going on back in Ithaca. When Telemachus arrives at Pylos with the disguised Athena, Nestor is in the process of making a sacrifice to Poseidon of 81 black bulls, and before his guests depart the aged king initiates a sacrifice of a cow with gilded horns to Athena, whom he has recognized. The passage is one of the most detailed descriptions of Greek sacrifice that survives.

> Leading the cow by the horns were Stratius and noble Echephron;
> Aretus came from indoors with a washbasin lovely with flowers
> And in his other hand a basket filled with barley.
> Steadfast Thrasymedes stood by, holding a sharp axe
> With which to butcher the heifer, and Perseus held the bowl
> That would catch the blood when it flowed.
> The skilled horseman elderly Nestor started things off,
> Taking hold of the basin and grain and offering prayers to Athena,
> As he cut some hairs from the head and threw them into the fire.
> When they were done praying and had strewn the grains of barley,
> Noble Thrasymedes approached and struck the deadly blow,
> And the axe sliced through the sinews of the creature's neck
> Sending shock waves through the animal.
> Nestor's daughters and daughters-in-law and his wife Eurydice,
> Who was the oldest of all the daughters of Clymenus,
> Took up the sacred chant, and the men raised the head of the heifer
> From the broad-wayed earth and held it, and Peisistratus leader of men
> Cut its throat. Its black blood flowed out; it was alive no more.
> Immediately they cut the body up, removing the thigh pieces in
>   due order,
> And covered them with double rows of fat, laying raw flesh
> Upon them. The aged man burned the pieces on the logs
> And poured the shining wine over them. (3. 439–60)

Only when these rituals have been completed do they proceed to carving up the animal for general consumption and roasting the meat on spits. The creature would have been decked out in ribbons, and water would have been sprinkled on its head in a rather creepy ritual designed to demonstrate its assent to the slaughter: when it moved its head instinctively to shake off the unexpected drops, the animal was perceived as nodding in consent to what was to befall it.

To understand what Greek religion was, it is helpful to understand what it was not. Greek temples, for example, were built to honor gods, not to enclose congregations of worshippers; rituals generally took place outdoors at an altar, not inside a building. There was no day set aside each week for worship; Greeks knew no weeks, no sabbaths. Greek priests were not considered to have such special knowledge of the gods that community members would see merit in sitting and listening to them expatiate on the nature of divinity, elucidate the proper relations between gods and mortals, or school them in how they might best conduct their lives. Pastoral counseling was unknown. Those who found themselves at a crossroads in their lives might seek guidance from a friend or a relative. Young people would probably turn to an older sibling or a parent of the same sex; those with sufficient leisure and bodily strength sometimes undertook the trip to an oracle such as that of Apollo at Delphi. But to nobody would it occur to sit down with a priest and hash the problem out. Priests and priestesses were there to serve the needs of gods, not those of worshippers.

Normally attached to the cult of one particular divinity, priests and priestesses were proud of the positions they held and wont to commemorate priesthoods on their tombstones. A priestess would often be depicted holding an enormous key (to a temple), the priest a knife, used in sacrifice, though customarily priests did not themselves do the killing, which was generally carried out by another male; it was viewed as man's work, although there were occasional exceptions.[6] Sacrifice did not play the same prominent role in all-female festivals, such as the Thesmophoria in honor of Demeter and the Brauronia for Artemis.[7] Priests were also in line for choice parts of the sacrificial animals, normally the skins, which could be sold for considerable sums. For this reason, priesthoods were often bought. They might also be obtained by lot or by election, but many of them simply ran in families. The most famous hereditary priesthoods in Greece were those that supervised the mystery religion at Eleusis, shared for centuries by the families of the Kerykes and Eumolpidae.

Greek religion operated on several planes at once. First, there was the individual. Greeks often devoted themselves to a particular divinity with whom they felt a close and nurturing bond. For many women, this was Artemis, goddess of childbirth and the wild and possibly the most

FIGURE 6.1. Priestesses at a sacrifice. On this late fifth-century Attic amphora attributed to the artist known as the Nausicaa painter, two priestesses, a younger one on the left and an older one on the right, prepare animals for sacrifice by draping them with garlands. British Museum E284. © The Trustees of the British Museum. All rights reserved.

popular deity in Greece; men worshipped Artemis as well. A special bond with one god, however, would not preclude appropriate worship of others, at least not if people knew what was good for them. Euripides' tragedy *Hippolytus* showed the devastation brought on his entire family by the title character's worship of Artemis to the exclusion of Aphrodite. Next, there was the religion practiced in the household, conducted by the oldest male, the father or grandfather. Then came the religious events of the village or, in Attica, the deme; then the religion of the polis, enacted in state festivals, of which there were always many; and last there were Panhellenic events such as the Olympics, dedicated to

Zeus, or the celebration of the Eleusinian Mysteries, open to anyone, slave or free, who was free of crime and a Greek-speaker. And just walking around would bring a Greek into contact with the physical manifestations of religion. A stroll through the countryside—and most Greeks either lived there or owned property there—was likely to result in an encounter with a heap of stones by the side of the road. Such a heap was believed to embody a god, and the wanderer might show his piety by adding a stone to it. Should our wanderer cross a river, he would have in his mind that rivers were holy, and he might remember the prescription of Hesiod: never cross a river without saying a prayer and washing your hands in its waters (*Works and Days*, 737–38). He would most certainly not, like Xerxes, curse the waters or order them to be whipped. Youths who cut their long hair often dedicated it to a nearby river.

The countryside was dotted with sanctuaries of various kinds. Whereas an urban sanctuary might be as much as a hundred yards on a side or more, a rural sanctuary was likely to be a small enclosure that doubled as a boundary marker of polis territory, containing a modest stone altar or even just a pile of ashes where offerings had been burned. Beginning in the seventh century, temples could also be seen in the vicinity of cities and inside the cities themselves, some humble, some glorious. More common were shrines, *hērōa* (sing. *hērōon*), to heroes both male and female, which cost far less in labor and materials. Although there were (fairly uncommon) Greek words for a female hero (*hērōinē* or *hērōissa*), I hesitate to use the English word "heroine," as it has degenerated to indicate any female "co-star," however passive, whose only accomplishment lies in maintaining the good looks necessary to attract the attentions of the hero, so I will usually say female heroes. Like their male counterparts, female heroes tended to be revered in the particular place where they were believed to have lived and died. Thus Antinoë, daughter of the Argonaut Cepheus, received heroic post-mortem honors in Arcadia after she had determined the proper site for the city of Mantinea (so it was said) by following the guidance of a snake.

Sanctuaries and temples were set off from the more ordinary grounds around them and were to be treated with reverence—*aidōs*. A bowl with lustral water was placed at the entrance to sanctuaries to facilitate washing off any pollution. It was unacceptable to have sex, give birth, or die in a temple. Temples were places of refuge. When Pausanias, seeing that he was about to be arrested, took refuge in a temple of Athena, the Spartans walled him up until he was on the point of dying from hunger but took care to avoid the pollution attendant on death in a temple by dragging him out at the last possible minute to die in the open air. Thucydides, who reports this event (1. 134. 2–3), cites the Corcyraeans' murder of suppliants inside temples as clear proof of the depravity of civil strife (3. 81. 5). No woman who had been found guilty of adultery or man convicted of prostituting himself could ever again enter a temple. During the Peloponnesian War the Spartans came right up to the temple of Poseidon at Cape Sounion on the southern tip of Attica, but though they ravaged the surrounding land, they prudently spared the temple, fearing the god's wrath, and they similarly spared the sanctuary of Artemis at Brauron in northern Attica.[8]

————

The Greeks had many more gods than the twelve associated with Olympus; several Christian writers complained that they had as many as 365, one for each day of the year.[9] For one thing, each god had many manifestations. Athena, for example, might be worshipped in civic affairs as Athena Polias, Athena of the City, or by craftspeople as Athena Ergane, Athena the Worker. The Athenians built a temple to Athena of Victory, Athena Nike, and erected magnificent statues on the Acropolis to Athena Parthenos, Athena the Virgin, and Athena Promachos, Athena who Fights in Front. In Argos Athena was worshipped as Athena Oxyderkes, Athena of the Penetrating Gaze; the Spartans built a temple to Athena Chalkioikos, Athena of the Bronze House, perhaps because the goddess's cult statue there was made of bronze, perhaps because the walls of the temple were decorated with bronze plaques. Artemis Agrotera (of the wild) had a temple outside Athens on the Ilissos River. At Megalopolis in the Peloponnesus, the Temple of Zeus featured a triad of impressive statues showing a seated Zeus flanked by the goddess Megalopolis herself and Artemis Soteira (the Savior). Also worshipped in Perge on the south coast of Anatolia, Artemis Soteira acquired a cult and an altar on the island of Thera when in the late third century BCE one Artemidorus relocated there and transplanted her worship along with him. Artemis Aithiopia (of Brightness) was worshipped in Hellenistic Erythrae on the north coast of Anatolia. Aithiops also meant Ethiopian and is the origin of the name; it meant "burnt-faced," since that was how the Greeks regarded the Ethiopians' appearance.

There were also numerous Apollos and seemingly infinite Zeuses. In his conduct of the family worship, the householder could not possibly be expected to call on each and every one of these divinities, but he probably did make regular offerings to Zeus Ktēsios (Zeus of the Household Stores), Zeus Herkeios (Zeus of the Fence), and Apollo Agyieus (Apollo of the Street); Apollo Apotropaios (Averter of Evil) would also be given his due. The patriarch might also participate as a priest in the cult of a god or hero honored in the family's village or, in Attica, deme. A typical calendar for a given month in an Attic deme might go like the one historian of religion Simon Price cites for the deme Thorikos in southern Attica near Laurium, probably during the 430s, including sacrifices for the deity Korotrophos/Kourotrophos, a goddess construed as a protector of children and young people who had a sanctuary in Athens, the Kourotropheion, and a cult; Kephalos and Prokris were heroes:

Boedromion [August–September]. The Proerosia [a pre-plowing festival]. For Zeus Polieus a selected sheep (and?) a selected piglet. (For Zeus?) to Automenai a bought piglet, to be burnt whole. The priest is to provide lunch for the attendant.

For Kephalos a selected sheep, for Prokris an offering-table. For Thorikos a selected sheep, for the Heroines of Thorikos an offering table.

To Sunium, for Poseidon, a selected lamb. For Apollo, a selected kid.

For Korotrophos a selected piglet, for Demeter a full-grown victim, for Zeus Herkeios a full-grown victim.

For Korotrophos a piglet, for Athena a sheep, to be sold. For Poseidon, at the salt-works, a full-grown victim. For Apollo a piglet.[10]

Festivals were grand affairs and operated on many levels—religious, social, political, and even nutritional. Meat was not widely available to

Greeks, who were on the whole a poor population, and the offer of food at these events was a significant part of their allure. The processions, the dances, the choral hymns, were inspiring; an opportunity to mingle amid food and drink in a party atmosphere is always appreciated; and performances of poetry and sometimes drama were a welcome add-on. Altogether the affirmation of the civic bond seemed important enough to the government and the elite to foot the bill.

Most festivals welcomed participants of both sexes, but some did not. Women were barred from the cult of Heracles, for example, and men from the Thesmophoria. Held in honor of Demeter, the Thesmophoria was dedicated to the fertility of both the land and its people. It lasted for a period of several days ranging from three in Athens and Sparta to ten in Syracuse. It must have been a remarkable experience for the participants, whose lives were otherwise ruled by the demands of marriage and motherhood; it seems that girls and unmarried women were not invited to participate. On call day and night for the rest of the year, for the duration of the Thesmophoria women were accountable only to themselves and to one another. It must have had something of the air of a high school reunion, where the attendees had the opportunity to leave their day-to-day responsibilities behind and reconnect with childhood friends from whom the demands of domestic life had cut them off.

Different activities were scheduled at intervals in the festival, such as a period of fasting, a period of sympathetic mourning to support Demeter in grieving for her lost daughter, and a ritual that involved retrieving the decayed bodies of piglets whom the women had tossed into a ravine along with phalluses sculpted from dough. Sacred to Demeter, the pig was also associated with fertility and with femaleness. The word for a young pig, *khoirion*, did double duty as the word pussy does in English, denoting both a small animal and the female genitalia. Just how the piglets had met their end is unclear, but evidently the manner of their death was not central and did not involve the sort of elaborate sacrificial ritual that was associated with festivals where men were present.

Most remarkable of all the events that made up the Thesmophoria was the period of *aischrologia*, the "speaking of shameful things" that evidently entailed a free-for-all in which women were not only permitted but required to cast off-color insults at their friends and relations while swatting one another playfully with impromptu scourges of braided bark.[11] Would that we knew the precise verbiage deployed, but of this there is no record, for strict taboos prohibited divulging the details of religious rites—Alcibiades was sentenced to death for acting out the rites at Eleusis in front of the uninitiated—and those who knew them belonged to a sex that only rarely learned to write. What we do know is that for the duration of the Thesmophoria profoundly irreverent, transgressive behavior was encouraged. It was a veritable Semonidean nightmare: whereas Semonides' ideal wife was the one who recoiled from talking with other women about sex (7. 90–91), the participants in the Thesmophoria were obligated to do just that, and in as crude a manner as possible. Sex played other roles in the festival as well. Women seem to have consumed pennyroyal, which was known for a variety of reproductive functions, slept on the stems of willows, which had similar properties, and spent the night in makeshift huts they had made of pine, believed to aid in lactation. Most important, perhaps, the Thesmophoria must have served as a clearing house for the kinds of gynecological information that older women traditionally pass down to younger ones. Sexual talk can serve more than one function.

Two tales that explained the proceedings at the festival seem to fall in the category of myths that were developed to explain a ritual. When Persephone was snatched by Hades and sank beneath the earth, it was said, the pigs of the swineherd Eubouleus were swallowed up as well. As we have seen in chapter 1, moreover, the *Homeric Hymn to Demeter* told how while pining at Eleusis for her lost child the despondent goddess was lifted out of her dejection by the wisecracks of Iambe, from whom iambic poetry derived its name, and by the equally irreverent antics of the elderly Baubo. Archaeologists have turned up a number of Baubo figurines. The specifics vary, but the vulva are always prominent. In one Baubo rides a pig; in another she is seated with enormous vulva clearly visible between her legs; in another she is a headless torso, her face in her body and sporting vulva in its chin. In exposing what decorum dictated should be concealed, Baubo established the paradigm that gave the women license to speak forbidden words at the Thesmophoria.

The nexus of pigs, jibes, lack of inhibition, and female sexuality/fertility was central to the proceedings.

While undeniably religious in intent, the Thesmophoria also served as a safety valve for a group of people whose lives otherwise were lived under substantial constraint and duress. Although limited to adult women, and very adult in its emphasis on fertility and sex, it afforded a unique opportunity for a return to the carefree days of childhood and the attendant same-sex bonding and sense of play. The longest surviving fragment of the poet Erinna is a lament for her beloved childhood friend Baucis, who left behind the companions and pastimes of her youth first to marry and then shortly afterward to die. Erinna looks back wistfully at the time they spent playing a game in which one girl would play the part of a tortoise, evidently a variant of tag. The lines are broken, but seem to have meant something like:

> "Oh, no, I'm caught!" I cried aloud.
> Then I became the tortoise!
> I chased you briskly all around
> The yard of the great court. . . . (22–23)

No doubt many Greek housewives were nostalgic for their comparatively unencumbered youth. The opportunity for women to fulfill their social role while at the same time regressing to childhood lack of inhibition must have been delicious.

The calendar of the famously pious Spartans was structured around a plethora of festivals. Prominent among them were the Carneia and the Hyacinthia. Held every year in late summer, the Carneia, honoring Apollo, had both an agricultural and a military aspect. During the festival nine select citizens lived and ultimately feasted in each of nine tents set up for the purpose in the countryside. Everything in them was to be done at command, the aim being to instantiate life in army camp. The agricultural basis of Greek society was manifest in another event, a scapegoat ritual in which a man handicapped by being draped with woolen fillets and evidently representing a vegetation spirit was pursued by a band of youths; it betokened good fortune for the city if he was caught, bad if he was not. A ram was also sacrificed—*karnos* may mean ram—and there are also suggestive echoes of human sacrifice in earliest times. Herodotus tells a story of ongoing sacrifice in northern Greece to Zeus Laphystius (the origin of the epithet is uncertain). The descendants of the legendary Phrixus, he maintains, who was rescued from sacrifice when the ram of the famous golden fleece carried him off, were themselves sacrificed after being led in procession covered with ribbons (7. 197. 2). Oedipus, of course, was lame and twice driven out as a scapegoat, both at his birth and after his identity as his father's murderer was discovered.

The Greeks were intrigued by the notion of human sacrifice and, as in many other cultures, were quick to attribute it to other peoples—the Scythians, the Taurians (in Crimea), the Egyptians. Archaeology confirms the allegations regarding Scythia but not Egypt or Tauris. In truth, the Greeks' own legends contain numerous instances of human sacrifice, including several of the myths that congregated around the Trojan War: Agamemnon's sacrifice of his daughter Iphigenia to gain a wind for the Trojan expedition; the sacrifice of Priam's daughter Polyxena on the funeral pyre of Achilles; Achilles' own sacrifice of twelve Trojan youths on the pyre of Patroclus; and the story that appears in Herodotus about how Menelaus, becalmed in Egypt, sacrificed two Egyptian children to gain a fair wind (2. 119. 2–3). (Did this proclivity run in the family, or is the Menelaus story a doublet of his brother's?) Several of the plays of Euripides deal with human sacrifice, particularly the sacrifice of daughters, a phenomenon also known in other cultures. The popularity of the "virgin sacrifice" motif is overdetermined. It reified the sacrificial role assigned still today to women, who are pressured to surrender their autonomy for the perpetuation of society; celebrated the perceived sex appeal of helplessness in females; and of course derived in part from the fact that girls were considered more expendable than boys, who would work hard on the farm and perpetuate the *oikos*.[12]

The late spring festival of Apollo known as the Thargelia celebrated the first fruits of the new season and included a striking ritual in which two scapegoats were amply fed, led in procession through the city, whipped with various kinds of vegetation, and expelled from the city. One man was draped with white figs around his neck and acted as a purification for the city's men, another with black figs for the women. Historically, the scapegoat was someone at the bottom of society. In Athens, slaves and those considered particularly ugly were chosen. On the island of Leucas a criminal was selected and thrown off a rock into the sea. His fall was evidently broken by feathers attacked to his body, as it was not generally intended that the scapegoat should die. In Abdera a poor man was fed well, led around the city walls, and finally chased to the borders of the territory, pelted with stones. The ritual could also be deployed separately from the festival. In the colony of Massalia (Marseille), a man volunteered for the position of scapegoat during a plague. After a year of hearty food, he was expelled from the city. Curiously, those at the top of society could serve as scapegoats as well as those on its margins. Kings and other royalty might also sacrifice themselves for the community and had rather more motivation to do so. When the Pythia at Delphi proclaimed that Athens would not be taken by the Peloponnesians if their mythical king Codrus was slain, Codrus, it was said, disguised himself as a beggar and went among the Peloponnesians in the hope of being dispatched. His hope was realized, and Athens was saved.[13] The sacrificial death of Leonidas at Thermopylae provided the historical corollary. The Athenians told how when Athens was at war with Eleusis and it was believed the city could be saved only by the sacrifice of the daughters of King Erechtheus, the young women voluntarily gave up their lives. When Orchomenos was assailed by a plague, so the story went, the daughters of the hunter Orion ended the pestilence by sacrificing themselves, and the Greeks told how in the reign of King Midas a huge cleft opened up in the earth, to close only when Midas's son Anchuros jumped on his horse and charged into it, sacrificing himself for the community.[14]

Though joyous (for those who were not the scapegoat, and probably sometimes even for those who were), religious festivals were serious business. At crucial junctures during both the Persian and the Peloponnesian Wars, their celebration of the Carneia kept the pious Spartans from participation in military campaigns. The Spartans also interrupted their campaigns to return home for the celebration of the Hyacinthia, held in early summer in honor of Hyacinthus, Apollo's beloved from the Laconian town of Amyclae who had perished in the discus accident; out of his blood Apollo created the red flower that bears his name. The festival began in mourning for Hyacinthus's death and continued in celebration of his floral rebirth, which was commemorated with song and dance and goat sacrifice. At Amyclae itself there were parades of carts decorated by Spartan women and girls.

The "mystery religion" practiced at Eleusis some thirteen miles northwest of Athens was Panhellenic and more: it was open to anyone, free or slave, who knew Greek, and in time the Roman emperors Hadrian and Marcus Aurelius were both initiated into the cult, which held out the promise of a happy life after death—something not much on offer in traditional Greek religion. The rites were tied to the ancient myth of Demeter and her daughter Persephone, more commonly known simply as Kore, "the maiden." Because initiates were sworn to secrecy on penalty of death, we are in the dark about just what transpired in the huge hall known as the Telesterion, which fit 10,000 worshippers. There were, it seems, *drōmena* (things done), doubtless a reenactment of the story of Demeter and Kore; *deiknumena* (things shown), the display of sacred objects; and *legomena* (things said—to accompany the things shown?). Participants were not so much taught as they were transformed: what happened at Eleusis was not intellectual but rather experiential, and initiates evidently departed feeling that they had undergone a profound change for the better.

———

Knowledge both arcane and mundane could also be gained by patronizing the various oracles. Equivocal prophecies protected oracles against the danger of being proven wrong, and in this they were aided by the human propensity to literalness in interpretation, not to mention wishful thinking. Oracular utterances were rife with grammatical and syntactic ambiguities. Thus King Pyrrhus of Epirus in northern Greece, when about to make war on Rome, received the response at Delphi, "I say that you, Pyrrhus, the Romans are able to conquer." As in English, the text hinted that Pyrrhus would conquer the Romans but was also susceptible of the opposite interpretation, which turned out to be the correct one.

The development of sophisticated political institutions in Greece led to a drop-off in oracular consultations by official delegations after the Persian Wars. Democratic governments in particular had better ways of reaching decisions in the give and take of public debate. The states that continued to send to Delphi tended to be those in which such debate was less developed. As we have seen, the anxious Spartans inquired of the Pythia whether they should make war on Athens even though they had already voted that the Athenians had violated the Thirty Years' Peace (1. 118. 3). More personal questions posed by individual consultants, however, persisted, often concerning family and career matters. Second in rank and popularity to Delphi was the oracle of Zeus and Dione at Dodona, located in Epirus in northern Greece. It was very old, perhaps older than the oracle at Delphi, and Herodotus maintained that it took its origins from Egypt (2. 55–57). Though the priests there had originally been male, in historical times they were, like the Pythia, women; at Didyma in Anatolia women replaced men as priests from the time of Alexander. Whereas the limitations placed on women's mobility meant that most consultants at oracles were men, starting in the fourth century a number of women evidently visited Dodona. Queries posed at Dodona were inscribed on lead tablets, many of which survive. Shall I marry? Who are my parents? Would it be profitable to raise sheep? And my personal favorite: About those missing pillows and blankets— did I just misplace them, or did someone steal them?[15]

At least one inquiry at Dodona concerned the wisdom of hiring a magician to communicate with the dead. Many Greeks believed in magic, and in negotiating the world around them they deployed magical arts on what seems to have been a fairly regular basis. Whereas the Greeks had no word for religion, they certainly did for magic: *mageia*, they called it, for the first practitioners of magic, they believed, were the Persian priests known as the *magoi*. Some of their number probably made their way in the later sixth century to the Greek cities of Anatolia and moved westward from there. The foreign, eastern element in their rituals may in part explain the unsavory connotations that came to surround both the practices and the people associated with them. Magic, Robert Parker has sagely observed, "differs from religion as weeds differ from flowers, merely by negative social evaluation."[16] Though both religion and magic sought to manage risk and minimize anxiety in a dangerous and unpredictable universe, religion channeled human effort through supplication of the gods and was thought always to aim at the good, whereas magic sought to bypass or even overcome the gods and was believed to work for selfish, often immoral ends. Religious practices occasionally took place in private, but magical ones nearly always did; priests were public officials, but the practitioners of magic were frequently men and women on the margins of society. The practice of magic so alarmed Plato that in his *Laws* he included it among the most serious of crimes punishable by imprisonment. Those, he argues, who "promise to persuade the very gods by bewitching them, so to speak, with sacrifices, prayers, and incantations, and who seek in this way to utterly destroy not only individuals but entire families and states for the sake of gain" should be locked away in prison away from intercourse with all free people and upon their deaths be cast outside the borders of the state without burial (*Laws* 909b–c).

Magic for the Greeks entailed the use of spells, drugs ranging from love potions to poisons, amulets, and curse tablets. Women sought with spells and potions to win back the affection of irate or wandering partners; men sought to instill passion in indifferent ones.[17] The curse tablets are particularly intriguing. The more than 1,600 tablets that have been found scattered across the Greco-Roman world dating from shortly before 500 BCE to after 700 CE offer enormous insight into how and why Greeks cursed one another. Rivals in love and business were regularly cursed both preemptively to ward off their success in competition and out of spite when they had already worsted the author of the curse. Typically these tablets were very thin sheets of lead. Once the cursing texts had been scratched on them, they were rolled up, folded, or punctured with nails and placed beneath the earth, buried in graves or tombs, hidden away in underground sanctuaries, or cast into wells, though they might sometimes be nailed to temple walls. Some were accompanied by small figurines, frequently also pierced with nails, representing the object of the curse; often both the hands and the feet of the figurine were bound. Many curses were aimed at opponents in the courts, or at their male and female supporters. Other inscriptions seem to have been trade-related, like this elaborate one found pierced with a nail:

> I bind Callias the neighborhood innkeeper and his wife Thraetta and the inn of the bald man and the nearby inn of Anthemion . . . and the innkeeper Philon. Of all these men I bind spirit, work, hands, feet, and their inns.
>
>   . . .
>
> I bind the innkeeper Mania, the woman near the spring, and the inn of Aristandros of Eleusis and their work and mind. Spirit, hands, tongue, feet, mind. All these I bind in the . . . grave in the presence of Hermes the Binder.[18]

Another fourth-century tablet reads on one side:

> O Lord Hermes, Binder, bind Phrynichus and his extremities, his feet, his head, his hands, his stomach, his spirit, the stuff of his fat. O lord Hermes, bind his rear end. Restrain Kittus and his extremities, his spirit and his eyebrows . . . and of her . . . spirit. . . .

And on the other:

> Lord Hermes, bind Chaerylle. Also bind her extremities. I bind these of Chaerylle . . . I bind her hands, her hands [sic], her mind, the stuff of her spirit, the stuff of her head, the stuff of her heart, the stuff, her tongue.[19]

Unlike practitioners of magic, seers like Calchas in the *Iliad* were highly regarded. It bolstered their standing that unlike the practitioners of magic, who were of both sexes, seers were almost invariably male. The Greek word was *mantis*. Divination, *mantikē*—the root is the same as mania—was practiced both in the civilian community in peacetime and in the army in wartime. On campaign, omens needed to be taken constantly before such things as crossing rivers or state borders, and special rites needed to be performed to take the omens prior to engaging battle (though among the Spartans these offices were discharged by the king). The anxious Athenian general Nicias always traveled with his own personal seer, Stilbides. After Stilbides' death in Sicily, it fell to other seers to interpret the eclipse that occurred just as the army was about to depart after a devastating defeat in a night battle. By acquiescing in their determination that the army must not move for 27 days, Nicias doomed the Athenians and their allies, some to slaughter and others to slavery (Thucydides 7. 50). Seers were believed capable of deducing the will of the gods by interpreting such things as celestial and natural phenomena—comets, eclipses, lightning (especially when unexpected, as from a clear sky); the movement of water; human spasms such as sneezes; and, most of all, certain kinds of behavior related to animals both living and dead. Birds, who moved easily from the sky to the earth and back, seemed obvious intermediaries between gods and mortals; just how and from what direction they flew was believed to reveal divine intent. Hieromancy, the art of inspecting the entrails of sacrificed animals, was paramount and its practitioners much in demand. Inspection of the livers was most important—onlookers at a sacrifice eagerly awaited news of the formation and coloration of the various lobes. The art originated in Mesopotamia and traveled through Ugarit and the Hittite Empire to Cyprus and finally to Greece, where it seems to have arrived around 700.

Since they could be found all over and hence little or no travel was involved, seers were easier and cheaper to consult than oracles. Just how Greeks believed these seers had acquired their powers of divination differed from one instance to the next. Myth told how some early seers had received their powers directly from a god, as Apollo had enabled the Trojan Cassandra to see the future, or through saliva, as when Melampus acquired his skills in understanding animals after a snake licked his ears; Iamos, who, like Melampus, founded a dynasty of seers, had honey dropped on his lips while still an infant (Apollodorus, 1. 9. 11–12; Pindar, *Olynthian* 6. 66). Cassandra's abilities fall into the "poisoned gift" category. When she rejected the god's advances, he added a rider that nobody would ever believe her. Some seers were fortunate enough to be born into a seer dynasty like Theoclymenus in the *Odyssey*, descended ultimately from Melampus (15. 225–54). These families often expanded into guilds of sorts, as aspiring seers would apprentice themselves to members of the actual biological family. The skill might also be acquired through reading. A speech of Isocrates dated to the early fourth century tells how one Thrasyllus compensated for the lack of an inheritance from his parents by the money he made from divination after inheriting some books on the subject from a soothsayer friend (19. 5).

Divine messages might also come through dreams. The gods, Xenophon wrote, "know all things, and in sacrifices, in omens, in voices and in dreams they send signs to those they have chosen to receive them" (*The Cavalry Commander*, 9. 9). Homer told how Zeus decided to send a "baneful dream" to Agamemnon (*Iliad* 2. 1–6). Herodotus portrayed Xerxes' uncle Artabanus reassuring him about a disturbing dream by suggesting that dreams really just arise from what one had on one's mind during the day, but he is forced to backtrack and concede a divine origin for his nephew's dream after a parallel vision appears to him when he puts on Xerxes' clothes and sits on his throne (*Histories* 7. 16b. 2–18. 3). Not everyone was convinced that dreams came from the gods. In the next century Aristotle in his thoughtful essay *On Divination through Dreams* rejected the idea that the gods would send important messages to people when they were not fully in possession of their faculties (463b 15ff, 464a 20ff). But Greeks spoke not of "having" a dream but of "seeing" one, and most believed they came from outside the person and might well be of divine origin. As today, specialists were at hand to make money by deconstructing these, but individuals often felt free to make their own interpretations. In 401 Xenophon accompanied some 13,000 mercenaries as they marched into the heart of the Persian Empire on an expedition intended to replace the king Artaxerxes II with his brother Cyrus. When the two brothers joined battle, however, Cyrus was killed, leaving the mercenary army stranded in the heart of hostile territory. Xenophon then dreamed that a bolt of lightning fell on his father's house and set it on fire. Waking, he interpreted the dream to mean that in the midst of great perils he had beheld "a great light from Zeus" (*Anabasis* 3. 1. 12), whereupon despite his youth he exhorted the army to depart from Persia under his leadership. Many years later Ptolemy I introduced the cult of the god Sarapis in Egypt as a result of a dream (Tacitus, *Histories* 4. 83–84).

Incubation—the practice of sleeping in a temple or shrine in hopes of being visited by a god in a dream—was common, particularly where a healing deity such as Asklepios was concerned. A painful number of veterans suffering from ghastly war wounds visited the god's shrine in Epidaurus in the Peloponnesus. Anticrates from Cnidus, stuck with a spear through both his eyes, had been blind, he said, until he slept in the temple, where he dreamed that the god removed the spear and then fit his eyes back under his eyelids; when he awoke, his vision had been restored. Poor Euhippus had carried a spearhead around in his jaw for six years, but he reported that after he spent the night in the temple he awoke feeling fine, with the spearhead in his hands. Infertility frequently brought would-be parents to Epidaurus. Nicasiboula of Messene visited the shrine in the hope of becoming pregnant, and

> sleeping here she had a dream that the god approached her accompanied by a snake that crept beside him, and with this snake she had sex. As a consequence, children were born to her within a year—twin boys.

Cures might also take place while the patient was awake: a man from Ceos was cured of his gout when he walked over to a goose that bit him in the feet.[20] Not surprisingly, the twin traumas of the Peloponnesian War and the plague prompted the establishment of a cult for the healing god in Athens itself: on its arrival in Athens the snake that was believed to be the god incarnate lived with the playwright Sophocles before becoming ensconced in its sacred space in a new sanctuary to the god, the Asklepeion, on the south slope of the Acropolis.

Some sought answers not from gods but in astrology, a Mesopotamian import, although this method of exploring one's place in the universe did not really flourish until the Hellenistic Age, when the fusion of Egyptian and Babylonian astrological traditions resulted in an explosion of interest in the interplay of planets and people. When life on earth had witnessed the disappearance of the familiar polis structure and many found themselves living far from their original homes amid people of alien cultures, many turned to the skies for guidance about navigating their discombobulation. Unlike in the Classical Age when philosophy was the province of an elite who had the leisure to study with Plato or Aristotle, in the Hellenistic Age many sought the solace that the new schools of philosophy provided. Epicureanism and Stoicism offered appealing guides to life in the new world that appealed to all social classes and functioned for some as meaningful alternatives to religion, or at the very least as complements to it.

At the same time, however, the age was marked by a powerful spiritual thirst that propelled worshippers in an increasing variety of directions. The elasticity of Greek polytheism also left the door open to gods from outside Hellas, and the fusion of cultures prompted a reaction that was powerful in its explosive force. Eastern gods were sometimes assimilated to Greek ones by a process of syncretism (as was the Egyptian Ammon with Zeus), sometimes worshipped independently in their own right. From Phrygia in Anatolia came Cybele. First practiced by Greek colonists in the area, by the sixth century her worship had spread to the Greek mainland and even as far west as Italy and Sicily. As a mother goddess, she was associated sometimes with Gaia, sometimes with Rhea, sometimes with Demeter. Throughout Greece she was known as *Potnia Therōn* (mistress of animals), associated with nature in its fertility and with feral animals, particularly lions, who were often depicted drawing her chariot. City walls too were within her purview, and she may have been conceived as a mediator between the civilized and the wild. Her cult shared much with that of Dionysus, another god associated with the east. Although born in Greece and indeed the son of Zeus, the outlier Dionysus, because of his travels in the east as far as India, had a distinctly non-Hellenic feel. He too was depicted arriving in a chariot drawn by big cats, and worship of both gods entailed frenzied abandonment to wild music featuring the tympanon, a hand drum rather like a tambourine. The tympanon was a distinctly non-Greek instrument, and despite—or perhaps because of—her popularity, Cybele, like Dionysus, was regarded in some quarters with suspicion. Not surprisingly, both Dionysus and Cybele were immensely popular in the Hellenistic world, where notions of Greekness had become permeable.

The spread of Greek civilization to the east and south occasioned a concomitant explosion of religious possibilities. In mainland Greece and the west, the focus continued to be on the ancestral gods, but even there new deities made their appearance. Sizable Jewish communities were found in Corinth and Athens. Already during Alexander's lifetime the Athenians had allowed Egyptians to establish a cult of Isis in the city's port, Piraeus, and although the cult was initially intended for Egyptian devotees exclusively, in time a number of Athenians began to worship Isis as well. The island of Delos, which became a focal point of international trade, was home not only to cults of the powerful siblings who had been born there, Apollo and Artemis, but to a variety of new cults as well. There a devotee from Anatolia erected a temple to the Syrian mother goddess Atargatis, who was worshipped along with her consort Hadad. By the end of the first century the priesthood of Atargatis had fallen to an Athenian, and she had come to be worshipped by Greeks as Aphrodite Hagnē (pure) and Hadad as Zeus Hadatos, though the many non-Greeks on the island made their dedications in her original Syrian name. Immigrants to Delos from Berytus (Beirut) worshipped the Semitic god Ba'al there in the guise of Poseidon. In 1912 archaeologists excavating on Delos discovered a second-century synagogue that may be the oldest ever found. Ionian Erythrae was home to more than fifty cults, including a number of hero cults, but the personified female divinities that were characteristic of the age also had their cults: *Aretē* (Excellence/Virtue), *Eirēnē* (Peace), *Nikē* (Victory), and *Agathē Tychē* (Good Fortune). Though these personifications dated to archaic poetry, it was only much later, in the late Classical and Hellenistic Ages, that they actually had cults and were worshipped with sacrifices. The upheaval and deracination attendant on life in the Hellenistic world and the strains occasioned by the constant wars of Alexander's successors provided a particularly receptive atmosphere for the worship of Agathē Tychē, whose cults were spread far and wide. Increasingly throughout the Hellenistic Age her image appeared on coins minted in the Aegean, and she had statues and temples in small cities as well as the major metropoleis of Antioch and Alexandria.

The worship of Isis exploded throughout the Mediterranean. Known in Egypt since the third millennium, by the Hellenistic Age Isis had come to be worshipped as womanpower in all its manifestations. Like

Kronos and the Titans, she and her siblings Osiris and Set were born of the union of Earth and Sky. Osiris and Isis got along so well that they married, but Osiris and Set were always at odds, and in time, Set killed Osiris and dismembered his corpse. In perhaps the first attested case of woman picking up after man, the devoted Isis managed through great effort to chase down her husband's body parts and reassemble them; Herodotus was struck by the parallel between Isis's search for Osiris with Demeter's for Persephone (and in fact some Hellenistic Egyptians chose to worship Demeter as well as Isis). The story of Isis and Osiris gave rise to the belief that Isis might restore the dead to life just as she had done to her husband. Isis was worshipped not only as a wife but also as a mother, for she and Osiris had a son, Horus, whom she protected sedulously against the designs of the conniving Set. She came to be known for her cunning and was believed to have magical powers. Known as "mistress of life, ruler of fate and destiny," by the Hellenistic Age she was credited with a sphere of influence that had come to embrace the entire cosmos. Rain and sun and moon—they were all within her purview. She governed over kings and kingship, and her Greek worshippers transferred to her inventions traditionally attributed to their own gods such as that of marriage, ascribed to Hera, and of law and agriculture, previously ascribed to Demeter. Tender and nurturant unlike the martial Athena or the volatile Artemis, Isis was worshipped widely throughout the Mediterranean, sometimes as herself alone and sometimes conflated with Demeter.

A long Greek inscription from Cyme in Anatolia around the turn of the era offers a dramatic picture both of the way Isis was integrated into Greek mythological tradition and of the breadth of the powers ascribed to her:

> I am Isis. . . . I was educated by Hermes, and together with Hermes I invented letters. . . . I imposed laws on people, and the laws which I laid down no one may change. . . . I am the eldest daughter of Cronus. I am the wife and sister of King Osiris. I am she who discovered the cultivation of grain for people. . . . The governments of tyrants I suppressed. I stopped murders. I compelled women to be loved by men.

I caused the just to be stronger than gold and silver. . . . I caused the
honorable and the shameful to be distinguished by Nature.

I conquer Fate. Fate heeds me. Hail Egypt who reared me.[21]

Another characteristic of Hellenistic religion was the deification or
near-deification of illustrious human beings. Already in fifth-century
Greece the Spartan commander Brasidas had become the object of a
cult at Amphipolis after he liberated it from the Athenian Empire, and
at the end of the fifth century the people of Samos had decreed divine
honors to Lysander, engineer of the Spartan victory in the Peloponnesian War, renaming the Heraea, their annual festival of Hera, as the
Lysandreia and celebrating him with sacrifices and paeans.[22] Alexander
encouraged the belief that his father was not Philip but rather a god, a
notion that plainly had implications for his own status. As throughout
the Hellenistic world rulers shored up their power by encouraging belief
in their own divinity, Ptolemaic queens came to be worshipped as both
Isis and Demeter. This notion was particularly easy to sell in Egypt,
where Alexander had been hailed as pharaoh, and pharaohs had always
put it about that they were living gods. (Greeks who had relocated in
Egypt were more skeptical.) To ensure that divine blood flowed in the
veins of their children, pharaohs had traditionally married their sisters.
Most of the Ptolemies consequently did so as well, and both king and
queen came to be advertised as divine. Just as Isis had been identified
with Demeter and Hera, other local deities were given Greek identities
to accommodate the new arrivals. Ptolemy I even enlisted the Egyptian
priest Manetho and an Athenian expert in religious matters, Timotheus,
to forge a brand-new hybrid deity. The new god, Sarapis, would serve as the
patron deity of the Ptolemaic dynasty. A fusion of Greek and Egyptian
elements, Sarapis combined the Underworld powers of Hades with the
helping features of Dionysus and Asklepios.

The existence of ruler cults tapped into a long-standing vagueness
about just what divinity was all about. Not all Greeks had seen this in
the same way, and in fact not all were persuaded that the Olympians
even existed.[23] The fact that Greek religion was not grounded in sacred
texts opened the door to considerable debate on the nature of gods,

though then as now, skeptics were often cautious about voicing their doubts. The Hippocratics, while not denying the existence of gods, certainly cut back their role in determining health. The Hippocratic treatise on epilepsy, known to the Greeks as "the sacred disease," began, "This is the way it is with the so-called sacred disease: it strikes me as in no way more divine or sacred than other diseases. . . . It is ignorance and awe that lead people to view its nature and cause as divine" (*On the Sacred Disease* 1). (A parallel ignorance and awe amplified Greek men's complicated feelings about women's bodies.) While doubts about the paramount role of the gods in directing the course of human affairs accelerated with the speculations of the sophists, when people like Protagoras alleged that it was impossible to be confident in the existence of gods, so did interest in quashing such thoughts. In Athens, to which the sophists gravitated, the seer Diopeithes moved a decree calling for the impeachment of anyone who "did not recognize the gods or who taught doctrines about the heavens" (Plutarch, *Pericles* 32. 1), and impeachment at Athens was a very serious procedure often resulting in the death penalty. According to Plutarch, our source for this decree, Diopeithes' purpose was to direct suspicion at Pericles on account of his friendship with Anaxagoras, who had suggested that the sun was not a god but rather a white-hot mass of iron larger than the Peloponnesus. In fact, Anaxagoras was brought to trial and condemned to death, though Pericles managed to spirit him out of town before the sentence could be carried out. Socrates too had friends in high places, but he refused their help after he was convicted of failing to recognize the gods of the state, teaching new gods, and corrupting the young. Political considerations played a large role in each trial, that of Anaxagoras being connected to his friendship with Pericles and that of Socrates sparked in part by his association with the traitors Critias and Alcibiades, but others seem to have gotten into trouble too. The sophist Prodicus of Ceos was evidently put to death in 390 for making so bold as to proclaim that "the gods in whom people commonly believe do not exist."[24] The sophist Hippo (probably from Samos), Diagoras of Melos, and Theodorus of Cyrene were all nicknamed *atheos* (whence the English word atheist) at Athens, and both Diagoras and Theodorus got into legal difficulties.[25]

Most iconoclastic thinkers, however, paid no price for their skepticism. The composite *Life of Thucydides* apparently assembled in the sixth century CE and published under the name of Marcellinus maintained that the historian was considered in his lifetime to be an atheist because he had studied with Anaxagoras (22), but the biography contains enough doubtful material to render it suspect; we also read there that Thucydides wrote his history sitting under a plane tree—and that he was descended from Zeus (25, 2–3). Still, Thucydides' narrative is strikingly devoid of divine causation and frequently showcases the futility of Olympian worship. Thucydides is scoffing where oracles are concerned. The plague that ravaged the city, he reported, persuaded Athenians of an old oracle to the effect that "A Dorian war will come, and with it, plague," but there was some uncertainty as to whether the oracle had actually said *loimos*, plague, or perhaps *limos*, famine, and, he wrote, "people adjusted their memory to fit their suffering" (2. 54. 2–3). Should a famine strike in future, he was convinced, people would read the oracle that way. In one of the most frequently cited passages in his text, Athenians and representatives from the small island state of Melos discuss the prospects of the neutral Melians submitting to Athens and joining the Delian League. In refusing, the Melians indicate that because they are righteous people opposing the unjust, the gods will favor them (5. 104). The gods do no such thing; the Athenians kill all the men they can get their hands on and enslave the women and children. Thucydides is scathing as he recounts the refusal of Nicias, "who was overly inclined to believe in the interpretation of omens and the like," to disregard the seers' advice to wait twenty-seven days before moving his army out of danger in Sicily, with catastrophic results (7. 50. 4). But Thucydides' legal troubles arose solely from his failure to hold the northern stronghold of Amphipolis against the Spartans in 424. We never hear of his being haled into court on suspicion of impiety.

Private rites and public festivals, though they served to organize a great deal of daily life in Greece, drew a wide spectrum of responses from the populace. The more pious took the gods they honored very seriously, and some certainly enjoyed deeply sustaining connections with individual deities. Others of a less spiritual bent welcomed the sense of connection they felt to both the gods and the community on the occasion of religious celebrations, and there was no doubt some overlap between this group and those who privately—or publicly—doubted the very existence of the pantheon. With the passage of time, the varieties of religious worship expanded enormously, so that by the end of the Hellenistic Age the veneration of the traditional Olympians thrived side by side with other beliefs and practices, and some found their solace not in religion but in philosophy. In religion as in other aspects of life, the Greek world manifested a striking multiplicity.

Suggested Readings

Burkert, Walter. 1985. *Greek Religion: Archaic and Classical*, trans. John Raffan. Oxford: Blackwell.

———. 1993. *Homo Necans: The Anthropology of Ancient Greek Sacrificial Ritual and Myth*, trans. Peter Bing. Berkeley: University of California Press.

Burkert, Walter, René Girard, and Jonathan Z. Smith. 1987. *Violent Origins: Ritual Killing and Cultural Formation*. Stanford, CA: Stanford University Press.

Connelly, Joan. 2007. *Portrait of a Priestess: Women and Ritual in Ancient Greece*. Princeton, NJ: Princeton University Press.

Dillon, Matthew. 2001. *Girls and Women in Classical Greek Religion*. London and New York: Routledge.

Eidenow, Esther, and Julia Kindt, eds. 2015. *The Oxford Handbook of Ancient Greek Religion*. Oxford: Oxford University Press.

Faraone, Christopher A. 1999. *Ancient Greek Love Magic*. Cambridge, MA, and London: Harvard University Press.

Flower, Michael. 2008. *The Seer in Ancient Greece*. Berkeley and Los Angeles: University of California Press.

Fontenrose, Joseph. 1978. *The Delphic Oracle: Its Responses and Operations with a Catalogue of Responses*. Berkeley and Los Angeles: University of California Press.

Girard, René. 1977. *Violence and the Sacred*, trans. Patrick Gregory. Baltimore, MD: Johns Hopkins University Press.

Graf, Fritz. 1997. *Magic in the Ancient World*, trans. Franklin Philip. Cambridge, MA: Harvard University Press.

Habicht, Christian. 1970. *Gottenmenschentum und griechische Städte*, 2nd edition. Munich: Beck.

Luck, Georg. 2006. *Arcana Mundi: Magic and the Occult in the Greek and Roman Worlds: A Collection of Ancient Texts*, 2nd edition. Baltimore, MD: Johns Hopkins University Press.

McGlew, James F. 1993. *Tyranny and Political Culture in Ancient Greece*. Ithaca, NY: Cornell University Press.

Mikalson, Jon D. 2009. *Ancient Greek Religion*. Malden, MA: Wiley-Blackwell.

Naiden, F. S. 2013. *Smoke Signals for the Gods: Ancient Greek Sacrifice from the Archaic through Roman Periods*. New York: Oxford University Press.

Nilsson, Martin. 1940. *Greek Popular Religion*. New York: Columbia University Press.

Ogden, Daniel, ed. 2007. *A Companion to Greek Religion*. Malden, MA: Blackwell.

O'Higgins, Laurie. 2003. *Women and Humor in Classical Greece*. Cambridge, UK: Cambridge University Press.

Parker, Robert. 1983. *Miasma: Pollution and Purification in Greek Religion*. Oxford: Clarendon Press.

———. 2011. *On Greek Religion. Cornell Studies in Classical Philology* 60. Ithaca, NY, and London: Cornell University Press.

Price, Simon. 1999. *Religions of the Ancient Greeks. Key Themes in Ancient History*. Cambridge, UK: Cambridge University Press.

Pulleyn, Scott. 1998. *Prayer in Greek Religion*. Oxford: Clarendon.

Stoneman, Richard. 2011. *The Ancient Oracles: Making the Gods Speak*. New Haven, CT: Yale University Press.

Van Oppen de Ruiter, Branko F. 2015. *Berenice II Euergetis: Essays in Early Hellenistic Queenship*. New York: Palgrave Macmillan.

Versnel, H. S. 2011. *Coping with the Gods: Wayward Readings in Greek Theology*. Leiden: Brill.

CHAPTER 7

The Thrill of Victory

There was not just one kind of strife alone,
But there are two all over the wide earth.

—HESIOD, *WORKS AND DAYS*, 11–12

Greek males were highly competitive. The disposition of the temperamentally rivalrous Greeks was beautifully captured by Hesiod, who devoted the opening of his *Works and Days* to delineating two kinds of strife, *eris* (not to be confused with *erōs*, desire). One, he says, is cruel and foments fell wars and battles; she is loved by nobody on earth. The other, however, is far kinder to men (that is Hesiod's word: *andrasi*, male people, not all mortals, and we have no idea whether Greek women were as competitive as Greek men):

> Even the lazy man she prompts to toil as he sees
> His wealthy neighbor plow and plant, putting his house in order.
> Neighbor will vie with neighbor as they both quest after abundance.
> This Eris is healthy for mortals. And potter vies with potter,
> Envious and begrudging, and carpenter with carpenter,
> And beggar is jealous of beggar, and minstrel of minstrel. (20–26)

Each kind of *eris* played a role in the *Iliad*, as the poet began by showing us Agamemnon and Achilles vying for honor in the Achaean camp even before we see them fighting the Trojans for that of Menelaus. Not only

Achilles' father but Glaucus's as well had sent his son off to Troy with the charge "always to be the best and preeminent over the others" (*Iliad* 11. 784, 6. 208, in the identical words). The bitter, begrudging jealousy at work in the more dangerous variety of rivalry was apparent in the suicide of Ajax, devastated when the armor of Achilles was awarded not to him but to Odysseus, and we still see it at work generations later in the Greeks' habit of impeaching and exiling so many of their leaders and in the practice of ostracism. The combative temperament that once manifested itself on the battlefield would drive feverish litigation in courtrooms, though not all societies were as litigious as the Athenians. When a character in a comedy of Aristophanes has Athens pointed out to him on a map of the world, he exclaims, "Impossible! I don't see any cases being tried!" (*Clouds* 207). Aristotle was an astute analyst of competitiveness and envy. Success and good fortune, he observes, spark envy, and not only that. People envy those who are in what modern sociologists would call their "reference group"—those

> who are close to them in time, place, age, and reputation. . . . For nobody tries to rival people who lived ten thousand years ago, or are yet to be born or already dead, or those who live near the straits of Gibraltar or . . . are either greatly inferior or superior to them. (*Rhetoric* 2. 10. 5)

It is those who aim at the same things of whom people are most envious, he concludes, citing indeed Hesiod's words "potter vies with potter." The same rivalrous temperament contributed to the frequency of deadly, corrosive wars among the Greek states. When unity came, it arrived with the steep price tag of Macedonian domination.

The agonistic ideal was ingrained in the Greek ethos. War, athletics, drama, politics, litigation, rhetorical display all afforded opportunities for Greek men to build themselves up in the zero-sum game of life, besting competitors in a wide variety of spheres. The sophists were intensely competitive with one another: a character in one of Plato's dialogues called the typical slippery sophist "an athlete in the competitions of words" (*Sophist* 231e), and in fact the Olympic festival featured competitions in declamation. Tragedies like *Oedipus the King* that still captivate viewers today were performed in the context of a competition among playwrights, and talented speakers not only competed for audiences but served as speech-writers for the rivalries that played themselves out in Athenian courtrooms.

The oldest and most famous of the Greek athletic festivals both in its own day and today was the Olympic Games, celebrated at Olympia in the western Peloponnesus in honor of Zeus every four years (since 776, so tradition had it). Other games brought Greeks from all over together in competition as well: the Nemean Games, also for Zeus, at Argos in the Peloponnesus; the Pythian Games for Apollo at Delphi; and the Isthmian Games for Poseidon at Corinth on the narrow isthmus that linked the Peloponnesus with central Greece. Athletic competitions replaced the opportunity that single combat in warfare had once offered, as now that a more egalitarian mode of fighting in units had evolved, a reputation for valor on the battlefield was no longer as easily come by. Greek males showed their *aretē* in running, chariot racing, boxing; in the shot put and the long jump; and in the ultimate test of strength and grit, the *pankration* (all-strength), a mixed martial arts event that combined wrestling and boxing: nothing was off limits in the *pankration* except gouging of the opponent's eye, nose, or mouth—or going for the genitals. One Arrachion had the dubious honor of winning the *pankration* when he was dead. While his opponent had his hands in a death grip around Arrachion's neck, Arrachion managed to dislocate the fellow's toe but then expired from the choking. When his opponent acknowledged defeat on account of the pain in his foot, the judges proclaimed Arrachion the victor and placed a crown on his corpse.[1]

The glory that could be won at the Olympics and the other Panhellenic Games was magnified by the fact that, in this highly competitive world, there were no team sports—and no bronze or silver medals. Either you won or you lost. Training for the games took time away from earning a living that poor people simply did not have; as today, a gifted athlete from a humble background would require the support and sponsorship of people with money. Travel to one of the Panhellenic games and paying for accommodations was costly as well, and without wealthy patrons the trip would be an impossibility. Although both governments and private citizens sometimes funded the careers of promising athletes from poor families who would bring glory to their states by victory at the games, the majority of competitors came from the elite. Events like the chariot race called for that most expensive of animals, horses, and the prizes went not to the intrepid jockeys but to the owners of the team, like the wealthy Athenian aristocrat Alcibiades, who boasted in the assembly of "his" Olympic victories, or the Spartan princess Cynisca, the first woman to win at the Olympics by entering a team in the chariot race. Cynisca's brother King Agesilaus, it seems, who had caught on to the fact that the event favored the rich sponsor rather than the valiant athlete, encouraged her to enter the team in the hopes that a woman's victory would call attention to the problematic nature of the competition.

Cynisca's victories in both 396 and 392 did not undermine the popularity of the event, though they did prompt a number of women from both Sparta and elsewhere to enter teams in subsequent years. Hellenistic queens certainly did. In celebrating the victory of Berenice II, wife of Ptolemy III, the Macedonian poet Posidippus, who had relocated in Egypt, included mention of earlier triumphs by her ancestors both male and female:

> Ptolemy my grandfather won the victory with his chariot
> Driving his horse at the stadium at Pisa;
> So did my father's mother Berenice,
> And once more with a chariot my father carried off the prize,
> A king, son of a king, bearing the same name as his father.
> Arsinoë as well won all three harness races in one contest.
> . . .
> Celebrate with song, O Macedonians, the crown of victory
> Won by your ruler Berenice with her team of horses. (AB78)

The games sparked a good deal of poetry in the form of epinician odes celebrating victors, and these poems—songs, really, since Greek poetry was sung—themselves took the form of performance, for Greek culture from its earliest days was both oral and performative. We lose a tremendous amount by encountering Greek poetry in the form of written texts, for these texts served not so much as scripts as they did as librettos, to be adorned and amplified by song, dance, gesture, and in some cases a good deal of ad libbing. Verbal skill was as highly esteemed in Greece as skill on the battlefield. Achilles' tutor Phoenix tells how the hero's father Peleus attached him to Achilles to teach him to be "both a speaker of words and a doer of deeds" (*Iliad* 9. 443). The Homeric epics were not read but rather heard, sung by itinerant professionals known as rhapsodes. Even Herodotus gave recitations of selections from his work. Victory odes were performed publicly, accompanied by dancing and music, and the events were spectacular. Although literacy both male and female increased over the centuries, it was always limited, and books were expensive. The written word played a far smaller role in people's lives than it does today: the notion of relaxing in the evening by curling up with a mystery story or a volume of poetry is a modern invention. The sung or spoken word played a far larger role. Unlike popular songs heard over the car radio, Greek poetry was, at least until the Hellenistic Age, heard in a group, whether a small number gathering in the evening at a symposium or a large number of citizens coming together for a festival. Literature for the Greeks was primarily social and communal.[2] Poetry, moreover, was a central vehicle for the transmission of myth, religious belief, traditional wisdom—in short, the Greeks' entire cultural heritage.

The best known of the epinician poets was Pindar (ca. 518–438). Born near Thebes, he traveled widely both to study and to perform. His odes capture the aristocratic ethos that underlay the Panhellenic games, contests of strength and skill that provided an arena in which young men from the upper classes could demonstrate their *aretē* and win glory. Before Hellenistic times the games were close to all-male events; until a single footrace for females was introduced, all events were open to men and boys alone, and at least in theory any married woman caught watching could be put to death, although, curiously, unmarried girls were allowed to observe. The enthusiasm for the beautiful young athletic body that thrived among the Greeks was actually admiration of the beautiful young male athletic body. The modern preoccupation with the female body was overshadowed in Greece by the preoccupation with the male physique, and athletes at the games competed naked. Pindar's odes contain numerous references to the physical beauty of athletes like Epharmostus, "in the prime of his youth: a handsome man who has accomplished handsome deeds" (*Olympian* 9. 94).[3] The notion that visual appeal correlated with other excellences was encapsulated in the expression *kalos k'agathos* (literally, "beautiful and good") regularly used to describe the ideal Greek aristocrat. Although Greeks, if pressed, could certainly see examples of beautiful people not being very good—Helen and Paris being prime examples—for the most part excellence was perceived as a package deal in which admirable moral qualities accompanied enviable physical characteristics (not to mention distinguished descent). Herodotus tells of the Olympic victor Philippus, who was by so far the handsomest Greek that the people of Segesta in Sicily worshipped him as a hero after his death, offering sacrifices at his shrine (5. 47. 1–2).

The handsome young male was considered beautiful even in death. Priam's sad words on the difference between a young corpse and an old one are deeply moving. Contemplating the painful prospect of the same dogs he has fed at his table lapping his blood as he lies dead in front of his palace, he muses that

> It's fitting for a young man, when he has been slain in war,
> That, though he's dead, he lie mangled by sharp and pitiless bronze:
> Nothing that then appears is dishonorable in the least.
> But when the dogs work shame on the hoary head, hoary beard
> And nakedness of an old man slain, this is the most pitiful thing
> That befalls wretched mortals. (*Iliad* 22. 71–76)

So much for the purported Greek reverence for elders. The Spartan Tyrtaeus expressed precisely the same sentiment some years later, writing that

> Shameful the sight when a man long in years falls among the first
>   fighters,
> Lying in front of the young, head white and beard flecked with gray,
> Breathing his last, pushing out his stout soul in the dust as he lies there,
> His own hands holding fast to his genitals covered in blood,
> Hard indeed on the eyes, so painful to the beholder,
> His flesh all naked as well; but for a man who is young,
> To die in the same way is seemly, provided the fair bloom of youth

Still is upon him: a wonder for men to behold, and by women
Desired as long as he lives, and fair in the very same way
As he falls in the front lines.[4]

The classic example that demonstrated the correlation of baseness with physical ugliness was Thersites, a commoner described by Homer as the ugliest man in the Greek army at Troy. When he rails against the commander-in-chief Agamemnon just as the handsome aristocrat Achilles had done, the poor and misshapen Thersites is soundly thrashed by Odysseus—who is promptly cheered by the other impecunious soldiers, siding instinctively with their rich and good-looking superiors against one of their own (*Iliad* 2. 244–77).

The games offered a proving ground for beautiful young aristocratic men to show their *aretē*, and for poets like Pindar to earn commissions by celebrating them. The enthusiasm for the aristocratic ethos that pervades Pindar's work is all the more striking when we bear in mind that he lived in the glory days of democracy. While Pericles was exalting the virtues of democracy and the open-minded Herodotus was celebrating the superiority of self-government over monarchy and highlighting the contributions to history of individuals like Themistocles, an Athenian admiral of unremarkable ancestry who masterminded the defeat of Xerxes, and Spaco, the Median shepherd's wife who saved the baby who would grow up to found the Persian Empire, Pindar's work underlined at every turn the importance of bloodlines: "There is no way to conceal inborn nature" (*Olympian* 13, 13). Divine favor plays a role in determining the outcome of the games, but inborn talent is key as well. On the occasion of the victory of Hippocleas of Thessaly in the boys' long sprint race at Delphi, he writes

Oh, Apollo, sweet is the end for mortals, and the
    beginnings bring success
When a god speeds it on. Surely you devised that Hippocleas
Should succeed in this. Heredity, though, also played a role,
As he has walked within the footsteps of his father,
Twice an Olympic victor in the race in sturdy armor.
    (*Pythian* 10, 10–14)

A seeming anachronism, Pindar's work is a salutary reminder that aristocratic values were by no means dead in fifth-century Greece. The drama both tragic and comic that was central to life in Athens already in Pindar's lifetime, however, was very much grounded in democracy.

———

Theater is an amazing phenomenon, creating as it does a venue in which spectators can lose themselves as they enter into the alternative universe upon the stage. Because Greeks had such a strong sense of community, it should come as no surprise that drama was integrated into a powerful communal experience. Universal in its appeal, it was also a quintessential product of the Athenian democratic polis, asking many of the same questions that Athenians asked themselves in the course of their daily lives. Tragic or comic, the theater mirrored the polis. Tragedy became central to the annual festival of the Dionysia early on, taking its first steps in the sixth century and erupting in its glory in the fifth. Comic drama, though it was not accepted as part of the festival until a bit later, developed quickly enough to become one of the defining genres of the fifth century, and its roots probably go back even further than those of tragedy; it was no doubt early in Greek history that someone first said, "I have an idea! Let's pretend we're somebody else! We could even make costumes!" Certainly the obscene invective of iambic poets like Archilochus and Hipponax and the spirited obscenities of fertility festivals like the Thesmophoria were antecedents.

Drama both tragic and comic grew out of earlier forms, probably from various kinds of choral performance. Dionysus was a fertility god, and much Greek ritual sought to guarantee fertility in both land and people. Phalluses were carried in procession at the Dionysia, and comic actors were normally portrayed not only with huge rumps and bellies but also outsize phalluses of leather that protruded unmistakably in front; foreigners were identifiable by their "circumcised" appendages. Like other forms of poetry, drama in Greece was as didactic as it was aesthetically pleasing.[5] The chorus of Aristophanes' *Frogs* identifies its role as instructing the citizenry (686–87). For what, Aeschylus asks Euripides there, should a poet be admired? For cleverness and giving good advice, Euripides replies, since we improve people (1008–10). To be sure, the register of the two genres differed dramatically. Euripides' Theseus in a rage with his son exclaims

An exile from your native land, you'll roam
Forever over foreign soil! (*Hippolytus*, 1048–49)

Aristophanes' sausage seller in quarreling with the slave Paphlagon cries out

I'll stuff your asshole like a sausage skin! (*Knights*, 364)

But there is more than one key in which to instruct.

At first the stylized subspecies of theater that is Greek tragedy may appear so much the product of its time and place that it has nothing to say to us today, composed as it was entirely in verse, performed with an all-male cast wearing masks, drawing its plots largely from Bronze Age myths, punctuated by running commentary from a chorus, informed by the presence of fate and the gods, and removed from the minutiae of everyday life. The truth could not be more different. Greek tragedy, after all, is about suffering, both suffering brought on by one's own actions and suffering eminently undeserved—and the challenge of distinguishing the two. It is about the difficulty of knowing the right thing to do. It is about bewilderment in the face of the unexplained and sometimes inexplicable. It is about the fragility of human happiness, indeed of human life itself. It is about identity, and about the challenge of imagining and interacting with those who are unlike us. It is about choice, and responsibility. It is about conflict. It is about rage, and vengeance. It is about family, and love—and sex. It is about racism and sexism. It is about ambition. It is about uncertainty and ambivalence and indecision. It is about causation, and about unintended consequences and collateral damage. It is about the costs of war and the perils of imperialism. It is about democracy. It is about anxiety and uncertainty in an era of changing values and mores. Tragedy expands our sensitivity to suffering, underlining as it does the mutability of fortune, the unpredictable nature of life, and the limited control we have over our futures. It reminds us always to expect the unexpected.

What could be more relevant to our own concerns?

In many respects tragedy perpetuated the ideals of epic. The course of events is determined by both human and divine actions, and characters continue to worry about their reputations, their *kleos*. While the heroic ideals encapsulated in Homeric epics were very much alive in classical Athens, however, they were also being called into question there. What, after all, would be the place of a man like Achilles in democratic society—or Glaucus, also sent into war with the charge *aiein aristeuein kai hypeirochon emmenai allōn*: always to be the best and stand out above the others (*Iliad* 6. 208)? Although this competitiveness remained a powerful motivator—in politics, in athletics, in war—it also occasioned a certain unease, for might not a man who stood out above the others aim at tyranny? We know from the machinery of accountability not only in Athens but also in other states—in Sparta, in Syracuse, in Argos—and from the peculiar tales that congregated around kings and tyrants that fear and envy often attended on those who wielded great power. Bearing in mind the advice of Thrasybulus to Periander about lopping off the heads of the highest stalks of grain, Greeks of the Classical Age regarded their great men with a wary eye. Values like *kleos* and *timē* remained a serious concern throughout Greek history, but how could a citizen of the polis justify, say, placing his fellow citizens in danger because of a slight to his honor as Achilles had done when he withdrew from the fighting at Troy? Once confident of their standing in the eyes of gods and mortals, aristocrats snatched from Bronze Age legend and transported to the tragic stage now had to contend with a new value system. In their noble ancestry and their exalted status in society, the revered heroes of old now represented an ethos at odds with the burgeoning democracy, precisely the ethos from which it needed to distance itself and against which it was struggling to define itself. The agonistic ideal was all very well when it came to the production of dramas, as playwrights competed for the privilege of having their work produced and elite citizens could show off their wealth by funding productions, but for the larger-than-life characters in those plays, the quest for honor and glory had become problematic, and the new genre sees them very much cut down to size.

And what of justice? The question, "what is justice" that would form the framework for Plato's *Republic* in the fourth century also troubled the men and women of the fifth, but there it formed the subject matter not of philosophy but of tragedy. Replete with references to the "justice of Zeus," tragedy also wrestles with the difficulty of understanding just what that justice is and questions whether the gods are always just. Justice in a polis that has been struggling to establish a democratic legal system will be different from the justice of the heroic world. The pervasiveness of legal and legalistic language in the tragedies underlines the new ethos of the democratic polis. Tragedy, as French structuralist Jean-Pierre Vernant points out, comes into being

> when a gap develops at the heart of the social experience. It is wide enough for the oppositions between legal and political thought on the one hand and the mythical and heroic traditions on the other to stand out quite clearly. Yet it is narrow enough for the conflict in values still to be a painful one and for the clash to continue to take place.[6]

Though the heroic past remained very much alive for the Athenians, it had come under a scrutiny that was intensely uncomfortable in the way that all reconsiderations of long-standing value systems are uncomfortable. Above all, tragedy was a genre of questioning. Whereas myth is designed to answer questions, tragedy is organized around asking them. Like the philosophy that would flourish in the next century, it tackled the most profound uncertainties about what it meant to be a human being, but unlike philosophy, it did not seek to resolve them; in tragedy the Athenians found stimulation in exploring the human condition without insisting that the great mysteries of life be settled. Even a single playwright might offer conflicting slants on a question in two different plays. In Sophocles' *Oedipus Tyrannos*, for example, Oedipus accepts full responsibility for having killed his father and murdered his mother as the oracle had predicted he would do, whereas in his later *Oedipus at Colonus*, the playwright portrays Oedipus as a victim.

Along with other kinds of poetry, Plato famously banished tragic drama from the ideal state he sketched out in the *Republic*. In his view, tragedy was simply an imitation of reality at two removes: actions were a poor copy of the ideal disembodied truths he considered the highest, perhaps the only, reality, and tragedy was but an imitation of those actions—an imitation of an imitation. It was created, moreover, through inspiration, not reason. Just as bad was the fact that it worked on the audience not via the intellect but by means of the emotions: the music and verse cast a spell on the spectators that led them to accept the playwright's ignorant representations of reality as truth. And a great deal of what poets depicted was intrinsically wrongheaded and corrupting— their portrayals of gods misconducting themselves, for example. So thoroughly was this prototypically Athenian art form woven into the fabric of Athenian consciousness, however, that speakers throughout the Platonic dialogues quote frequently from tragedies; Plato in his youth wrote tragedies that he later burned in a fit of remorse, an incalculable loss. Reading, however, is not enough, for a text is not a production. The texts that have come down to us contain no musical scores or notes on choreography, and much must be supplied by the imagination. The Dionysia involved not only music but considerable dancing—the stage on which the chorus appeared, in front of the actors and a little below them, was called the *orchestra*, which meant a place for dancing. A total of over a thousand dancers participated in a single festival, and the Dionysia was considered so central to the life of the polis that dancers were exempted from military service in order to rehearse.

Drama was highly competitive at every stage. Aspiring dramatists needed to apply to the archon in charge for a chorus well in advance of the festival at which they wished their plays to appear. Though men whose previous plays had been well-received might be able to count on their reputations to propel them to success, others would need to provide a good deal of information about what they were planning, perhaps even reciting some selections that had already been sketched out, and all plays had to follow a prescribed format in terms of the interaction of chorus and actors. In addition, in the case of tragic drama, plays were presented not individually but in groups of four, three tragedies followed by a lighter drama also authored by the tragedian called a "satyr play." Sometimes, as in Aeschylus's *Oresteia* trilogy, the plays were closely connected, but more often they were not. The comic dramatists, though they submitted plays singly, were equally challenged by the need to produce dramas with prescribed alternations between choral pieces and dialogue among actors.

Once a chorus had been granted, the expense of training it was one of the several liturgies that affluent Athenians undertook to demonstrate their commitment to the common welfare—and to showcase their wealth. Although the state provided a flute player and paid the actors and the playwright, the man serving as *choragos* was required to foot the bill not only for a trainer, costumes, rehearsals, and room and board for the chorus members, but also for props, masks, scenery, special effects, and the remainder of the musicians. He did not direct the production, a task that fell to the playwright. It was not unusual for a *choragos* to find himself laying out a sum well in excess of over a year's salary for most Athenians. The actual production of the plays provided the next stage in the competition. Ten citizens chosen as judges ranked the performances and assigned prizes for best play, best *choragos*, and from around the middle of the fifth century, best actor. All parts were played by men, but masks and costumes enabled a man to portray a woman (and a single actor to play more than one part). Splendid monuments were erected in honor of successful *choragoi*, and Pericles' stature was considerably enhanced early in his career when he served as *choragos* for Aeschylus's prizewinning *Persians* in 472. Drama was very much a production by the city itself. Lysicrates, who won the prize for best *choragos* in 354, erected a beautiful monument bearing not only his name but those of several others involved with the festival. It stood among many other choragic monuments on the street near the Acropolis that led to the theater of Dionysus.

Forming as they did a central element in the festivals at which they appeared, tragedies and comedies were deeply embedded in the life of the community. The Greater Dionysia, usually held in March, began with a boisterous parade in honor of Dionysus. Citizens and even metics were welcome to join in though they might not have been assigned specific roles in the procession, a cavalcade that grew in numbers as it moved. Singing competitions followed and then a lavish sacrifice of bulls. Key among the ceremonials that preceded the dramas were several of a military and imperial nature: the parading of the generals and of war orphans across the stage and the laying out of the tribute brought in by the subject allies. The plays that followed, however, took on the issue of power and power struggles in a far more nuanced way. As classicist Simon Goldhill has written,

> The ceremonials before the play can bring the generals on the stage, and tragedy will then reveal the misplaced arrogance, disastrous overconfidence and failure of control of those in authority. The ceremonials before the plays may assert the military values of the state—yet drama after drama, set in a time of war, undermines all jingoism and certainty of purpose.[7]

The celebratory and profoundly androcentric cast of these rituals stands in stark contrast to the richness and depth of the dramas the audience was about to see, in which comfortable conventions about the joys of empire and the military ethos were undercut and the challenges confronting both sexes explored in depth.

The experience of actors and audience alike was radically different from what it is today. The theater of Dionysus, like other Greek theaters, was carved out of stone more or less in the shape of the letter C into the hillside—in this case, the south slope of the Acropolis. There spectators sat, thousands at a time, watching and listening, often in less than temperate weather, to an elaborate production that resembled a modern musical. Considerable endurance was required on the part of performers and audience alike, as a trilogy would begin in the morning and end in the late afternoon with the satyr play. The actor who played Clytemnestra in Aeschylus's *Oresteia* trilogy must have been made of stern stuff, as Clytemnestra appeared in each of the three plays. Members of the audience willed their eyes and ears to take in a spectacle that for many of them was taking place hundreds of yards away, and they could not remain passive throughout the performance, for the soaring poetry, particularly in the choral songs, was often complex and demanded close attention. Most of all, attending the theater was a civic and not a private experience. At some point tickets came to be distributed free of charge to all citizens, and though the audience might include metics and visitors from outside Athens, citizen attendees were arranged in their tribes, just as they were during battle. The audience may also have resembled military formation in an additional respect: gender. Metic women were probably allowed to attend the theater, but it is questionable whether citizen females could, and spectators looking around them would see mostly men.

Those in the audience were well aware throughout the performance that a large percentage of their friends were watching too, not just their army buddies sitting close to them, and that these friends would have thoughts about the plays and their production. In this respect viewing a Greek play was more similar to, say, attending a major sports event like the World Cup (or indeed the Olympics) or watching the season finale of a popular television series than going to see a play would be today. Although no two people would have precisely the same reaction to any play, edge-of-the-seat feelings of terror, relief, and jubilation would have united the audience at numerous junctures. For the Athenians, drama was an integral part of life, not a highbrow cultural experience for an elite. When thousands of Athenians were enslaved after their catastrophic defeat in the harbor of Syracuse in 413, a number improved their situation by charming their captors with recitations from the plays of Euripides, which were evidently very popular in Sicily.

———

All eleven complete plays that survive from the fifth century genre known as Old Comedy are by Aristophanes, although we know the names of a number of other comic dramatists whose works were popular. Cratinus carried off the prize for comedy on some ten occasions, Eupolis on eight, but the remains of their works are fragmentary. Nearly all the tragedies that survive intact date from the fifth century and were (probably) the work of the "big three": seven generally attributed to Aeschylus (although one attribution has been challenged), seven to Sophocles, and, by a quirk of fate, seventeen to Euripides, though one of these may have been written by someone else after Euripides' death. These represent a tiny fraction of the number actually composed. Sophocles was said to have written over a hundred plays, and other playwrights whose works are lost wrote many as well, including Aeschylus's nephew Philocles. What would one not give to have the lost tragedy with which Philocles won first prize in the competition over Sophocles' *Oedipus the King*? Aeschylus's son Euphorion took first prize at the Dionysia of 431, edging out both Sophocles and Euripides (who had submitted *Medea*), and some have suspected that he was actually the author of *Prometheus Bound*, normally classed with the works of Aeschylus. Sophocles' son Iophon and grandson Sophocles the Younger both followed in the famous tragedian's footsteps, writing tragedies of their own.

Despite the success of Aeschylus's *Persians*, plots were nearly always taken from mythology, and so tragedians were often faced with the challenge of devising a new twist on an old tale. So for example Aeschylus, Sophocles, and Euripides all wrote plays about the murder of Clytemnestra and Aegisthus by Orestes to avenge his father Agamemnon, but each play approached the event differently and assigned different roles in the murders to the various dramatis personae. The tragedian Agathon, a friend of Euripides and Aristophanes, won a prize in 416 with a play whose characters and plot he had invented from whole cloth, but the habit never caught on. In tragedy the number of characters was always small, the number of actors even smaller; their identities concealed behind their masks, silent actors often played more than one of the small parts of nonspeaking characters like attendants. Comedies featured both more speaking actors and more silent ones. The tragic chorus, which danced as well as sang, started out at twelve and then expanded to fifteen. At twenty-four, comic choruses were bigger. A key element in staging was provided by the device known as the *mechanē* or crane, used to display gods and occasionally others high above the action on the stage, hence the Latin expression *deus ex machina*, "a god out of a machine," to describe the resolution of crises by miraculous intervention.

Certain rules later codified by Aristotle guided the structure of the plot. All action was to take place in a single day in a single place, and no violence was permitted on stage; the (often gruesome) deaths that formed key parts of the story were narrated by those who had observed them rather than witnessed by the audience. Because the role of the chorus was to offer a running commentary on the action but not to intervene in it, choruses were often composed of women, slaves, or elderly people—groups whose failure to prevent, for example, an impending murder would not appear incongruous. Inevitably, these rules were sometimes violated. In Aeschylus's *Eumenides* the action extends over more than a day, and the Eumenides who form the chorus are important characters in the plot. In addition to commenting on the action as it unfolds, the chorus served to give voice to the core beliefs of the polis. Chief among these were the fragility of happiness, the perils of pride, the excellence of democracy, the limitations on human freedom, and the concomitant power of the gods, most particularly Zeus but certainly others as well. Oh, you generations of mortals, exclaims the chorus in *Oedipus the King*,

> I count your lives as nothing but a dream.
> Where is the man who ever has attained
> A happiness that's not just some illusion,
> Destined to vanish into empty air?
> From your unhappy ending, Oedipus,
> I shrink from calling any mortal blessed. (1185–91)

The centrality of drama to Athenian culture led Aristotle to feature it prominently in his *Poetics*. The disappearance of his section on comedy is a great loss, but the surviving section on tragedy has been very influential—indeed, too influential—in subsequent ages. Tragedy, Aristotle wrote,

> is a representation of an action that is lofty, complete, and of a certain magnitude, by means of language embellished with all kinds of ornament, the several kinds being used in the different parts of the play; in the form not of narrative but of action; and effecting through pity and fear a catharsis of such emotions. By "language embellished" I mean that which makes use of rhythm and harmony and melody, and by "in the different parts" I mean that some effects are produced by the medium of verse alone and some by song. (*Poetics* 1449b20)

Aristotle's notion of catharsis contrasted strikingly with the view of his teacher Plato and may have been designed specifically to counter it. As classicist Ruth Scodel has observed, "Plato had argued that tragedy harmed its audience by encouraging self-indulgent emotionality . . . so Aristotle claimed that it actually did not make people more emotional but less: viewing tragedy relieved excessive pity and fear." She knows, she says, of "no empirical basis for this claim, although it surely rests on the experience of feeling, after seeing a play, that one has passed through an emotionally wrenching experience. Nobody really knows what the longer-term effects of tragedy are."[8]

Tragedy, Aristotle added, should recount the fall of a fundamentally decent person of high station and good fortune whose misery is brought about "not by baseness or depravity but on account of a certain *hamartia*" (*Poetics* 1453a). The word derives from the Greek verb *hamartanō*: to miss the mark, specifically while hurling a spear or shooting an arrow, and more broadly to err, to fail; sometimes, but certainly not always, to commit a grave moral wrong. *Hamartia* is a failing, an inadequacy, a mistake in judgment, and, yes, sometimes—again, not always— something that might loosely be called a sin. Those who fall into misfortune through *hamartia* suffer from some frailty or other, but often it is one that would not result in disaster under ordinary circumstances. Frequently a series of events transpires that leads a weakness that might otherwise be harmless to prove catastrophic. *Katastrophe* is a good Greek word that means literally "overturning."

Through no fault of Aristotle's, *hamartia* has usually been translated as "tragic flaw," and because of Aristotle's high reputation, this passage in the *Poetics* has done great harm to the understanding of tragedy for centuries, prompting readers to exert untold energies in putting one play after another into an ill-fitting straitjacket as they quest fervidly after tragic flaws to explain the action. The surviving corpus of Greek tragedy does not bear out this blanket interpretation of tragedy's dynamic. Only by a grotesque oversimplification could Aeschylus's *Oresteia* trilogy be made to fit this paradigm. Sophocles' *Antigone* focused on the fatal conflict between the king of Thebes, Creon, who has forbidden the burial of his nephew Polynices on the grounds that he is a traitor, and Antigone, Creon's niece and Polynices' sister, who is determined to fulfill the religious obligation of burying a relative. The play examines the disaster that ensues from the clash of two strong temperaments and two radically different ways of looking at the human community, not the story of a great man's fall—or a great woman's. Euripides' *Medea* treats the title character's response to her abandonment by her husband, Jason of Argonaut fame, who aspires to make a political marriage to the local princess. Jason is most distinctly not a decent man, and Medea has much too much of the murderess in her life history for the killing she perpetrates in the play to qualify as an aberration. Like *Antigone*, *Medea* treats the tragic collision of two immovable objects. In the tableaux of the *Persians* or the *Trojan Women*, no such character appears. Sophocles' play about the death of Oedipus, *Oedipus at Colonus*, shows us no flawed character at the center of the play. Achilles and Hector and even Patroclus suit the picture of the flawed hero far better than most tragic protagonists.

The questions addressed by the tragedians were so many that it would be impossible to explore them all in a short space—perhaps even in a long space. Much, however, can be learned by focusing on three:

1. How much control do we have over the way our lives turn out?
2. Is justice separable from vengeance?
3. In what way is the human community to accommodate its division into two sexes?

The oldest of the playwrights, Aeschylus, grappled with every one of these questions in his masterpiece, the *Oresteia*, the only complete trilogy that has survived. A member of the "greatest generation" of the *Marathonomachoi*, those who had stood up to the invading Persians at Marathon, Aeschylus was the most conservative of the three major tragedians in his outlook. He does not tend to question the wisdom of the gods or the fundamental rightness of the way the world of gods and mortals has been ordered. He did not doubt that the human condition was fraught with pain, but, as the chorus sings repeatedly in *Agamemnon*, the first of the plays:

Sing a song of sorrow, but may good prevail in the end. (159)

Wisdom, they say, comes to the person who sings victory songs for Zeus—Zeus, who has set down the law that "through suffering comes wisdom" (177).

The audience would have been familiar with the story of the unfortunate house of Atreus, Agamemnon's father. Cursed from the time his own grandfather Tantalus tried to trick the gods into eating human flesh by serving up his son to them at dinner, King Atreus, feuding with his brother Thyestes, invited him to a banquet at which the main dish was a casserole featuring the dismembered bodies of Thyestes' sons, whom the king had murdered. In this tale we see reprised the motif of inappropriate eating that we saw in the *Odyssey* first with Penelope's suitors and then with the Cyclops Polyphemus: signs of a profound failure to respect hallowed norms. When Atreus revealed the nature of the mystery meat by displaying the severed heads to his brother, Thyestes understandably placed a further curse on him. Atreus's son Agamemnon, moreover, has also committed child murder. The chorus recalls the famous episode toward the beginning of the play. Becalmed en route to Troy and with stores running out, Agamemnon is told by the seer Calchas that an angry Artemis is holding back the winds and only the sacrifice of his young daughter can make them blow again. The king does not ask how he can possibly sacrifice his child, does not exclaim, as many men might, "my wife would kill me!" (which in his case would have been prophetic). Rather, he sees himself between a rock and hard place:

A heinous fate it is to disobey,
But surely heinous too to kill my child,
The glory of my house, and to pollute
My father's hands with streams of virgin blood
Beside the altar. Neither course is free
Of evil. How can I desert my fleet,
How fail my allies? For they have the right
To call for this. . . . (205–17)

Despite Iphigenia's frantic cries of "Daddy!" Agamemnon bids his henchmen raise her high above the altar as if she were a baby goat, her mouth gagged lest she call down further damnation on his already cursed house. Muted by the gag, she shoots supplicating glances at each one of the sacrificers,

Just like a picture wishing it could speak. (242–43)

Justice, the chorus concludes, inclines her scales so wisdom comes only to those who suffer (250–51).

As Agamemnon does not appear to have gained wisdom, we have to ask how much he really suffered. But suffer he will. On his return from Troy, Clytemnestra does indeed kill him (as well as the Trojan princess Cassandra who has been forced to share his bed) and exults in the murder along with Thyestes' youngest son, born after the casserole incident: her lover Aegisthus. The next link in the chain is explored in the middle play, named *The Libation Bearers* after the women of the chorus who bring offerings to Agamemnon's tomb. Just as Clytemnestra killed to avenge her daughter, Orestes will kill to avenge his father. For he is under a stern injunction from Apollo to repay his father's murderers. This, though, is a hard business. How many of us have been confronted with the uncomfortable choice between killing our mother and letting our father's death go unpunished? Much of tragedy is about uncomfortable choices, and Aeschylus exploited the conventions of tragedy to lend drama to Orestes' ambivalence. His friend Pylades in tow, Orestes returns home from the exile his mother has imposed on him since childhood, determined to kill Clytemnestra and Aegisthus. Face to face with a pleading Clytemnestra, however, his resolve begins to weaken. "What shall I do?" the paralyzed youth asks Pylades. When Pylades replies, gasps must have been audible throughout the audience in the echoing stone theater. As Pylades had not spoken in the play before, nobody could have doubted that he was simply one of those "extras," the silent, untrained actors who accompanied major characters on the stage in one capacity or another. But reply he does:

> What will become, then, of Apollo's oracles,
> Straight from the Pythia? of your sworn oaths?
> Count men your foes before you cheat the gods! (900–902)

No sooner is the matricide accomplished, however, than Orestes sees before him the bloody avenging spirits of Clytemnestra: the Furies. These belonged not among the gods of Olympus but rather among the powers associated with the Underworld and known as "chthonic" (of the earth)—Hades, to be sure, but also the grim watchdog Cerberus and sometimes other divinities, like Demeter and Dionysus, connected with things that grow in the ground, and of course Persephone, who bridged the gap between the living and the dead, and Hermes, who conducted the dead to their final resting place and thus, like Persephone, moved back and forth between the two worlds. And so the playwright sets the stage for the last phase of the trilogy. There Orestes takes refuge in Athens, the Furies in hot pursuit. At the instigation of Athena, Orestes is to be tried by a jury of Athenian citizens. Upon cross-examination by the Furies, Orestes is quick to point out that Apollo, after all, had commanded Clytemnestra's murder. Clytemnestra, furthermore, deserved her death because of her murder of Agamemnon.

And here is where things get really interesting. Enter Apollo. Orestes, he explains, was not actually related to Clytemnestra, because women make no genetic contribution to their children:

> The mother of the one who's called her child
> Is not its parent. No, she is the nurse
> Of what is newly sown in embryo.
> The one who mounts—he is the parent. She,
> A stranger acting for a stranger, serves
> To shelter the young shoot within, at least
> If no god intervenes to do it harm. (658–61)

And he calls as witness Athena, born from the head of her father Zeus (although if one is going to talk about the baby-sitting of embryos, Zeus himself would be a good example). Not only was Clytemnestra merely a surrogate mother; that, in Apollo's view, is the only kind there is. Though not all Greeks subscribed to Apollo's peculiar theory, the god's curious view of genetics, as we have seen, would later be articulated by Aristotle (*Generation of Animals* 737a25). Tickled to have her birth drawn into the argument, Athena then casts her vote for Orestes, breaking the jury's tie. The irate Furies, however, must also be accommodated, and she offers them a new role as patron goddesses of Athens under a new name. From the Furies, they now become the Eumenides— the kindly ones—and from this new designation the play takes its title.

This denouement was portentous for Athenian democracy. To break an unending cycle of murderous avenging, private feuds will now be settled in public courts. As justice replaces vengeance and government takes over from the family, the female will be subjugated to the male: citizen jurors, all of them men, now arbitrate disputes. There are to be no more Clytemnestras—women who take on the traditional male roles of ruling and killing—and the frightening force of the (female) Furies is broken and thus tamed. Their characteristic female emotionality is to be rechanneled from avenging to nurturing, while the serious business of life is transferred to male rationality. In the words of feminist theorist Nancy Hartsock, the Furies

> appear as elements of the archaic "old religion," primitive, lawless, regressive, and tied to the forces of earth and nature, while the male, "bright Apollo," is seen as leading toward the future—law abiding, orderly, and by implication part of the world of reason. Because of the danger the female presents to the male world, the plays can be read as a statement of the importance fifth-century Athenians gave to domesticating the forces of disorder. Failing this domestication, they feared, the male community could not survive.[9]

And not only that; women's unique contribution to the community, their fertility, is now denied.

All this was in keeping not only with human justice but with the justice of Zeus, and other gods play their parts as well. Artemis's demand for a sacrifice sets the action of the trilogy in motion, Apollo moves the action forward, and Athena is indispensable to its resolution. To be sure, not everyone benefits from divine intervention—certainly not Iphigenia or Cassandra, whose lot it is to serve as collateral damage. But Aeschylus never suggests that we live in the best of all possible worlds, only in one guided by the divine. While this releases the characters from some responsibility—Orestes, for example—it does not absolve everyone. Agamemnon remains guilty of a horrific act. As Aristotle would observe, the choices people make reveal their character (*Poetics* 1450b), and the comparative ease with which Agamemnon chose the death of his child reveals much. Irrespective of Artemis's intrusion, Agamemnon by virtue of his character set in motion the chain of killings.

The role of character even in a world directed by the gods is also central to the most famous play of antiquity, Sophocles' *Oedipus the King*, a play that does in fact correspond to Aristotle's notion that a tragedy should demonstrate the fall into wretchedness of an otherwise worthy character because of a precarious flaw in his make-up. Not surprisingly, Aristotle held the play in the highest regard; I myself am sorely tempted to label it the best play ever written. The roller coaster ride experienced by the audience as Oedipus comes to acquire more and more evidence of his identity; the irony of his repeated condemnations of a criminal who turns out to be none other than Oedipus himself; the chilling interaction of fate and character; the way the play picks up speed and judders along relentlessly as it hurtles to its denouement—nothing can match it. The suspense created by Sophocles in an audience that knew full well how the play would turn out is a formidable tribute to his artistic talent.

Like the story of Agamemnon's family, the legend of which Sophocles made use to explore the human condition involved a curse. When it had been prophesied that his child would grow up to kill him and marry his wife, King Laius of Thebes sought to thwart the prophecy by handing the newborn over to a shepherd with instructions to do away with it. Unfamiliar as he was with the corpus of world mythology, Laius could not know that this strategy inevitably fails. Sure enough, the shepherd has no stomach for the deed, and baby Oedipus comes to be adopted by the childless king and queen of Corinth, Polybus and Merope. After some years have passed, a drunken partygoer insinuates that Polybus and Merope are not Oedipus's biological parents. Badly shaken, the young man undertakes a visit to Apollo's oracle at Delphi to inquire about his origins. When instead of answering his question the Pythia informs him that he will kill his father and marry his mother, a second attempt is made to thwart the oracle: panic-stricken, Oedipus flees Corinth, leaving Polybus and Merope behind forever.

In his flight, he gets into a brawl over the right of way at a crossroads and in a burst of road rage kills a few people. One of them, of course, turns out to be King Laius, his biological father. He then encounters the Sphinx, a hybrid creature with a woman's head, a lion's body, and a bird's wings who has been destroying the crops of nearby Thebes and killing passersby who cannot solve her riddle. What, she demands to know, walks on four legs in the morning, two in the afternoon, and three at night? Oedipus becomes the first to unravel the brainteaser: Man, he replies, who crawls on all fours as a baby, walks on two legs as an adult, and leans on a walking stick in old age. The devastated Sphinx jumps to her death, and Oedipus proceeds on the road to Thebes, where he receives a warm welcome, marries Laius's widow Jocasta, and rules as king. Once more, time passes and Thebes is suffering anew, assailed by a horrible plague. When the oracle at Delphi reveals that the plague has been caused by the polluting presence of Laius's killer in the city, Oedipus immediately vows to flush the perpetrator out and punish him. As the truth finally emerges, Jocasta commits suicide and the devastated Oedipus blinds himself. The discombobulation one might expect anyone to feel in the circumstances was compounded by the Greek dread of *miasma*, unspeakable pollution: a horror that served to nullify any attempts to absolve Oedipus on grounds of ignorance. While it is his marriage to his mother that most unsettles moderns, for the Greeks the patricide disturbed the order of society every bit as much, for murder within the family polluted the relationship between the killer and all the surviving relatives. In the state outlined in Plato's *Laws*, a killer returning from exile is forbidden to resume association with his family if it is a relative whom he has killed (868c–869a).

It was Sophocles' genius that rightly judged the optimal way to approach the story: dramatizing Oedipus's dawning realization of his own identity. The play exemplifies the technique of dramatic irony, as we, the audience, are all too keenly aware that Oedipus himself is the killer on whom he is calling down fire and brimstone when he vows to rid the city of its *miasma*, declaring

> I pray the man who did this, whether he
> Bears all the guilt, or has confederates,
> May in the dreadful way that he deserves
> Wear out a life as evil as himself;
> And should it prove to be the case that he

With my full knowledge dwells in my own house,
I call these curses down upon myself as well. (246–51)

The ironies are excruciating, and it is easy to imagine the audience recoiling in horror. Why, Oedipus says, Laius and I are practically related! If only he and Jocasta had been blessed with offspring,

Then children to a single mother born
Would have united us with family bonds. (261)

Therefore, he promises,

As if he were my father, I will fight
In his behalf, and I will stop at nothing
In my attempt to catch his murderer. (264–66)

And so on and on throughout the play. With every new utterance of this nature, the ironies multiply and the tension is heightened. When will Oedipus learn the true meaning of his words, thus resolving the unnerving disconnect between the level of the audience's knowledge and his own?

On hearing the details of Laius's death from Jocasta's brother Creon, Oedipus is skeptical of the suggestion that robbers were responsible and surmises that it must have been a professional hit. Surely someone in the city commissioned the assassination. At the time, his conjecture appears reasonable, but it soon becomes clear that he is prone to see conspiracy everywhere around him. When Teiresias accuses him of being Laius's killer, he instantly suspects that Creon has put the blind seer up to it. Oedipus ignores the chorus's pointed warning about the dangers of a quick temper. He dares not relax his guard, he says, when an enemy is plotting against him in secret, and he threatens Creon with execution. This is not the last time he will threaten violence against those who stand in his way (nor was it the first).

As Oedipus gathers more and more information about the circumstances of Laius's murder and the disposition of the infant prince born to the king and his wife, he finds himself growing increasingly anxious. As I listen to these things, he tells Jocasta,

My soul ... it wanders suddenly. ... My mind
Is racing. ... (726–27)

Now the disjunction is operating on a different plane. Jocasta remains ignorant, while Oedipus suspects the truth that he may be the very man on whose head he has been calling down curses. "Oh, Zeus, what have you planned to do with me?" he cries (738).

It looks briefly as if Oedipus has received a reprieve. A messenger arrives from Corinth to report Polybus's death. Aha! cries Oedipus. What a mistake to trust oracles! Plainly this business about my killing my father was nonsense. Yet no sooner does he voice his remaining anxiety about incest with his mother than the messenger, hoping to allay his fears, seeks to reassure him by informing him that Polybus and Merope were not his real parents.

Terror. Despair. The shoe of ignorance is now on the other foot. It is the messenger who is clueless and Oedipus the one who knows more.

Icy fear now holds Oedipus firmly in its grip. Jocasta, recognizing the truth of Oedipus's identity, hangs herself. When at last he hears the truth from the shepherd to whom Jocasta had long ago consigned the newborn with instructions to kill it, Oedipus cries out in agony and rushes from the scene.

The conventions of Greek tragedy strictly forbade violence on stage, hence a long catalogue of "messenger speeches" in which a third party announces such acts and brings them vividly before us in description. It is through a speech of just this nature that we learn of Oedipus's final act: cutting his wife/mother down and laying her body on the ground, he plucks the golden brooches from his wife's clothes and with them stabs each of his own eyeballs, shouting:

> "No longer will you see the things I suffered,
> No more the things I did! For long enough
> You looked on those you never should have seen,
> Failing to know the ones I longed to know.
> From this day on, you will be dark forever."
> Over and over, keening in his pain,
> He struck and struck. . . .
> At every blow the eyeballs spurted blood,
> Wetting his beard. The blood that issued forth
> Came not in dribs and drabs but fell like hail,

Descending in a torrent. (1271–79)

The play has been rife with references to sight, beginning with Teiresias who, though blind, saw everything. It now comes full circle as Oedipus, once blind to the truth, now is on a par with the blind prophet, seeing at last with his mind, but no longer with his eyes. The chorus has the last word, bidding the Thebans give thought to the case of Oedipus, at one time a powerful figure envied by all, and recognize that we must count no one happy until his life has ended free of pain.

> Who of the Thebans did not envy him
> On looking at his abundant good fortune?
> At what a sea of misery has he arrived.
> No, we must wait until the final fated day
> When he has crossed life's border free from pain
> To count a mortal creature truly blessed. (1524–30)

The last lines here offer a strong parallel to Solon's words to Croesus at Herodotus 1. 32. 9 (earlier, pp. 90–91). (We cannot know who wrote first, Herodotus or Sophocles; the two men were said to be friends.)

Oedipus curses himself when at last he can no longer escape the truth, but where, really, does the responsibility for his actions lie? Did Apollo's oracle not doom him even before his birth? Sophocles proposes two answers, one here in *Oedipus the King* and a different one later in *Oedipus at Colonus*, written at the end of his life and produced posthumously. In *Oedipus the King*, Oedipus tries to distinguish between divine supervision and human responsibility. When the chorus inquires what spirit moved him to put out his eyes, he replies

> It was Apollo, to be sure, my friends,
> Who brought about my dreadful, dreadful pain.
> The hand that struck me, though—that was my own. (1329–31)

But we can go further. For throughout the play Oedipus manifests a temperament that easily accounts for the fulfilling of the oracle. He is quick to anger, prone to see himself embattled by others—by Teiresias, by Creon. More than once he threatens violence, first against Creon and then against the trembling shepherd terrified to reveal the secret of his birth. He is precisely the kind of man who would, when feeling under attack, raise his hand against a man old enough to be his . . . Fate and character go hand in glove in this excruciating drama, and it is this interplay that accounts for its force.

And yet. Oedipus's misfortune could be construed very differently, and this is precisely what Sophocles does in his revisionist *Oedipus at Colonus*. There it is revealed that Oedipus is both cursed and blessed. Purified by his suffering, he will bring the gods' grace to the place where he dies, and he chooses to end his life in Sophocles' native Athens— indeed in the part of the city where the playwright was born. Now Oedipus is portrayed as a victim, cursed in his fortune but blameless in his unwitting misdeeds. Forgotten are the dangerous character traits presented in the earlier play as complicit in his downfall. How, in the light of prophecies preceding his birth, he asks, can he be held responsible for what happened?[10] No, he says,

> I won't be judged to be an evil man—
> Not in my marriage, not in Laius's death. . . . (989–90)

Think about it, he tells Creon. If someone tried to kill you here and now, what would you do: defend yourself, or pause to ask him if by chance he happened to be your father? You know the answer as well as I do. And that's precisely the situation in which I found myself.

Sophocles' construction of events here differs from that in the earlier play not only in substance but in tone. The ethos of *Oedipus the King* was firmly grounded in myth; the commission of unholy acts brings upon a man *miasma* that affects everyone around him. *Oedipus at Colonus*, taking a more rationalistic approach, engages the more modern question of intent. At the end of his life, and a quarter century after the earlier play, Sophocles construed the matter of responsibility differently. The later Oedipus is a victim of circumstances, indeed of the divine.

The relationship between divine and human causation is paramount in Euripides' *Hippolytus*, whose prologue is spoken by the deity who sets the action in motion. Although a contemporary of Sophocles—the two died within months of each other—Euripides puts before our eyes

FIGURE 7.1. Cleveland Medea Vase. This dramatic Attic krater from around
400 BCE depicts the ending of Euripides' *Medea*, as Medea escapes in a chariot
drawn by dragons while the nurse and tutor stand below with the corpses of her
slain children; above left and right are two Furies, symbols of revenge. The
Cleveland Museum of Art, Leonard C. Hanna, Jr. Fund 1991.1.

and ears a different world, one infused with wild passions, the rhetoric
of the sophists, and novel twists on old myths. As the success of the
Oresteia and the Oedipus cycle attests, Aristotle was certainly correct
that the most effective tragedies involved dreadful actions taken within
the family (*Poetics* 1453b). Euripides certainly knew this as well. In the
Bacchae, Dionysus's worshipper Agave thinks she has killed a lion in

the god's ecstatic nocturnal rites only to discover that the head she is bearing triumphantly on a pike is that of her own son. *Medea* detailed the unraveling of the household that resulted from Jason's voyage to retrieve the golden fleece, as his subsequent abandonment of his helper Medea leads her to kill their children.

Hippolytus treats the family of the Athenian hero Theseus and portrays the disaster that ensues when a person motivated by white hot passion comes into conflict with an individual of a far chillier temperament. While Theseus, as so often, is traveling on business, his wife Phaedra has become desperately lovesick for young Hippolytus, Theseus's grown son by an Amazon, and appears to be starving herself to death in her misery and shame. The hopelessness of her longing is overdetermined. Not only is Hippolytus an eminently inappropriate love object—a married woman in love with her stepson!—but the youth has devoted himself to a life of virginity, spending his days hunting in the forest and worshipping only his fellow hunter, Artemis, goddess of the wild. He despises all that Aphrodite represents, declining to accord her even the most minimal reverence. Phaedra's torment is double-edged. She is both perishing of unrequited love and consumed with self-hatred because of her adulterous thoughts. She contemplates death as superior to living on and risking adultery, which would stand in the way of her children growing up in Athens *eukleeis*: with good *kleos* (423). Realizing her mistress is in danger of dying, Phaedra's nurse delivers a long sophistic speech in favor of yielding to her passion, citing the universality of love, cataloguing the affairs of the gods (at least one of them not so consensual), and stressing the impossibility of perfection. After all, she says, look at the roof beams in your house! Do you think they are laid out perfectly straight (468–69)? Not even construction workers are perfect. Come, she concludes; give up this misery:

> It's hybris plain and simple
> To want to be superior to the gods! (474–75)

Ironic words in light of the superiority complex that seems tied up with Hippolytus's ostentatious chastity.

Phaedra and the chorus are shocked by her speech, whose sophistry Phaedra decries. It is this, she says,

> This art of speaking fair, deceptive words
> That ruins cities, destroys people's homes. (486–87)

No, she insists, what the occasion calls for is words that conduce to *kleos* (489). No whit discouraged, the nurse proceeds to spill her charge's secret to Hippolytus, with predictably catastrophic results. Though he has been sworn to silence, Hipppolytus cannot contain himself. When the nurse reminds him of his promise, he exclaims in a line later deployed by Aristophanes to characterize the shiftiness of Euripides' characters:

> It was my tongue that swore it, not my heart. (612; cf. Aristophanes,
> *Frogs* 1471)

He then erupts in a long misogynistic tirade. Oh Zeus, he cries, why did you saddle us with this cheating race of women? Surely you could have found a better way to propagate the race:

> Men might have dedicated images
> Of bronze or iron or gold in your temples
> According to their means, the purchase price
> To buy the seed of progeny, and in this way
> Live in our houses free of womankind. (620–24)

Marriage he derides as at best a mixed affair. If the wife is acceptable, the in-laws are bad, and vice versa. A man can only hope that the woman he marries proves to be a nonentity, for an intelligent wife is a disaster. I hate smart women, he says:

> May there never be
> In my own home a woman who has got
> A sharper intellect than suits her sex.
> Lust will breed mischief in the smarter ones.
> At least the limits of their slender wits
> Keep the less gifted ones from acting up.

No slave should be allowed to see a woman.
Instead, we ought to give them for companions
The wildest beasts, voiceless (but with sharp teeth!)
So they cannot converse with anyone.
But as it is, the wicked ones lay plots
Indoors, and slaves then spread their schemes abroad. (640–50)

Damn you women, he concludes, every last one of you:

I'll never get enough of hating you.
Some say I rail at you incessantly,
But women's vileness is incessant too! (664–66)

Hippolytus has said a mouthful. His words go far beyond those of
Hesiod, who had said of marriage:

There's nothing better than a worthy wife,
Nothing more horrid than a dreadful one—
A parasite, she'll scorch a man to ash
Without a flame, no matter how robust
He seems to be, and hasten his old age. (*Works and Days*, 702–5)

It is not surprising that Aristophanes should have organized his *Women
at the Thesmophoria* around the notion that the women of Athens put
Euripides on trial for slandering females in his plays.

Overhearing this rant, Phaedra is so mortified that she hangs herself,
but not before leaving a note in which she claims that Hippolytus
prompted her suicide by raping her. In so doing she both saves her reputation and strikes at the man who has so brutally rejected her—and has
given voice to all the reproaches she feels she deserves. Words, Euripides' play makes clear, are problematic; Phaedra was correct in her claim
that deceptive language brings ruin to families (486–87). The nurse
used words to mislead Phaedra about her intentions, and then to betray
her to Hippolytus; Hippolytus used them to shame Phaedra; and Phaedra now uses them to destroy Hippolytus. Words are particularly problematic in the intensely chatty world of Athens, where reputation is
easily undone by slander.[11]

Dazed by the unexpected death of his young wife, Theseus disbelieves Hippolytus's indignant denials, and Hippolytus, who up until now has behaved execrably, does the honorable thing and keeps the oath he swore to the nurse not to reveal Phaedra's passion for him. Only after all this has ended in Hippolytus's death does a devastated Theseus learn how deeply he has wronged his son. As in *Medea,* a conflict between a man and a woman over love has disastrous results not only for them, as the woman takes vengeance on the man who has both rejected and wronged her, but for others as well. In both dramas the playwright explores the line between vengeance and justice—and it is important to remember that few Greeks perceived any daylight between the two. The standard definition of justice that Socrates was at pains to debunk was doing good to your friends and harm to your enemies.

But there is more. Perched high on the roof of Theseus's house, the first character to appear in *Hippolytus* is Aphrodite herself. She characterizes herself in the very first word of the play as *pollē*: mighty, powerful. And she is, for she directs the baneful action of the drama almost to the end. The chaste young hunter Hippolytus, she explains, has slighted her:

> He says I am the worst, the very worst
> Of all the gods there are. He shrinks from sex,
> Recoils from marriage—honors Artemis,
> And her alone. (13–15)

Indeed he has a close personal relationship with Artemis unusual for a mortal, even closer in some ways than that of Odysseus with Athena; they seem actually to "hang out" together in the woods. For this, Aphrodite says, he will pay. She has made his father's wife Phaedra fall hopelessly in love with him. Though she regrets the collateral damage that will ensue, she will not be satisfied until she has exacted *dikē,* just recompense, from her enemies (50). It is the same word that Medea uses: Jason will give her *dikē* for his transgressions (*Medea,* 802).

Just as Oedipus's fate was decreed by an oracle before his birth, so Phaedra is the plaything of a vengeful deity, and as is the case with Oedipus, the unraveling of the disaster of Phaedra's and Hippolytus's lives owes much to their own characters—Phaedra's emotionality, Hippolytus's

tunnel vision. Hippolytus is not merely committed to chastity, certainly
a strange position for a Greek man. Obsessed both with his chastity and
with the superiority he believes that it brings with it, he has lost sight of
the need to give all Olympians their due. Far wiser than his master, Hippolytus's slave worries about this exclusive cultivation of Artemis, cautioning Hippolytus not to disdain Aphrodite in his enthusiasm for the
goddess of the hunt; thus Hippolytus's prudent slave attendant serves
as a counterweight to Phaedra's imprudent slave nurse. Aphrodite, the
priggish Hippolytus announces, "I greet only at a distance; I am pure"
(102), adding that he has no use for any deity who is worshipped at
night. The fastidious avowal of chastity he puts forward in his defense
against Phaedra's wrongful charge of rape reveals what Greeks would
have considered a profoundly peculiar attitude to human sexuality. His
body, he says,

> has not known erotic love:
> I know the act from others' words alone
> Or pictures I have seen. My virgin soul
> Recoils even from viewing things like this. (1003–6)

Although Theseus is too quick to assume the truth of Phaedra's dying,
lying accusation, he is right on the mark in his assessment of his son:

> So you, a close companion of the gods,
> Not like the rest of us, are special—
> Modest and chaste and pure of every vice? (948–49)

He does not fail to note Hippolytus's unctuous self-satisfaction:

> You work so hard at worshipping yourself
> That justice and respect for parents both
> Fall by the wayside; no time left for that! (1080–81)

But of course Theseus is mistaken in his belief that Hippolytus has
violated his wife. Though his denunciations of Hippolytus suggest that
in some ways he knows his son well, he is surprisingly quick to label him
a smarmy hypocrite, professing purity and chastity while in reality guilty
of the worst of transgressions. At this juncture, however, Hippolytus

redeems himself somewhat, and our sympathies shift dramatically to the beleaguered youth. Even in the face of his father's sweeping moral condemnation, even under the threat of exile, he will not break his oath. Sworn to secrecy, he remains silent about Phaedra's motive in writing the damning farewell note.

The reward for his honorable silence is death, a hideously painful death of which we learn in a messenger speech. For the incensed Theseus is not just the king of Athens. In addition to his human father, his predecessor King Aegeus, he also has a divine one, Poseidon, and Poseidon has granted him three curses. O father Poseidon, he prays with chilling directness,

> With one of these fell curses kill my child! (888–89)

His prayers are answered as the sea god sends a particularly savage bull from inside a monstrous wave. Hippolytus's skilled hand is no match for the panic of his spooked horses, and his car capsizes. Then, the messenger reports,

> Confusion reigned. The axle-pins all leapt
> Into the air; Hippolytus himself,
> Entangled in the reins was dragged along,
> Bound in a knot that couldn't be untied.
> His head now smashed against the rocks, his flesh
> All torn, he uttered cries it hurt to hear. (1234–39)

Too late, Artemis appears and shares with Theseus the awful truth that the child whose death he has brought about was guiltless with respect to Phaedra. Aphrodite's revenge is now complete. It may be that Theseus, the only one in the triad left alive, suffers the most, having to live out his life knowing that he caused his son's death. Divine meddling has cooperated with human character to undo him. The passionate Phaedra, the prissy Hippolytus, the rash Theseus all had their parts to play in moving the action of the drama forward, and we are left uncertain as to just why life turns out as it does.

Hippolytus raises many questions: about passion and madness, about divine interference and mortal responsibility. While Euripides was putting together his play, Socrates was conversing with the youth of Athens about central questions of life such as why people behave as they do. Ignorance of the good, he maintained, alone explained the existence of evil. Those who through spirited debate and hard thinking gain a genuine understanding of good and evil would never choose evil, which harms the perpetrator even more than it hurts the victim. *Hippolytus* calls this tenet seriously into question, and this may have formed part of the poet's intent. Phaedra was not blind to the implications of her actions, but she chose them just the same, in the grips of passion. It is such passions, Euripides seems to be suggesting, rather than any intellectual apparatus, that determine human action, regardless of what philosophers may have to say.

———

The centrality of tragedy in the life of the polis is clear in the other dramatic genre of the fifth century, Old Comedy. The plays of the comic dramatist Aristophanes assume substantial familiarity with tragedy; audiences were plainly expected to recognize the purple passages and plot twists to which his plays make reference. During the competition in the Underworld between Aeschylus and Euripides, the chorus in his *Frogs* assures the playwrights that they will be judged by people of discernment:

> If you're worried our spectators just can't appreciate
> Delicate subtleties, intricate arguments,
> Banish all fear, for the world's been transmogrified.
> Everything's different now: people are veterans.
> Folks now own books and have come to appreciate
> All of the fine points: they're naturally smart as well! (109–15)

Aristophanes' subject matter was both wide and narrow, for he wrote about human nature broadly but also quite specifically about his native Athens, on which his plays cast an eye that was both critical and loving: he loved an idealized Athens of the past and criticized the all too real Athens of the present. Each play presents an ordinary citizen with a problem that the polis is not solving, indeed has sometimes created—like the Peloponnesian War. He or she develops a solution that is at the same time completely logical and utterly fantastic: women will take over the government; a farmer will fly up to Olympus to interrogate the gods about ending the war; disgruntled Athenians will metamorphose into birds and join their feathered friends in establishing a new polis in the sky, *Nephelokokkygia* (Cloudcuckooland); a debt-ridden man will send his son to study with Socrates so that he can sweet-talk his creditors. From there the plays take flight, and the game is afoot.

The contrast between the degenerate Athens of the present and the idealized Athens of the past is embodied in the *Frogs* in a contest between Aeschylus and Euripides, both lately arrived in Hades. When the play was produced, Sophocles had only just died, and the few references to him seem to have been added at the last minute to a play written when he was still alive. I'm in a bad way, we hear Dionysus confessing to Heracles as the play opens. He has been overcome, it seems, by a powerful longing, the force which he tries to convey by comparing it to the sudden craving for . . . pea soup. Have you ever been seized by an uncontrollable desire for pea soup, he asks Heracles? Have I ever! the god replies. Thousands of times! Well, Dionysus explains, that's precisely the kind of longing that is consuming me, but it's for Euripides. The god is immovable in his determination to retrieve the playwright from the Underworld. All the really good poets, he complains, are dead, and no one is left to say anything adventuresome like "a tongue that swears without the mind's consent," paraphrasing Hippolytus's famous line to Phaedra's nurse at Hipppolytus (*Frogs* 102; *Hippolytus* 612). Knowing that Heracles has himself visited Hades in the course of his last labor, when he was required to retrieve the dog Cerberus, he seeks travel tips from his fellow god—and resolves to disguise himself as Heracles himself, who is familiar to the powers below.

Crossing the river, he encounters the play's chorus of frogs, who punctuate their song with the Aristophanic equivalent of "ribbit":

Brekekekex koax koax!

Upon introducing himself as "the mighty Heracles," Dionysus finds his plan backfiring. So far from welcoming him on his supposed return,

Cerberus's guardian is perfectly horrified to see him—the damned do-gnapper is back!—whereupon the same god who had been portrayed only months before as himself a formidable deity in Euripides' *Bacchae* collapses, terrified, in a pool of diarrhea. Things go from bad to worse when he is "recognized" by the staff of the eating establishment Heracles had bankrupted with his gluttony.

The chorus, as so often in Aristophanes' plays, sets itself up as the arbiter of morals. It's right, says its leader,

> that the job of advising and teaching
> What's good for the city should fall to our chorus,
> A sanctified choir; we will share all our thinking. (686–88)

Just as it makes no use of the finest of its long-standing coins but rather uses inferior ones fresh out of the mint, they say, the city despises the *kaloi k'agathoi* trained in the old-fashioned way in athletics, dancing, and music, relying instead on Johnnie-come-latelies, "rascally children of rascally parents" (731). This, the chorus announces, must change.

We now learn that Euripides has challenged Aeschylus for the privi-leged position of sitting next to Hades and enjoying free meals in the Prytaneum, a reference to the privileges awarded to outstanding athletic or military achievement at Athens, but comical in light of the fact that for all its other drawbacks, the Underworld does operate on an "full board" basis: everyone's meals are free! In the upcoming contest that is to settle the matter, what better judge than Dionysus, with his background in theater? There ensues a tit-for-tat mudslinging as, amid parodic quota-tions of one another's work, each playwright seeks to persuade Diony-sus that he is worthy of the chair. Euripides accuses Aeschylus of being bombastic and obscure, and Aeschylus lambastes Euripides for putting ordinary people in everyday situations on the stage. Euripides makes clear that in fact he takes pride in this:

> I didn't leave a single person out:
> A slave would speak as much as any wife—
> Who spoke as well; the master, the young girl,
> And the old woman—everybody spoke. (947–49)

For this, Aeschylus says, he should have been executed. No, replies Euripides,

> Rather, it was a democratic act. (952)

Aeschylus then turns to the heart of the matter, the value of the poet to the community, asking for what qualities a poet should be admired. For his sound advice, Euripides replies; because we make people better citizens.

There is no disagreement between the playwrights as to the moral obligations of the poet. Throughout history, Aeschylus says, poets have improved people by their teaching. Orpheus revealed mystic rites and the importance of abstaining from taking life; Musaeus told us all about oracles and how to cure diseases; in agriculture, we learned from Hesiod, and in warfare, from Homer (1030–36). Euripides, Aeschylus alleges, had turned the stalwart infantrymen shaped by Aeschylean drama into deserters, loafers, dishonest politicians, and men who are so unfit they can't even run a race—and turned respectable women's thoughts to adultery by stories like that of Phaedra to boot (1013–17, 1044, 1083–88). It is not only Aeschylus, Aristophanes suggests, who represents the morality of the good old days. Athenians as a group were also better in the generation of the Persian Wars. To Euripides' response that the story of Phaedra was already well known when he wrote *Hippolytus*, Aeschylus replies:

> Of course. The poet, though, must make a point
> Of hiding wicked things, not staging them
> Or teaching them. The young, the children, learn
> From teachers, but adults from poets. Thus
> We have to teach them lessons that are good. (1053–56)

Despite his original commitment to Euripides, Dionysus ends by siding with Aeschylus, announcing his intention to bring him back to Athens, whereupon Aeschylus bequeaths the chair of tragedy to Sophocles. When an indignant Euripides reminds him that he had sworn by the gods to choose him, Dionysus has the perfect riposte. "It was my tongue that swore," he replies, quoting the specious argument of Hippolytus when he betrays Phaedra's confidence:

It was my tongue that swore it, not my heart. (*Hippolytus*, 612)

The chorus rejoices that Athenians will now have something better to do with their time than split hairs in idle chatter with the likes of Socrates, and Hades himself in his farewell bids Aeschylus educate the dummies there—of whom, he says, Athens has many—and sends him away with (presumably fatal) gifts for a bunch of squirrely politicians, bidding them to hurry on down to his kingdom.

The appeal of Athenian drama is universal, knowing few limits of time and place. Tragedy was popular in its own day outside Athens. Both Aeschylus and Euripides ended their lives in other parts of Greece where they received patronage, Aeschylus in Sicily and Euripides in Macedonia, and Athenian soldiers enslaved in Sicily after their catastrophic defeat in the harbor of Syracuse often won their freedom by entertaining their captors with recitations from Euripides' plays. The splendid Greek theater Alexander made a point of building in Babylon still stands. Romans both produced the originals and adapted them in the dramas of Seneca and others. The much-heralded opening performance of the new Olympic Theater in Vicenza, Italy, on March 3, 1585, was *Oedipus the King*, and so eager was the audience to see it that spectators began pouring into the theater nearly ten hours before the play was slated to begin.[12] Greek tragedy, which formed the basis of so much Renaissance drama—Marlowe and Shakespeare in England, Lope de Vega and Calderón de la Barca in Spain, Racine in France— continues to influence theater on every continent except Antarctica, whether in revivals or in adaptations; we will examine some of the variations rung on Sophocles' *Oedipus* in the epilogue. Although *Lysistrata* has been adapted many times as a rallying cry for women to be taken seriously as full persons, Aristophanes has enjoyed an influence far more diffuse than the tragedians. His heirs are as different as madcap comedians like Mel Brooks and Carol Burnett in the United States, Charlie Chaplin and Monty Python in England, and the late-evening talk show hosts whose nightly commentary on current events is so hilarious—and so very on target—as to be quoted in the morning papers the day after. But while Aristophanes plainly did not invent humor, it is sometimes easy to believe that all the men and women who have earned their living by making people laugh owe something to his genius.

Laughter abounded as well in the third genre to grace the Attic stage, the satyr play. Only one satyr play has survived intact, the *Cyclops* of Euripides, which takes its plot from Odysseus's encounter with Polyphemus, but fragments of several others can still be read. A mixed genre, the satyr play combined elements of comedy and tragedy and was labeled by an unknown writer of the second century CE "tragedy at play."[13] It resembled comedy in its zany humor and even in the make-up of the chorus: the chorus of satyrs that was universal in satyr drama and gave it its name often appeared in lost comedies as well. Rarely, however, did satyr plays lampoon public figures as did Old Comedy, and they took their plots, like tragedy, from the myths of the heroic age, producing comic results from the incongruous overlap of the august heroes of myth and the eminently undignified satyrs cavorting around them. The survival of more satyr plays is a particular loss in view of the close connection between the hybrid satyrs and the god in whose honor the plays were produced: Dionysus, gender-fluid and closely connected to nature and animal life. Along with fourth-century tragedy, nearly the entirety of this enigmatic genre has perished, and without the satyr plays we are left with much the same distorted picture of Greek drama as we get of Greek art and architecture from the shining white statues and temples time has stripped of their paint.

Suggested Readings

Billings, Joshua. 2021. *The Philosophical Stage: Drama and Dialectic in Classical Athens*. Princeton, NJ: Princeton University Press.

Bromberg, Jacques, and Peter Burian, eds. 2020. *A Companion to Aeschylus. Blackwell Companions to the Ancient World*. Malden, MA: Wiley-Blackwell.

Cartledge, Paul. 1991. *Aristophanes and His Theatre of the Absurd*. London: Bristol Classical Press.

Critchley, Simon. 2019. *Tragedy, the Greeks, and Us*. New York: Pantheon.

Easterling, P. E. 1997. *The Cambridge Companion to Greek Tragedy. Cambridge Companions to Literature*. Cambridge, UK, and New York: Cambridge University Press.

Ehrenberg, Victor. 1951. *The People of Aristophanes: A Sociology of Old Attic Comedy*. Cambridge, MA: Harvard University Press.

Hall, Edith. 2010. *Greek Tragedy: Suffering under the Sun*. Oxford: Oxford University Press.

Henderson, Jeffrey. 1993. *The Maculate Muse: Obscene Language in Attic Comedy*, 2nd edition. Oxford and New York: Oxford University Press.

Goff, Barbara. 1990. *The Noose of Words: Readings of Desire, Violence and Language in Euripides' Hippolytos*. Cambridge, UK: Cambridge University Press.

Goldhill, Simon. 2004. *Love, Sex & Tragedy: Why Classics Matters*. London: John Murray.

———. 2012. *Sophocles and the Language of Tragedy*. Oxford and New York: Oxford University Press.

Gregory, Justina. 2008. *A Companion to Greek Tragedy*. Malden, MA: Wiley-Blackwell.

Kyle, Donald G. 2014. *Sport and Spectacle in the Ancient World*. Ancient Cultures, Book 5, 2nd edition. Malden, MA: Wiley-Blackwell.

McClure, Laura. 1999. *Spoken Like a Woman: Speech and Gender in Athenian Drama*. Princeton, NJ: Princeton University Press.

McCoskey, Denise E., and Emily Zakin, eds. 2010. *Bound by the City: Greek Tragedy, Sexual Difference, and the Formation of the Polis*. Albany: State University of New York Press.

Mikalson, Jon D. 1991. *Honor Thy Gods: Popular Religion in Greek Tragedy*. Chapel Hill: University of North Carolina Press.

Miller, Stephen G. 2006. *Ancient Greek Athletics*. New Haven, CT: Yale University Press.

Nelson, Stephanie. 2016. *Aristophanes and His Tragic Muse: Comedy, Tragedy and the Polis in 5th Century Athens*. Mnemosyne Supplement. Leiden: Brill.

Nussbaum, Martha C. 2001. *The Fragility of Goodness: Luck and Ethics in Greek Tragedy and Philosophy*, updated 2nd edition. Cambridge, UK, and New York: Cambridge University Press.

Ormand, Kirk, ed. 2012. *A Companion to Sophocles*. Malden, MA: Wiley-Blackwell.

Rehm, Rush. 2017. *Understanding Tragic Theatre (Understanding the Ancient World)*, 2nd edition. Abingdon, UK, and New York: Routledge.

Rusten, Jeffrey, ed. 2011. *The Birth of Comedy: Texts, Documents, and Art from Athenian Comic Competitions, 486–280*. Baltimore, MD: Johns Hopkins University Press.

Scodel, Ruth. 2010. *An Introduction to Greek Tragedy*. New York: Cambridge University Press, 2010.

Sommerstein, Alan H. 2002. *Greek Drama and Dramatists*. New York: Routledge.

Stoneman, Richard. 2014. *Pindar (Understanding Classics)*. London and New York: I. B. Tauris.

Taafe, Lauren. 2016. *Aristophanes and Women*. Routledge Revivals. New York: Routledge.

Tyrrell, William Blake. 2004. *The Smell of Sweat: Greek Athletics, Olympics, and Culture*. Waukonda, IL: Bolchazy-Carducci Publishers.

Vernant, Jean-Pierre, and Pierre Vidal-Naquet. 1988. *Myth and Tragedy in Ancient Greece*, trans. Janet Lloyd. New York: Zone Books.

Vetter, Lisa Pace. 2005. *Women's Work as Political Art: Weaving and Dialectical Politics in Homer, Aristophanes, and Plato*. Lanham, MD: Lexington/Rowman & Littlefield.

Winkler, John J., and Froma I. Zeitlin, eds. 1990. *Nothing to Do with Dionysos? Athenian Drama in Its Social Context*. Princeton, NJ: Princeton University Press.

Wohl, Victoria. 2015. *Euripides and the Politics of Form*. Princeton, NJ, and Oxford: Princeton University Press.

Zeitlin, Froma I. 1995. *Playing the Other: Gender and Society in Classical Greek Literature (Women in Culture and Society)*. Chicago: University of Chicago Press.

CHAPTER 8

The Search for Meaning

The path of philosophy turns away from the sacred imagery of myth toward empirical and conceptual models of thought. This entails a turn from the existential lived world toward abstract representations of the world. Now the world is measured according to principles of unity, universality and constancy, and the mind aims for empirical and conceptual foundations which permit a kind of certainty.

—LAWRENCE J. HATAB, *MYTH AND PHILOSOPHY: A CONTEST OF TRUTHS*

The unexamined life is not worth living.

—SOCRATES AS IMAGINED BY PLATO, *APOLOGY* 38A

Myth and religion never lost their grip on the Greek imagination. Generation after generation, century after century, no social, cultural, and political transformations could alter the fact that Greek life was both overlaid with and undergirded by a rich and ever-growing body of thought about the gods and the imagined heroic past. Beginning around 600, however, thinkers in Ionia began to explore alternative ways of explaining the cosmos. Not long afterward this speculation crossed the sea and took root in the communities of Magna Graecia, and a variety of provocative theories about the creation and workings of the universe sprang up and were promulgated throughout the Greek world. A number of these ideas were later adapted by Plato and Aristotle. Lectures at Plato's Academy and Aristotle's Lyceum were directed at a highbrow elite who had the leisure to think about ideas, many of whom looked forward to using their education to play an important role in shaping the life of the polis. When Alexander of Macedon died in 323 after changing the shape of the world, followed by Aristotle the following year, philosophy came to be directed rather to the ordinary man—and woman—in the street. While very different, each successive school of thought drew profit from the thinkers who had gone before and frequently incorporated aspects of their ideas.

———

The advancement of knowledge begins with the asking of a question, and Greece's earliest philosophers asked question upon question. In the absence of laboratories, the equipment that lay to hand in their search for answers was their own restless intellects, with an occasional assist from thinkers to the east who had applied themselves to similar questions before. How had the world come into being, and of what was it made? Is the universe composed of one essential substance or many? Is it organized according to fixed principles, and if so, what are those principles, and where did they come from? Is it a complete and unified structure the function of whose parts conduces to its smooth operation, or is it merely the outcome of a collection of random developments? Can nature alone account for the regularity of the cosmos without the guiding hand of a sentient intelligence?

Had there been a time when the universe did not exist? What implications did the structure of the universe carry for how people should live their lives? What role was played by the gods in shaping the universe—and in molding a person's life? What is the soul made of? What happens when we die? Is it really possible to obtain certain knowledge about these questions? Do the senses help in the acquisition of this knowledge, or do they stand in the way? Historian of science Geoffrey Lloyd is probably correct to suggest that this speculation was fueled by the spirit of competition identified by both Hesiod and Aristotle as an essential building block of society, as one thinker after another strove to develop a more accurate paradigm.[1] The speculative thinkers who posed these questions and sought to answer them have been known since the nineteenth century as the "Presocratics." What a nod that is to Socrates, especially since one of them, Democritus, was in fact his contemporary! Modern philosophical thought has found the Platonic dialogues, in which Socrates generally appears, to be such a watershed in the history of thought as to warrant the division of Greek thinkers into those independent of Socrates and those who succeeded him. Understandably so, yet the Presocratics—those whom modern scholars conceived as living in a benighted intellectual universe not yet blessed with the deathless wisdom of Socrates, Plato, and Aristotle—themselves formed a first watershed, the first wave (to mix aquatic metaphors) of that tide that moved reflection on the world into a new order.

Although they often disagreed vehemently with the Presocratics and sometimes misunderstood them, later Greeks were fascinated by these thinkers and not only preserved portions of their work but enjoyed telling colorful stories about them. In one of Plato's dialogues, Socrates cites Thales as a prime example of the absent-minded professor, telling how one day Thales was so preoccupied in looking up at the stars that he fell into a ditch, prompting the caustic remark of a Thracian slave girl to the effect that he was "so eager to understand the things in the sky that he could not see what was right in front of him" (*Theaetetus* 174a). Pythagoras and Empedocles, it was reported, put it around that they were gods, and both claimed to have enjoyed a variety of incarnations. Pythagoras believed that he had been the Trojan War hero Euphorbus in an earlier life, and Empedocles insisted that he had been once a boy, once a girl, once a plant, once a bird, and once a fish. Pythagoras was said to have appeared in several different places at once, and it was reported that one of his thighs was made of gold.

Not long before the first of the Presocratics began to apply himself to understanding the composition of the universe, similar issues had exercised Hesiod, moving him to compose the *Theogony*. Hesiod's brain, however, got a very different kind of exercise, for Hesiod took it as his mission to work into an artistic form the traditions about the world current in his

day, not to set forth a new way of looking at the cosmos. Hesiod felt no
obligation to cite any evidence for his claims about the origins and
workings of the universe; for him it was sufficient to claim that he had
heard all about them from the Muses. For Hesiod and Homer, it was
the gods who accounted for meteorological phenomena: Zeus for lightning, Poseidon for earthquakes, Iris for rainbows. The Presocratics, however, sought natural explanations, Xenophanes, for example, writing:

> And she whom they call Iris is as well
> The work of nature, purple and bright red
> And greenish-yellowish to look upon. (D39 [B32] Scholia on
>   Homer's *Iliad*)

In the view of Anaxagoras, people gave the name to the reflection of the
sun on the clouds (Aetius, *Oldest Tenets* 3. 5; 373).

It is probably no coincidence that the first of these early scientists—
protoscientists, we might call them—lived in Miletus, which sat at a
great navigational crossroads on the fringes of the Persian Empire and
whose citizens traversed the seas, bringing back not only novel wares
but also novel ideas. Identified by Aristotle as the first of these thinkers,
Thales was reported to have been of Phoenician descent. Certainly
proximity to eastern speculation fueled the beginnings of Greek cosmo-
logical thought, and, as a trader, Thales probably moved around quite a
bit in the fringe area where the Greek and Near Eastern worlds inter-
sected. Thales maintained that the original state of the universe was
water, and that, appearances to the contrary, everything we see is actually water in one form or another (Aristotle, *Metaphysics* 983b). It may
be significant that Thales was familiar with Mesopotamian creation
myths and had traveled in person to Egypt. The Babylonians and the
Egyptians had a variety of myths tracing creation to water. The somewhat younger Milesian Anaximander agreed that the seemingly diverse
elements in the universe all derived from a single original ingredient,
but for him this underlying substance was not water but rather something he called the *apeiron*, the "boundless." This *apeiron* generated the
opposite powers hot and cold, which acted on one another so as to
produce the regulated structure of the world—a far tidier system than

the chaotic realm directed by an assemblage of capricious, quarrelsome gods. A third Milesian, Anaximenes, believed that the underlying element was something he called *aēr*: not quite air, but a sort of dense mist. Different substances were created by the motion of the eternal *aēr*, which was in constant motion, and these substances had different natures depending on how much *aēr* they contained and in what condition; rarefied and condensed, *aēr* might become something as pliable as seaweed or as hard as rock.

All three of the Milesians were Monists, that is, they believed that a single substance underlay the universe and changed its form to create the variety of matter present in the world. It is no coincidence that the age of the Presocratics was also the lyric age when individual poets set forth conflicting notions about a different kind of bottom line. For Sappho, it was love that made the world go around; for Tyrtaeus, martial valor; for Archilochus, staying alive. Xenophanes awarded the palm to wisdom.

Inevitably, other views were possible. Empedocles, from Acragas in Sicily, saw the world as made up of four elements and two forces. The elements were Earth, Air, Fire, and Water, and the forces were Love and Strife. Love, the force of attraction, drew things together in a variety of combinations and arrangements, whereas conversely Strife, the force of repulsion, separated them out. Parmenides, from Elea in south Italy, held radically different views. For Parmenides, just as it was meaningless to say that something did not exist—if it did not exist, it was not something but nothing—so it was impossible for there to be empty space in the universe where nothing existed. It followed from this, moreover, that as there was no space through which to move, there was in fact no motion. In his (mostly) lost poem *On Nature* he maintained that since something that changed was no longer the same and had thus ceased to exist, change was logically impossible. Meanwhile in Ephesus a very different thinker was staking out a diametrically opposite position. For Heraclitus, famous for saying one cannot step in the same river twice, motion was the one constant in a cosmos that was always in flux—very much in fact like a river: always moving, always flowing, now approaching, now receding. Both Parmenides and Heraclitus saw coherence in the cosmos, but each man's coherence was of a radically different kind. For

Parmenides the coherence lay in the unity and stability of all matter; for Heraclitus it lay lie in the inexorability of flux. Nothing ever moves; everything moves constantly: each of these opposing worldviews formed part of the legacy of the thinkers who would come after them.

A generation later, still another of the Ionian Presocratics, Anaxagoras, relocated in Athens, where he became a friend and mentor of Pericles. Anaxagoras was also intrigued by the question of change. How, he wanted to know, did it happen that the grain and meat and fish that people ate became in time skin, bone, teeth, and so forth? "How," he asked, "could it be that hair could ever come from not-hair and flesh from not-flesh?"[2] His answer was that matter was composed of infinitely divisible particles each one of which contained the seeds of everything. Bone took the form that it did because of a preponderance of seeds that were predominantly bone, wood from a preponderance of seeds that were predominantly wood, and so forth. These seeds, Anaxagoras argued, moved quickly throughout the cosmos, organized by a force to which he gave the name *nous*, intellect, and he soon found himself known by that very nickname, Nous ("The Mind"). "All things," he wrote, "contain a portion of everything" and "circulate and are separated off by force and speed. The speed causes the force, and their speed is not like the speed of anything that now exists among humankind, but rather many times as fast."[3] All living things, he maintained, are ruled by *nous*.

The notion of matter as composed of particles was also put forward by the shadowy Leucippus and his better-known disciple Democritus, who gave the name "atoms" (from the Greek word *a-tomos*, "un-cuttable") to the tiny particles that comprised the make-up of the universe. Unlike Anaxagoras, Leucippus and Democritus conceived of these particles as indivisible. Too small to be perceived by the naked eye, these particles, varied in size and shape, sped through empty space—void—and collided in different ways to form the various substances we can see, touch, smell, feel. The differences in the atoms' shapes accounted for the qualities that we perceive in them. Spicy food, for example, was made of sharp atoms, honey from round ones.

Perhaps the most charismatic of the Presocratics was Pythagoras, plainly something of a cult figure in his day. Originally from Samos in

Ionia, he relocated in Croton in south Italy around 518, but not before traveling in those hotbeds of scientific and mathematical speculation, Egypt and Babylon. In Italy he established a community of men and women who shared his interests, which included pure mathematics— for the Pythagoreans, mathematical principles explained the whole world—and metempsychosis: the transmigration of souls. Being immortal, Pythagoras maintained, the soul would move from one body to the next, relocating after the death of its host in another creature, whether human or animal. For this reason the Pythagoreans were vegetarians and thus proof against the danger of inadvertently feasting on a departed friend or relation. The road to Purification, the Pythagoreans were convinced, was through the life of inquiry and contemplation. In their view, the underlying principles that governed the universe could best be grasped by a lifelong study not only of mathematics but of related fields such as astronomy and music as well, both of these being governed by mathematical principles. They saw numbers everywhere. As Aristotle wrote,

> those called Pythagoreans took hold of mathematics and were the first to advance that study, and being brought up in it, they believed that its principles are the principles of all things that are. . . . Since they saw the attributes and ratios of musical scales in numbers . . . and numbers seemed to be primary in all nature, they supposed the elements of numbers to be the elements of all things that are. (*Metaphysics* 985b23–986a2)

The Pythagoreans may have been the first Greeks to discover the value and the joy of studying mathematics for its own sake rather than for its practical applications. In the course of his studies, Pythagoras produced a proof of the theorem that took his name to the effect that the sum of the squares of the two sides of a right triangle is invariably equal to the square of the hypotenuse, although it is likely that this so-called Pythagorean theorem had already been discovered in Babylon, where he may have encountered it in the course of his travels.

In general, we are ignorant about female followers of the Presocratics, but the Pythagoreans offer a striking exception. There were reported to have been some twenty-eight women in the community Pythagoras established in south Italy. The active participation of women in

Pythagoreanism—a first, as far as we know, in Greek history—probably has something to do with the higher status of women in western Greece, although some of the women no doubt came from elsewhere; a number were from Sparta, where women also enjoyed comparatively high status. Precisely what role these women played in the Pythagorean community remains a puzzle. Pythagoras required men to refrain from adultery, an unusual notion in Greece. Various tracts ascribed to female Pythagoreans circulated after Pythagoras's death, and Theano (wife? daughter?) was believed by many to have taken over as head of the community after he died. Understanding the prevalence and work of female Pythagoreans is made difficult by the alternating fascination and horror Greek men felt at the prospect of women doing philosophy, which could have led them alternatively to ascribe male-authored texts to women or to deny the existence of female-authored texts altogether.[4] The presence of women among the Pythagoreans is in curious conflict with the treatment of gender in the Pythagorean "table of opposites" recorded by Aristotle, whose *Metaphysics* contained a list of ten tantalizing Pythagorean polarities in which the female does not come out well, classed with darkness, crookedness, evil, and the disfavored left side:

Finite	Infinite
Odd	Even
Unity	Polarity
Right	Left
Male	Female
Rest	Motion
Straight	Crooked
Light	Darkness
Good	Evil
Square	Oblong

(*Metaphysics* 986a)

———

But what of life? How did life begin? Anaximander suspected that all creatures had originated in the interaction of the sun with what he called "the moist element." In this he echoed the belief in the centrality of moisture in the creation of life that was central to the system of Thales (and the Babylonians, and the Egyptians). He also developed a theory that was in many ways the forerunner of evolution. The long period of dependence in human babies suggested to him that humans must have derived from another animal. He suspected it was fish, who dwelled in an extremely moist environment. Anaximander, wrote the Roman polymath Censorinus, "believed that there arose from heated water and earth either fish or animals very like fish. In these humans grew and were kept inside as embryos up to puberty. Then finally they burst and men and women came forth, already able to nourish themselves."[5] Empedocles foreshadowed Darwin's notion of the survival of the fittest in his speculation about maladaptive life forms that died out through failure to thrive, writing that in early times faces appeared without necks, arms without shoulders; eyes wandered around alone without foreheads:

> Creatures sprang up who had faces and chests on both sides of
>   their bodies,
> Offspring of oxen with faces of humans, and some to the contrary
> Rose up as ox-headed creatures whose bodies were human, compounded
> Of men and of women at once, with their sexual organs all shaggy.[6]

As Love combined with Strife to assemble the various parts, the resulting creatures that were put together in such a way as to be capable of surviving continued to exist, but the ones that could not survive, such as a human head joined to a cow's body, perished (D156.3). One cannot help wondering if there was a Mesopotamian source for his speculation. The third-century BCE Babylonian priest Berossus, citing an obscure earlier source, wrote of a time when the universe was as yet undeveloped and "in it there were wondrous beings with peculiar forms who were able to engender other living beings. For men with two wings were born, as were other men with four wings and two faces." Bulls, he says, were born with human heads and dogs with four bodies—and fish tails. Some people had two heads, one male and one female, as well as two sets of genitals, and there were most definitely centaurs.[7]

The protoscientists adapted a good deal of their mythic heritage and transmuted it into a new and systematized form of rational discourse. So far from standing at an opposite pole to philosophy, myth had laid the groundwork for philosophy by addressing profound questions about the human condition. Rather than imagining the evolution of the world they knew as guided by a series of rebellions of sons against fathers, however, pushing history forward from the time of Uranus to the age of Kronos to the rule of Zeus, the protoscientists used observation and reason to construct explanatory systems. Even in specifics, their constructs at times parallel those found in Greek myth, which put forward sometimes water, sometimes earth, sometimes an interaction of the two as the source of life. Both Thebans and Athenians reveled in myths that imagined them as "earthborn," myths that the inhabitants of both cities considered authoritative well after speculation about natural science had become popular. In order to found Thebes, so the story went, Cadmus had to kill a waterdragon who guarded the nearby spring. When he then sowed the serpent's teeth in the ground on the advice of Athena, a crop of armed men sprang up—men who in Theban tradition became known as Spartoi (sown men; no relation to Spartans), ancestors of the Theban nobility. The Athenians, as we have seen, came to bolster their sense of superiority over poleis with more mixed populations, or indeed any other poleis at all, by adducing their origins in the soil of Attica. This belief was contemporary with Athenian democracy and in fact closely tied up with democratic civic ideology. "Pure" birth from the soil was held to make a population superior in both strength and virtue to mixed citizen bodies composed of migrants from all over. The constructs of the protoscientists, then, held sway concurrently with a residual attachment to myth that was impossible to extinguish— and in some cases was not that different from their theories.

Despite their naturalistic explanations for the workings of the cosmos, the protoscientists often mouthed conventional pieties concerning the gods. "Always to have respect for the gods," Xenophanes wrote, "that is good" (*Athenaeus* 11. 462c); the gods, said Democritus, "are givers of all good things, both in the past and now" (B175). In their open-minded search for truth, however, they inevitably raised new questions about the nature of divinity. Xenophanes suggested that the gods had been created by humans rather than the other way around. While mortals believed that gods had the same voice and body as humans, he wrote, and even wore the same kinds of clothes,

> if oxen and horses or lions had hands, or if they could draw,
> and create works of art like the ones men make, why horses
> would draw pictures of gods that were shaped just like horses,
> and oxen would make ones of gods that were shaped very much like
>> oxen,
> and they would make the forms and bodies of their gods
> along the same lines as the form that each species itself possesses.[8]

After all, he contended,

> Ethiopians have gods with snub noses and dark skin,
> and Thracians have gods with light eyes and red hair.[9]

In his view, the nature of divinity was very different:

> There is one God, among the gods and mortals the greatest,
> not at all like humans in body or in mind. . . .
> He sees as a whole, thinks as a whole, and hears as a whole. . . .
> But without effort he set everything in motion, by the organ of his mind.
> He always stays in the same place, stock still;
> It is not fitting that he move around.[10]

Notions of a nonanthropomorphic deity were also put forward by Empedocles. God, he says, is

> A perfect sphere. His limbs are not equipped
> With human head, nor do two branches shoot
> Forth from his back; he has no feet, no knees,
> No shaggy genitals, but he is Mind
> Holy and ineffable, and only Mind,
> Darting through the whole cosmos with swift thoughts.[11]

But is this deity responsible for the workings of the universe? Not according to any of the Presocratics. In the words of Heraclitus, "It was none of the gods or mortals who made this ordered cosmos."[12]

The speculations of the Presocratics had moved the Greek world a giant step forward by replacing mythological explanations with materialistic/naturalistic ones. Now in the last third of the fifth century that world would be moved still further in its intellectual journey by a new assortment of iconoclasts who hailed from all over Greece but gravitated toward the cultural and commercial mecca of Athens. Sometimes lumped in with the Presocratics, these itinerant intellectuals shared the Presocratics' proclivity for challenging traditional assumptions and questioning the powers of the gods. In applying their speculation to embrace the world of ethics, these men (we know of no women among them) introduced new and critical elements in Greek thinking about the human community. Some, like Protagoras, were profoundly interested in ethics, while others like Gorgias gravitated toward the teaching of rhetoric. They were called variously know-it-alls, gurus, highbrows, sages, wordsmiths, brains, savants, professors, pundits, and pedants, but the one word that was applied to all of them was sophist.[13]

There was a crying need for such people. In the fifth century, Greek education consisted entirely of imprinting the values of society on the young, who, it was hoped, would in the best of all possible worlds grow into people just like their parents. Although children (mostly boys) whose families could spare them from the farm received instruction from teachers until adolescence, the real education of life went on in the family, where mothers would impart training in home economics to daughters and fathers would model adulthood and citizenship for sons, and for young elite males at symposia, where appropriate social behavior was learned from older men. At school, moreover, education was entirely literary. Boys and the occasional girl would learn poetry and then more poetry as, through repeated recitation, they soaked up the wisdom of Homer, and in time that of some other poets as well. Osmosis was all; absent was the analysis, questioning, and argumentation that now plays such a large role in education. So was the imparting of information not contained in the works of the poets. Except for some basic mathematics, students received no instruction in many of the subjects that fill the curriculum today: social studies, natural science, composition, art, and architecture. Only by tripping over a tidbit in the poets might one be exposed to such things. It would not have occurred to a Greek that being an educated person entailed knowledge of any language other than Greek. Schoolchildren were not given the choice between the Persian track and the Egyptian track; no phrasebooks promising "Scythian in 30 Days" have come down to us. Although Alexander had brought Egypt under Macedonian control in 332, it was not until nearly 300 years later that a Macedonian ruler of Egypt, Cleopatra VII, thought to learn the language.

City life, however, particularly in Athens, had created a need for well-informed men prepared to question authority and argue positions in the assembly and the lawcourts. The expansion of horizons through travel, colonization, and even warfare had exposed more and more people to new ways of thinking and acting, and some began to wonder whether perhaps the values with which they had grown up were not in fact absolute and dictated by the gods but rather relative to different societies and shaped by humans. Herodotus certainly thought so. The notion that reality could be constructed in the mind of an individual person was both intoxicating and unsettling. There was no telling where this might end. In the intensely verbal and competitive democracy of the Athenians, where a young man could hope to succeed in the rough and tumble world of politics, there was plainly money to be made by those who could teach ambitious pupils to play around with ideas and work their thoughts up into clever speeches. In the up-and-coming youth of Athens a niche market lay ready to hand.

Although many sophists were highly esteemed both in the cities of their birth and in Athens, to which they gravitated, they also sparked considerable hostility in conservative quarters. Had the natural scientists with their denials of divine involvement in the workings of the cosmos not been bad enough? In fact, those who associated the sophists' speculations about society and politics with developments in scientific thought were not entirely mistaken, for behind both lay the same commitment to open-minded, rational inquiry into the relationship of appearance to reality, the same curiosity about the relationship between the immutable and the ephemeral. Although she was alluding to the suspicion that had fallen on her because of her training in witchcraft,

Euripides' Medea hit on something when she spoke of the Greek propensity to suspect the overeducated. No right-thinking person, she observed, ought to give his children an above-average education, for this sparks envy and resentment in others (*Medea*, 294–97).

The currency of the sophists was words, and for the Athenians, as for other Greeks, words were every bit as sound a currency as coins. From the time of the first iambic poets, words had been invested with almost magical properties. They could even kill, or so the stories went. Archilochus, as we have seen in chapter 1, had been going to marry a young woman named Neobule, and when her father Lycambes for some reason broke off the engagement, he attacked the family in such forceful vituperative verses that ... that what? In some versions Lycambes hanged himself, in others all his daughters did as well, or perhaps instead. It may be that the tale derived from a misunderstanding, and that the family members had merely hung their heads in shame; or one of the versions of the story may be true. In his commentary on the *Odyssey*, the twelfth-century Byzantine scholar Eustathius maintained that many people had been driven to hang themselves because of their misfortunes, "as according to the old story the daughters of Lycambes did, being unable to bear up under the onslaught of Archilochus's taunts. For the man was fearful in his attacks." For this reason, he maintained, people said to those who were the victim of this kind of jibe, "you have stepped on Archilochus" just as one would say "you have stepped on a scorpion or a snake or the sharp acanthus," and, he concludes, offering an alternative explanation for the word *iambos*, it was said that "a certain girl named Iambe hanged herself, having been shamefully outraged (*hybristheisa*)."[14] In poetic—and later prose—recitations in the courts, on the stage, in the assembly, words transfixed the listeners. Greeks listened with remarkable concentration to the complex choral odes of tragedy, to speakers in the assembly, to plaintiffs and defendants in the courts, to sophists holding forth in the agora or in private homes. No wonder Socrates railed against the primacy of rhetoric in Athenian politics, as we see him doing in Plato's dialogue *Gorgias*, named after one of the founders of Greek rhetoric, Gorgias from Leontini in Sicily. Rhetoricians, Socrates complains there, are like cooks whose aim is to provide not healthful, nourishing food but rather foods that appeal to the senses. Both cooking and rhetoric are just different forms of flattery. "As self-adornment is to exercise," he concluded, "so is sophistry to governing, and as cooking is to medicine, so is rhetoric to justice" (*Gorgias* 465c). When Gorgias arrived in Athens in 427 from Leontini, his verbal pyrotechnics took the city by storm. One of his more famous pieces was a rhetorical tour de force in which he defended the much-maligned Helen, blamed in song and story for causing the Trojan War by decamping with Paris. Gorgias lists several possible reasons for Helen's action, each of them exculpatory. Perhaps it was the will of the gods; perhaps she was taken by force; surely in neither of these instances could she be blamed. And if she was persuaded by words? Even in that case:

> it is not difficult to defend her and free her from blame. For consider this: speech is a powerful master that with the smallest and least evident body manages to work the most divine feats. It can put an end to fear, relieve pain, create joy, and increase pity. . . . How many men on how many subjects have persuaded and do now persuade how many others by molding a false speech! (*Encomium of Helen* 8, 11)

How many, indeed; this was not a fact that most Athenians wished to celebrate, or a strategy they wanted to see taught to smart-alecky young whippersnappers, but many Greeks were enamored of this kind of play. Consider the famous paradoxes of Parmenides' friend and follower Zeno of Elea. Let us imagine, Zeno said, a race between the famously swift-footed Achilles and, of all things, a tortoise. Because of his reputation, Achilles will be given a handicap: the tortoise is permitted a head start. Once he is allowed to start running, Achilles heads for the tortoise, but of course by the time he arrives at the spot where he had last seen it, some time has passed, and the tortoise has progressed along the track. So Achilles keeps running, but by the time he gets to the place where the tortoise had last been, it has moved still farther forward. Although he keeps on moving at a far greater speed than the sluggish amphibian, he is never able to catch up. According to another one of Zeno's paradoxes, the tortoise doesn't win the race either. First he gets halfway to the goal; then he covers half the remaining distance, then half the distance that remains after that, and so on ad infinitum, but he can never actually reach the end. But we all know that in real life it is possible to complete a race—and that Achilles will overtake the tortoise and win. A third Eleatic, Melissus from Samos, seems to have had considerable tolerance for paradox as well. His denial of both change and motion is puzzling in light of the only detail known about his life: his military experience. We know from Plutarch that Melissus was a commander in the Samian fleet, and during the war between Athens and Samos he won a battle against an armada led by Pericles. Did he somehow believe that the ships in question were both moving and not moving?[15]

Many Greek parents worried that there was no limit to what their sons might use rhetoric to defend. Had not the sophistic treatise the *Dissoi Logoi* (*Double Arguments*) suggested that sickness could be good if you were a doctor, and death if you were an undertaker or gravedigger? Just as the protoscientists had viewed the creation and operation of the cosmos as the work of natural forces rather than of the gods, it was now suggested by many of the sophists that the laws that governed the human community were not of divine origin either. Inevitably, moreover, their new ways of looking at the world had serious implications for relations between gods and mortals. One of the most renowned of the sophists who came to teach in Athens was Protagoras (ca. 490–420) from Abdera in northern Greece. "Each person," Protagoras claimed, "is the measure of all things—of things that are, that they are, and of things that are not, that they are not" (cited in Sextus Empiricus, *Against the Mathematicians* 7. 60). Human opinion, in other words, rather than any god, was the arbiter of reality.

————

Socrates (469–399) and his pupil Plato (ca. 429–347), who most decidedly rejected Protagoras's relativism, nonetheless shared the sophists' concern with human affairs to the exclusion of speculations about the cosmos. The fundamental question that exercised Socrates was, how should a person live? He had no school and charged no fees (though no doubt he received gifts from appreciative pupils); he simply engaged in animated and provocative conversation in private homes and public spaces with those who wished to converse with him—and some who would have preferred not to. Plato was understandably eager to stress the difference between Socrates' thought and that of the sophists. In his view, he and his teacher upheld the primacy of absolute truth and pure reason against the morass of subjectivity that was the sophists' province. Where the sophists had held out the promise of professional success, what Socrates and Plato offered was enlightenment: the understanding of reality that could arise from the back and forth of conversation about the nature of such things as truth, virtue, and beauty, all of which were for them very much tied up together. In replacing the commonsense experience of the everyday with reasoning and analysis as a valid basis for understanding, they followed in the footsteps of the protoscientists but went further in maintaining that this reasoning and analysis would lead to virtue. For nobody, Socrates claimed, does wrong willingly but only from a failure of understanding.

Plato shared Pythagoras's conviction that the abstract properties of mathematics made it the ideal basis for a wider understanding of the world. Like Pythagoras, he was committed to a dualistic worldview that separated the mortal body from the immortal soul. Pythagoras, after all, had believed in a split between body and soul so complete that there was nothing to prevent a human soul from taking up residence in the body of a dog or a fish. While Parmenides denied the reality of the sensible world, Plato acknowledged it and, like Heraclitus, saw the material world of the everyday as in constant flux, but he also considered it a cheap and tawdry "imitation" of a reality that, like the cosmos of Parmenides, was eternal, unchanging, and perfect. In his concept of a Prime Mover, in turn, Plato's student Aristotle evoked the concept of divinity evident in the thought of Xenophanes, who, as we have seen, had written of a god who sets everything in motion using only the power of his mind, never moving himself.[16]

Conversing in the agora with young men who lionized him, Socrates fell foul of Athenian fathers whose sons preferred his conversation to theirs. His reputation was not enhanced by his association with high-profile traitors like the renegade Alcibiades and Critias, the ringleader of the infamous Thirty Tyrants, and the merciless scrutiny to which he subjected democracy aroused further suspicion about his loyalties. The amnesty of 403 precluded charges being brought that related directly to activities during the war or under the Thirty, but this technicality was circumvented by accusing Socrates of corrupting the young, failing to acknowledge the gods in which the state believed, and teaching new gods. While the precise grounds for the religious charges are unclear—new gods?—the Athenian jurors' concern with the spiritual welfare of the state was certainly legitimate in Greek terms, for if the gods did not receive the reverence due to them, the citizens could not expect their crops to flourish, or—perhaps more germane here—their armed forces to win wars. And might not the horrific plague have resulted from neglect of the gods? Both the war and the epidemic had contributed to heightened anxiety as well as short tempers, and Athenians had no more sense of "separation of church and state" than any other Greeks.

Socrates' defense speech has not been preserved. The most famous of the retrospective renditions composed in antiquity was by Plato in his *Apology of Socrates* (not an apology in the modern sense; the Greek word means simply "refutation"). Although Plato's rendering does not accord with Athenian courtroom protocol and thus cannot reproduce what Socrates really said, it remains a magnificent defense of the value of open inquiry, unfettered reason, and the life of the mind; it contains the famous dictum "the unexamined life is not worth living," and in it Socrates reprised his central assertion that "no harm can come to a good man either in life or in death" (*Apology* 38a, 41d). There is no reason to doubt that it paints an accurate picture of a man who had spent his life seeking to persuade people not to put looking after their bodies or their possessions before "seeing to it that their souls may be in the best possible condition" (*Apology* 30a–b7). The word in question is *psychē*, and it has come a long way from its meaning in Homer as essentially the breath of life that escapes at the moment of death. In Plato's dualistic worldview it is noncorporeal and of far more value than anything one could see or touch. The word had also developed in tragedy to mean the essence of a person. When Creon accuses the guard he has set to watch over Polynices' body of collusion in his burial, he accuses him of having sold his soul, his *psychē*, for money (*Antigone* 322), and in defending himself to his father Hippolytus argues that he has such a virgin soul that he can't bear even to look on pictures of lovemaking (*Hippolytus*, 1006).

Socrates' speech also contains a telling reference to one source of the animus directed at him. For many years, Socrates says, people have been making accusations against him, one of them a writer of comedies (*Apology* 18c–d). In 424 Aristophanes produced his *Clouds*, set in a preposterous school run by Socrates in the sky, the Thinkery. There the philosopher is surrounded by a chorus of "Clouds"—lovely young goddesses of rhetoric and hairsplitting (played, of course, by men) who, he explains, are the only true divinities. Zeus, he claims, does not even exist (368). The Thinkery offers education in both science and sophistic argument to paying pupils. The first prospective student we meet is the elderly farmer Strepsiades, who had been bankrupted by his spendthrift son Pheidippides' habit of throwing money away on horses and hopes to learn how to argue his creditors out of pressing for repayment of the debts the youth has incurred. When Socrates dismisses him as a dunce incapable of learning, Strepsiades decides to send Pheidippides himself instead. The intellectual crisis of the age is exemplified in a debate between two of Socrates' associates, Just Argument and Unjust Argument, who are portrayed as wrangling with one another as to which can provide the best education. Predictably, Unjust Argument triumphs as it shows how it offers young men a good life grounded in an ability to talk their way out of trouble and into Athenian politics.

Pheidippides, however, does nothing to help Strepsiades when the creditors come calling; rather, he not only beats his aged parent but also uses his new skills in argumentation to justify his actions. When he announces that he's planning to beat his mother as well, Strepsiades instructs his slaves to grab torches and sets fire to the Thinkery that is doing so much harm to Athens and its time-honored values.

It is not surprising that Athenians who had seen the play, as many had, would have had their dislike of the moral relativism of the sophists with their rhetorical tricks intensified, as well as their suspicion that Socrates was no different from the rest of them: a man who wasted his time—and that of Athens's youth—on abstruse argumentation that bore no relation to real-life concerns. Socrates' execution formed a turning point in Greek thought. Gutted by the loss of his mentor, Plato made it his mission to disseminate Socrates' teachings by imaginative re-creations of his conversations in dialogue form. As Socrates, like Jesus and Mohammed, never wrote anything, it is maddeningly difficult to disentangle his ideas from those of Plato, though it is likely that the earlier dialogues more closely reflect Socrates' thought, the later ones being more purely Platonic.

Plato sought to turn attention away from the mundane universe of everyday experience to the rarefied world of abstraction. Like the protoscientists, he was confident that there existed a realm of pure thought more precious than the material world visible to the naked eye. In this realm could be found the ultimate realities of courage, justice, love, piety, and, perhaps most important, truth and beauty, which for him were synonymous. Acts of courage performed by individual people, justice as rendered in particular court decisions, were of less interest than these abstractions. Socrates' interlocutors tended to hold commonsense workaday beliefs such as Plato's readers themselves might cherish—readers much like you and me. Socrates would chip away gradually at their arguments, pointing out illogicalities and inconsistencies, with the result that little by little a higher and more truthful reality would be revealed, as when a sculptor takes an undifferentiated piece of marble and slowly molds it into a beautiful form.

Turning the eyes of Socrates' associates away from the array of diverse actions and events in their daily lives, Plato sought to replace the messy multiplicity of the mundane with a higher, purer truth. While a casual observer contemplating a sunrise and a mathematical proof and a statue of Hermes might perceive three distinct phenomena, Plato saw not what distinguished one from the other but rather different concrete manifestations of the single abstract idea of beauty. To such an abstraction Plato gave the name of *eidos*: a Form, an Ideal. Though a grapefruit, the sun, a marble would evoke the Form of a sphere, unlike the Form they would not be perfectly round, as by definition nothing in the world of the concrete can be perfect. The only perfect sphere is the one defined by the mathematical formula: the locus of all points equidistant from a given point in a three-dimensional space. No wonder Plato was so invested in mathematics.

Although Plato was highly critical of existing Greek myths because of the unflattering light in which they so often painted the gods, he was himself a marvelously inventive mythmaker and storyteller. To illustrate the relationship between the visible world of everyday life and the Forms, he inserts into his dialogue the *Republic* a brilliant parable that has since become famous. Imagine, Socrates says, people who have been living since childhood in a dark cave with chains on their legs and necks so that they have to stay in the same place and are unable to turn their heads side to side. They can't see one another very well, and all they perceive of the world above is the shadows of handmade figures of people and animals being carried like puppets above a low wall. Would they understand anything of the rich three-dimensional world above besides the shadows of these figures illuminated by a faraway fire burning in the distance? "How could they," Plato's half-brother Glaucon replies, "if they were prevented from moving their heads all their lives?" (*Republic* 515a–b). They would mistake these simulacra for reality, and when, like puppeteers, the people holding them spoke, they would imagine that the voice came from one of the shadows. If someone were released from the cave and enabled to see the objects as they really were, surely he would have a terrible time adjusting to the new reality. Once he did, though, would he not feel very fortunate to be in touch at last with reality in its full richness? But imagine his relations with his fellow cave-dwellers if he were to return to his old habitat and try to explain things to them. They would believe he had gone mad, and communication would be impossible. Indeed, Socrates adds in a plain reference to his own fate, if someone were to try to drag them up to the light, would they not lay hands upon him—and kill him? This he says, is precisely the situation of those who have glimpsed the Forms. And so, he says to Glaucon, "you would be correct if you were to surmise that the ascent from the cave and the contemplation of the world above represents the soul's ascent to the realm of true knowledge" (*Republic* 517b).

At the outset of the *Republic*, Socrates is groping after a definition of justice with a number of young men, and one older man, who soon has to leave. (No women are present in any of Plato's dialogues, although Socrates twice claims to be reporting a woman's words.) The sophist Gorgias defined the *aretē* of a man as not only being competent in public affairs but helping friends and harming enemies (DK 19), and the age-old saw about benefiting friends and injuring enemies is one of the facile definitions that Socrates is at pains to reject. After all, one might be wrong about just who was one's friend and who one's enemy. Besides, since the *aretē* of the human being, Socrates claimed, was justice, then harming people would make them less just, and who would want to live surrounded by unjust people?

When he has demonstrated the inadequacy of all the slipshod definitions his interlocutors put forward, such as helping friends and harming enemies, he suggests that it might be possible to extrapolate from an understanding of the just state to a definition of the just soul—and then proceeds to outline his ideal state (*Republic* 368d–369a). Like the soul of the individual, Socrates argues, the just state divides into three parts. At the top are the Guardians, who represent the reasoning part of the soul. Their supreme rationality, the product of both temperament and education, qualifies them to govern. After them come the Auxiliaries, representing the spirited element; they are ideally suited for the military. Last come the majority: in Plato's view, the great unwashed. Being neither especially bright nor particularly brave, these correspond to desire in the soul and live only to satisfy their own material yearnings. All the jobs in the state other than governing and fighting will fall to them.

But how to persuade people to buy into this division? Initially, a myth about different races born of the earth and composed of different metals—Plato's so-called noble lie—will assign people to classes. After that, the three groups will reproduce themselves biologically. Plato imagined a governing class of both men and women. Although, Socrates says, the average woman is inferior to the average man in everything except homemaking, there will nonetheless be some women who are brighter than some men. A child who appears to have been born into the wrong class—which Plato plainly does not expect will happen often—will be transferred (generally down). Plato devotes considerable attention to the education and habits of the Guardians, who will study for many years. The Guardians' lives were to be unusual in many respects. Private property, though it exists for the other two classes, will be abolished in their case. Just as they lack individual property, moreover, they have no individual spouses; to perpetuate the system, an elaborate mathematical scheme was to dictate short-term couplings. All Guardian children conceived around the same time would be raised in common nurseries, with the result that no parents will know their own children and vice versa.

The analysis of existing constitutions contained in the *Republic* makes clear Plato's alienation from his native Athens. Although he is dismissive of all the shoddy excuses for government common in fourth-century Greece, his attack on democracy is particularly unsparing. In discussing the constitutions of the various poleis, he equates the freedom of speech Athenians so proudly associated with their democracy with license to do exactly what one pleases in every respect. In a democracy, Socrates argues in a passage jarringly disconnected from reality, the man who does not want to go to war when the state declares war or keep a peace on which the state has agreed is not compelled to do so; one will go ahead and hold an office to which he is not entitled by law, and indeed people who have been condemned to exile can nonetheless be seen roaming the streets pretty as they please. In its tolerance of all kinds, he concludes, democracy is much like the sort of multicolored garment that appeals to women and children, "anarchic and motley" (557b–558c). To what degree Plato hoped any of this blueprint would be adopted, or even adapted, in any existing state is uncertain. The philosopher made two trips to Syracuse, hoping to obtain from the tyrant Dionysius II land and settlers to establish an experimental new state in Sicily and even to transform Dionysius into a philosopher-king much like the Guardians of the *Republic*, but he was unsuccessful on both fronts. He had greatly hoped that the tyrant might find the study of philosophy improving. He did not. In fact, Plato was fortunate to escape with his life.

Plato was not only a profound and complex thinker; he was also a brilliant and engaging stylist. Though he burned his youthful tragic compositions, Plato the playwright is very much alive in his philosophical writings, for the dialogue format afforded the opportunity for an approach to the search for truth that was both dynamic and dramatic. One of his liveliest compositions is his dialogue on love, the *Symposium*, in which the men who had gathered together for the evening presented various explanations of the mechanics of love, some earnest, some less so; the account of the comic poet Aristophanes is predictably hilarious. The quite serious explanation Socrates puts forward is undergirded by the notion of Forms. Socrates claims, however, that what he has to say was told to him by a prophetess from Mantinea in the Peloponnesus, Diotima. As Diotima is otherwise unattested in surviving texts, it is possible that she is a fictional character—but not likely, as nearly all the personalities in Plato's dialogues have been identified as historical personages.

Love, Diotima has told Socrates, entails a grasp at immortality and is grounded in an apprehension of the divine. From finding himself excited by beautiful bodies, the lover will proceed to an understanding that what is really to be loved is the beautiful soul and will come to appreciate beautiful souls even when they are housed in not particularly attractive bodies. In time, he will come to love the idea of beauty itself—its Form. Love, Diotima says, is a longing for immortality that prompts one to want to possess the beautiful and beget upon it. Although she pays lip service to the notion of heterosexual coupling that issues in mortal offspring, most of her discourse focuses on the beloved as a young male and concerns the deathless ideas to which men give birth in philosophical dialogue with one another. When a man has been sufficiently tutored in the art of love, she says, and

> by the right use of the love he feels for boys he ascends from these particulars and starts to discern that beauty, he is very close to laying hold of the final secret. This is the right approach, the right initiation to matters of love. Beginning from obvious beauties he must for the sake of that highest beauty be ever climbing higher as on the rungs of a ladder, from one example of physical beauty to two, and from two to all beautiful bodies [and from there] to moral beauty . . . until from various different kinds of beauty . . . he comes to know the very essence of beauty. (*Symposium* 210e–212a)

At that point, she concludes, he will have attained true virtue and become, if anyone can, immortal.

Plato shared his ideas not only in his written work but in the world's first university, the Academy, which he founded in 387 by the grove of the ancient Greek hero Academus. In accordance with the principles he had set forth in the *Republic*, he accepted students of both sexes, although we only know of two women who studied there, both from the Peloponnesus: Axiothea of Phlius and Lasthenia of Mantinea. By far the most famous pupil at the Academy was Aristotle. The son of a court physician in Macedon, after studying at the Academy for some 20 years he went on to found his own school, the Lyceum, named for the sanctuary of Apollo Lyceius, *lykos* being Greek for wolf; evidently Apollo was worshipped in some connection with wolves, perhaps as a defender against them. There Aristotle and his pupils engaged in conversation and debate while ambling through the beautiful colonnaded walks known as *peripatoi*, from which followers of Aristotle are still known today as "peripatetics." Athens's most illustrious metic, Aristotle was born in Stagira in northern Greece and lived most of his life away from home—in Athens, in Macedonia, in Assos not far from Troy in Anatolia, and in Macedonia, where he had a famous pupil of his own: Philip II of Macedon hired him to tutor the young Alexander.

That Aristotle loved science while Plato loved mathematics is diagnostic. Embracing with delight the material world Plato had disdained, he found great satisfaction in organizing flora and fauna in categories. Alexander made sure that all new species he encountered in the course of his campaigns were sent to his teacher to be catalogued. A man of restless energy, Aristotle ascribed a great deal of the excitement of mental life to the dynamic power of change. Where Plato had gravitated to a Parmenidean world in which what really mattered was eternal and unmoving, Aristotle saw everything in the universe moving toward a specific goal: "teleology," his orientation is labeled from the Greek *telos* (end/goal/purpose). Ultimately this *telos* was god, but not god as most Greeks would have imagined it. Utterly removed from any notion of anthropomorphism, Aristotle's god was rather a perfect, ageless being who existed outside time and space. Where the traditional Olympians and their associates had been changeable—indeed, mercurial—it rather was the agent of all change in the universe. To this being Aristotle gave the name the "Prime Mover."

Aristotle no doubt inherited his interest in physiology from his father, the court physician to the Macedonian Amyntas, father of Philip II. For Plato, understanding was to be gained by the application of reason, but like any good doctor, Aristotle placed tremendous importance on observation and the gathering of data. Whereas Plato's quest for the best government led him to establish an ideal state in the *Republic* and later in the *Laws*, Aristotle's approach to the problem of the best government was to set his students at the Lyceum to writing up the constitutions of 158 existing states (of which sadly only *The Constitution of the Athenians* has survived), and he classified in his *Politics* all the political arrangements of his day known to him. To Aristotle, moreover, the notion that the Forms were more real than their various physical manifestations made no sense. For him—as for most people—Forms were not real at all. For something to be real, it had to arise from a combination of form and matter; the notion of form as separate from matter struck him as ludicrous. Aristotle's political philosophy also differed from Plato's. Being more pragmatic and down-to-earth, Aristotle believed in collective wisdom. Put enough people together, he argued, and the sum of their wisdom might well exceed the wisdom of the few smartest men (unlike Plato, he did not believe in the existence of smart women), just as potluck dinners may prove to be more rewarding than those hosted by a single individual, since "some appreciate one thing, some another, and taken together they appreciate everything" (*Politics* 1281b). For this reason, he is grudgingly amenable to opening up the franchise to the poor who had no opportunities for education, although he drew the line at allowing them to hold office.

In addition to being a polymath who wrote extensively on subjects as varied as rhetoric, biology, physics, politics, and aesthetics, Aristotle founded the discipline of logic. It is to him that we owe the articulation of the basic principle of the syllogism—the principle that tells us that if A yields B and B yields C, then A by itself must yield C. If Sardis is in Persia and Persia is in Asia, then Sardis is in Asia. Since Plato and

Socrates believed that nobody does wrong willingly and that moral transgressions invariably arise from ignorance of the good, they envisioned virtue as arising from an education that culminated in apprehending the Forms. Aristotle shared their concern with virtue but conceived it not as the consequence of fancy education but rather as something one instantiates in virtuous activity. Virtue needed to be reinforced constantly by the performance of virtuous deeds. For him, *eudaimonia*—well-being—lay in "acting in accordance with virtue" and arose from action, not contemplation (*Nicomachaean Ethics* 1098b). The more common-sensical Aristotle did not agree with Plato and Socrates that no harm can come to a virtuous person. There are certain externals, he contends—birth into a "good" (reasonably affluent) family, children who have turned out all right, passable looks, friends—without which it is difficult to perform virtuous deeds and thus attain happiness:

> You cannot really regard as happy someone of very ugly appearance or low birth, someone without children or other connections—or, worse yet, someone who has children or friends who are rotten through and through, or whose friends, though outstanding, are no longer living. As I said, then, happiness does seem to require a modicum of external good fortune. (*Nicomachaean Ethics* 1098b)

Most people, he believed, had no capacity for true happiness or meaningful friendship and could only experience the fleeting pleasures occasioned by food or sex or recreation. "The utter boorishness of the herd of men," he complained, "is reflected in the way they opt for the kind of life suitable to a cow" (*Nicomachaean Ethics* 1095b).

———

Already before Aristotle's death in 322, a number of important thinkers had developed a radically different take on the average person's relationship to philosophy. Among the founders of the schools of thought that would flourish in the Hellenistic Age, Diogenes had already died, and Pyrrho had already returned from a trip to India with Alexander that had important consequences for the Skeptical school of thought that he

originated, or at least inspired. Plato and Aristotle had addressed themselves to those who had the leisure to spend significant stretches of time
in contemplation and the status conducive to putting virtue into action
in the service of the polis. Although their ideas had incalculable influence
on the history of philosophy, the schools of thought that became popular
upon the collapse of the independent polis spoke to a broader range of
people, and some of them underpin the self-help books that flood the
market today. They also addressed both sexes—or at least tried to. Even
Hellenistic philosophers, though, often found themselves assuming that
"person" and "man" were synonymous. Prominent Cynics included
Hipparchia from Maroneia in Thrace; Epicurus had many female followers; the Stoics believed that women as well as men could attain virtue
through the practice of philosophy, and when Stoicism became popular
in Rome, there were a number of prominent female Stoics there. The
Skeptic Pyrrho denied that there was any particular reason to assign roles
to one sex or another, and he cheerfully performed household chores
normally carried out by women (Diogenes Laertius, 9. 66).

Constantly shaken by bloody clashes among Alexander's successors,
the Hellenistic world also saw not only cultural syncretism of an unprecedented scope but also migrations so frequent that even those who had
stayed put found themselves joined by constant floods of newcomers
from afar. Despite major differences among them, all the new schools of
thought focused on the attainment of inner peace in a world that was
becoming increasingly unfamiliar and chaotic. Concomitantly, each
built in distinct ways on the primacy Socrates had awarded to
independence of externals. Nobody, Socrates argued, could injure a
good person, and the Hellenistic thinkers agreed. There was nothing good
or evil, they believed, but thinking made it so. As Ray Bolger sang in *The
Churkendoose*, "It all depends on how you look at things." In this they
harked back both to the relativism of Protagoras and the provocative
rhetorical pyrotechnics of the *Double Arguments*. Not for these new
thinkers Aristotle's acknowledgment that the absence of fundamental
creature comforts tended to inhibit happiness; rather they followed
Plato and Socrates in cultivating a self that was proof against the intrusion of any externals whatsoever. The founders of the first of these

movements, Cynicism, seem to have been Socrates' follower Antisthenes (ca. 446–366) and a proudly eccentric thinker from Sinope on the Black Sea, Diogenes (ca. 400–325). Like the other philosophies of the day, Cynicism rejected the trappings of wealth and prestige, encouraged self-sufficiency, and advocated conducting one's life in accordance with nature. Living at a basic level and carrying around with them the few possessions they had not given away, Cynics cultivated asceticism and rejected pleasure. Antisthenes was apparently in the habit of saying "I'd rather be insane than feel pleasure" (Diogenes Laertius, 6. 3). The Greek word for dog is *kuōn*, and the colorful Diogenes probably earned for himself the name of Cynic ("canine") by not only insisting that humans should follow their instincts just as animals do but acting on this belief at every opportunity, cheerfully defecating and masturbating in public.[17]

It may be, though, that Cynicism derived its name from Cynosarges, the gymnasium frequented by *nothoi* and where the Cynic Antisthenes had his school. An ambiguous word, *nothos* was used to refer to people whose background, whether in having one noncitizen parent or in having unmarried parents, marked them off from the rest of the citizen population; such people would have been singularly receptive to the Cynics' rejection of externals. Though Diogenes proudly pronounced himself a "citizen of the world" (*kosmopolitēs*, hence the English word "cosmopolitan") rather than of any particular polis, he also went out of his way to flout the customs of any polis of which the Greeks had ever heard.

The "power couple" of Cynicism was Crates (ca. 365–285) and the much younger Hipparchia (born ca. 335). Born into a wealthy family in Thebes, Crates gave his money away and moved to Athens to study, it seems, with Diogenes. Captivated by Crates' teachings, Hipparchia was smitten by the man himself despite the gap in their ages and horrified her upper-class parents by not only marrying him but also embracing his lifestyle, wearing the same clothes and attending symposia where she engaged in philosophical debate. It was claimed that she and Crates consummated their marriage outdoors on a public porch, in view of all. The Cynics were so iconoclastic that it may well be true, but colorful stories about philosophers formed a little subgenre of their own in antiquity, and we might do well to reserve judgment.

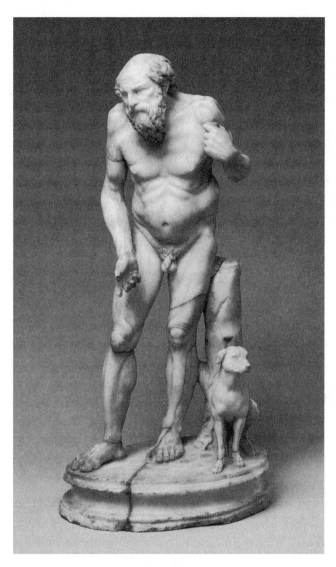

FIGURE 8.1. The philosopher Diogenes. Because Diogenes decried artificiality and advocated a life lived in accord with the dictates of nature, he was often portrayed accompanied by a dog, as in this statue. The Metropolitan Museum of Art, New York, Rogers Fund, 1922, https://www.metmuseum.org/art/collection/search/251181.

Pyrrho, whose name is associated with the Skeptic school, hailed from Elis in the western Peloponnesus, but he moved around a good deal, and it is likely that his way of looking at the world owed something to his experiences in the east, where he traveled as part of Alexander's entourage. Conversing with the so-called gymnosophists—the "naked philosophers"—in India, he would have been exposed to a variety of ideas. In particular, Buddhist notions of the attainment of tranquility through dissociation from the minutiae of life have a great deal in common with the tenets of skepticism, as do the tenets and practices of the Jains, the sect of Hinduism to which the naked philosophers probably belonged. Certainly there is a parallel between the Buddhist goal of nirvana and the goal of Skepticism, *ataraxia*—untroubledness, tranquility—which went on to be the watchword of much subsequent Hellenistic philosophy as well. Skepticism (or Pyrrhonism, as it is sometimes called after its founder) was not so much an intellectual system as a prescribed way of being in the world. *Ataraxia*, Pyrrho believed, could be attained only by holding no beliefs whatsoever. In light of the impossibility of certain knowledge, he argued, nothing should be perceived as either good or bad, safe or dangerous, desirable or undesirable (except, of course, *ataraxia*). Nothing was even real or unreal (except, again . . .). In his belief system, then, sensations such as pain and hunger were not to be feared, as there was no way of knowing whether they were desirable or undesirable. Diogenes Laertius relates an illustrative story about Pyrrho's imperturbability. When the ship on which he was traveling ran into a storm that badly unnerved his companions while a little pig who happened to be on board went on blithely chomping away as if nothing unusual were happening, Pyrrho calmly held up the *ataraxia* of the piglet as an appropriate role model for the wise person. Diogenes does not report the response of his apprehensive fellow passengers to this rather tall order.[18] But how, realistically, could one live by this philosophy, when peace of mind is more commonly associated with certainty than with its polar opposite? Going through life without any opinions about whether, say, one's food is poisoned would seem a rather heavy burden to bear, even for those who have managed to persuade themselves that there is no way of knowing whether food poisoning is good or bad. And on what basis could one ever make a decision? Skeptics, however, were permitted to have impressions as long as they did not pretend to any certainty, and on the basis of these impressions courses of action could be chosen.

Much in the writings of both the Presocratics and the sophists foreshadowed Pyrrho's teachings. Xenophanes had claimed that "nobody knows or ever will know the truth concerning the gods," and even if someone should happen to be right, "one would not know it: it is all a matter of opinion" (DK 34). Among the sophists, the relativist Protagoras had certainly argued against holding firm opinions, and Gorgias had declared that "Nothing you could mention actually exists; if it did, it would be unknowable; and even if it did exist and could be known, it would be impossible to communicate it to others" (DK 3). Still, striking parallels link Pyrrho's way of thinking to the Indian philosophers whom he evidently met while traveling with Alexander. The naked philosophers appear to have lived simple lives in the forest and regarded such amenities as food and clothing as obstacles to clarity of thought. They saw no difficulty in contradicting themselves in describing the world around them. Most of all, they defined their belief system in terms of negatives/ absences. All matters/questions, Pyrrho argued, were marked by three characteristics. They were *adiaphora*, without a clear identity; *astathmēta*, unstable/not measurable; *anepikrita*, undecided. It is no coincidence that all these words begin with the Greek letter *alpha*, corresponding to the Roman letter *a*. For the Greeks made use of what they called the *alpha* privative, the *alpha* that indicates the absence of something, a custom that has come into English not only in Greek-derived words like atypical and anarchy and anesthetic but in some other words as well, like asexual, a Latin-derived word. As this is an old Indo-European practice, we find it in Sanskrit as well, and significantly, two of the three defining characteristics of all matter/questions put forward by the Buddha are marked by the same prefix. In addition to being *duhkha*, unsatisfactory/unsteady, they are *anātman*, without a clear identity, and *anitya*, variable/unfixed.[19]

A-taraxia—the absence of agitation—was certainly the watchword of Epicurus, who may have studied with Pyrrho and in any case was known to admire him immensely. Epicurus established his school at Athens around the same time as Zeno from Citium in Cyprus (a different Zeno from Parmenides' disciple Zeno of Elea). A former student of the Cynic Crates, Zeno lectured in the covered portico in the Athenian agora known as the Stoa Poikile (Painted Portico), from which his followers were soon dubbed Stoics: "Porchers." Although almost nothing that Zeno and his disciples wrote survives, three prolific men who lived three centuries later under the Roman Empire—the freed slave Epictetus (ca. 55–135 CE); the philosopher Seneca (4 BCE–65 CE), tutor to the emperor Nero; and the emperor Marcus Aurelius (121–180 CE)—have left extensive writings advocating the Stoic way of thinking and living.

Following the dictates of nature meant something different to the Stoics from what it meant to Cynics like Zeno's teachers. For the Stoics, living in accordance with nature meant that just as Zeus ruled over the gods, so the system of monarchy was the divinely ordained organization for mortals. Since one building block of tranquility was certainty that one had fulfilled one's civic duty, a large dose of public service was recommended, though not the kind that might entail activism aimed at reforming society; because the existing order was in keeping with cosmic harmony, such behavior was discouraged. Thus the same Stoics who preached the universal dignity of humankind and made a great deal of the notion that slaves were just as free as their owners never agitated for the abolition of slavery.

The Stoics agreed with the Cynics (and with Socrates and Plato) that the concerns around which people ordinarily organized their lives— possessions, power, prestige—were extrinsic to well-being. While they were not bad things, neither were they good unless in some way they conduced to the practice of virtue, such as, for example, holding a government job that made it possible to mete out justice, or having the wherewithal to contribute to good causes. They were, in the Stoics' words, "indifferents": neutral. We all have preferences, and Stoics were no exception (nor are they today, as there are still many around). Even Stoics would prefer wealth to poverty and health to illness. But a preference is not the same thing as an attachment or a need. In their identification of virtue as the sole good, the Stoics echoed Socrates' claim that no harm can come to the good person and that doing injustice is far worse than being on its receiving end. Those sages who have come to an understanding of the way things really are, the Stoics believed, will be proof against whatever life may throw at them, be it physical pain, poverty, bereavement, or any other seeming calamity. Indeed, all these could be reframed as challenges and opportunities for growth. A proper Stoic would be immune to the excesses of pleasure as well. Correct reasoning offered the key to equanimity. In the words of Epictetus, "It is not the things that happen that disturb people but rather what people believe about those things. . . . So when we are hindered or upset or aggrieved, let us never blame others, but rather ourselves—that is, our beliefs" (*Enchiridion* 5).

Zeno's contemporary Epicurus (341–270) shared the Stoics' belief that the means of achieving *ataraxia* lay in reframing reality. A number of Epicurean tenets correspond to those of the Stoics. "If you want to make Pythocles rich," Epicurus was reported to have said, "what you need to do is subtract from his desires, not add to his bank balance" (Seneca, *Epistles* 21. 7). Similarly the Stoics argued that freedom was achieved "not by satisfying desires but by removing them" (Epictetus, *Discourses* 4. 1. 175). In many respects, however, Epicurus's views differed. Where the Stoics' preoccupation was virtue, that of the Epicureans was pleasure, which Epicurus identified as dictated by nature. Even children and animals, he argued, were programmed to seek pleasure. In 306 Epicurus established a school called the Garden in his home in Athens. There men and women gathered to apply themselves to his teachings and enjoy the blessings of companionship, which he considered one of the highest goods. In the garden they could emulate the gods by living tranquil, untroubled lives devoted to contemplation and the study of philosophy, evoking Plato's suggestion that to attain wisdom through philosophy is to become "as much as possible like a god" (*Theaetetus* 176b). Unlike the Stoics, Epicurus advocated disengagement from society rather than public service; not for him the rough and tumble world of politics and office-holding. Not only were his followers to eschew the chancy quests after money and political power as much as any Stoic; he also placed high importance on not falling in love (although sex presented no problem unless there were complications such as irate spouses or unwanted pregnancies). Whereas Plato had been uncomfortable about physical sex but a great enthusiast of erotic passion, seeing it as a step on the road to passion for beautiful ideals, Epicurus, like other Hellenistic philosophers, was comfortable with sex but argued strongly against passion, which ran the risk of ending in heartbreak. Food and drink were also fine, provided one practiced the moderation that would ward off indigestion and hangovers. Were Epicurus to be brought back to life today, he would be mystified to find the word "epicurean" associated with gourmet dining, for his definition of pleasure as the absence of pain precluded immoderate indulgence of any kind.

The sixth-century poet Anacreon spoke for many when in old age he wrote of his fear of death and what lay beyond:

> My temples now are gray, my head all white,
> And graceful youth abides with me no more.
> My teeth are aged, and the span of life
> That now remains is not so very long.
> > These days I'm in a state of constant dread,
> > Facing the awful pit of Tartarus,
> > The fearful recesses that lurk below.
> > Grievous enough the journey down:
> As for getting back up—that's not an option. (Stobaeus 4. 51. 12)

The last line is a sexual pun reflecting the incapacity of old age: it might also be translated "As for getting it up . . ." For Epicurus, banishing fear of death and the Underworld was key to expunging pain from life on earth. Following Leucippus and Democritus, he argued that all things were comprised of atoms, maintaining that after death the atoms that had made up the body and soul of each person simply dissolved, to re-form in other humans yet to come. Epicurus's atomism, however, was atomism with a difference. Unable to subscribe to the determinism of his predecessors, he ascribed the vast diversity of substances in the universe to periodic swerves in the atoms' paths, swerves that resulted in the atoms colliding at a variety of random angles. This new atomism eliminated not only the gods but fate from the equation: what operated in the shaping of the Epicurean universe was chance. The difference in texture between iron and roses, then, was a product of the different angle at which the atoms comprising them had collided. A dedicated materialist, Epicurus insisted that the soul was a physical entity, taking up space in the body, and that it was mortal. Like the body of which it formed a part, it came into being at a particular time and would at a particular time cease to exist.

Epicurus was certainly interested in science, but like other Greeks during the Archaic and Classical Ages he relied for his understanding of the material world more on a combination of observation and conjecture than on experiment. Although the same was true to some extent of Aristotle, the meticulousness with which he devoted himself to observation went a long way to compensate for the absence of controlled experiments. Science took a dramatic step forward in the Hellenistic Age with the advent of experimentation, vivisection—and patronage. The Ptolemies attracted many brilliant minds to Alexandria, which became a remarkable center for the study of biology, astronomy, geography, physics, and mathematics, and the scientific advances of the Hellenistic Age were far more dramatic than anything during the centuries that would follow. Although significant discoveries were made by Islamic scholars during the intervening years, it was not until the time of Galileo that serious scientific research would pick up in Europe.

To be sure, numerous important discoveries were made all over the Greek world. In Syracuse the brilliant mathematician Archimedes (ca. 287–ca. 212) proved a number of important theorems, discovering for example the formula for calculating the area of a circle, the surface area of a sphere, and the volume of a sphere. The story is told how when stumped as to how to calculate the volume of an irregularly shaped crown Archimedes, who was bathing, suddenly realized that his body had displaced a volume of water identical to its irregular size. He was so excited at realizing that his problem could be solved by simply immersing the crown in water and measuring the amount of water it displaced, so the tale went, that he jumped out of the tub and ran naked through the streets exclaiming *eureka*: "I have found it!" The patronage of Hiero II facilitated a number of Archimedes' inventions, several of which were designed for the defense of Syracuse against the Romans. Sadly, this very conflict led to the inventor's death. During the siege of Syracuse in 212, a Roman soldier apparently came upon him with his scientific instruments and, having no understanding of what he or they were all about, killed him, to the great sorrow of his commander Marcellus.[20] On the other side of the Greek world, Hipparchus from Anatolia (ca. 190–ca. 120), sometimes regarded as the inventor of trigonometry, catalogued 850 stars and successfully predicted both lunar and solar eclipses.

In Alexandria, the think tank of the Museum and the resources of the library combined with Ptolemaic patronage to draw a variety of fertile minds. Not all focused on the sciences: Zenodotus of Ephesus (ca. 330–ca. 260) worked on standardizing the texts of the *Iliad* and the *Odyssey*; Callimachus wrote broadly in both poetry and prose, and his 800-odd works, as we have seen, included a catalogue of the library's holdings, a formidable project. Around the same time Apollonius came from Rhodes to Alexandria, where he worked on his epic the *Argonautica*. A native of Byzantium, Aristophanes (not the comic dramatist: ca. 257–ca. 185/180) studied with Zenodotus and Callimachus and developed punctuation and line breaks in Greek poetry, working in particular on the texts of Homer, Hesiod, and Pindar: he was evidently the inventor of the comma. Among the scholars at work in Alexandria were numerous mathematicians and scientists. Active during the reign of the first of the Ptolemies, Alexander's general Ptolemy I, Euclid spent his working life in Alexandria, where he produced his *Elements*, the foundation of the geometry we still call Euclidean. The third-century astronomer Aristarchus came from Samos to work on his theory that the earth and other planets rotated around the sun, but his system was not widely accepted.

Perhaps the most remarkable of the Alexandrians were Herophilus, Erasistratus, and Eratosthenes. Hailed as the father of both anatomy and neuroscience, Herophilus (335–280) from Chalcedon near Byzantium spent most of his life in Alexandria, where together with Erasistratus, who seems to have come from one of the islands off Anatolia, he performed public dissections in front of rapt audiences. The two drew students from many corners of the world to the medical school at Alexandria.[21] He was the first to perform systematic dissections of human cadavers and was reported to have cut open hundreds of prisoners supplied by the government even while they were still alive. Greeks believed firmly that pollution attached to dead bodies, but the hybrid culture of Ptolemaic Egypt provided a different atmosphere more open to tampering with corpses, and the Ptolemies themselves were eager supporters of scientific research. His work on human bodies living and dead was of immeasurable assistance to Herophilus, whose work enabled him to distinguish between motor and sensory nerves. Herophilus made dramatic advances in the field of gynecology; he identified the fallopian tubes, and his demonstration that the uterus was attached to the pelvis by the peritoneal fold known as the broad ligament should have put paid to the popular "wandering womb" thesis of female disturbance, but the belief proved surprisingly hardy and persisted for centuries. He was the first to offer an accurate description of the liver and the first to investigate the pancreas, and he accurately described the various parts of the eye: the cornea, the retina, the iris, and the vitreous humor.

Equally significant was the work the polymath Eratosthenes (ca. 276– ca. 195) from the Greek settlement of Cyrene in Libya. Having distinguished himself intellectually at both Cyrene and Athens, he attracted the attention of Ptolemy III, who appointed him chief librarian at Alexandria. There he pursued a variety of interests: geography (he may have been the first to use the word), mathematics, history, poetry, and astronomy. He is credited with inventing a system of latitude and longitude and made a map of the known world. In the three volumes of his *Geography*—literally, "writing up the earth"—he included a map with freezing, temperate, and tropical zones and the locations of more than 400 cities. Probably his most stunning achievement was his calculation of the earth's surface. Although by the time of Aristotle most Greek scholars had abandoned the notion of the earth as a flat disc and recognized that it was a sphere, its size remained a mystery. Aware that on the summer solstice the sun shone directly into the Egyptian city on the Nile that is now Aswan, he set up a pole in Alexandria and measured the angle of the shadow that it cast. Knowing the distance between the two cities, he was able to develop the following equation:

$$\frac{360 \text{ degrees}}{7.2 \text{ degrees}} = \frac{\text{circumference of the earth}}{\text{distance from Alexandria to Aswan}}$$

Calculating the distance between the two cities at about 5,000 stadia or around 500 miles, he came up with a circumference of about 25,000 miles (a little more than 40,000 kilometers), quite close to the actual circumference. A century later, however, the astronomer Posidonius of Rhodes (ca. 135–51) made a similar calculation but used the wrong distance between Rhodes and Alexandria, resulting in a number over a quarter too small. It was Posidonius's calculations rather than those of Eratosthenes that Columbus used when he sailed west from Spain in search of India. One cannot help wondering if he might not have scrapped the expedition had he known of Eratosthenes' calculations, and from there the possibilities for a major rearrangement of world history are endless.

The development from a mythical to a philosophical way of approaching the world corresponds to the change from a receptive self privileged to soak up messages about the world and its sacred stories to an active self capable of analyzing the world with no divine assistance or support. Philosophy, however, never entirely supplanted myth, which continued to be the foundation of Greek literature and the visual arts, and when the Romans co-opted Greek culture many more of them became invested in the stories of Zeus/Jupiter and Athena/Minerva (and Apollo/Apollo) than in the principles of *ataraxia* or the tripartite soul; Vergil's *Aeneid* drew to it far more readers than Lucretius's Epicurean manifesto *On the Nature of Things*.

Suggested Readings

Three superb Internet encyclopedias of philosophy have outstanding articles on individuals and topics:

Internet Encyclopedia of Philosophy
Routledge Encyclopedia of Philosophy
Stanford Encyclopedia of Philosophy

Adamson, Peter. 2014. *Classical Philosophy: A History of Philosophy without Any Gaps.* Vol. 1. Oxford: Oxford University Press.

———. 2015. *Philosophy in the Hellenistic and Roman Worlds: A History of Philosophy without Any Gaps.* Vol. 2. Oxford: Oxford University Press.

Allen, Danielle S. 2011. *Why Plato Wrote.* Malden, MA: Wiley-Blackwell.

Bremer, Jan. 1983. *The Early Greek Concept of the Soul.* Princeton, NJ: Princeton University Press.

Brunschwig, Jacques, and G.E.R. Lloyd, eds., with Pierre Pellegrin, trans. Catherine Porter et al. 2000. *Greek Thought: A Guide to Classical Knowledge.* Cambridge, MA: Belknap Press of Harvard University Press.

Clayman, Dee L. 2009. *Timon of Phlius: Pyrrhonism into Poetry*. Berlin and New York: Walter de Gruyter.

Diels, H., and W. Kranz. 1974. *Die Fragmente der Vorsokratiker*. 3 vols., original ed. 1903; reprint. Dublin and Zürich: Weidmann.

Dutsch, Dorota M. 2020. *Pythagorean Women Philosophers: Between Belief and Suspicion*. Oxford: Oxford University Press.

Farnsworth, Ward. 2018. *The Practicing Stoic: A Philosophical User's Manual*. Jaffrey, NH: David R. Godine.

Graham, D. W. 2006. *Explaining the Cosmos: The Ionian Tradition of Scientific Philosophy*. Princeton, NJ: Princeton University Press.

———, ed. 2010. *The Texts of Early Greek Philosophy: The Complete Fragments and Selected Testimonies of the Major Presocratics*. 2 vols. Cambridge, UK: Cambridge University Press.

Guthrie, W.K.C. 1971. *The Sophists*. Cambridge, UK: Cambridge University Press. Originally published as *A History of Greek Philosophy*, volume 3, part I, 1969. Cambridge, UK: Cambridge University Press.

———. 1975. *The Greek Philosophers from Thales to Aristotle*. New York: Harper & Row.

Hankinson, R. J. 2001. *Cause and Explanation in Ancient Greek Thought*. Oxford: Clarendon.

Hatab, Lawrence J. 1990. *Myth and Philosophy: A Contest of Truths*. La Salle, IL: Open Court.

Kahn, Charles H. 2001. *Pythagoras and the Pythagoreans: A Brief History*. Indianapolis, IN: Hackett.

Kerferd, G. B. 1950. "The First Greek Sophists." *Classical Review* 64, 8–10.

Kirk, Geoffrey S. 1970. *Myth: Its Meaning and Functions in Ancient and Other Cultures*. Cambridge, UK, and Berkeley: University of California Press.

Kirk, G. S., J. E. Raven, and M. Schofield. 1983. *The Presocratic Philosophers: A Critical History with a Selection of Texts*. Cambridge, UK, and New York: Cambridge University Press.

Laks, André, and Glenn W. Most, eds. 2016. *Early Greek Philosophy*. 9 vols. Cambridge, MA, and London: Harvard University Press.

Nussbaum, Martha C. 1994. *The Therapy of Desire: Theory and Practice in Hellenistic Ethics*. Princeton, NJ: Princeton University Press.

Pappas, Nickolas. 2013. *The Routledge Guidebook to Plato's Republic*. London and New York: Routledge.

———. 2020. *Plato's Exceptional City, Love, and Philosopher*. London and New York: Routledge.

Pomeroy, Sarah. 2013. *Pythagorean Women: Their History and Writings*. Baltimore, MD: Johns Hopkins University Press.

Sassi, Maria Michela. 2020. *The Beginnings of Philosophy in Greece*. Princeton, NJ: Princeton University Press.

Sedley, David. 2007. *Creationism and Its Critics in Antiquity*. Berkeley and Los Angeles: University of California Press.

CHAPTER 9

Life after Life

I'm a Frisbeetarian. We believe that when you die, your soul goes up on
the roof and you can't get it down.

—ATTRIBUTED ALTERNATELY TO STEVE MARTIN
AND GEORGE CARLIN

Sooner or later, all Greeks died. All philosophical schools addressed the
question of mortality. Socrates described the practice of philosophy as a
kind of preparation for death. Consider this, Plato portrays him saying:
philosophers are in every way hostile to the body, desiring to have the
soul all by itself. Why, then, should they be frightened when the body
and the soul separate? "When you see someone troubled because he is
going to die," he asks, "does this not make clear that he was not a lover of
wisdom but a lover of the body?" (*Phaedo* 68b). Not everyone, however,
is a philosopher, and despite the heroic efforts of philosophers of many
stamps, most Greeks were as anxious about death as anyone else.

They were also profoundly curious about what might await them afterward. At least in the long run: for the next month or so, time-honored
protocol dictated what would be going on around them, although not
what would be happening in their minds. It is not clear how much ceremony attended the death of a slave—one suspects there was pitifully
little—but in the case of free people, elaborate rituals were prescribed,
particularly for men who were heads of households but also to some

degree for women and children. Women of the family, preferably over sixty, would wash the corpse, anoint it with oil, and dress it in garments specially chosen for the occasion. Adorned with ribbons (and sweet-smelling flowers to offset the encroaching odor of decay), the body was then placed on a high bier in the home. In keeping with the connection between sleep and death, the bier was dressed like a bed, with blankets and pillows. Associations between sleep and death transcend cultures, but they may have been particularly tight for Greeks: had Hesiod not identified Thanatos, Death, and Hypnos, Sleep, as brothers, sons of Night (*Theogony*, 756)? The geographer Pausanias described in loving detail an ornate cedar chest dedicated by the Corinthian tyrants at Olympia early in the sixth century that purported to be the container in which his mother had hidden the infant Cypselus to save him from the murderous designs of the ruling Bacchiads. On it was carved a female cradling two infants in her arms along with an inscription identifying the triad as Night and her children Thanatos and Hypnos.[1]

Homer describes funerals far from home in Troy, especially the extravagant obsequies of Patroclus, in whose honor Achilles sacrificed not only two prized dogs and four horses but twelve unfortunate Trojan youths he had captured for the purpose. Excavation of a tenth-century hero shrine in Lefkandi on the island of Euboea opposite Attica revealed not only three horse skeletons but two humans: the ashes of a man, plainly the hero in question, and the skeleton of a woman, presumably his wife or other consort sacrificed on the occasion of his burial. Despite its popularity in myth, human sacrifice was rare in Greece during the centuries for which we have records, and though horses were occasionally buried with their masters well into the Classical Age, nothing has been found that compares with the unnerving Scythian funeral customs recorded by Herodotus. Archaeology has confirmed sacrifice of dozens of hapless subjects and their mounting on sacrificed horses in a Scythian king's grave a year after his burial: and this on top of the earlier sacrifice of a strangled concubine and a variety of other humans and animals on the occasion of the original interment.[2]

It was more common for bodies, or at least urns, to be transported home and buried there. During the Archaic and Classical Ages, both

FIGURE 9.1. Dipylon vase. This eighth-century Geometric amphora from the Dipylon Cemetery at Athens stands some five feet tall and is one of the finest of many depictions of the *prothesis*. © Vanni Archive / Art Resource, NY.

inhumation and cremation were common, although inhumation prevailed in the Hellenistic Age. For a period of three days the family would welcome visitors. Women sang dirges, the lead singer customarily cradling the head of the deceased in her hands. This ritual, known as the *prothesis* (the "setting out"), was a common subject in art: over fifty representations on Geometric vases have survived.

On the third day the body was carried to its final resting place and either buried or burned, the ashes then placed beneath the earth in an urn. In part this interval was observed in order to give guests the opportunity to pay their respects and family members to mourn, but it was also designed to make sure that the individual was truly dead. Greeks do not appear to have regarded death as instantaneous. Rather, it was perceived

as an ongoing process: it was possible to be just a little bit dead. It took
time, moreover, for the departed to become fully integrated into the world
of shades beneath the earth's crust. On the thirtieth day, additional rites,
the *triakostia*, were performed by the survivors. Although those who died
in battle might well be memorialized en masse in a state ceremony, funerals
were fundamentally the business of families; professionals were conspicuous by their absence. There were no such things as funeral homes, and
it would never have occurred to a bereaved Greek to involve a priest in
obsequies, the purpose of Greek religion being not to console the afflicted
but to regulate relations between gods and mortals. Some priests were
actually barred from having anything to do with a funeral, such as the
priestess of Demeter on the island of Cos and those who presided over
the mystery rites at Eleusis. Along the same lines it is worth noting that
after the Archaic Age gods could not be present either. Apollo in the *Iliad*
took tender care of the corpse of Sarpedon, washing it in the river and
anointing it with ambrosia (16. 676–81), whereas in Euripides' *Alcestis* he
leaves as soon as he sees Thanatos approaching, explaining that he must
not be polluted by the *miasma* death entails (22–23). As Hippolytus lies
dying, Artemis announces that she must be getting a move on:

> Farewell; it's not allowed for me to look
> Upon the dead or to defile my eye
> With the last breath of someone as he dies. (1447–48)

Hippolytus actually seems a bit thrown by her abandonment of him,
commenting, in effect, yes, well, sure, goodbye to you too, although . . .
I must say you do seem awfully casual about abandoning our long association. . . . (1440–41). Not until the *triakostia* had been duly carried
out could the survivors get on with their lives confident that their loved
one was firmly ensconced in the afterlife. Even after this, however, relatives were expected to attend to the tomb of the deceased indefinitely.
This responsibility was so great that it was often put forward as a reason
for those not favored with offspring to adopt, as dying without an heir
would mean not only the dreaded end of one's *oikos* but the lack of tomb
visits and offerings. In *The Libation Bearers* Aeschylus portrayed
Agamemnon's long-separated children Electra and Orestes reunited

when they bring offerings to their father's grave at the same time. An Athenian seeking public office could not proceed unless he was able to show that he maintained a family tomb.[3]

Not only would the deceased suffer should these honors be withheld: the well-being of those who were still alive was often perceived as contingent on maintaining good relations with those who were no longer. If properly honored, many thought, the dead had the power to confer benefits on not only their relatives but indeed their entire polis. If disgruntled, on the other hand, all manner of disaster might ensue, from drought to disease. Tombstones commemorated the dead and proclaimed the attachment of the bereaved. In Athens, following the dual-descent law of 451, citizenship could be advertised in the form of a tombstone commemorating a wife and mother. Boasting about one's father could be taken as elitist, but honoring one's mother affirmed one's citizenship. Those who had died in battle were honored not only with public orations but, in the case of major battles like Marathon, with monuments of various kinds. Public benefactors were often heroized, as were many founders of colonies. Battus, founder of Cyrene in Libya, was honored as a hero after his death and granted a tomb in the agora. The Spartan general Brasidas was heroized in Amphipolis in northern Greece after he liberated the city from the Athenian empire in 424, and annual festivals complete with games were held in his honor.

Death was a social event as well as a biological one. Ceasing to be members of one community, the dead had also joined another. The variety of rituals prescribed sought to honor this shift and to heal the rupture death occasions in the social fabric. These healing activities were divided according to gender, with females in charge of the physical and emotional, males in charge of the verbal and cerebral. Women took the lead in the family, largely indoors, and men led in the community, largely outdoors. Thus it was women, always involved in rites of passage—birth, weddings, deaths—who washed the body and prepared it for display and then burial, rent their cheeks, beat their breasts, and cried out in lamentation, while men composed and delivered funeral speeches celebrating the war dead as citizens of the polis. There was a large element of ritual in the conduct of both sexes. Hired female mourners, of whom many were available (it was a good job and one of the few open to women), might well never have met the deceased, but they wailed piteously just the same.[4] They still do. Hired mourners feature in numerous cultures all over the world today.[5] In the Mani peninsula in the Peloponnesus a cadre of women known as "moirologists"—fate-tellers—can be hired to sing an improvised lament recounting the life of the deceased.[6] Meanwhile funeral orations for those who had died in battle deliberately glossed over any individuality among the dead. Generals and common soldiers, rich cavalrymen and poor sailors, were homogenized into a heroic mass of patriots and in this way received *kleos aphthiton* much like the elite war heroes of an earlier age. The war dead in classical Athens became in essence heroized, commemorated in prose as the aristocratic elite of old had been in verse.

It helped to have a body to bury, or at least an urn of ashes. The bodies of those killed in war were frequently returned to their families, although the Athenians and Plataeans who died at Marathon were honored with a tumulus on the spot.[7] It was a sacred obligation for generals to retrieve the bodies of their dead from the battlefield and for the victorious side to return them to the losers. After the Athenians had defeated the Corinthians in battle in 425, the general Nicias discovered to his horror that in gathering up the dead he had left two men unnoticed on the battlefield. Although petitioning the Corinthians to allow him to return for the bodies meant renouncing the claim of victory and the attendant right to erect a commemorative trophy, Nicias, Plutarch reports, "preferred to abandon the honor and reputation of his victory to leaving two of his fellow citizens unburied" (*Nicias*, 6. 4–5). It was a great sorrow to the bereaved to be deprived of the body of their lost relative, as often happened in war and in the case of drowning. Greeks had an intense love-hate relationship with the sea. It was the sea, after all, that was a Greek's ticket out of his little city-state, a highway to riches and adventure, but the mysterious deep also held many perils and secrets. Beneath the surface lay not only shoals, caves, giant weeds, and powerful currents but also water nymphs, dragons and other sea monsters, and the bones of countless lost sailors, picked dry by aquatic scavengers. Mass hysteria broke out in Athens in 406 after Athenian admirals neglected to retrieve their men from the choppy waters in a storm off Anatolia, resulting in the execution of the six who made the mistake of returning home. The assembly's concern was not merely the failure to rescue the living but the inability to give a proper burial to those who had already drowned.

Penelope's ruse about Laertes' shroud makes clear that distinguished families at one time buried their dead in finely wrought garments, but beginning perhaps around the sixth century sumptuary laws discouraged this as well as other forms of flamboyance. Funerary legislation was often organized around clamping down on ostentatious display on the part of the rich—and relieving the not-so-rich of the pressure to compete with their more affluent compatriots: because funerals took place outdoors, lavish pageantry was open to public view. The law code of Ioulis on the island of Ceos, birthplace of the poet Simonides, banned the rites of the *triakostia* and specified that a maximum of three choes (about two gallons) of wine and one of olive oil were to be carried to the tomb, that the cloaks in which the deceased was garbed must be plain white, and that they should not number more than three, costing not more than a fixed amount. The Labyad clan at Delphi prescribed gray clothing—plainly relatives left to their own devices often opted for flashier garb—and forbade more than 35 drachmas' worth of items to be deposited in (or perhaps on) the tomb, a drachma or two being the probable daily pay of a skilled worker. Only one cloth could be placed on the bier and one pillow under the head, and all wailing was to take place at the tomb of the deceased: extracurricular lamentation next to the tombs of those who had died previously was strictly forbidden. Similarly at Mytilene around 600 the lawgiver Pittacus forbade people outside the family from attending a funeral.[8] In early centuries soldiers might be buried in their armor. The unmarried or newly married were often dressed as if for their wedding, particularly poignant for young girls who had died before fulfilling their destiny as mothers of future citizens. At Gambreion near Pergamum in Anatolia a third-century law prescribed that women in mourning were to wear brown garments that were unsoiled, presumably a slap at the melodramatic custom of sporting torn and dirty clothing to signal one's anguish. When he was on the point of death the Syracusan tyrant Gelon ordered that the sumptuary laws providing for modest funerals be respected in his case, but Diodorus claimed that the whole populace accompanied Gelon's body on foot to his tomb more than twenty miles away.[9]

At Sparta a law ascribed to Lycurgus placed similar restrictions on funerary ritual—nothing at all was to be buried with the dead—and required a dead man to be laid out in a scarlet military cloak strewn with olive leaves. Only men who died in battle and women who died in childbirth were permitted to have their names inscribed on tombstones. In a remarkable departure from Greek practice, he prescribed that the Spartans bury the dead not outside the city walls but in the city itself, the purpose being to discourage the young from superstitious fear of corpses by making them accustomed to the idea of dead bodies.[10] At the same time, however, Lycurgus was credited with the laws that specified elaborate mourning for Sparta's kings. Although he does not ordinarily set forth the customs of the various Greek states, Herodotus plainly found Spartan ways sufficiently distinctive as to warrant full ethnographic treatment. When Spartan kings die, he wrote,

> Riders are dispatched throughout Laconia to announce the event, while in the city women go around beating bronze cauldrons. When this happens, two free persons from each house, a man and a woman, are required to defile themselves in mourning on pain of heavy fines. (6. 58)

The *perioikoi*, moreover, were required to send a specified number of mourners to the funeral, where they mingled with the helots and the Spartiates, both male and female, in tens of thousands, beating themselves about the head and breasts and proclaiming the late king to have been the best one ever.

When Athens was at war with Megara and Salamis, Plutarch reports, and still reeling from Cylon's attempted tyranny and the execution of his followers, the seers "interpreted the sacrifices as indicating pollutions that required expiation." Consequently they summoned the sage Epimenides from Crete, who made the Athenians more moderate in their religious observances, in particular cracking down on the "harsh and barbaric practices in which their women had previously been accustomed to indulge" (*Solon* 12. 5). Solon went on to restrict both the deceased and the mourners to no more than three cloaks, placed a limit on the value of the food and drink brought to the tomb, and forbade the sacrificing of an ox (an expensive animal) on the grave. His restrictions were part of a broader package of checks specifically on women:

> He also subjected the behavior of women in public—their mourning and their festivals—to a law doing away with disorder and lack of discipline. They were not permitted to go out wearing more than three garments or to carry food or drink worth more than an obol [a sixth of a drachma] or a basket over a cubit high, or to travel around at night at all unless they rode in a wagon with a lamp to give light. (Plutarch, *Solon* 21. 4)

He also limited the degree of kinship within which women were allowed to participate in funerals. His laws, Demosthenes reported, specified that

> when the deceased is carried out, the men shall walk in front and the women behind. And no woman under sixty years of age shall be allowed to enter the chamber of the deceased, or to follow the deceased when he is carried to the tomb, unless she is within the degree of children of cousins. (43. 62)

Under Solonic law the poignant Homeric lamentations of Briseis for Patroclus and Helen for Hector would never have been heard.

While it was clear what the bereaved should and would be doing after a death in the family, it was less obvious what lay ahead for the departed. Would they feel pain—and would they be capable of feeling pleasure? Would there be opportunities for sex? Some thought so, although there was evidently a marked decline in fertility after death: no babies had been reported born in the Underworld, not even to Persephone and Hades. Would the dead have the power to wreak vengeance on those who had harmed them—or confer blessings on those who paid them homage? Would they indeed have any agency at all, or were they fated to wander aimlessly as shades in Hades, eking out a feeble existence in the gloom?

Most important, dared people hope that they might perhaps, by dint of something they had done when alive, actually escape the gloom and enjoy a life even more pleasant than the one they had left behind?

Practitioners of the cult known as Orphism believed in reincarnation, but only as a fallback for those who had not attained ritual purity. The mythical bard Orpheus, whose music was credited with the ability to move even animals and mute stones, was believed to have descended to Hades and returned safely to the earth's surface, albeit without the wife he had hoped to regain. Having granted his wish that his deceased bride Eurydice might return home with him, Hades imposed a fairy tale condition: "whatever you do, make sure you never . . ." Orpheus was not to look at his wife until their ascent from the kingdom of the dead was complete. When he proved unable to resist temptation and turned to check on her, Eurydice vanished forever from his sight and his life. That he himself had made a successful round-trip, however, put him in a category with Dionysus, who had also descended to Hades but returned, and Orpheus was believed to have originated the god's mystery cult. When he turned against the affections of women in his mourning for his wife, outraged devotees of Dionysus were said to have killed him and dismembered his body, and tradition had it that his head lived on after his death endowed with the gift of prophecy.

The central myth of this cult concerned the murder of the infant Dionysus by the Titans. After the Titans had dismembered and eaten their victim, the story went, his enraged father Zeus struck them with a thunderbolt, turning them to ashes from which the human race was in turn born. Mortals, consequently, were believed to possess a dual nature. In their bodily incarnation, they were the polluted descendants of cannibals and murderers, but in spirit they had inherited a divine spark derived from the ingested remains of Dionysus. Initiation into the cult of Dionysus and the practice of asceticism (including vegetarianism) were required to achieve and maintain the ritual purity that would lead to an enviable afterlife passed alongside Orpheus and other heroes; death alone could provide a thorough escape from pollution. The uninitiated, however, would undergo an indefinite series of reincarnations. Similar notions were put forward about initiation into the Eleusinian mysteries.

FIGURE 9.2. The Muses with the oracular head of Orpheus. This mid-fifth-century hydria (jar for carrying water) may be the first visual representation of the legend that Orpheus's detached head prophesied after it was torn from his body. © Antikenmuseum Basel und Sammlung Ludwig.

The archaic *Homeric Hymn to Demeter* indicated that those who had participated in the rites of Persephone at Eleusis would fare well in the Underworld, while the uninitiated would not.[11] Some centuries later these initiates formed the chorus of Aristophanes' *Frogs*, set in the Underworld. There the self-seeking politicians to whom the playwright ascribes the disasters that befell Athens in the Peloponnesian War are condemned to wallow in muck while the initiates, who represent the suffering populace of the city, enjoy a delightful existence in the sunlight, singing:

> The sun shines here for us alone;
> For us alone the joyous light.
> We who are the initiates
> And tread the road of piety

Toward strangers and toward ordinary folk
Who do not know the secrets that we do. (455–59)

The fifth-century poet Pindar certainly believed that conduct in one's lifetime would shape life after death. Although, as he concedes,

The rich and poor alike must make their way
Along the road to death (*Nemean* 7. 19)

nonetheless

Those who have gladly kept their oaths enjoy
A life that's free of tears; the others, though,
Suffer harsh labors miserable to watch. (*Olympian* 2, 66–67)

Both the notion of reincarnation and the idea of differential afterlives depending on one's conduct on earth appear in the writings of Plato, who gave a lot of thought to what might await us after death. It often seems, however, that his conflicting visions varied according to the dramatic needs of his dialogues. Toward the end of his trial, for example, in speculating on what might lie ahead for him Socrates alludes to the existence of two schools of thought about death. Being dead, he muses playfully, is one of two things. Either the dead have no awareness at all, or else death is some sort of migration of the soul to another place. Now, if there is indeed no awareness, and death is like an amazingly sound sleep, who among us would not welcome that? On the other hand, if it is indeed true, as we are told, that everyone who has died is in that other place to which we all pass, what in the world could be a greater good? Imagine, he says, how wonderful it would be to meet the poets of old, like Homer and Hesiod and Orpheus! He would be willing to die many times over if he could look forward to meeting such people in the Underworld. The greatest pleasure, he concludes,

would be to pass my time in examining and investigating the people there, as I do those here, to discover who among them are wise and who think they are when the truth is that they are not. How much would one give, jurors, to examine the man who led the great host against Troy, or Odysseus, or Sisyphus, or the countless others whom one might mention, both men and women? To enter into conversation with them and examine them would be a delight beyond measure. In any case, they don't kill people down there for this reason, since, if what we hear is true, they are immortal for all time, besides being more fortunate in other respects than people are here. (*Apology* 41b–c)

Last he reiterates his lifelong claim that no evil can befall a good man—and extends it to the afterlife: no evil can befall a good man, living or dead. For this reason, too, death is nothing to be feared by the just person.

Other possibilities are explored in the *Republic*, as Socrates recounts a myth of his (or, more likely, Plato's) own making, telling how the Greek warrior Er, having died on the field of battle, revived on the funeral pyre to recount his time in the afterlife. There, Er reports, he had come upon openings both up to the sky and down into the earth, between which sat judges who guided the virtuous to the heavens and the wicked down below. Down from the sky floated pure souls who recounted wonderful experiences full of beautiful sights and feelings of elation. Those who came up from under the earth, however, were filthy and haggard and had only wretched experiences to report, for they were forced to pay tenfold for all evil deeds they had committed when they were alive. The expiation of their sins in fact took so long that they had spent fully a thousand years below ground. Those whose crimes were particularly heinous were bound, flayed, and carded before being hurled into the very bottommost pit, the dread Tartarus. The distance between Hades and Tartarus, Homer and Hesiod agreed, was as great as that between heaven and earth. (In some later writers, however, Hades and Tartarus seem to be used interchangeably, perhaps depending on the demands of meter.) After some days, he related, all the souls were offered the opportunity to choose their next lives. Predictably, a combination of temperament and the degree of wisdom one had attained dictated the choices. The first soul in line chose the life of a tyrant, "not recognizing that his choice fated him, among other evils, to devour his own children" (*Republic* 619b–c). The last soul was that of Odysseus, who, exhausted after all the struggles forced upon him in his earlier existence, opted for the life of a private citizen, free from arduous responsibilities.

Although the notion of reincarnation appears in the dialogue *Timaeus* as well, there the system of allotment differs. The divine craftsman, Socrates explains, once he had created the universe, set about molding humanity so that each person would grow into the most god-fearing individual. These new creatures if they lived justly and did a creditable job of handling the powerful sensations of desire, pleasure, pain, fear, anger, and so forth, would in consequence enjoy a blessed afterlife. Those who failed to do so, however, would be reborn as women, and anyone who persists in misconducting himself would be changed first into one animal, then another and another in accordance with the nature of his misdeeds. Not until he finally pulls himself together and lives in accordance with reason will he be reborn in his original human state (*Timaeus* 41e–42d). Socrates, or Plato, seems to forget here that some people are born female in the first place. Do unjust women proceed immediately after death to the animal kingdom?

Both these systems were at odds with the views of the Pythagoreans, who evidently regarded the allotment of souls into new bodies as a haphazard affair. Empedocles, however, envisioned a different scenario. Human souls, he suggested, were in fact fallen spirits who had been banished from Olympus after committing bloodshed and perjury. They then enter a cycle of rebirth whereupon those who purify themselves come to be reincarnated in such respected professions as seer, poet, or physician. Leaders in their communities, they eventually take their place among the gods.[12] The various systems for the transmigration of souls, then, included reincarnation contingent on ritual purity; reincarnation dependent on the soul's degree of development; and reincarnation in random new bodies. Most Greeks, though, were not so hopeful about what might await them after death and perceived it as the ultimate equalizer.

A handful, to be sure, went to places both better and worse. Well-connected individuals like Menelaus, who had married a daughter of Zeus, might be transported to the Isles of the Blessed, where great heroes lived "untouched by sorrow" and crops flourished three times a year (Hesiod, *Works and Days*, 170–73). In Homer's construct,

> The place is untouched by snow, harried by no worrisome storms;
> It never even rains, but constantly Ocean sends blasts
> Of welcome soothing winds that blow out of the west
> And offer cool air to mortals. (*Odyssey* 4. 566–68)

It is sometimes suggested that Cadmus, the founder of Thebes, who married the daughter of Ares and Aphrodite, enjoyed the same fate, and Hesiod, as we have seen, claimed that Zeus transported some of his fourth race of men there as well. Particularly heinous criminals like Tantalus, Ixion, and Sisyphus, on the other hand, were consigned to unremitting punishment in Tartarus. Significantly, all three men had violated traditional boundaries that kept order in the world by separating gods and mortals. Both Tantalus and Ixion had been granted the rare privilege of consorting with the gods on Olympus—and abused it. Tantalus thought it would be a neat trick to test the gods' power of discernment by killing his son Pelops and serving him up to the Olympians at dinner: would the gods detect the inappropriate fare and reject it? Most did, but Demeter, pining for her missing daughter, nibbled absentmindedly on the boy's left shoulder. A stern Zeus ordered the boy reconstituted (with an ivory shoulder to replace what Demeter had eaten) and consigned Tantalus to eternal punishment in Tartarus, compelling him to stand for eternity in a pool of cool water that receded whenever he reached down to drink—beneath a fruit tree whose branches receded whenever he reached up to eat (hence the English word "tantalize"). Ixion for his part took advantage of Zeus's hospitality by plotting to rape his wife, surely an extreme violation of *xenia*, the sacred bond between guest and host. Zeus foiled his plan by creating a Hera-shaped cloud with which the deluded Ixion coupled, fathering the race of centaurs. Eternity found Ixion bound to a fiery wheel, endlessly spinning: perpetual vertigo. And then there was Sisyphus. Who of us has not identified with poor Sisyphus? Founder and king of Ephyra (probably the original name of Corinth), Sisyphus showed an early disrespect for *xenia*, regularly killing guests at his palace. When he betrayed one of Zeus's secrets—these were early days, when a mortal might be privy to such a thing—Zeus ordered Thanatos to chain him in Tartarus. Thinking to outdo the king of the gods in cleverness, Sisyphus asked Thanatos to show him how the chains worked, and by the time the demonstration had finished, poor Thanatos was in chains and Sisyphus was free. As long as Thanatos was bound by the sturdy fetters, nobody on earth could die. Galled by pointless battles in which nobody on either side perished, an exasperated Ares intervened, freeing Thanatos and handing Sisyphus over to him. It gets better: when Sisyphus had been on the point of death, it seems, he had cleverly instructed his wife not to bury him but rather to cast his body naked into the public square. This set him up for a plea to Persephone to the effect that he had been disrespected on earth and needed to return in order to remedy the disgraceful situation. His plea was successful, but when he then refused to return to the Underworld, Hermes was sent to drag him back. Fed up with his shenanigans, Zeus condemned him to an eternity of rolling a boulder up a hill only to have it tumble back to the starting point just as it approached the top.

The average person, however, anticipated neither bliss nor torture nor peaceful sleep but rather a lackluster eternity in a dreary Underworld, the musty kingdom of Zeus's brother Hades and the bride he had kidnapped as a child, who might or might not be away for the summer holidays. The Greeks' grim view of the afterlife is a testament to their underlying pessimism. To be sure, this shadowy existence might be punctuated by periodic banqueting on the couches often portrayed on funeral monuments, at least after a bit: the earliest Greeks do not seem to have imagined that shades ate and drank. (One wonders where the food that was ingested wound up, as we hear nothing of sanitary facilities in Hades.) Reliefs depicting the deceased enjoying a symposium, wine in hand, number in the hundreds, and the dead are often portrayed passing the time (of which there was so very much) playing games such as dice, which have been found in a number of seventh- and sixth-century Greek tombs. Board games were evidently also popular, a notion possibly taken over from Egypt. Still, it was not a pleasant place, far away from the light and guarded by the unprepossessing hound of hell,

Cerberus. Although the notion of Cerberus as a three-headed creature has ensconced itself firmly in the modern imagination, ancient sources were inconsistent about how many heads he had. Sometimes they numbered as many as fifty, and all we can say for certain is the Greeks believed the number to be a positive integer greater than one.

Curiously, Hades himself was not always portrayed negatively. Often it was the commonality of death that was stressed: for Antigone he is

Hades, the one who lays all folk to rest (*Antigone*, 810)

and the chorus in Sophocles' *Ajax* calls his kingdom "a home common to many" (1193). Hades is certainly no respecter of persons; if he were, he would not have kidnapped and raped a child. He was often described ironically as a fabulous host, a model of *xenia*. Faced with the prospect of a forced marriage, the daughters of Danaus in Aeschlyus's *Suppliant Women* threaten to hand themselves over to the

Zeus down below, a very gracious host. (156)

The chorus in *Oedipus at Colonus* refers to Thanatos as a helper who comes at the end to all alike (1220). The notion of Thanatos—not necessarily personified—as soothing to those in pain is often stressed: the dying Hippolytus expresses the wish that *thanatos* come to him as a physician and free him from his suffering. Although Hades and Thanatos were sometimes interchangeable, Thanatos was often perceived separately; Hades tended to stay in, well, Hades, whereas Thanatos roamed the earth doing his dismal duty. He could not kill of his own accord but only if he was under orders. Along with Hypnos, Thanatos appears on vases carrying off both mythical figures and ordinary Greeks—even, starting around 400, women.

The Homeric dead were quite literally shadows of their former selves, lacking in energy and agency, although under exceptional circumstances they might make trouble—the unburied dead, for example, returning to harry those who had neglected to bury them. In time, however, many Greeks came to perceive the dead as able to act, and a variety of practices sprang up calculated to shape the form that action might take. As grave offerings were thought essential to remaining in the good graces of the departed, liquids such as wine, oil, and milk were frequently poured over the graves of the dehydrated dead in the expectation of gaining their favor—or averting their displeasure. Both motives appear in the scene in Sophocles' *Electra* that shows Agamemnon's daughter Chrysothemis under instructions to take offerings to her father's grave on behalf of the mother who murdered him. Frightened by a dream, Clytemnestra sought to appease his wrath, but Electra suggests they pray instead

> That he might come in kindness from below
> And help us go against our enemies. (453–54)

The deceased were most certainly not at the top of their game. Relatives sometimes put a false bottom in the painted funeral vessels known as *lekythoi* so that a very small amount of liquid would appear to have filled it. Plainly it was believed that the dead could be fooled.

The shift to a different belief system may have been sparked by contact with Mesopotamia and Egypt. From their earliest history both cultures assumed that the dead interacted with the living on a regular basis, sometimes when summoned, sometimes spontaneously. Many rituals were available in Mesopotamia for contacting and influencing the souls of the dead. The Egyptians suspected that various family conflicts and ailments were caused by resentments on the part of those who had died prematurely or by violence as well as those who not been properly buried. Similarly Plato writing in the fourth century cautioned that a man freshly slain, "being himself perturbed at the sight of his murderer going about the very same places he had frequented when alive, is filled with horror, and being perturbed himself, he takes the awareness of the wrong done to him as his ally and sees to it that his killer is perturbed in all he does" (*Laws*, 865e). And not only that; since the unhappy dead might trouble the entire city, the proper care of the deceased was the concern of the community as well as the immediate family.

It was also possible for the dead to cause frightful harm for reasons entirely of their own and through no fault of the living. In antiquity as today, pregnant women were vulnerable to miscarriage as well as death in childbirth, and small children, particularly newborns, were subject to sudden and seemingly inexplicable death. Far more convenient to assign agency to the spirits of the disgruntled dead than to point the finger at living women who might envy the fertility of a friend or relation, or living people of either sex who might wish to prevent the birth or maturation of an heir. Rather, such misfortunes, extending even to the deaths of adolescent girls who died before they could be married, might be laid at the door of various demonic spirits held to be the jealous and resentful souls of women who had lost their children or had died before realizing their roles as mothers. Queen of the Underworld, Persephone herself never had children. One wonders whether the sterility of her marriage was connected to the famous story that Demeter had to settle for joint custody of Persephone because she had eaten a few pomegranate seeds that Hades had offered her, binding her to spend part of her life in the Underworld. Classicist Laurie O'Higgins has made the ingenious suggestion that Persephone ate the seeds on her own initiative, a persuasive hypothesis: why would Hades wish his wife to consume such a thing when pomegranate was commonly used in Greece as a contraceptive?[13] By eating them, Persephone asserts her identity as her mother's child, not as her husband's wife, for the Greeks did not consider a girl fully a woman until she had given birth to her first child. The arrangement on which Demeter and Hades agree would have been unworkable had Persephone herself become a mother. Persephone came to be known simple as Kore, the maiden—always a girl, never fully a woman. That the life of a newly married female was considered just as incomplete as the life of a virgin is attested by the stress in epitaphs for young women on the fact that they had never married or had only just married. Women's poetry in particular commemorated the deaths of friends who died before or just after marriage. Sappho wrote of Timas, "dead before her marriage," mourned by her female companions.

> This is the sad dust of Timas, whom, dying before she was married,
> Persephone's gloomy house took. Mourning her death, all her friends
> Cut off their beautiful locks with blades sharpened just for the purpose.
> (*Greek Anthology* 7. 489)

Anyte mourned the death of her friend Antibia, whose many suitors' hopes had been dashed by destructive Fate, and grieved for devastated Cleina, whose daughter Philaenis had crossed into Hades before her wedding:

> Here I lament the young virgin Antibia. Eager to wed her,
>   Suitors in droves would appear, seeking her father's consent,
> Led by reports of her beauty, her prudence; now each one's discovered
>   All his hopes rolling away, victims of most baneful Fate.
>   (*Greek Anthology* 7. 490)

> Often upon this, the tomb, of her much-cherished but short-lived daughter
>   Did Cleina call on her child, wailing in heart-rending tones,
> Summoning back from the dead the dear soul of departed Philaenis,
>   Passed beyond Acheron's pale stream before she could be wed.
>   (*Greek Anthology* 7. 486).

The notion that the young were particularly vulnerable to the machinations of evil spirits was a useful tool in exacting obedience. Greek children were frightened into submission by the stories that circulated about Gello. Her name probably derived from the Mesopotamian word *gallu*, meaning "evil spirit." Particularly feared in Lesbos, where she had lived before her death, Gello was reputed to "spirit" little children away and gobble them up, and parallel figures known as *Gelloudes* are still believed to haunt the Greek countryside. A beautiful Libyan woman, daughter of the eastern god Ba'al, the "bogeywoman" Lamia was another source of terror. Like the Mesopotamian Lamashtu, from whom she seems to derive, Lamia specialized in causing the deaths of women, fetuses, infants, and small children, her own children having been killed by a jealous Hera after her affair with Zeus. While these malign Greek spirits may indeed have derived from eastern counterparts, it is also possible that the Greeks were more comfortable casting such distasteful figures as essentially foreign even though in fact they were not.[14] Various mixtures were marketed that could be rubbed on the body during pregnancy for protection against these spirits, and there was a thriving business in apotropaic amulets.

The abundance of lore that congregated around the afterlife afforded Greeks a great deal of variety in what to believe. As people will do, they picked and chose from among the various tales, and conflicting beliefs often settled in a single mind. Knowledge of myths, moreover, is not the same as belief in them. I know a good deal about Santa Claus, but I do not believe in him. I know that Hell is excruciatingly hot, but I do not believe in Hell. I do not believe in Heaven either, yet after my father's death I did find myself imagining that he was looking down on me disapprovingly from above if I went home directly after class rather than stopping in to check on my mother. What any individual Greek believed is anyone's guess. When it came to Greek notions about life after death, inconsistencies abounded; it was not just the number of Cerberus's heads that was in dispute. Not only the afterlife but also death itself is presented inconsistently in the Homeric epics. At times life is identified with consciousness or vision, but at others it seems to escape through a wound. Does it then reside in the blood? At times it seems to be equated with breath. Sometimes the strength of the limbs is broken; at others a mist covers the eyes. Myth told how newly arrived souls would drink of the river Lethe to forget all the pain of their past lives, but Agamemnon never forgot his murder at the hands of the adulterous Clytemnestra and welcomed any opportunity to complain of it, and Socrates in expressing enthusiasm for interrogating the shades below plainly expected them to have total recall of their earthly existence. Did the dead reside in Hades or in their tombs? Certainly those who cultivated the tombs of heroes, regarded as protectors of the surrounding territory, perceived the heroes as being quite immediately present. Circe tells Odysseus that Tiresias was the only soul whom Persephone permitted to retain his wits, the others all having been deprived of their faculties upon their deaths, yet the souls who converse with Odysseus upon his arrival in Hades do not appear cognitively impaired in the least.[15]

The shades of the dead were often perceived as only marginally corporeal, yet war heroes were frequently portrayed as covered with blood and wounds; Oedipus plainly expected his vision problems to persist after death, as he attributes his blinding to his unwillingness to look his parents in the eye in the Underworld (*Oedipus the King* 1371–73);

Sisyphus sweats as he labors endlessly with his boulder; and the punishment of Tantalus would carry no weight if the poor man did not experience hunger and thirst. The truth is that incorporeal figures of negligible energy and consciousness were entirely unsuited to literature: a good story required characters with a little more pizazz. Along the same lines the complete absence of light in Hades was artistically inconvenient, with the result that when Odysseus travels there he is perfectly able to see people, or what remains of them, and they to see him.

Given the subject matter, the inconsistencies and illogicalities are inevitable. As classicist Emily Vermeule has written,

> The manifold self-contradictions in Greek ideas and phrasing about death are not errors. They are styles of imagining the unimaginable, and are responsive both to personal needs and to old conventions. The same conflicts surge up in many cultures. They are necessary ambiguities in a realm of thinking where thinking cannot really be done, and where there is no experience. Logic is not fruitful in the sphere of death.[16]

And some Greeks were just plain skeptical about just what went on beneath the earth's crust. Being dead, Andromache says in Euripides' *Trojan Women*, is no different from never having been born in the first place:

> To never have been born and to be dead
> Are just the same, it really seems to me.
> Death is far better than a life of misery.
> The dead do not know sorrow, have no griefs. (636–38)

Socrates, as we have seen, raised the possibility that death was merely an extraordinarily sound and restful sleep; Aristophanes in his *Frogs* made great capital of the comic potential inherent in Greek myths of the Underworld; and the third-century Alexandrian Callimachus shared his irreverence, writing in an epigram:

> "Yo, Charidas! What are things like down there?"
> "Dark. Darker. Darkest."
> "The ways up?"
> "A lie."

"What about Pluto?"

"A myth."

"Dang it. You've ruined my whole day." (Epigram 15. 3–4)

Inevitably, beliefs changed over time, although Hades continued to be perceived as a Bronze Age kingdom of sorts, with formidable gates, a central palace, and a great hall; the dead not only go down in space but back in time. The notion that the dead are shepherded to Hades by Hermes in his role as psychopomp—literally, soul-conductor—appears in the Homeric epics only in the last book of the *Odyssey*; elsewhere the Homeric dead descend as independent travelers, perfectly capable of making their way to the Underworld under their own steam.

Beginning in Alexandria over two thousand years ago, the inconsistency has led some scholars to believe that *Odyssey* Book 24 was the work of a different poet.[17] This conclusion strikes me as extreme, although not impossible; more likely the disjunction should be taken as further evidence that the *Odyssey* was composed later than the *Iliad*. Hermes was always a traveler and had already appeared as a guide associated with the dead in the last book of the *Iliad*, where he gave safe conduct to Priam as the Trojan king journeyed to the Greek camp to retrieve his son's body. Around 500 the figure of Charon appears in Greek myth and art. His name and origin may well be Egyptian, as Diodorus maintained, and he remained a fixture in the Underworld throughout the Classical and Hellenistic Ages.[18] It was Charon's job to ferry the souls of the newly dead across the river dividing the world of the living from that of the dead, usually the Acheron but in some later accounts the Styx, and sometimes not so much a river as a lake. It was sometimes, but not always, thought necessary to place a small coin in or on the mouth of the deceased to pay Charon's fare, although it's difficult to imagine just what Charon could have been saving up for. Dared he hope to buy his way out of his peculiar job, thus avoiding occupational hazards? They were certainly substantial: when Heracles was charged with retrieving Cerberus as one of his twelve labors, he had browbeaten Charon into ferrying him across, for which dereliction of duty poor Charon was said to have been confined to chains for a year.

Frequently portrayed as winged miniature replicas of the deceased, the fluttering souls that had parted from the body should certainly have been able to fly across the dividing waters even if they were not strong swimmers; they had after all made it safely to Hades for centuries before Hermes and later Charon got into the act. It may be that dying became a source of greater anxiety and required props and helpers to give structure to the process—and to reassure the living that they will not be alone when their mortality catches up with them but rather will have trained assistants to help them in the inevitable process ahead. The two sides of Charon are diagnostic in terms of Greek attitudes to death. On the one hand he was often perceived as kindly in assisting souls on their necessary passage, but on the other he was ferocious in guarding the boundary between the world above and that below. Consequently some depict him as welcoming and benevolent, others as disagreeable and sinister.

The two psychopomps served to establish boundaries that were both ritualized and permeable. On the one hand souls now required intermediaries to gain entry to their final resting places. On the other hand, those who let them in might also under certain circumstances let them out: Hermes, the god of travel who was expert at crossing boundaries, was the perfect deity to monitor the boundary between the upper and lower worlds, the Checkpoint Charlie of antiquity. Hermes had always had a special connection with the Underworld. He accompanied Heracles on his trip to capture Cerberus and was also sent by Zeus to persuade Hades to allow Persephone to return to the earth on a part-time basis to pacify her distraught mother.

Although the trip to Hades was normally a one-way proposition, several Greeks were believed to have made successful round-trips: Persephone, of course, with her commuting marriage; the sneaky Sisyphus; Odysseus, whose journey in Book 11 of the *Odyssey* was a major source when it came to Greeks' understanding of the afterlife; Orpheus, although he failed in his quest to bring his bride back with him; and, along with those whom he liberated from the clutches of death, Heracles, who made at least four round-trips: one to retrieve Cerberus, another to return him, still another to rescue Theseus when he had rashly descended to the Underworld with his friend Peirithoos in the vain hope of carrying

FIGURE 9.3. Cerberus with Hermes and Heracles. The dog Cerberus was a popular subject of vase painting; here he is portrayed drawn along by Heracles as Hermes looks on. Photograph © 1931, Museum of Fine Arts, Boston.

off Persephone (the less fortunate Peirithoos was left below), and one to restore to life Alcestis, the wife who had generously volunteered to die in her husband's place.

The reunion of families in Hades was warmly regarded and eagerly anticipated. Those who had already spent some time in the Underworld could offer tips on negotiating it like the upperclassmen who when not in hazing mode provide guidance to first-year students, while recent arrivals could bring news of development in the world above—filling in the established residents about the grandeur of the funerals that had followed their deaths. Agamemnon seems to have been particularly delighted to see new arrivals, since each one gave him a new opportunity to expatiate on the sins of his faithless wife. Other reunions, to be sure, were less promising and offered both misery and comic potential. One would give much to be a fly on the wall at the reunion of Agamemnon and Iphigenia, who might not have been the most receptive audience for his condemnation of Clytemnestra. Creon's intransigence in the face of Antigone's defiance led not only to her suicide but to those of his wife and son; do they really want to spend eternity with him? Would soldiers who shortly before had been striving with might and main to end one another's lives find themselves awkwardly reunited below? In light of the role his *Clouds* had played in stirring up public sentiment against Socrates, Aristophanes surely would have organized his afterlife around avoiding Plato, and those of whom Socrates had made mincemeat in conversation when they were alive would surely be horrified to find that they had not escaped him in death. On the other hand, the Presocratics might have greatly enjoyed being together in the same place at the same time to hash out their conflicting theories. Or perhaps not: Heraclitus was prone to decrying the failings of other thinkers, and he might have been aghast at the prospect of their eternal company. Did the shades simply wander, or did they have assigned seats? It is amusing to contemplate Hades and Persephone sitting down to work out placement like a seating chart at a wedding: oh no, we've got Clytemnestra next to Electra; that won't do. What about Penelope next to Helen? The fur would fly, but it would be worth watching. . . . The rulers of the Underworld did not have an easy job, but on the whole the denizens of their dusky kingdom had it far worse.

Suggested Readings

Bremmer, Jan N. 2002. *The Rise and Fall of the Afterlife*. London and New York: Routledge.

Dimakis, Nikolas, and Tamara M. Dijkstra, eds. 2020. *Mortuary Variability and Social Diversity in Ancient Greece: Studies on Ancient Greek Death and Burial*. Oxford: Archaeopress Archaeology.

Edmonds, Radcliffe G., III. 2013. *Redefining Ancient Orphism: A Study in Greek Religion*. Illustrated edition. Cambridge, UK: Cambridge University Press, 2013.

Erasmo, Mario. 2012. *Death: Antiquity and Its Legacy. Ancients and Moderns*. New York: Oxford University Press.

Garland, Robert. 1985. *The Greek Way of Death*. Ithaca, NY: Cornell University Press.

González González, Marta. 2019. *Funerary Epigrams of Ancient Greece: Reflections on Literature, Society, and Religion*. London and New York: Bloomsbury Academic.

Håland, Evy Johanne. 2014. *Rituals of Death and Dying in Modern and Ancient Greece: Writing History from a Female Perspective.* Newcastle upon Tyne, UK: Cambridge Scholars Publishing.

Johnson, Sarah Iles. 1999. *The Restless Dead: Encounters between the Living and the Dead in Ancient Greece.* Berkeley and Los Angeles: University of California Press.

Long, Alex G. 2019. *Death and Immortality in Ancient Philosophy. Key Themes in Ancient Philosophy.* Cambridge, UK, and New York: Cambridge University Press.

Mirto, Maria Serena, trans. A. M. Osborne. 2012. *Death in the Greek World from Homer to the Classical Age. Oklahoma Series in Classical Culture* 44. Norman: University of Oklahoma Press.

Morris, Ian. 1992. *Death Ritual and Social Structure in Classical Antiquity.* Cambridge, UK, and New York: Cambridge University Press.

Renfrew, Colin, Michael J. Boyd, and Iain Morley, eds. 2015. *Death Rituals, Social Order and the Archaeology of Immortality in the Ancient World: "Death Shall Have No Dominion."* Cambridge, UK, and New York: Cambridge University Press.

Sourvinou-Inwood, Christine. 1995. *"Reading" Greek Death: To the End of the Classical Period.* New York and Oxford: Oxford University Press/Clarendon.

Vermeule, Emily. 1979. *Aspects of Death in Early Greek Art and Poetry.* Berkeley and Los Angeles: University of California Press.

The Greeks among Us

I say that someone will remember us
Even in another time.

—SAPPHO, 147

We must stay hopeful;
We must stay patient—
because when they excavate the modern day
they'll find us: the Brand New Ancients.

—KATE TEMPEST, *BRAND NEW ANCIENTS*

In light of the general perception of Hades' realm as a drab and dreary world decorated in fifty shades of gray, it is no wonder that Greeks placed so much importance on attaining *kleos* in life. In the words of Pindar,

> Posthumous fame is all that will reveal
> The way of life of those who have departed
> For storytellers, and for singers too. (*Pythian* 1.92–94)

The Greeks would be pleased by the amount of *kleos* they have continued to enjoy throughout history, though they would be mystified by the obloquy that has come to attend on their slaveholding, misogyny, and ethnocentrism. For the Greek heritage has continued powerfully into our own time in the form of a legacy that is both rich and problematic, as the Greeks are cited as models and anti-models alike. Greek culture lives on all over the globe. Brought to a wider audience by colonialism, it persisted after independence, often as a vehicle for exploring colonialism itself.[1] Colonialist traces are evident all over the world in not only the verbal but also the visual arts, not least in the white column buildings evident from Australia to Africa. Classically inspired buildings dot the globe today, from Brisbane City Hall begun in 1920 to the elaborate sculptural program at Rockefeller Center developed over a period of years in New York City to the Rhodes Memorial on Devil's Peak in Cape Town and the National Academic Theatre of Opera and Ballet of Mongolia inaugurated in 1963; the striking Ionic columns in the Old Parliament Building (completed in 1930) in Colombo featured prominently in media coverage of the civil unrest in Sri Lanka in 2022. Even the design for Sydney's eminently modern opera house was based on the ancient Greek semicircular theater. The Mausoleum in Herodotus's hometown of Halicarnassus has enjoyed reincarnations from the Shrine of Remembrance in Melbourne to the National Diet Building in Tokyo to Grant's Tomb a few blocks from my home in New York City, where it stands less than two miles north of the Soldiers' and Sailors' Monument modeled on the choragic monument of Lysicrates in Athens.

It is probably myth most of all that draws us back to the Greeks and guarantees their immortality. Any number of plays, operas, and films—high-brow, middle-brow, and extremely low-brow—have been grounded in Greek myth. Heracles, most frequently in his Roman incarnation as Hercules, has such a high profile in popular culture that papers about his significance in modern times have been offered for purchase to students on the Internet. He has appeared in countless television shows, comic books, and films, not the least of which, *Hercules in New York* (1970), starred 22-year-old Arnold Schwarzenegger in his film debut (credited as Arnold Strong, "Mr. Universe") and involves the superhero's conflict with the Mafia during his visit to New York City in the twentieth century, a high point being a showdown with a grizzly bear in Central Park [sic]. The amazing 1963 *Jason and the Argonauts* and the 1981 *Clash of the Titans* have enthralled generations of both children and adults. In presenting Ray Harryhausen with a Lifetime Achievement

Award for his electrifying special effects for these and other films, actor Tom Hanks proclaimed *Jason and the Argonauts* "the greatest film ever made."

The legendary bard Orpheus certainly lives on. His head, it was said, prophesied as it rolled down the Hebrus River after his death, washing up on the island of Lesbos. As Milton put it in 1637,

> His goary visage down the stream was sent,
> Down the swift Hebrus to the Lesbian shore ("Lycidas," 51–52)

where an oracle was established in his name. The head continued to prophesy, so the story went, until Apollo, envious at the attention being drawn away from his shrine at Delphi, ordered it to stop. The story of Orpheus eventually made its way into many paintings and several twentieth-century plays and films: in *The Blood of a Poet*, for example, a cinematic trilogy by the French surrealist Jean Cocteau (1952); in Brazilian writer and musician Marcus Vinicius da Cruz e Mello Moraes's 1956 musical drama *Orpheus of the Conception* and its two screen adaptations, Marcel Camus's *Black Orpheus* (1959) and Carlos Diegues's 1999 remake. Over half the tales in Kate Bernheimer's edited 2013 collection *xo Orpheus: Fifty New Myths* are of Greek origin, and Tracy Barrett titled her hilarious 2019 collection of new myths of her own making *The Song of Orpheus: The Greatest Greek Myths You Never Heard*.

The philosophers of Greece have also continued to exercise thoughtful minds (as well as some that are not so thoughtful). The eighteenth-century framers of the American constitution were steeped in Stoic philosophy. Karl Marx received his doctorate from the University of Jena in 1841 for a dissertation on Democritus and Epicurus. An early edition of Darwin's *Origin of Species* featured Aristotle's summary of Empedoclean evolution on the flyleaf. Handbooks of Greek philosophy are published in dozens of languages on six of the seven continents—still waiting on Antarctica. In the eyes of twentieth-century Nazis, however, Hellenistic philosophy was vitiated by a blending with the decadent peoples of the east that had fatally undermined the purity of the Greek race.[2] Seizing on the fact that Zeno hailed from an area of Cyprus where the population included some Phoenician settlers, prominent Nazi

FIGURE E.1. Monument of Lysicrates and Soldiers' and Sailors' Monument.
(a) To commemorate the honor he earned when he was awarded a tripod as best
choragos in 335, the Athenian Lysicrates erected this monument on Tripodon Street
(street of the tripods) leading to the Theater of Dionysus. It has served as a model
for many modern monuments. HIP / Art Resource, NY. (b) Soldiers' and Sailors'
Monument. Monuments modeled on that of Lysicrates dot the globe. This one, located
on Riverside Drive in Manhattan, commemorates the soldiers and sailors who fought
for the Union in the American Civil War. It was designed by the firm of Stoughton
and Stoughton and completed in 1902. © Vanni Archive / Art Resource, NY.

FIGURE E.1B. (*continued*)

classicist Fritz Schachermeyr spoke for many in expressing revulsion for Stoicism, a philosophy "elaborated by Semites and bastards."[3]

Stoicism has fared better in the United States, and not just among the founders. Hellenistic philosophy has undergone a revival as people struggle to cope with the increasing challenges and frustrations of modern life. In 1965 pilot James Stockdale was shot down over Vietnam and imprisoned for over seven years. In his essay *Courage under Fire: Testing Epictetus's Doctrines in a Laboratory of Human Behavior*, Stockdale explored the many aspects of Epictetus's thought that nourished him during this dark period when his external circumstances were far beyond his control. He ended his memoir with the last verse of William Ernest Henley's Stoic poem "Invictus," a work that famously gave heart to Nelson Mandela during his years of imprisonment in South Africa:

> It matters not how strait the gate,
> How charged with punishments the scroll,
> I am the master of my fate:
> I am the captain of my soul.

Stoicism also underpinned the so-called Serenity Prayer composed by Reinhold Niebuhr and adopted by Alcoholics Anonymous in 1941: "God grant me the serenity to accept the things I cannot change, courage to change the things I can, and wisdom to know the difference." In 1955 American psychologist Albert Ellis put forward his new treatment Rational Emotive Behavior Therapy (REBT). Citing the Stoics' contention that people are made unhappy not by external events but by the views that they take of them, he gratefully expressed his profound debt to Zeno and his followers. The first form of Cognitive Behavior Therapy, REBT is still widely practiced today.[4]

The Stoic heritage has a long history in China. In 1601, Jesuit missionary Matteo Ricci became the first European to enter the forbidden city. Sensing that foregrounding the story of a poor man who was executed by crucifixion would not win converts, he set about conveying fundamental Christian teachings through the filter of Stoicism. His "Twenty-five Paragraphs," published in 1605, basically constituted a modified and abbreviated version of Epictetus's *Enchiridion*. In this new rendition multiple divinities became one and explicit sexual material wound up on the cutting room floor.[5]

Stoicism has enjoyed a high profile in the twenty-first century in what is known as the manosphere, a loose collection of malcontents who communicate mostly on the Internet.[6] United by a conviction that the liberation of women has resulted in a degenerate society, members of this community believe that the world around them is salvageable only if men cultivate a hyper-masculinity that will restore traditional sex roles. Ignoring the Stoics' unisex approach to philosophy, citizens of the manosphere have been drawn rather to their advocacy of cultivating a self that is proof against adversity and rejects the prevailing value system of the world around them. In countless websites the movement appeals to Stoicism in proclaiming the superiority of men, who operate on the basis of reason, to women, who are governed by emotion. Action plans are provided to counter purported efforts to cripple society by feminizing young men. One of the most remarkable books in the manosphere is the 2018 anonymously self-published and deliberately provocative *Bronze Age Mindset*. Widely believed to be the work of Costin Alamariu, a right-wing journalist and Internet personality who holds a doctorate in political science from Yale, it is mixture of impressive learning and misogynistic ravings that was highly regarded and much read in the Trump White House.[7] "With the liberation of women in the 19th [sic] century," the author complains, "the West has given itself an infection and can be saved from complete collapse only if a few exceptional men dare to emulate the Greeks and recover the unbridled ambition of the Bronze Age heroes" (91). The author identifies himself as simply Bronze Age Pervert, though his use of the term Bronze Age is not consistent; at times he distinguishes it from the Classical Age, but at others it seems to refer more loosely to ancient Greek civilization as a whole. He identifies the Greek state as the product of "free men accepting the rigors of training together so they can preserve their freedom by force against hostile outsiders and against racial subordinates at home." These men, he explains, could never have subscribed to any abstraction like "equality" or "the people," which they would have rightly seen as deferring "to the opinion of slaves, aliens, fat childless women, and others who have no share in the [sic] actual physical power" (72). In Greece, "The real man was a man filled by courage and daring that all came from an excess of being," an idea "shared by other Aryan cultures" (45).

The Spartans so admired by that champion of Aryan culture Adolf Hitler also afforded role models to American gun rights activists, a number of whom have appropriated Leonidas's reputed response to Xerxes' request for his weapons, *molōn labe*—"come and take them." When the Capitol building in Washington, DC, was stormed on January 6, 2021, several rioters wore reproductions of Greek helmets, and gun rights advocate Representative Marjorie Taylor Greene, who had refused to wear a mask during the Covid pandemic, then appeared in Congress sporting one on which was emblazoned *molōn labe*. The pandemic itself prompted a re-examination of famous Greek plagues and the responses to them—the plague of the *Iliad*, Thucydides' account of the plague during the Pelopon-nesian War, the plague in Sophocles' *Oedipus the King*—in countless books and magazine articles as citizens of the twenty-first century sought to ground their experience in those of astute thinkers of the past.[8]

Greece has served as both model and comfort zone for champions and practitioners of homoerotic love. Combined with the power of her verses, Sappho's unique position in the canon of Greek literature has guaranteed a long tradition in reception. Sappho inevitably became an icon for the lesbian community, as crystallized in the title of Sidney Ab-bott and Barbara Love's 1972 book *Sappho Was a Right-On Woman: A Liberated View of Lesbianism* (Stein and Day). For numerous Beat Gen-eration writers in New York City in the 1960s, Sappho was a cherished muse, offering as she did a model of open sensuality and strong emotions eminently congenial to the self-identified beatniks. Poet, publisher, and activist Ed Sanders, who completed a degree in Greek at New York Uni-versity in 1964, identified Sappho as the muse of the avant-garde, under-lining her rejection of war-oriented patriarchal power and valorization of passion. His mixed prose-verse "Sappho on East Seventh" tells how his fellow NYU Greek student and poet John Barrett was visited by Sappho in his apartment, where Barrett was constructing a lyre—as the Greeks had done—from a tortoise shell. Summoned by his song, Sappho appears and takes him on a magical journey through time, teaching him to use his tongue not only to sing verses but to satisfy a woman through cun-nilingus, offering him detailed hands-on instruction

> this way
> that way
> steering with fondly grabbed ears
> . . .
> Showing him pressures
> motions
> patterns.[9]

In the late twentieth century the very definition of Greek civilization became an object of scrutiny. In 1987 Rutgers University Press published the first volume of Cornell professor Martin Bernal's provocative *Black Athena: The Afroasiatic Roots of Classical Civilization*, a work that sparked an unprecedented firestorm in the world of Classics.[10] During the last decades of the eighteenth century and the first of the nineteenth, Bernal argued, a variety of forces such as the Atlantic slave trade and European colonialism ushered in a new construction of Greek civilization that disregarded the foreign influences that Herodotus had found worthy of note. In its place they put forward a racialist "Aryan" model that set the Greeks apart as unique and ascribed what was distinctive (not to mention admirable) in Greek civilization solely to their Indo-European heritage. Discarding the Greeks' own view of their world—a view, in Bernal's opinion, quite hospitable to the notion of eastern influence—these thinkers became convinced that the burst of creativity still sometimes known today as "the Greek miracle" was entirely original with the Greeks. Bernal argued instead for extensive eastern influence—indeed for Egyptian and Phoenician colonization of the Greek mainland. While a number of Bernal's theories were rejected by classical scholars, his fundamental claim that the culture of the Greeks was a hybrid one is beyond question. Still more important than his emphasis on the multiple strands that went to make up Greek civilization is the attention Bernal called to the racist underpinnings that underlay the glorification of Greek culture.

More recent takes on the Greeks are profoundly skeptical of such glorification. Feminist thinkers have seen ancient Greece as a laboratory for the study of the gender relations that are still problematic today. Thus Marilyn Arthur Katz's long 1973 article on Greek thinking about women in the journal *Arethusa* is titled "Early Greece: The Origins of the Western Attitude Toward Women."[11] In her 1985 study of gender dynamics in Athens, Eva Keuls identified classical Athens as "a kind of concave mirror in which we can see our own foibles and institutions magnified and distorted."[12] Journalist Jess Zimmerman has undertaken to explore Greek mythology in order to get at the underpinnings of some of the problematic modes in which many men still think about women today—and how women are taught to think of themselves. In *Women and Other Monsters: Building a New Mythology*, Zimmerman zeroes in on the ways in which women are confined by Procrustean standards of beauty that leave almost everyone out. For women, she writes "the 'correct' form is so narrowly defined that almost anyone's physical form can be deviant. We don't have to have two heads to be monstrous. It's enough to have two chins." Scylla and Charybdis appear in Zimmerman's chapter "Voracious." Though not every monster devours, she concedes, nonetheless "the drive to consume . . . is considered a monstrous trait. Outsize hunger is the province of the monster, and for women, all hungers are outsize. . . . A man's appetite can be hearty, but a woman with an appetite is always voracious: her hunger always overreaches, because it is not supposed to exist." The challenge of navigating the straits through which Odysseus and his crew must pass represents the danger of a man losing his identity by being literally swallowed up by one voracious female or another.[13]

When Odysseus has spent seven years on the island of Ogygia with its resident nymph, Calypso, Zeus sends Hermes to have a stern talk with his hostess/lover, making clear to her that she must let Odysseus go. Calypso has some strong words for Hermes as well:

> Hard of heart you gods are, and quicker to envy than anyone,
> Begrudging as you do that goddesses should mate with men
> Openly, if any makes a bedfellow of a mortal. (5. 118–20)

Isn't this always the way, she asks bitterly. Despite their countless liaisons with mortal women, the gods clamp down on goddesses for precisely the same behavior. When Dawn took the Hunter Orion for a lover, Artemis slew him with her arrows; when Demeter lay with Iasion, Zeus killed him with a thunderbolt; and now once more you begrudge a goddess a relationship with a mortal man.

This condemnation of Olympian sexism provides a woman's viewpoint normally lacking in the Homeric poems. A female reader of the *Odyssey* offered a compelling rendition of that vantage point already in a poem she wrote in her diary in October 1875. The haunting verses of

Jemimah Makepiece Sturt cast into sharp relief the barriers that will continue to divide Odysseus, constantly in motion, and Penelope, ever still, even after his return:

> I know thee not, yet know thee well,
> Thine eyes have seen the deeps of Hell.
> Thy limbs have lain in witches' arms,
> I know the cunning of thy charms.
> Why have you come to claim my heart,
> When we so long have dwelt a'part?
> When I can hear within your blood
> The changing dalliance of the flood?
> Stay with me, if you must, a'while.
> The stars shine cold in your soft smile,
> The desert winds sing in your breath,
> I know I'll be alone at death.[14]

The notion that the behavior of Homer's "heroes" was problematic was already adumbrated in Greek tragedy, and beginning in the last years of the twentieth century, a spate of female-authored takes on Homeric tales have appeared, including Margaret Atwood's *Penelopiad*, Madeline Miller's *Circe*, Natalie Haynes's *A Thousand Ships*, and Pat Barker's *The Silence of the Girls*. The year 2016 witnessed the publication of the first translation of the *Iliad* into English by a woman, Caroline Alexander, and 2017 the first of the *Odyssey* by Emily Wilson. A classicist at the University of Pennsylvania, Wilson has written extensively about her project translating this "text which inscribes and valorizes androcentric values," a work in which "the female characters are defined in terms of their relationships with the male protagonist, as either obstacles or helpers on his mission" as he seeks to return to his home and his "voluntarily subordinate wife."[15] In discussing her work, Wilson focuses on the slave girls' killing by Telemachus at his father's insistence. In their treatment of this episode, male anglophone translators have engaged in an enormous amount of what can only be called slut-shaming. This may indeed reflect the intention of the poet, the product of a specific time and place—an approximate contemporary of Hesiod, after all—but it may well not. Robert Fagles has Telemachus say, "You sluts // the suitors' whores!" For Stanley Lombardo's Telemachus they are "the suitors' sluts."[16] As Wilson points out, the Greek text is actually value-free and nonjudgmental on that score, stating simply that the slave women "lay beside the suitors," as she has rendered the text in her own translation. She reproduces her own account of their grisly deaths:

> The girls, their heads all in a row,
> Were strung up with the noose around their necks
> To make their death an agony. They gasped,
> Feet twitching for a while, but not for long.

She hoped, she explains, "that using 'gasped' might make readers feel the women's desperation during this torturous murder—and that 'twitching' might underline the fact that, as slaves, their movements were never wholly their own."[17]

She has called them "girls" here, she reported, "to make clear their vulnerability and youth—with a little nod to the enslaved 'girls' of *The Handmaid's Tale*."[18] Though this was the Margaret Atwood novel that had been in the public eye while Wilson was working because of the immensely popular television series it had just inspired, Atwood had also engaged the fate of enslaved women in her 2005 *Penelopiad*, a take on the Odyssey both sidesplitting and savage—a novella that begins with a jump-rope rhyme, that looks ahead to the manner of the girls' deaths:

> We are the maids
> The ones you killed
> The ones you failed
> We danced in air
> Our bare feet twitched
> It was not fair.[19]

When Odysseus departs for Troy and leaves her alone with his disapproving mother the chilly Anticleia and his bossy nurse Eurycleia, Penelope loses not only her only companion but her only protector against these women. She is friendless—until the slave girls who have been raised along with Telemachus reach adolescence. Then everything changes. Penelope now has confidants, and when she hits upon her ruse to put the suitors off by unraveling Laertes' shroud by night, she has partners in crime, a relationship calculated to engender intimacy.

Her relationship with these twelve young women and its tragic consequences stand at the novella's center. Throughout, Penelope's wary eye offers a new angle on Odysseus. Atwood's Penelope recognizes her husband as soon as she sets eyes on him after his return, but she keeps this knowledge to herself, mindful of how much he was "looking forward to the big revelation scene, the part where I would say, 'it was you all along! What a terrific disguise!'" After all, she points out, "If a man takes pride in his disguising skills it would be a foolish wife who would claim to recognize him; it's always an imprudence to step between a man and the reflection of his own cleverness" (170–71, 137). But it is his treatment of the hapless slave girls, Penelope's only friends, that affords the principal indictment of Odysseus—and Telemachus as well. The slaves' flirtations with the suitors, we learn, were undertaken at Penelope's instigation, so that they could be her eyes and ears, keeping her abreast of what alarming plans her unwelcome guests might be hatching. The discovery of her action's unintended consequence devastates her.

In her 2018 *Circe*, another feminist meditation on patriarchy and power, American classicist Madeline Miller shows us a Circe taken aback upon learning about the girls' fate from Telemachus, who has come to visit her. After Odysseus had enlisted his help killing the suitors, Telemachus tells her,

> He commanded me to gather up all the slave girls who had ever lain with one of them and make them clean the blood-soaked floor, and when they were finished, I was to kill them as well.

The words, Circe reports, jolted her: "The girls would have had no choice. Odysseus would have known that."

"'Odysseus told me to carve them into joints like animals.' His eyes held mine. 'Do you disbelieve it?'" (309).[20] Thinking back on the stories

Odysseus had recounted to her during his sojourn on her island of Aeaea, she does not. "He had always loved his vengeances," she recalls. But to gentle Telemachus, who could not face the butchery and hanged the girls instead, the experience was traumatic. "I have never known such ugly, drawn-out deaths," he says. "I will see their feet twisting the rest of my days."

A sea change in perceptions of Greek models underlies the difference between Benevenuto Cellini's sixteenth-century statue *Perseus with the Head of Medusa*, which stands in the Piazza della Signoria in Florence, and Luciano Garbati's subversive 2008 statue of *Medusa Holding the Head of Perseus* displayed in Collect Pond Park in Lower Manhattan in 2020, opposite the courthouse where, as the artist pointed out, cases of violence against women are tried. As we have seen, the Greek tragedians themselves laid the groundwork for using Bronze Age myth to analyze and criticize the dynamics of their own society. French historian Pierre Vidal-Naquet observed in 1997 that "Every Athenian tragedy is a reflection on the foreigner, on the Other, on the double."[21] South African poet Guy Butler engaged questions of race in his rendition of Euripides' *Medea* as *Demea*, begun in the 1950s and finally performed in 1990. There the title character, a princess of the Tembo tribe, abandons her royal heritage to marry a white European, much as Medea had done to marry Jason, only to have him abandon her to marry the daughter of a Boer leader. Chicano playwright Luis Alfaro reworked *Medea* as *Mojada* (*Wetback*), a flexible text about immigration that he adapted to fit the various cities in which it was performed; in the version I saw on stage at The Public Theater in Manhattan in 2019, the immigrant woman's struggles are set in New York City and the script modified accordingly. Adaptations of Aristophanes' *Lysistrata* have powerful appeal not only for the anti-war movement but for the movement of the Greeks' ultimate "other," women. The poster child for civil disobedience, Antigone has found herself the subject of numerous reworkings as one playwright after another deals with the way her plight—and, a fortiori, that of her brother Polynices—represents those who do not quite belong. In South Africa, playwright

Athol Fugard modeled his adaptation *The Island* (co-authored with actors John Kani and Winston Nshtona) on a true story. In a prison reminiscent of the one on Robben Island where Nelson Mandela was imprisoned for twenty-seven years, two political prisoners are depicted rehearsing scenes from Sophocles' play for an upcoming performance as they struggle with their circumstances. Puerto Rican playwright Cristina Pérez Díaz's 2016 *Western (A play starring Antigone and her brothers)* deals with issues of citizenship and national borders, as Antigone carries the body of her dead brother around while seeking to overcome the legal obstacles to his burial.[22]

The compelling myth of Oedipus has been reworked since antiquity in any number of cultures.[23] The building blocks of Oedipus's story have opened themselves up to a seemingly unlimited number of permutations and combinations: identity, reality, fate, religion, humanism, immigration, ethnicity, free will, divinity, incest, pride, and leadership are only some of the themes that appear in its variants. Productions of Sophocles' play were particularly popular in the last decades of the nineteenth century, and seeing the play performed had an electric effect on the Viennese physician Sigmund Freud. The story of Oedipus gained a firm footing in the mind of the general public when Freud made it the linchpin of his theory of human development. Adaptations multiplied in the twentieth and twenty-first centuries as the story of the unfortunate Oedipus came to be mined for what it might reveal about the world around us.[24]

In his 1930 *Oedipus*, the future Nobel Laureate André Gide used Sophocles' play and the story it told to explore the tensions between different sides of humanity that exercised the author throughout his life. What drives the drama is the conflict between the humanistic worldview of Oedipus and his sons and the religious outlook of Tiresias and Antigone. Tensions between the studied piety of Antigone and the irreverence of her iconoclastic brother Polynices run the length of the play, and Oedipus comes down on the side of Polynices. "I would rather believe in heroes," Polynices says, "than in gods," to which Oedipus, seeing himself in his son, replies, "Well said!" (27). The answer to the Sphinx's riddle, he points out, was man. No matter what riddle the Sphinx should pose, he cautions his children,

> You must persuade yourselves that the answer is always the same. Yes, there is only this one same answer to those many and various questions; and that this one answer is Man; and that this one man, for each and all of us, is: Oneself. (28)

Tiresias scolds Oedipus for the values he is instilling in his sons, arguing that "All knowledge that starts from man, not from God, is worthless" (29). And indeed not only Oedipus but, after his death, his sons come to terrible ends. One discounts the divine at one's peril.

A variety of modern reworkings of Oedipus's story focus on the tensions that arose from Oedipus's situation as an outsider in Thebes. Composed against the background of the ongoing Civil War in Nigeria in 1968, Ola Rotimi's *The Gods Are Not to Blame* was grounded in the ethnic strife that attended the decision of military leaders to divide Nigeria into separate regions based on ethnicity as well as geography. Rotimi has forged a remarkable cultural hybrid in his blending of African proverbs with declarations of the inherent sorrows and challenges of life that would be at home in any Greek tragedy. Many of the concerns are the same: the suffering intrinsic in the human condition, the problem of knowledge, the paranoid tendencies of absolute rulers. But when tensions start to build in the play, the anxieties of King Odewale focus on the fact that he is of a different ethnicity (or so it would appear) from his people; in reality, he is decidedly of the same ethnicity, indeed the exposed son of the king and queen. Raised among the Ijekun when the attempt of his Kutuje parents to make away with him at birth has failed, Odewale had suddenly appeared out of nowhere when the Kutuje king Adetusa had just been killed. Leading the Kutuje to victory over neighbors from whom they have been getting the worst of it, he married the king's widow. Years later, when a pestilence falls on the city and the word comes down from the blind seer Baba Fakunle that the murderer of the previous king must be rooted out, Odewale comes to believe that people are against him because of his ancestry. "If Adetusa, a son of Kutuje, could be killed in violence, and the murderer be hidden from vengeance in the same land, what will the people of Kutuje not do to me of Ijekun tribe?" he later asks, praying before his household shrine (Act 2, Scene 4). In an interview the playwright revealed that the gods of the title referred not to actual divinities but rather to political actors like the United States, Russia, France, and England—that in his view it was not these forces but rather the Nigerians' ethnic divisiveness and mistrust that was responsible for the bloodshed in his country.[25]

In 1994 Rita Dove, the first African American poet laureate, published her own reworking of the Oedipus myth, *The Darker Face of the Earth*, a verse drama that also deals with matters of colonization and ethnicity. Set on a plantation in antebellum South Carolina, it depicts the unsettling of the Jennings estate when the mistress of the household, Amalia, purchases a bright and educated young mulatto slave, Augustus Newcastle. Many slaveowners in the United States proclaimed their allegiance to the cultured, slaveowning societies of Greece and Rome by giving classical names to slaves; other characters in the play bear the names Phebe, Scylla, Diana, Alexander, and Hector. The most central of these is Hector, Amalia's beloved childhood companion before they were separated by the realities of race and slavery—but not entirely: they are lovers even as she is living in the "big house" with her white husband. As is made clear to the audience from the outset, Hector and Amalia in fact are the parents of Augustus, who, like Oedipus, had been sent away at birth and grown up elsewhere. Both parents were devastated by the fate of the baby who, the slaves were told, had died just after birth. Amalia, the slave Alexander reports,

> went crazy in the head
> the day she lost that baby boy. (34)
> Hector, when it was announced that his child had died,
> fell to his knees
>> and ate dirt like a worm.
>> Now he lives alone
>> and catches snakes in the swamp. (38)

Predictably, Amalia is charmed by Augustus and in time makes him her lover as well; just as predictably, in time he inadvertently kills his father

Hector in a tragic accident. Though hard on her slaves, Amalia is not entirely unlikable. Of the slave revolts in Haiti she says,

> It was a brilliant revolution.
> I've often wondered why our niggers
> don't revolt. I've said to myself:
> "Amalia, if you had been a slave,
> you most certainly would have plotted
> an insurrection by now." (87)

A woman of promise, Amalia is shunted by society into the roles of both oppressor and oppressed. Encouraged by what they learn from Augustus about the revolution in Haiti and on the ship *La Amistad*, the slaves revolt as the play ends, bearing Augustus on their shoulders as their chosen leader, but it is plain that the strained relations between the races, as encapsulated in Amalia's connections with both Hector and Augustus, will persist, as in fact they have done.

From Stoicism in the manosphere to the battle over gun rights in the United States, the Greek heritage is now in the twenty-first century undergoing repurposing as well as reexamination. Its identification with whiteness has prompted even some professors of Classics to raise questions about the viability of their discipline. Dominican-born Princeton professor Dan-el Padilla Peralta has laid out a savage indictment of the field as "equal parts vampire and cannibal," a dangerous force that has been used to justify all manner of oppression. "Far from being extrinsic to the study of Greco-Roman antiquity," he claims, "the production of whiteness turns on closer examination to reside in the very marrows of classics."[26] Certainly the study of classical antiquity has historically been tied up with matters of race. For centuries Europeans, and then Americans, identified the peoples of Greece and Rome as their unique, and uniquely admirable, cultural ancestors. Nowhere was this more conspicuous than in the slaveholding southern states of the new American experiment in government. Educators in the south were given to appealing to the slaveholding societies of classical antiquity as models for their own nation, Thomas Dew, president of the College of William and Mary in Virginia, claiming that slavery in the United States fostered a spirit of

freedom and equality similar to that in Greece and Rome, as the relega-
tion of menial labor to slaves removed divisions among citizens.[27]

The amorphous creature known as "western civilization" has frequently been credited with all manner of fair-sounding ideals: democracy,
rationality, scientific thought, individualism, freedom, toleration,
monotheism, the separation of "church" and state. History has made
plain the absence of many of these ideals from the thought and practice of
"western" (European and American?) societies. The notion that we must
study the societies of ancient Greece and Rome in order better to appreciate the roots of these principles is profoundly peculiar. Many Greeks and
Romans disliked democracy and did not practice it. America's founders
certainly neither liked nor practiced it, declaring that power must follow
property. The ancients would have been appalled by notions of the separation of church and state. On trial for his life, Socrates never thought to
suggest that there was anything inappropriate in taking a man to court for
his religious beliefs. Greeks and Romans were certainly not monotheistic,
and their idea of freedom entailed freedom from domination; it did not
suggest that no person could enslave another, or that citizens were free to
think whatever they liked. "Western," moreover, is often a code word for
White and Christian. The people of Greece and Rome were not particularly White, and until late in their history they were decided not Christian. Individualism was generally perceived in antiquity as antisocial. But
the link between the classical world and "western civilization" persists in
people's minds; the editors of *The Guardian* chose a color photograph of
the Parthenon to illustrate Kwame Anthony Appiah's essay "There is no
such thing as western civilisation" (November 9, 2016). Greece thus remains the emblem even of the western civilization that does not exist.

The white column mansions that slave labor erected throughout the
American south sent out a clear advertisement for better living through
slavery. Revulsion for the imperialism and racism of British mining
magnate Cecil Rhodes has now sparked distaste for the enormous
classical columned monument dedicated to him in Cape Town. A bust
of Rhodes at the memorial was vandalized during protests in 2015 and
again in 2020, and the statue of Rhodes at the nearby campus of the
University of Cape Town was removed after protests.

FIGURE E.2. Cecil Rhodes Monument. Modeled on the altar at Pergamum in Anatolia and the Temple at Segesta in Sicily, the Rhodes Monument at the foot of Devil's Peak in Cape Town has been the object of considerable controversy in light of Rhodes's racist and imperialist views. HIP / Art Resource, NY.

Now in the twenty-first century architecture that proudly proclaims a connection to the ancient world has become for that very reason problematic. These buildings tend to be a glistening white (although the white columns of the Mongolian theater are engagingly set off by a cupcake-icing pink background). For some time now this whiteness has been called into question, and rightly; the Parthenon whose white columns are so instantly recognizable today was in ancient times, like other Greek buildings, elaborately decorated in a variety of bright colors, and the gleaming white statues displayed in museums today were painted in reds and blues and yellows. Careful scholarship is beginning to reconstruct what the originals must have looked like. Not everyone has been pleased by this development. When ancient historian Sarah Bond at the University of Iowa began speaking and writing about the fact that classical sculpture and statuary were in fact polychromatic and often depicted individuals who were not particularly White, she found herself the object of death threats.[28]

In 2020 American president Donald Trump drafted an executive order to make classical architecture the "preferred and default style" for federal buildings, requiring such buildings to display not the modernist values of "brutalism and deconstructivism" but those of democratic Athens and republican Rome. The proposal horrified a majority of architects and classicists alike. Not only did it denigrate the creativity that had gone into American architecture across the generations, but it also seemed of a piece with a consistent White supremacist position on Trump's part. Support for this intrusive step confirmed its racial underpinnings. Defending the executive order in his article "Leftists Rage against Classical Architecture," White nationalist Gregory Hood maintained that

> Architecture that alienates whites from their past makes them feel helpless, rootless, and weak. As part of a larger wave of hostility, this may be driving whites to despair or even suicide. In a healthy society, buildings connect people to their heritage and history. They offer comfort, beauty, and connectedness.... President Trump's proposed executive order is one small step towards reuniting white Americans with our civilizational tradition.[29]

But, like the myth of a classically inspired "western civilization," the white architectural and sculptural style "inherited" from the Greeks is in reality a modern invention.

Yet the Greece that was not in fact the fountainhead of this nonexistent civilization nonetheless has a tremendous amount to teach about the question that exercised Socrates: how shall we live? The Greek preoccupation with combat, for example, has been repurposed to benefit those who have been scarred by today's wars. While working at the U.S. Department of Veterans' Affairs in Virginia, American psychiatrist Jonathan Shay became interested in posttraumatic stress disorder, and encouraged by Homerist Gregory Nagy he published two books linking the experiences of Vietnam veterans in particular to those of Homer's protagonists, *Achilles in Vietnam: Combat Trauma and the Undoing of Character* (1994) and *Odysseus in America: Combat Trauma and the Trials of Homecoming* (2002).[30] Greek historian Lawrence Tritle drew on his experiences in the US Army in Vietnam to publish *From Melos to*

My Lai: Violence, Culture, and Survival in 2000, placing the atrocities in Vietnam in the context of Thucydides' account of the Peloponnesian War. Since that time extensive work has been done bringing veterans together to explore the treatment of war in Greek civilization, particularly in tragedy. The Theatre of War project founded by Bryan Doerries has staged war-related Greek tragedies to audiences of veterans and their families in a therapeutic setting, and the project's work reached a broad audience when its productions, followed by discussion, began to be livestreamed via Zoom during the Covid-19 shutdown. The works of the ancient tragedians, Doerries has written, "have something urgent to show us about ourselves, something that we desperately need to see."[31] Once weaponized in the advocacy of amorphous "western" thought patterns, the Greeks are now examined in a more nuanced way for what they can tell us about the human condition.

———

To engage with the ancient Greeks is to join a long conversation that began when the lyric poets exchanged views of life's priorities and the Presocratics debated one another across wide seas and over several generations. It continued when the classical philosophers Plato and Aristotle in turn engaged with the Presocratics, and when the Hellenistic philosophers engaged with Plato and Aristotle. Classical and Hellenistic writers never ceased to hearken back to the heritage of Homer, and the Athenian tragedians regarded the great heroes of the Trojan War with a new eye. In his *Andromache*, Euripides put a striking indictment of the Greek glorification of men like Agamemnon and Menelaus in the mouth of Achilles' father Peleus:

> Alas, the way we do things here in Greece!
> Each time our army routs the enemy,
> Who gets the credit? Not the grunts. Oh, no.
> The tributes congregate around the general,
> A man who did the same as all the rest,
> Brandished his spear as one man among thousands,
> But winds up with the lion's share of praise.

Yes, sitting high and mighty in their jobs
They think they're better than the folk below.
In truth, they're great big nothings. . . .
You and your brother sit there, all puffed up
Over the war at Troy and your commands in it:
The toil of others lifts you to the skies! (693–705)

The Christian writers of late antiquity were profoundly influenced by
Plato, and in the thirteenth century Thomas Aquinas adapted the teachings of Aristotle to fit a Christian framework. The Italian Renaissance
was in many ways a dialogue with the classical past. Greek civilization
does not come to us unmediated. When we converse with the Greeks,
we converse as well with all the generations that separate us from them,
each of which has interpreted the Greek world in its own way. At the
beginning of the twenty-first century the study of Greek and Roman
civilization is on the defensive. The notion that Greek and Latin texts
are somehow the only "classical" ones that have seen the light of day
puts many people off, and neither Greek ethnocentrism nor Roman
imperialism does anything to improve the image of a field that is now
tainted with the stain of colonialism. It is indisputable that knowledge
of Greek and Latin has often been the mark of a distasteful elitism, and
lack of such knowledge has served to exclude people from the centers
of power. In the 2020s, conferences began to be held to explore the wid-
ening of the field to include both more examination of the cultures with
which Greeks and Romans interacted and more variety in the ethnicity
of those who study Greek and Roman antiquity. There has been an explosion of books and articles studying the Greek and Roman heritage
in non-western cultures; representative examples are listed in the suggested readings at the end of this chapter. Departments once labeled
"Classics" have begun scrambling to rebrand themselves as Greek and
Roman Studies; Greek, Latin, and Ancient Mediterranean Studies
(what could be more enticing than the acronym GLAM?); and the like.
So far nobody seems to have picked up on Cambridge classicist Krish-
nan Ram-Prasad's suggestion of DAWS: Decolonized Ancient World
Studies. Where it will end, nobody knows. But surely to study the remarkable creativity of the Greeks is not to endorse the seamy side of

their civilization; a profession in which some half of the doctorates are awarded to those whom Aristotle labeled "deformed males" is unlikely to idealize the ancient world.

The attack on the study of Greece and Rome is hardly a modern phenomenon. Thomas Jefferson's favorite architect, Benjamin Latrobe, fulminated against the use of the *Iliad* as a school text, maintaining that "It poisons the minds of young men, fills them with a rage for military murder, glory, and conveys no information which can ever be practically useful."[32] The exaltation of Greek and Roman classics was a source of great distress to the Philadelphia physician and social reformer Benjamin Rush, founder of Dickinson College. Who, he asked,

> are guilty of the greatest absurdity—the Chinese, who press the feet into deformity by small shoes, or the European and Americans, who press the brain into obliquity by Greek and Latin? Do not men use Latin and Greek as the cuttlefish emit their ink, on purpose to conceal themselves from an intercourse with common people?[33]

The notion that the study of Greek and Latin is elitist certainly lives on today, but it has on the whole weathered a long succession of attacks: it encourages militarism, it is useless, it is colonialist, it is racist, it smacks of snobbery. So far, however, the creativity of the Greeks and Romans has served to sustain belief in the value of studying their achievements, as people have been doing for hundreds of years. In the words of British classicist Mary Beard, "Studying Classics is to enter a conversation—not only with the literature and material remains of antiquity itself, but also with those over the centuries before us who have tried to make sense of the Greeks and Romans, who have quoted them or recreated them."[34] It is my hope to have added in some way to this ongoing dialogue.

Suggested Readings

Andújar, Rosa, and Konstantinos P. Nikoloutsos, eds. 2020. *Greeks and Romans on the Latin American Stage. Bloomsbury Studies in Classical Reception.* London: Bloomsbury Academic.

Brinkmann, Vinzenz. 2017. *Gods in Color: Polychromy in the Ancient World.* New York and Munich: Prestel.

Burton, Diana, Simon Perris, and Jeff Tatum, eds. *Athens to Aotearoa: Greece and Rome in New Zealand Literature and Society.* Wellington, New Zealand: Victoria University Press, 2017.

Chapoutou, Jacques. 2015. *Le nazisme et L'Antiquité.* Paris: Presses Universitaires de France, 2015.

Cook, William W., and James Tatum. 2012. *African American Writers and Classical Tradition.* Chicago: University of Chicago Press.

Edmunds, Lowell. 1985. *Oedipus: The Ancient Legend and Its Later Analogues.* Baltimore, MD, and London: Johns Hopkins University Press, 1985.

Edmunds, Lowell, and Alan Dundes. 1995. *Oedipus: A Folklore Casebook.* Madison: University of Wisconsin Press.

Kennedy, Rebecca Futo. 2018. *Brill's Companion to the Reception of Aeschylus.* Leiden and Boston: Brill.

Laird, Andrew, and Nicola Miller, eds. 2018. *Antiquities and Classical Traditions in Latin America. Bulletin of Latin American Research Book Series.* Hoboken, NJ: Wiley.

Lauriola, Rosanna, and Kyriakos N. Demetrious, eds. 2017. *Brill's Companion to the Reception of Sophocles.* Leiden and Boston: Brill, 2017.

Nguyen, Kelly. 2020. "Pham Duy Khiêm, Classical Reception, and Colonial Subversion in Early 20th Century Vietnam and France." *Classical Receptions Journal* 12, 340–56.

Pérez Díaz, Cristina, ed. 2022. *Antígona by José Watanabe: A Bilingual Edition with Critical Essays. Classics and the Postcolonial.* Abingdon, UK: Routledge.

Rankine, Patrice D. 2006. *Ulysses in Black: Ralph Ellison, Classicism, and African American Literature.* Madison: University of Wisconsin Press.

Rawson, Elizabeth. 1969. *The Spartan Tradition in European Thought.* Oxford: Clarendon.

Richard, Carl. 1994. *The Founders and the Classics: Greece, Rome, and the American Enlightenment.* Cambridge, MA: Harvard University Press.

Roberts, Jennifer T. 1994. *Athens on Trial: The Antidemocratic Tradition in Western Thought.* Princeton, NJ: Princeton University Press.

Sharpe, Matthew. 2018. "Into the Heart of Darkness, Or: Alt-Stoicism? Actually, No . . ." *Eidos: A Journal for Philosophy of Culture* 4, 106–13.

Tritle, Lawrence. 2000. *From Melos to My Lai: A Study in Violence, Culture, and Social Survival.* London and New York: Routledge.

Walters, Tracey L. 2007. *African American Literature and the Classicist Tradition: Black Women Writers from Wheatley to Morrison.* London: Palgrave-Macmillan.

Winterer, Caroline. 2009. *The Mirror of Antiquity: American Women and the Classical Tradition, 1750–1900.* Ithaca, NY: Cornell University Press.

Zimmerman, Jess. 2021. *Women and Other Monsters: Building a New Mythology.* Boston: Beacon.

Zuckerberg, Donna. 2018. *Not All Dead White Men: Classics and Misogyny in the Digital Age.* Cambridge, MA: Harvard University Press.

NOTES

Chapter 1. A World of the Imagination

1. K. K. Ruthven, *Myth* (*The Critical Idiom Reissued*, vol. 30) (Oxford and New York: Routledge, orig. Methuen, 1976), 24.

2. A. J. Levin, "The Oedipus Myth in History and Psychiatry," *Psychiatry* 11 (1948), 283–99; Luis Feder, "Adoption Trauma: Oedipus Myth/Clinical Reality," *International Journal of Psycho-Analysis* 55 (1974), 491–93; Sofie Lazarsfeld, "Did Oedipus Have an Oedipus Complex," *American Journal of Orthopsychiatry* 14 (1944), 226–29; N. Atkins, "The Oedipus Myth, Adolescence and the Succession of Generations," *Journal of the American Psychoanalytic Association* 18 (1970), 860–75; Leonard Schengold, "The Parent as Sphinx," *Journal of the American Psychoanalytic Association* 11 (1963), 725–51; all cited in Robert Eisner, *The Road to Daulis: Psychoanalysis, Psychology, and Classical Mythology* (Syracuse, NY: Syracuse University Press, 1987), 46.

3. Pseudo-Acron on Horace, *Epodes* 6. 14; Pliny, *Natural History* 36. 4. 12.

4. William Hansen, *Classical Mythology: A Guide to the Mythical World of the Greeks and Romans* (New York: Oxford University Press, 2004), 41.

5. Fr. 654, P. Berol. 284,15–18.

6. Cited in Athenaeus 11.491b.

7. *The Orientalizing Revolution: Near Eastern Influence on Greek Culture in the Early Archaic Age* (Cambridge, MA, and London: Harvard University Press, 1992), 98.

8. A full exploration appears in Ian Rutherford, *Hittite Texts and Greek Religion: Contact, Interaction, and Comparison* (Oxford: Oxford University Press, 2020).

9. A good treatment of cannibalism in Greek thought appears in Christopher Weimer, *Eating People Is Might: Power and the Representation of Anthropophagy in Antiquity* (PhD dissertation, City University of New York Graduate Center, 2022).

10. See Richard Janko, "The Derveni Papyrus: An Interim Text," *Zeitschrift für Papyrologie und Epigraphik* 141 (2002), 1–62.

11. Luc Ferry, *The Wisdom of the Myths: How Greek Mythology Can Change Your Life*, trans. Theo Cuffe (New York: Harper Perennial, 2014), 380.

12. Palaephatus, 37. All translations from Palaephatus are from Jacob Stern, ed., *Peri Apistōn/ On Unbelievable Tales* (Chicago: Bolchazy-Carducci, 1996).

13. Plutarch *Moralia* 149c–e.

14. John Colarusso, ed. and trans., *Nart Sagas: Ancient Myths and Legends of the Circassians and Abkhazians*, updated with an introduction by Adrienne Mayor (Princeton, NJ: Princeton University Press, 2016).

15. A good case for the historicity of the Amazons, Amezan, and an exploration of other connections between the Amazons and warrior women of the Caucasus appears in Adrienne Mayor, *The Amazons: Lives & Legends of Warrior Women across the Ancient World* (Princeton, NJ: Princeton University Press, 2014.)

16. See the discussion in Walter Penrose, Jr., *Postcolonial Amazons: Female Masculinity and Courage in Ancient Greek and Sanskrit Literature* (Oxford and New York: Oxford University Press, 2016).

17. See Mayor, *The Amazons*.

18. Morales, *Antigone Rising, The Subversive Power of the Ancient Myths* (New York: Bold Type Books, 2020), 72.

19. Servius at Vergil, *Aeneid* 4. 402.

20. Plato also underlines the erotic element in the Ganymede story at *Phaedrus* 255b–c.

21. Morales, *Antigone Rising*, 66.

Chapter 2. The Heroic Past

1. Parry's experiences in Serbia are recounted in the updated edition of Albert Lord, *The Singer of Tales*, ed. Stephen Mitchell and Gregory Nagy (Cambridge, MA: Harvard University Press, 2000).

2. Two scenes of hospitality during Meho's first journey to Buda duplicate themselves; see Albert Lord, "Composition by Theme in Homer and Southslavic Epos," *Transactions and Proceedings of the American Philological Association* 82 (1951), 71–80. Avdo's description of an assembly is virtually identical to one in another of his works.

3. Lowell Edmunds has explored the parallel in his *Stealing Helen: The Myth of the Abducted Wife in Comparative Perspective* (Princeton, NJ: Princeton University Press, 2015).

4. See, in addition to Edmunds, Martin L. West, *Indo-European Poetry and Myth* (Oxford: Oxford University Press, 2007), 186–90, 232–37, 438.

5. *The Discovery of the Mind: The Greek Origins of European Thought*, translated into English by Thomas Rosenmeyer in 1953; 2nd ed. (Tacoma, WA: Angelico Press, 2013).

6. These examples and many others are collected in Bernard Williams, *Shame and Necessity* (Sather Lectures 57) (Berkeley and Los Angeles: University of California Press, 1993), and related arguments were made in 1951 by Williams's teacher E. R. Dodds in an earlier Sather Lectures volume, *The Greeks and the Irrational* (Berkeley and Los Angeles: University of California Press, 1951).

7. Gilgamesh 10 / 3. A perceptive analysis of Patroclus and Enkidu as "second selves" appears in Thomas Van Nortwick, *Someplace I Have Never Traveled: The Hero's Journey* (New York: Oxford University Press, 1996). On Gilgamesh and Homer, see Michael Clarke, *Achilles beside Gilgamesh: Mortality and Wisdom in Early Epic Poetry* (Cambridge, UK: Cambridge University Press, 2020). Egbert Bakker's perceptive "The Greek Gilgamesh, or the Immortality of Return" in M. Païsi-Apostolopoulou, ed., *Eranos: Proceedings of the 9th International Symposium on the Odyssey* (Ithaka, 2001), 331–53, is very useful; see also Walter Burkert, *The Orientalizing Revolution: Near Eastern Influence on Greek Culture in the Early Archaic Age* (Cambridge, MA, and London: Harvard University Press, 1992), *Babylon, Memphis, Persepolis: Eastern Contexts of*

Greek Culture (Cambridge, MA, and London: Harvard University Press, 2004), and Martin L. West, *The East Face of Helicon* (Oxford and New York: Clarendon Press, 1997).

8. See Gregory Nagy, *Comparative Studies in Greek and Indic Meter* (Cambridge, MA: Harvard University Press, 1974), 229–61.

9. In his book *The Making of the "Odyssey"* (Oxford and New York: Oxford University Press, 2014), Martin L. West, a scholar for whom I have enormous admiration, makes a compelling case for different authorship.

10. *The Last Scenes of the Odyssey, Mnemosyne Supplement* 52 (1978), 74–75.

11. These elements of the fairy tale evident in the Odyssey have been assembled by Barry Powell in *Homer* (*Blackwell Introductions to the Classical World*), 2ⁿᵈ ed. (Malden, MA: Blackwell Publishing, 2007), 155–56. Martin West has documented the "winning a bride in an archery contest" motif in Indian literature both before (*Mahabharata*) and after (*Ramayana*) Homer in *Indo-European Poetry and Myth* (Oxford and New York: Oxford University Press, 2007), 433–34, 439–40.

12. On *Gilgamesh* and the *Odyssey*, see Bakker, "The Greek Gilgamesh, or the Immortality of Return."

13. Translated by Stephanie Dalley in *Myths of Mesopotamia: Creation, The Flood, Gilgamesh, and Others* (New York: Oxford University Press, 1989), 50.

14. The Greek word that I have translated "of many devices" is *polytropon*, "many turning." *Poly*, of course, means many, as in polygon or polygamy. *Tropos* is a richer word: a turn, a way, a manner, a characteristic. *Polytropon* has been translated into English in Homer's famous opening line variously as "many-sided" (Lovelace Bigge-Wither), "adventurous" (George Palmer), "shifty" (William Morris), "ingenious" (Samuel Butler), "of many devices" (Augustus Murray), "restless" (Francis Caulfeild [sic]), "never at a loss" (W.H.D. Rouse). Recent translations include Richmond Lattimore's "of many ways," Robert Fitzgerald's "skilled in all ways of contending," Robert Fagles's "of twists and turns," Stanley Lombardo's "cunning," Barry Powell's and Peter Green's "resourceful," and Emily Wilson's "complicated"; and this is just a sample of some sixty translations into a single language. Much as I would like to take credit for gathering these examples, I did not do the legwork myself: most of these translations are culled from Wyatt Mason and Emily Wilson, "The First Woman to Translate the 'Odyssey' into English," *New York Times Magazine*, November 2, 2017.

Chapter 3. Meeting the Greeks

1. Cited in Theophilus, *To Autolycus* 2. 53.

2. Cited in Stobaeus, *Anthology* 105. 24.

3. A detailed study of this phenomenon appears in Renaud Gagné, *Ancestral Fault in Ancient Greece* (Cambridge, UK, and New York: Cambridge University Press, 2013).

4. Although rather vaguely defined, hybris was a crime in classical Athens; allegations of hybris in court normally entailed assault, and in conversation hybris was sometimes a euphemism for rape. As S. C. Todd has written in *The Shape of Athenian Law* (Oxford: Clarendon, 1993), the statute regarding hybris quoted at Demosthenes 41. 47 "notably presupposes rather than explains the nature of the offence" (270).

5. Cited in Eusebius, *Preparation of the Gospel* 14. 3. 7.

6. "Women and Culture in Herodotus's Histories," *Women's Studies* 8 (1981), 94.

7. Eric H. Cline, *The Trojan War: A Very Short Introduction* (Oxford: Oxford University Press, 2013), 59–60. On the collapse of the Bronze Age more generally, see Cline, *1177 B.C.: The Year Civilization Collapsed: Revised and Updated* (Turning Points in Ancient History) (Princeton, NJ: Princeton University Press, 2021).

8. Walter Scheidel, *The Great Leveler: Violence and the History of Inequality from the Stone Age to the Twenty-First Century* (The Princeton Economic History of the Western World) (Princeton, NJ: Princeton University Press, 2017), 273.

9. Much has been written about the Greeks' purposes in developing an alphabet; see in particular Peter W. Rose, *Class in Archaic Greece* (Cambridge, UK, and New York: Cambridge University Press, 2012), 94–98.

10. Cited in Plutarch, *Solon* 2. 2.

11. Jeffrey Henderson, *The Maculate Muse: Obscene Language in Attic Comedy*, 2nd ed. (Oxford and New York: Oxford University Press, 1993) provides a detailed account of obscenity in Aristophanes' plays.

12. For a social history of immigrant women in Athens, see Rebecca Futo Kennedy, *Immigrant Women in Athens: Gender, Ethnicity, and Citizenship in the Classical City* (New York: Routledge, 2016), and for the intellectual history of immigration, citizenship, and democracy, Demetra Kasimis, *The Perpetual Immigrant and the Limits of Athenian Democracy* (Classics after Antiquity) (Cambridge, UK, and New York: Cambridge University Press, 2018).

13. Arrian describes the immolation at *Anabasis* 7. 3.

14. A discussion of the inscription in context appears in Rachel Mairs, *The Hellenistic Far East: Archaeology, Language, and Identity in Greek Central Asia* (Berkeley and Los Angeles: University of California Press, 2014), 73–74.

Chapter 4. The Polis—City and State

1. Cited in Pausanias, 1. 3. 4.

2. An excellent treatment of Athenian autochthony and imperialism appears in Vincent Rosivach, "Autochthony and the Athenians," *Classical Quarterly* 37 (1987), 294–306.

3. J. S. McClelland, *The Crowd and the Mob: From Plato to Canetti* (London and Boston: Unwin Hyman 1989), 1–2.

4. An astute analysis of the way Pericles makes a point of praising Athens for strengths that were commonly associated with Sparta appears in Paula Debnar, "Sparta in Pericles' Funeral Oration," in Paul Cartledge and Anton Powell, eds., *The Greek Superpower: Sparta in the Self-Definition of Athenians* (Swansea: Classical Press of Wales, 2018), 1–32.

5. An excellent analysis of this phenomenon appears in Ellen Millender, "Athens, Sparta, and the Technē of Deliberation," in Cartledge and Powell, eds., *The Greek Superpower*, 33–60.

6. The frequency of impeachment in Athens and its role in the democracy is explored in Mogens Herman Hansen, *Eisangelia: The Sovereignty of the People's Court in Athens in the Fourth Century B.C. and the Impeachment of Generals and Politicians*, Odense University Classical Studies, vol. 6 (Odense, Denmark: Odense University Press, 1975); P. J. Rhodes, "*Eisangelia* in Athens,"

Journal of Hellenic Studies 99 (1979), 103–14; Jennifer T. Roberts, *Accountability in Athenian Government* (Madison: University of Wisconsin Press, 1982); and Debra Hamel, *Athenian Generals: Military Authority in the Classical Period* (Mnemosyne Supplement 182) (Leiden: Brill, 1998).

7. Aristotle, *Politics* 1302b18–19 (Argos); Diodorus 11. 87 (Syracuse). A good discussion of procedure in Greek democracies outside Athens is offered in Eric W. Robinson, *Democracy beyond Athens: Popular Government in the Greek Classical Age* (Cambridge, UK, and New York: Cambridge University Press, 2011).

8. On divorce in Athens, see Signe Isager, "The Marriage Pattern in Classical Athens; Men and Women in Isaios," *Classical et Medievalia* 33 (1981–82), 81–96; Vincent J. Rosivach, "Aphairesis and Apoleipsis: A Study of the Sources," *Revue internationale des droits de l'antiquité* 31 (1984), 193–230; and Louis Cohn-Haft, "Divorce in Classical Athens," *Journal of Hellenic Studies* 115 (1995), 1–14.

9. Cited in Aristotle, *Rhetoric* 1418.42b.

10. *History of Animals* 618a31.

11. A detailed analysis of all the philology surrounding Cypselus's name appears in Daniel Ogden, *The Crooked Kings of Ancient Greece* (London: Duckworth, 1997), 88–91.

12. Alcaeus and Pittacus Ogden, *Crooked Kings*, 97–99.

13. Herodotus 4. 154–55.

14. Limp: Olivier Masson, "Myskelos fondateur de Crotone et le nom 'Myskel(l)os," *Revue de Philologie* 63 (1989), 61–66; hunchback: Ogden, *Crooked Kings*, 62–72.

15. Diogenes Laertius, *Lives of the Philosophers* 1. 94.

16. A different version of the story appears in Aristotle's *Politics* 3.1284, where the advice is given by Periander to Thrasybulus.

17. Plutarch, *Nicias* 27. 6.

18. Strabo 6. 1. 8.

19. See James Redfield, *The Locrian Maidens: Love and Death in Greek Italy* (Princeton, NJ: Princeton University Press), 263.

20. Plainly I believe in the authenticity of this work of art, but not all are convinced. Its authenticity is defended ably in B. Ashmole, "Locri, Epizephyrii and the Ludovisi Throne," *Journal of Hellenic Studies* 42 (1922), 248–53, and endorsed in Redfield, *The Locrian Maidens*, 332–45. See, for example, S. Sande, "The Ludovisi 'Throne,' the Boston 'Throne' and the Warren Cup: Retrospective Works of Forgeries?" *Acta ad archaeologiam et artium historiam pertinentia* (2018), 29 (15 N.S.), 23–51.

21. A thorough edition, translation, and commentary on the Gortyn code appears in Michael Gagarin and Paula Perlman, eds., *The Laws of Ancient Crete, c. 650–400 BCE* (Oxford and New York: Oxford University Press, 2016).

Chapter 5. Foreigners, Slaves, and Sex[ism]

1. See for example *Republic* 557c and 563b; *Timaeus* 42b–c. I have explored Plato's treatment of women in "Myths of Democracy and Gender in Plato's 'Republic': A Reply to Arlene Saxonhouse," *Thamyris: Mythmaking from Past To Present* 2 (1995), 259–72. See also Prof. Saxonhouse's reply to me in the same issue, 273–76.

2. In John Rich and Graham Shipley, eds., *War and Society in the Greek World* (London and New York: Routledge, 1993), 112–13.

3. Herodotus 4. 184 (Atlantes); 2. 35; 3. 99. 1–3 (Padaeans); 1. 216. 2–3 (Massagetae); 4. 26. 1–2 (Issedones); 4. 194 (Gyzantes).

4. Herodotus 4. 61 (Scythia); 1. 196 (Babylon); 3. 113 (Arabia).

5. Incisive commentary on Herodotus's long Egyptian excursus can be found in Alan Lloyd's treatment of Book Two in Oswyn Murray and Alfonso Moreno, eds., *A Commentary on Herodotus Books I–IV*, by David Asheri, Alan Lloyd, and Aldo Corcella (Oxford: Oxford University Press, 2007), 219–378.

6. See still the classic 1966 study by Geoffrey E. R. Lloyd, *Polarity and Analogy: Two Types of Argumentation in Early Greek Thought* (Cambridge, UK: Cambridge University Press).

7. *The Gift of the Nile: Hellenizing Egypt from Aeschylus to Alexander* (Berkeley and Los Angeles: University of California Press, 2001), 217.

8. Mukhtasar Kitab al-buldan, ed. M. J. De Goeje (Leiden, 1885), 162. The translation is that of John O. Hunwick, based in part on that of Bernard Lewis, cited in Hunwick's article "A Region of the Mind: Medieval Views of African Geography and Ethnography and Their Legacy," *Sudanic Africa* 16 (2005), 103–36 at 126–27.

9. Data on Greek enslavement of other Greeks is collected in Vincent Rosivach, "Enslaving 'Barbaroi' and the Athenian Ideology of Slavery," *Historia* 40 (1999), 129–57.

10. It is unclear whether we should class along with this observation the words attributed to the sophist Hippias in Plato's *Protagoras*, set shortly before the production of this play: "All of you gentlemen who are present here, consider that I regard you as kinsmen and intimates and fellow-citizens by nature rather than by law; for like by nature is akin to like, whereas law, the tyrant of the human race, frequently constrains us against nature" (*Protagoras* 337c–d). It is possible, however, that Hippias was speaking merely of Greeks from different poleis.

11. Aristotle, *Politics* 1267b. On Plato's laws concerning slavery, see Glenn R. Morrow's detailed study *Plato's Law of Slavery in Its Relation to Greek Law*, Illinois Studies in Language and Literature, 25. 3 (Urbana: University of Illinois, 1939; reprinted New York: Arno Press, 1976), vitiated as it is by the peculiar contention that "The condition of slaves at Athens seems to have been an exceedingly happy one," a claim not borne out by the evidence; as well as Trevor J. Saunders, *Plato's Penal Code: Tradition, Controversy, and Reform in Greek Penology* (Oxford: Clarendon, 1991).

12. Plutarch, *Lycurgus*, 28. 4; Myron of Priene cited in Athenaeus, *Deipnosophists*, 14, 647d.

13. Peter Hunt, *Slaves, Warfare, and Ideology in the Greek Historians* (Cambridge, UK: Cambridge University Press, 1998), 31–32.

14. On this poem, Robin Osborne, "The Use of Abuse: Semonides 7," *Proceedings of the Cambridge Philological Society* 47 (2001), 47–64, with ample bibliography, is very useful.

15. "Early Greece: The Origins of the Western Attitude Towards Women," *Arethusa* 6 (1973), 50 (published under the name Marylin Arthur).

16. On Hippocrates and the diseases of virgins, see Helen King, "Bound to Bleed: Artemis and Greek Women," reprinted in Laura McClure, ed., in *Sexuality and Gender in the Classical World: Readings and Sources* (Malden, MA: Blackwell, 2002), 77–93.

17. The ways in which Athenian women managed to circumvent the restrictions on their initiative and mobility are explored in Virginia Hunter, *Policing Athens: Social Control in the Attic Lawsuits, 420–320 B.C.* (Princeton, NJ: Princeton University Press, 1994), 21–29.

18. Appian, *Syrian Wars* 9. 59; Plutarch, *Demetrius* 38.

19. For a presentation and analysis of the flimsy evidence out of which the notion of this alleged school has been constructed, see Holt N. Parker, "Sappho Schoolmistress," *Transactions of the American Philological Association* 123 (1993), 309–51.

20. Plutarch, *Lycurgus* 18.4.

21. "Divided Consciousness and Female Companionship: Reconstructing Female Subjectivity on Greek Vases," *Arethusa* 30 (1997), 35–74, esp. 64–69.

22. Susan M. Sherwin-White and Amélie Kuhrt, *From Samarkhand to Sardis: A New Approach to the Seleucid Empire* (Berkeley and Los Angeles: University of California Press, 1993), 150–53.

23. *Women in Hellenistic Egypt* (New York: Schocken Books, 1984), 149–51, 163.

24. P. Col. Zen. I. 6; P. Lond. 7. 1976; and P. Mich. I. 29., translated in Roger S. Bagnall and Raffaella Cribiore, with contributions by Evie Ahtaridis, *Women's Letters from Ancient Egypt, 300 BC–AD 800* (Ann Arbor and New York: University of Michigan Press, 2006).

25. P. Lond 42 (UPZ_1.59), http://www.attalus.org/docs/select1/p97.html, translated in Bagnall and Cribiore, *Women's Letters from Ancient Egypt*.

26. Gutzwiller, "Genre Development and Gendered Voices in Erinna and Nossis," in Yopie Prins and Maeera Shreiber, eds., *Dwelling in Possibility: Women Poets and Critics on Poetry* (Ithaca, NY: Cornell University Press, 1997), 202–3.

27. Zenobius *Proverbs* 4. 21 (i 89 Leutsch-Schneidewin) (cod. Coisl.).

28. On the double entendres in the seventh mimiambos, see Alan Sumler, "A Catalogue of Shoes: Puns in Herodas Mime 7," *Classical World* 103 (2010), 465–75.

Chapter 6. Giving the Gods Their Due

1. For examples, see Aeschylus, *Seven against Thebes*, 602–4; Antiphon 5. 82.

2. Parker, *Miasma: Pollution and Purification in Early Greek Religion* (Oxford: Clarendon, 1983), 257.

3. *Homo Necans: The Anthropology of Ancient Greek Sacrificial Ritual and Myth*, trans. Peter Bing (Berkeley and Los Angeles: University of California Press, 1983).

4. *The Cuisine of Sacrifice among the Greeks*, with essays by Jean-Louis Durand, Stella Georgoudi, François Hartog, and Jesper Svenbro, trans. Paula Wissing (Chicago: University of Chicago Press, 1989).

5. *Smoke Signals for the Gods: Ancient Greek Sacrifice from the Archaic through Roman Periods* (New York: Oxford University Press, 2013). The intriguing topic of sacrifice has been the subject of an enormous amount of speculation: see in addition to Burkert, Vernant, Detienne, and Naiden in particular René Girard, *Violence and the Sacred*, trans. Patrick Gregory (Baltimore, MD: Johns Hopkins University Press, 1977), and Sarah Hitch and Ian Rutherford, eds., *Animal Sacrifice in the Ancient Greek World* (Cambridge, UK: Cambridge University Press), 2017; and for a collection of visual images of sacrifice, Folkert T. Van Straten, *Hierà kalá : Images of Animal Sacrifice in Archaic and Classical Greece* (Leiden and New York: E. J. Brill, 1995).

6. The parallel situation of punishment, a process from which women (at least in Athens) were excluded, is explored in Danielle S. Allen, *The World of Prometheus: The Politics of Punishing in Democratic Athens* (Princeton, NJ: Princeton University Press, 2000).

7. On women's relationship to sacrifice, see Robin Osborne, "Women and Sacrifice in Classical Greece," *Classical Quarterly* 43 (1993), 392–405, and Joan Connelly, *Portrait of a Priestess: Women and Ritual in Ancient Greece* (Princeton, NJ: Princeton University Press, 2007), 179–84.

8. This author did not exercise equal discretion and was captured on film clambering gracelessly over the wall.

9. For example, Theophilus, *To Autolycus* 3.2; Lactantius, *Divine Institutes* 1. 7. 6–7.

10. Simon Price, *Religions of the Ancient Greeks* (*Key Themes in Ancient History*) (Cambridge, UK: Cambridge University Press, 1999), 172.

11. The Thesmophoria was not unique in its encouragement of transgressive language. Male and female choruses exchanged insults at the festival of Demeter in Pellene in the Peloponnesus; ritual abuse also took place at the women's festival of the Stenia a couple of days before the Thesmophoria and at the midwinter festival of the Haloa in Eleusis, also an all-female event. A rich discussion of this aspect of the Thesmophoria appears in Laurie O'Higgins, *Women and Humor in Classical Greece* (Cambridge, UK: Cambridge University Press, 2003), and D. M. O'Higgins, "Women's Cultic Joking and Mockery: Some Perspectives," in André Lardinois and Laura McClure, eds., *Making Silence Speak: Women's Voices in Greek Literature and Society* (Princeton, NJ: Princeton University Press, 2018), 137–60.

12. E.A.M.E. O'Connor-Visser, *Aspects of Human Sacrifice in the Tragedians of Euripides* (Amsterdam: B. R. Grüner, 1987); Dennis Hughes, *Human Sacrifice in Ancient Greece* (London and New York: Routledge, 1991); Rush Rehm, *Marriage to Death: The Conflation of Wedding and Funeral Rituals in Greek Tragedy* (Princeton, NJ: Princeton University Press, 1994); Ruth Scodel, "Domōn agalma: Virgin Sacrifice and Aesthetic Object," *Transactions of the American Philological Association* 126 (1996), 111–28; James M. Redfield, *The Locrian Maidens: Love and Death in Greek Italy* (Princeton, NJ: Princeton University Press, 2004); Pietro Pucci, "Human Sacrifices in the Oresteia," in Ralph Hexter and Daniel Selden, eds., *Innovations of Antiquity* (New York: Routledge, 2013), 513–36; Anthony F. Mangieri, *Virgin Sacrifice in Classical Art: Women, Agency, and the Trojan War* (Abingdon, UK: Routledge, 2021).

13. On Codrus, see Walter Burkert, *Structure and History in Greek Mythology and Ritual* (Berkeley and Los Angeles: University of California Press, 1979), 62–63, and Hughes, *Human Sacrifice*, 74–75.

14. Scapegoats and sacrifice are discussed at length with bibliography in Jan Bremmer, "Scapegoat Rituals in Ancient Greece," *Harvard Studies in Classical Philology* 87 (1983), 299–320.

15. For these and other questions asked of Greek oracles, see Richard Stoneman, *The Ancient Oracles: Making the Gods Speak* (New Haven, CT: Yale University Press, 1911).

16. *Polytheism and Society at Athens* (Oxford: Oxford University Press, 2005), 122.

17. The gender difference and other aspects of this phenomenon are explored in Christopher A. Faraone, *Ancient Greek Love Magic* (Cambridge, MA, and London: Harvard University Press, 1999).

18. R. Wünsch, *Corpus Inscriptionum Atticarum, Defixionum Tabellae Atticae, Inscriptiones Graecae*, vol. 3, pt. 3, 87 (Berlin, 1897).

19. R. Wünsch, *Corpus Inscriptionum Atticarum*, vol. 3, pt. 3, 89 (Berlin, 1897).

20. Lynn R. LiDonnici, *The Epidaurian Miracle Inscriptions: Text, Translation, and Commentary* (*Society of Biblical Literature Text and Translations*) (Atlanta: Scholars Press, 1995), B 12 (32), A 12, B 22 (42), B 23 (43).

21. *Inscriptiones Graecae* 12. 14, translated by Stanley Burstein in *The Hellenistic Age from the Battle of Ipsos to the Death of Kleopatra VII* (Cambridge, UK, and New York: Cambridge University Press, 1985), 147.

22. For the Samian cult of Lysander, see Paul Cartledge, *Agesilaos and the Crisis of Sparta* (Baltimore, MD: Johns Hopkins University Press, 1987), 83–86 with notes. A good treatment of ruler cults in the Hellenistic world is Angelos Chaniotis, "The Divinity of Hellenistic Rulers," in E. Erskine, ed., *A Companion to the Hellenistic World* (Oxford: Blackwell, 2003), 431–45.

23. An excellent treatment of atheism in Greece and Rome is offered in Tim Whitmarsh's *Battling the Gods: Atheism in the Ancient World* (New York: Knopf, 2015).

24. Herculaneum Papyrus 1428, fragment 19 (fragment 72 in Robert Mayhew, *Prodicus the Sophist: Texts, Translations, and Commentary* (Oxford: Oxford University Press, 2011).

25. Prosecutions for atheism at Athens are discussed in Whitmarsh, *Battling the Gods*, 115–24.

Chapter 7. The Thrill of Victory

1. Pausanias 8. 40. 1–2.

2. For the role of performance in Greek society, see Eva Stehle, *Performance and Gender in Ancient Greece: Nondramatic Poetry in Its Setting* (Princeton, NJ: Princeton University Press, 1997).

3. Compare *Olympian* 8. 19 on Alcidamas and *Nemean* 3. 19 on Aristocleides.

4. Cited in Lycurgus *Leocrates* 107, 21–30.

5. See Lilah Grace Canevaro and Donncha O'Rourke, eds., *Didactic Poetry of Greece, Rome and Beyond: Knowledge, Power Tradition* (Swansea, UK: Classical Press of Wales, 2019).

6. In Jean-Pierre Vernant and Pierre Vidal-Naquet, *Myth and Tragedy in Ancient Greece*, trans. Janet Lloyd (New York: Zone Books, 1990) 27.

7. Goldhill, *Love, Sex and Tragedy: How the Ancient World Shapes Our Lives* (Chicago: University of Chicago Press), 231.

8. Scodel, *An Introduction to Greek Tragedy* (Cambridge, UK, and New York: Cambridge University Press, 2010), 7. Plato's observations are at *Republic* 376e–398b and 595–608b.

9. Nancy C. M. Hartsock, *Money, Sex and Power: Towards a Feminist Historical Materialism* (Boston: Northeastern University Press, 1985), 192; see also Froma Zeitlin's important article, "The Dynamics of Misogyny: Myth and Mythmaking in the Oresteia," *Arethusa* 11 (1978), 149–84.

10. *Oedipus at Colonus* 266–67, 962–64, 969–73.

11. See for example Bernard Knox, "The Hippolytus of Euripides," *Yale Classical Studies* 13 (1952), 3–31, and Laura McClure, chapter 4, "Phaedra and the Politics of Reputation," in *Spoken*

Like a Woman: Speech and Gender in Athenian Drama (Princeton, NJ: Princeton University Press, 1999), 112–57.

12. Pierre Vidal-Naquet, "Oedipus in Vicenza and in Paris," in Pierre Vidal-Naquet and Jean-Pierre Vernant, *Myth and Tragedy*, trans. Janet Lloyd (New York: Zone Books), 365.

13. [Demetrius], *On Style* 169, wrongly attributed to Demetrius of Phalerum, an Athenian politician and man of letters who governed Athens under the Macedonian king Cassander from 317 to 307. An excellent collection of essays on satyr drama appears in George W. M. Harrison and Z. Philip Ambrose, eds., *Satyr Drama: Tragedy at Play* (Swansea, UK: Classical Press of Wales, 2005).

Chapter 8. The Search for Meaning

1. Geoffrey Lloyd, *The Revolutions of Wisdom: Studies in the Claims and Practice of Ancient Greek Science* (Berkeley and Los Angeles: University of California Press, 1989), esp. 83–103.

2. D21 (< B10) Scholia on Gregory of Nazianzus.

3. D25 [B6] and D14 [B9] Simplicius, *Commentary on Aristotle's Physics*.

4. Two recent studies of female Pythagoreans are Sarah B. Pomeroy, *Pythagorean Women: Their History and Writings* (Baltimore, MD: Johns Hopkins University Press, 2013), and Dorota M. Dutsch, *Pythagorean Women Philosophers: Between Belief and Suspicion* (*Oxford Studies in Classical Literature and Gender Theory*) (Oxford: Oxford University Press, 2020).

5. D39 (A30) Censorinus, *The Birthday*.

6. D156 [B61] Aelian, *On the Nature of Animals*.

7. Berossus, *History of Babylonia*, F1 52 in Gerald P. Verbrugghe and John M. Wickersham, *Berossos and Manetho Introduced and Translated: Native Traditions in Ancient Mesopotamia and Egypt* (Ann Arbor: University of Michigan Press, 1996), 45.

8. D14 [B15] Clement of Alexandria, *Stromata* 5.109.1.

9. D13 [B16] Clement of Alexandria, *Stromata*.

10. D19 [B26] Simplicius, *Commentary on Aristotle's Physics*.

11. D93 [B134] Ammonius, *Commentary on Aristotle's On Interpretation*.

12. D85 [B30)] Clement of Alexandria, *Stromata*.

13. Excellent histories of the word "sophist" can be found in two older but still very useful works: G. B. Kerferd, "The First Greek Sophists," *Classical Review* 64 (1950), 8–10, and W.K.C. Guthrie, *The Sophists* (Cambridge, UK: Cambridge University Press, 1971; originally published as *A History of Greek Philosophy*, vol. 3, part I [Cambridge University Press, 1969]), 27–34.

14. *Commentary on the Odyssey* 11. 227; see also C. Carey, "Archilochus and Lycambes," *Classical Quarterly* 36 (1986), 60–67.

15. Plutarch, *Pericles* 26.

16. D18 [B25] Simplicius, *Commentary on Aristotle's Physics*.

17. Diogenes Laertius 6. 46.

18. Diogenes Laertius 9. 68.

19. See Christopher Beckwith, *Greek Buddha: Pyrrho's Encounter with Early Buddhism in Central Asia* (Princeton, NJ: Princeton University Press, 2015), 25–33. For an interesting

exploration of the possibility of Eastern influence on Pyrrho, see Everard Flintoff, "Pyrrho and India," *Phronesis*, 25 (1980), 88–108; Richard Bett, *Pyrrho, His Antecedents and His Legacy* (Oxford: Oxford University Press, 2000); Adrian Kuzminski, *Pyrrhonism: How the Ancient Greeks Reinvented Buddhism* (Lanham, MD, and Plymouth, UK: Lexington Books, 2008); and Richard Stoneman, *The Greek Experience of India From Alexander to the Indo-Greeks* (Princeton, NJ: Princeton University Press, 2019), 346–57. An excellent examination of Pyrrhonism appears in Dee Clayman's study of Pyrrho's disciple Timon of Phlius: *Timon of Phlius: Pyrrhonism into Poetry* (*Undersuchungen zur antiken Literatur und Geschichte Book* 98) (Berlin: De Gruyter, 2009).

20. Plutarch, *Marcellus*, 19. 4.

21. For a very detailed study of Herophilus and Erasistratus at Alexandria, see James Longrigg, "Anatomy in Alexandria in the Third Century B.C.," *British Journal for the History of Science* 21 (1988), 455–88.

Chapter 9. Life after Life

1. Pausanias 5. 18. 1.

2. On the royal Scythian burials, Herodotus 4. 71–72 with Aldo Corcella in Oswyn Murray and Alfonso Moreno, eds., *A Commentary on Herodotus Books I–IV*, by David Asheri, Alan Lloyd, and Aldo Corcella (Oxford: Oxford University Press, 2007), 632–35.

3. Pseudo-Aristotle, *Constitution of the Athenians* 55. 3.

4. The centrality of women to the rituals surrounding death in Greece is discussed in Karen Stears, "Death Becomes Her: Gender and Athenian Death Ritual," in Sue Blundell and Margaret Williamson, eds., *The Sacred and the Feminine in Ancient Greece* (London and New York: Routledge, 1998), 113–27, and Janett Morgan, "Women, Religion, and the Home," in Daniel Ogden, ed., *A Companion to Greek Religion* (Malden, MA: Wiley-Blackwell, 2010), 297–310.

5. See Teresa Matthew, "Professional Mourners' Laments from Quarantine," published during the Covid-19 shutdown (*New Yorker*, June 9, 2020).

6. Photographer Ioanna Sakellaraki has documented the work of these women in her project *The Truth Is in the Soil*, at https://ioannasakellaraki.com/the-truth-is-in-the-soil/.

7. The burial of fallen soldiers in Greece is examined in Noel Robertson, "The Collective Burial of Fallen Soldiers at Athens, Sparta and Elsewhere: 'Ancestral Custom' and Modern Misunderstanding," *Echos du monde Classique: Classical Views* 27 (1983), 78–92.

8. Robert Garland, "The Well-Ordered Corpse: An Investigation into the Motives behind Greek Funerary Legislation," *Bulletin of the Institute of Classical Studies* 36 (1989), 8–9.

9. Diodorus 38. 2–4.

10. Plutarch, *Lycurgus* 27. 1.

11. *Homeric Hymn to Demeter*, 480–81.

12. D39 [B146] Clement of Alexandria, *Stromata*.

13. Laurie O'Higgins, *Women and Humor in Classical Greece* (Cambridge, UK: Cambridge University Press, 2003), 55.

14. Jonathan Z. Smith, "Towards Interpreting Demonic Powers in Hellenistic and Roman Antiquity," *Aufstieg und Niedergang der Römischen Welt* II 16.1 (1978), 425–39, esp. 429; Walter

Burkert, *The Orientalizing Revolution: Near Eastern Influence on Greek Culture in the Early Archaic Age* (Cambridge, MA, and London: Harvard University Press, 1992), 82–87; and Sarah Iles Johnson, chapter 5, "Childless Mothers and Blighted Virgins: Female Ghosts and Their Victims," in *The Restless Dead: Encounters between the Living and the Dead in Ancient Greece* (Berkeley and Los Angeles: University of California Press, 1999), 161–200.

15. *Odyssey* 10. 494–95.

16. *Aspects of Death in Early Greek Art and Poetry* (Berkeley and Los Angeles: University of California Press, 1979), 118.

17. Detailed arguments to the effect that Book 23. 297–372 and all of Book 24 were composed by a different person from the author of the rest of the *Odyssey* and of the *Iliad* appear with substantial bibliography in Christine Sourvinou-Inwood, *"Reading" Greek Death to the End of the Classical Period* (Oxford: Clarendon, 1995), 94–106. I am more inclined to lean toward the arguments of Dorothea Wender in *The Last Scenes of the Odyssey, Mnemosyne Supplement* 52 (Leiden: Brill), 1978.

18. Diodorus 1. 92. 2.

Epilogue. The Greeks among Us

1. The scholarship on this phenomenon has exploded in recent years; sample work includes Kevin J. Wetmore, Jr., *The Athenian Sun in an African Sky* (Jefferson, NC, and London: McFarland, 2002); Barbara Goff, *Classics and Colonialism* (London: Bristol Classical Press, 2005); Patrice D. Rankine, *Ulysses in Black: Ralph Ellison, Classicism, and African American Literature* (Madison: University of Wisconsin Press, 2006); Lorna Hardwick and Carol Gillespie, *Classics in Post-Colonial Worlds* (Oxford: Oxford University Press, 2007); Barbara Goff and Michael Simpson, *Crossroads in the Black Aegean: Oedipus, Antigone, and Dramas of the African Diaspora* (Oxford: Oxford University Press, 2007); Justine McConnell, *Black Odysseys: The Homeric Odyssey in the African Diaspora since 1939* (Oxford: Oxford University Press, 2013); and Elisa Rizo and Madeleine M. Henry, eds., *Receptions of the Classics in the African Diaspora of the Hispanophone and Lusophone Worlds* (Lanham, MD: Lexington/Rowman & Littlefield, 2016). Additional titles appear in the suggested readings for this chapter.

2. Hitler's wish is reported in Otto Strasser, *Hitler and I*, trans. Gwenda David and Eric Mosbacher (1940; reprinted New York: AMS Press, 1982), 214–15; for the use of the Thermopylae motif, see R. Watt, "'Wanderer, kommst du nach Sparta': History through Propaganda into Literary Commonplace," *Modern Language Review* 26 (1985), 871–83.

3. "Die Aufgaben der alten Geschichte im Rahmen der Nordischen Weltgeschichte," *Vergangenheit und Gegenwart* 23 (1933), 599, n. 15. The Nazi dismissal of Stoicism as a fundamentally debased and Semitic school of thought is discussed in Johann Chapoutot, *Le nazisme et L'Antiquité* (Paris: Presses Universitaires de France, 2015), and Matthew Sharpe, "Into the Heart of Darkness, Or: Alt-Stoicism? Actually, No . . . ," *Eidos: A Journal for Philosophy of Culture* 4 (2018), 106–13.

4. A good explanation of this Stoic-based treatment appears in Donald Robertson, *The Philosophy of Cognitive-Behavioral Therapy (CBT): Stoic Philosophy as Rational and Cognitive Psychotherapy*, 2nd ed. (Oxford and New York: Routledge, 2019).

5. Matteo Ricci and the use of Stoicism to convey Christian teachings in China are explored in Shadi Bartsch's fascinating *Plato Goes to China: The Greek Classics and Chinese Nationalism* (Princeton, NJ, and Oxford: Princeton University Press, 2023), 21–25.

6. The manosphere's appeal to classical civilization is the subject of the first chapter ("Arms and the Manosphere") in Donna Zuckerberg's *Not All Dead White Men: Classics and Misogyny in the Digital Age* (Cambridge, MA: Harvard University Press, 2018).

7. Self-published via Amazon Publishing, 2018.

8. See for example Joel Christensen, "Plagues Follow Bad Leadership in Ancient Greek Tales," *Brandeis Now*, April 12, 2020; Ryan M. Antiel, "Oedipus and the Coronavirus Pandemic," *Journal of the American Medical Association* 323 (2020), 2231–32; Nicholas A. Christakis, *Apollo's Arrow: The Profound and Enduring Impact of Coronavirus on the Way We Live* (New York: Little, Brown Spark, 2020), 8, 10, 131, 198, 232, 285. A wide variety of additional references are collected in Daniel Levine, "Philokleon Goes Viral: Re-Reading Aristophanes' Wasps through a Covid-19 Lens," *Athenaeum Review* 7 (Summer 2022), 28–38.

9. "Sappho on East Seventh," in *Tales of Beatnik Glory* (New York: Thunder's Mouth Press/ Avalon, 1975).

10. The three volumes were reprinted as a set by Rutgers in 2020. The literature sparked by Bernal's work was both passionate and voluminous. A good overview of the controversy can be found in Stanley M. Burstein, "The Debate over *Black Athena*," *Scholia* ns 5 (1996), 3–16.

11. *Arethusa* 6 (1973), 7–58.

12. Keuls, *Reign of the Phallus: Sexual Politics in Ancient Athens* (New York: Harper & Row, 1985), 12.

13. Zimmerman, *Women and Other Monsters* (Boston: Beacon, 2021), 19, 32.

14. Cited in Sheila Murnaghan, "Homer's Odyssey: The Adventure of Homecoming," 81–95, in Deborah Boedeker and Anna Lea, eds., *The "Iliad," the "Odyssey" and the Real World: Proceedings from a Seminar Sponsored by the Society for the Preservation of the Greek Heritage and Held at the Smithsonian Institution, Washington, D.C. on March 6–7, 1998* (Washington, DC: Society for the Preservation of the Greek Heritage, 1998), 94. See in particular the comprehensive study by Ian Rutherford, *Hittite Texts and Greek Religion* (Oxford and New York: Oxford University Press, 2020).

15. Wilson, "Epilogue: Translating Homer as a Woman," in Fiona Cox and Elena Theodora-kopoulos, eds., *Homer's Daughters: Women's Responses to Homer in the Twentieth Century and Beyond* (Oxford: Oxford University Press, 2019), 279–80.

16. Both cited in Wilson, "Epilogue," 288–89.

17. Wilson, "Epilogue," 291.

18. Wilson, "Epilogue," 291.

19. Atwood, *The Penelopiad* (Edinburgh: Canongate, 2005), 5.

20. Page numbers are from *Circe* (New York and Boston: Back Bay, 2018).

21. "The Place and Status of Foreigners in Athenian Tragedy," in C. Pelling, ed., *Greek Tragedy and the Historian* (Oxford: Clarendon Press, 1997), 119.

22. Volumes dealing with adaptations of Antigone include George Steiner, *Antigones* (New York: Oxford University Press, 1984), and Erin B. Mee and Helene P. Foley, eds., *Antigone on the Contemporary World Stage* (Oxford and New York: Oxford University Press, 2011).

23. Classicist Lowell Edmunds and folklorist Alan Dundes have collected dozens of these renditions: Lowell Edmunds, *Oedipus: The Ancient Legend and Its Later Analogues* (Baltimore, MD, and London: Johns Hopkins University Press, 1985), and Lowell Edmunds and Alan Dundes, *Oedipus: A Folklore Casebook* (Madison: University of Wisconsin Press, 1995).

24. Examples include André Gide, *Oedipus* (France, 1930); Ali Ahmad Bakathir, *The Tragedy of Oedipus* (Egypt, 1948); Tawfiq Al-Hakim, *King Oedipus* (Egypt, 1949); Luis Alfaro, *Oedipus el Rey* (United States, 2010); Fawzi Fahmi, *The Return of the Absent* (Egypt, 1977); Ali Salim, *The Comedy of Oedipus: You're the One Who Killed the Beast* (Egypt, 1979); Walik Ikhlasi, *Oedipus* (Syria, 1978); Gabriel García Márquez, Stella Magagon, and Jorge Alí Triana, *Oedipus Mayor* (Colombia,1996); Garon Rsuchiya, Nobuaki Minegishi, and Park Chan-wood, *Oldboy* (South Korea, 2003).

25. Cited in Bernth Lindfors, *Dem-say: Interviews with Eight Nigerian Writers* (Austin: University of Texas, African and Afro-American Studies and Research Center, 1974), 62.

26. Cited in Rachel Poser, "He Wants to Save the Classics from Whiteness: Can the Field Survive?" *New York Times Magazine*, February 2, 2021.

27. *Review on the Debate in the Virginia Legislature of 1831 and 1832* (reprint Westport, CT, 1970), 112. University of Mississippi president George Frederick Holmes cited Aristotle's *Politics* approvingly for its treatment of slavery, commenting that "Nature has clearly designed some men for freedom and others for slavery:—and with respect to the latter, slavery is both just and beneficial." "Observations on a Passage in the Politics of Aristotle Relative to Slavery," *Southern Literary Messenger* 16 (1850), 193. Similarly Virginian George Fitzhugh, the proud author of *Sociology for the South, or the Failure of Free Society*, who made the advancement of slavery his life's mission, came to see himself as the very incarnation of Aristotle, exclaiming upon reading his works for the first time, "All these things which I thought original with me, I find in Aristotle" and claimed that he had quite unknowingly adopted not only his ideas but indeed his very words! Cited in Edwin A. Miles, "The Old South and the Classical World," *North Carolina Historical Review* [1971], 266–67. A good discussion also appears in Page duBois, *Slavery: Antiquity and Its Legacy* (New York: Oxford University Press, 2009), 69–75.

28. Sarah Bond, "Why We Need to Start Seeing the Classical World in Color," *Hyperallergic*, June 7, 2017; Maya Mackrandial, "The Aesthetics of Empire: Neoclassical Art and White Supremacy," https://contemptorary.org/the-aesthetics-of-empire-neoclassical-art/.

29. *American Renaissance*, February 7, 2020.

30. Vietnamese American classicist Kelly Nguyen, whose work has explored classical reception in Vietnamese contexts, has called attention to Shay's neglect of the Vietnamese experience and point of view in several blogposts, including https://blogs.brown.edu/humanities/archives/513 and https://classicalstudies.org/scs-blog/kelly-nguyen/blog-%E2%80%98vercingetorix-vietnam%E2%80%99-addressing-intersection-classics-and-vietnamese, contending that Shay's Achilles in Vietnam "relegates Vietnamese people to the margins of history, either victimizing or demonizing them."

31. Bryan Doerries, *The Theater of War: What Ancient Greek Tragedies Can Teach Us Today* (New York: Knopf, 2015), 8.

32. *Journal of Latrobe* (New York, 1905), 74. The poet Joel Barlow also deplored study of the *Iliad*, which, he believed, filled the young with eagerness for military conquest, glorified violence and war, and, worse still, encouraged belief in the divine right of kings, writing "How much of the fatal policy of states and of the miseries and degradations of social man have been occasioned by the false notions of honor inspired by the works of Homer, it is not easy to ascertain." The existence of the Homeric epics, he lamented, "has really proved one of the signal misfortunes of mankind" (*The Columbiad* [Philadelphia, 1809], I, v–vii).

33. Cited in Carl Richard, *The Founders and the Classics, Greece, Rome, and the American Enlightenment* (Cambridge, MA: Harvard University Press, 1994), 200.

34. *Confronting the Classics: Traditions, Adventures, and Innovations* (New York and London: Liveright, 2013), preface.

INDEX

Page numbers in *italics* denote figures.

Abbott, Sidney, and Barbara Love: *Sappho Was a Right-On Woman: A Liberated View of Lesbianism,* 364
abduction/kidnapping, 89; of adolescent boys, 204; of children, 49, 345–46; and woman-snatching, 89 (*see also under individual names, e.g.,* Helen)
abolitionism, 191, 194, 322
abstraction, 10, 309, 363
Academus, 314
Academy in Athens, xvi, 209, 291, 314
acanthus, 303
Achaean League, 142
Achaeans, 53, 57, 60, 64, 68–70, 82, 247
Acheron (river), 349, 352
Achilles: and Agamemnon, 70–71, 74, 80–81, 247; appearance/visual appeal of, 253; armor of/and Odysseus, 81, 248; Athena and, 58–59, 67–68, 219; and Briseis, 59, 62–64, 70–71; and Chiron the centaur, 19; death of, 66, 69; and Hector, 62–71, 74, 85, 97–98, 181, 219, 265; and parents Peleus and Thetis, 21–23, 43, 56, 59–60, 88, 248, 251, 378–79; and Patroclus, 21, 48, 64–67, 70, 204, 230, 331, 384n7; Phoenix as tutor of, 251; and son Neoptolemus, 193; in the Underworld, 80–81; wrath of, 53, 56. See also *Iliad* (Homer)
Achilles in Vietnam: Combat Trauma and the Undoing of Character (Shay), 377
Acragas, Sicily, 170, 294
Acropolis, 119, 146, 225, 238, 259–60

action: *vs.* contemplation, 316; divine, 256; human, 74, 256, 283
activism, 322, 363, 364
actors, 135, 254, 258–60, 262, 267, 371. *See also specific topics, e.g.,* masks
Ada (Queen of Caria), 172
Adea Eurydice (wife of Alexander's brother), 135
adolescence, 10, 21, 46, 84, 301, 348, 369; and marriage of young girls, 9, 28, 149, 163; and paederastic relationships, 203–8
Adonis, 109, 212–13
"Adonis of Praxilla," 213
adultery, 48, 56, 163, 225, 277, 286, 297, 350. *See also individual names*
Aeacus (son of Zeus), 36
Aeëtes (Medea's father), 164
Aegean basin, 88
Aegean Sea, *ii,* 4, 88, 96, 99–100, 119, 131, 144, 240
Aegeus, King, 24, 282
Aegisthus, 262, 267
Aegospotami, 125; Battle of, 190
Aeneas, 59
Aeneid (Vergil), 46, 328
Aeolian ethnic group, 116
aēr (a sort of dense mist), 294
Aeschylus, 121, 200, 258–66; *Agamemnon,* 265; death of, 287; the *Eumenides,* 20, 33, 175, 218, 263, 268; *The Libation Bearers,* 267, 333–34; *Oresteia,* xv, 200, 258–60, 264–65, 276; *Persians,* 171, 180–83, 259,